Meaning Reconstruction & the Experience of Loss

Meaning Reconstruction & the Experience of Loss

Edited by Robert A. Neimeyer

American Psychological Association

Washington, DC

First printing December 2000
Second printing January 2002
Third printing October 2003
Fourth printing July 2005
Fifth printing March 2007

Published by
American Psychological Association
750 First Street, NE
Washington, DC 20002

Copies may be ordered from
APA Order Department
P.O. Box 92984
Washington, DC 20090-2984

In the U.K., Europe, Africa, and the Middle East, copies may be ordered from
American Psychological Association
3 Henrietta Street
Covent Garden, London
WC2E 8LU England

Typeset in Goudy by Monotype Composition, Baltimore, MD
Printer: Sheridan Books, Ann Arbor, MI
Cover Designer: Anne Masters, Washington, DC
Technical/Production Editor: Emily I. Welsh

The opinions and statements published are the responsibility of the authors, and such opinions and statements do not necessarily represent the policies of the APA.

Library of Congress Cataloging-in-Publication Data

Meaning reconstruction and the experience of loss / Robert A. Neimeyer, editor.—1st ed.
    p. cm.
    Includes bibliographical references and indexes.
    ISBN 1-55798-742-4
  1. Loss (Psychology) 2. Meaning (Psychology) 3. Grief. 4. Bereavement—Psychological
    aspects. 5. Death—Psychological aspects.   I. Neimeyer, Robert A., 1954–

BF575 D35 M43 2000
155.9'37—dc21   00-060602

British Library Cataloguing-in-Publication Data
A CIP record is available from the British Library.

Printed in the United States of America

CONTENTS

CONTRIBUTORS

Marla J. Arvay, PhD, Department of Counseling Psychology, University of British Columbia, Vancouver, Canada

Thomas Attig, PhD, Professor of Philosophy Emeritus, Bowling Green State University, Bowling Green, OH

Sheri Kathleen Bélanger, BA, Department of Psychology, Atkinson College, York University, Toronto, Ontario

Lawrence G. Calhoun, PhD, Department of Psychology, University of North Carolina, Charlotte

Heather R. Carlson, MA, LCPC, Department of Counseling Psychology, Loyola University, Chicago

Christopher G. Davis, PhD, Department of Psychology, St. Francis Xavier University, Antigonish, Nova Scotia, Canada

Megan M. Farrell, MS, Department of Counseling and Educational Psychology, State University of New York, Buffalo

Stephen J. Fleming, PhD, Department of Psychology, Atkinson College, York University, Toronto, Ontario, Canada

Thomas T. Frantz, PhD, Department of Counseling and Educational Psychology, State University of New York, Buffalo

Melinda A. Green, BA, Department of Psychology, University of Iowa, Iowa City

George Hagman, LCSW, Director, Outpatient Services, Greater Bridgeport Community Mental Health Center, Bridgeport, CT; Private Practice, New York City and Stamford, CT

John H. Harvey, PhD, Department of Psychology, University of Iowa, Iowa City

Tamara M. Huff, BA, Department of Psychology, University of Iowa, Iowa City

Dennis Klass, PhD, Department of Religious Studies, Webster University, St. Louis, MO

Elizabeth Moulton Milo, PhD, Department of Psychology, Washington School of Professional Psychology, Seattle

Janice Winchester Nadeau, PhD, Minnesota Human Development Consultants, Inc., Minneapolis, MN

Robert A. Neimeyer, PhD, Department of Psychology, University of Memphis, Memphis, TN

T. Anne Richards, MA, Department of Medicine, University of California, San Francisco

Sandra A. Rigazio-DiGilio, PhD, School of Family Studies, Marriage and Family Therapy Program, University of Connecticut, Storrs, CT

Bronna D. Romanoff, PhD, Department of Psychology, The Sage Colleges, Troy, NY

Henk Schut, PhD, Department of Social and Organizational Psychology, University of Utrecht, Netherlands

Kenneth W. Sewell, PhD, Department of Psychology, University of North Texas, Denton

Margaret S. Stroebe, PhD, Department of Clinical Psychology, University of Utrecht, Netherlands

Richard G. Tedeschi, PhD, Department of Psychology, University of North Carolina, Charlotte

Barbara C. Trolley, PhD, Department of Counseling and Educational Psychology, State University of New York, Buffalo

Amy M. Williams, PhD, Department of Psychology, University of North Texas, Denton

PREFACE

When my father died on the eve of my 12th birthday, one world ended, and another began. Long depressed and increasingly isolated by the progressive glaucoma that had robbed him of his vision and that now threatened to take from him the family pharmacy he had founded 20 years before, he decided on one cold January evening to relinquish a life that had for him become unlivable. Our awareness of his suicide—meticulously planned, drawing on the same pharmaceutical skills that once had sustained his life—burst in on my sleeping 9-year-old brother and me the next morning in the form of our mother's panicked announcement that she could not wake our father. Frightened and bewildered, we scrambled out from under our cowboy quilt and stood peering around the doorjamb of our parent's bedroom, as our mother approached our father's lifeless body, touched him, and then recoiled in horror and a convulsion of tears. With that one abrupt gesture, most of what constituted the themes of our family narrative were swept away, and we were thrown collectively into a tumultuous renegotiation of who we were, how we would manage, and what his death meant. Many of the subsequent emotional, relational, and occupational choices made by my mother, my brother, my little sister, and me can be read as responses to my father's fateful decision, although their meaning continues to be clarified, ambiguated, and reformulated across the years.

As this book goes to press, my mother now lies in a nursing home, firmer of mind than body. Frail and emaciated, she may be nearing the end of her long struggle against heart problems, emphysema, and the emotional aftermath of my father's death. My feelings about this, more vivid and fresh than my still-accessible sadness and questioning about the loss of my father, rise in me as I type these words. With trembling lips and moist eyes I anticipate her absence and also grieve for her lost vitality that now is captured only in decades-old photographs. This liminal period between living and dying is indefinite and prolonged, in sharp contrast to the abruptness—at least to my child's mind—of my father's passing. It has therefore afforded different possibilities for negotiating the meaning of our mother's illness and eventual death in conversations with my brother, sister, wife, children, friends and, most centrally, with my mother herself. Although much about this experience is indescribably sad and sometimes openly conflictual, it is also often sweet, affirming the best in each of us and our relationships with one another. And although the immediacy of this real and impending loss makes any very specific anticipation of its meaning impossible, I sense a premonition of its role in further redefining our individual and collective identities in the years to come.

Of course, these are only the two most evident of the defining losses of my life, and there have been many others, not all of which have involved death. The reader can no doubt access stories of his or her own losses that are equally figural and whose meanings may be more or less clear in the broader context of his or her biography. Indeed, I have come to believe that loss, and our personal, relational, and cultural responses to it, are definitional of human life, not because of its intrinsic significance—if there is any—but precisely because it initiates a quest for meaning in deeply personal and intricately social terms.

This book is premised on this assumption, that meaning reconstruction is the central process in what we conventionally refer to as grieving. In the pages that follow, I have invited some of the leading theorists, researchers, and clinicians who are jointly authoring this "new view" of bereavement to articulate their visions, share their findings, and contemplate their implications for the practice of grief counseling and psychotherapy. Just as loss is central to life, I have come to regard a nuanced sensitivity to the legacy of loss as a core feature of psychotherapy, not as a specialized service that is provided only to the recently bereaved. My hope is that something in the chapters that follow will speak to the minds and hearts of the academicians who study loss in all of its human complexity, as well as to the helping professionals who assist people with the reconstruction of their lives in the wake of unbidden transition. I also hope that readers will at least occasionally connect these words to their own loss experiences, so that their professional engagement with grief might be enriched by a more delicate grasping of its role in their own lives.

I conclude with a note of thanks to the many people who have supported me in the development of this book project and the larger life project of which it is the most recent expression. Peggy Schlegel, my acquisitions editor at the American Psychological Association, has been unflagging in her patience and unparalleled in her editorial perspicacity as the book has moved, and sometimes inched, forward. Professional colleagues in the Association for Death Education and Counseling and the International Work Group in Death, Dying, and Bereavement have provided both inspiration and support in various measures, as we have respectfully witnessed one another's real-life losses, celebrated one another's gains, and struggled together toward a more adequate conception of grief in human life. Dennis Klass, Tom Attig, Stephen Fleming, Danai Papadatou, Janice Nadeau, Ken Doka, and Bill Worden deserve special mention in this regard. Most essentially, my wife, Kathy Story, and my children, Eric and Michael, have been supportive beyond expectation in accommodating the inconveniences caused by my pursuit of this project, and more important, in demonstrating their love for me and for my mother at this emotional juncture. I dedicate this book to all three living generations of my family, as we collectively and individually attempt to make meaning of our shared passages.

Robert A. Neimeyer, PhD
Memphis, TN

INTRODUCTION

MEANING RECONSTRUCTION AND LOSS

ROBERT A. NEIMEYER

Like most practicing psychotherapists, theorists, and researchers, I came of age after the dawning of the "death awareness movement," a cultural shift toward greater acknowledgment of the place of death in human life, which emerged in popular consciousness in the 1960s and has continued unabated to the present day. Foreshadowed by the work of pioneering psychologists, sociologists, and physicians (Feifel, 1959; Glaser & Strauss, 1969; Shneidman & Farberow, 1961), this contemporary re-engagement with the ancient problems of death and loss gained impetus with the publication of Elizabeth Kübler-Ross's (1969) paperback *On Death and Dying*. More than any other volume, this book focused popular attention on the psychosocial transitions of the dying person and the grief of survivors, ultimately gaining such wide acceptance that it has become the primary resource on the topic in professional schools in both North America and Europe (Downe-Wambolt & Tamlyn, 1997). A groundswell of scholarship and social advocacy followed, laying the foundation for vigorous research on topics such as grief, suicide, and death attitudes and fostering revolutionary changes in the health care system (e.g., the development of hospice) in the closing decades of the 20th century (Strack, 1997; Wass & Neimeyer, 1995).

My decision to edit this book reflects both my excitement and disenchantment with the fruits of this movement. On the one hand, the burgeoning literature on death and loss has yielded a good deal of data about typical and atypical psychosocial responses to trauma, dying, and bereavement. Partly in response to this growing understanding, such professional specialties as thanatology (the study of death and loss), grief counseling, suicidology, and traumatology have emerged, and nonprofessional bereavement support programs have been organized in countless hospitals, community centers, churches, and synagogues in the United States and abroad. On the other hand, close scrutiny of this literature and these movements suggests that fervid developments in research and social organization have not been matched either by a consistent sophistication in our conceptual models of loss or the generation of new insights into clinical practice. As a result, contemporary researchers are too often constrained by adherence to dated theories that restrict the field of questions they can address, the range of methods they can use, and the conceptual resources on which they rely to interpret their findings (Neimeyer & Hogan, 2001). Likewise, practicing counselors are left operating on the basis of outmoded and increasingly suspect models of loss and its aftermath or are forced to jettison explicit models of grieving altogether in an attempt to work in a way that has greater fidelity to the lived experience of their clients. This situation suggests that the time is ripe for the formulation of new models of grieving that can help integrate and give direction to current research and that carry fresher and more helpful implications for clinical practice.

A GRIEF THEORY FOR THE 21ST CENTURY

For most of the 20th century, bereavement was understood in quintessentially "modern" terms, as a process of "letting go" of one's attachment to the deceased person, "moving on" with one's life, and gradually "recovering" from the depression occasioned by the loss so as to permit a return to "normal" behavior. Reflecting both early psychodynamic formulations of mourning and a contemporary zeitgeist emphasizing individualism, medicalization of suffering, and self-control, this distinctive cultural discourse soon largely displaced a more romantic Victorian understanding of grief as the lasting sign of a "broken heart" resulting from the loss of a love (Stroebe, Gergen, Gergen, & Stroebe, 1992). As the professional and lay literature on loss grew in the past 50 years, this modern conceptualization of grief was gradually expanded to detail the symptomatic manifestations of both "complicated" and "uncomplicated" bereavement and the presumed stages through which it would be "resolved." The latter focus on seemingly universal phases or tasks associated with recovery proved especially popular, offering an apparently authoritative road map through the turbulent emotional terrain associated with acute loss and grief. As a consequence, it was embraced by generations of bereaved people and their caregivers as the preferred framework for understanding grief and facilitating its resolution.

The popularity of this modernist framework notwithstanding, the limitations of conceiving of mourning as the relinquishment of emotional ties and a stagic progression toward recovery have gradually been recognized by increasing numbers of grief scholars, researchers, and counselors (Neimeyer, 1998). At the most obvious level, scientific studies have failed to support any discernable sequence of emotional phases of adaptation to loss or to identify any clear endpoint to grieving that would designate a state of "recovery." Neither is it clear that a universal and normative pattern of grieving exists that would justify the confident diagnosis of symptomatic deviations from this template as "disordered" or "pathological." More subtly, some critics have begun to draw attention to ways in which conventional models indirectly disempower both the bereaved person and would-be caregiver by implying that grieving people must passively negotiate a sequence of psychological transitions forced on them by external events. Similarly, other dissenters have called into question the tacit assumption that emotional states should occupy center stage in theories of grieving, marginalizing both meanings and actions. Finally, some theorists have begun to cast doubt on the highly individualistic nature of traditional theories, which construe grief as an entirely private process, experienced outside the context of human relatedness.

Spurred by these criticisms, and supported by a contextualist, constructivist, and interpretive shift in psychology and allied disciplines (Neimeyer & Mahoney, 1995; Neimeyer & Raskin, 2000), a "new wave" of grief theory is emerging that reflects a changing *zeitgeist* about the role of loss in human experience. Among the common elements of these newer models are

- skepticism about the universality of a predictable emotional trajectory that leads from psychological disequilibrium to readjustment, coupled with an appreciation of more complex patterns of adaptation;
- a shift away from the presumption that successful grieving requires withdrawal of psychic energy from the one who has died, and toward a recognition of the potentially healthy role of continued symbolic bonds with the deceased person;
- attention to broadly cognitive processes entailed in mourning, supplementing the traditional focus on the emotional consequences of loss;
- a de-emphasis on universal syndromes of grieving and a focus on "local" practices for accommodating loss among specific categories of the bereaved or various (sub)cultural groups;

- greater awareness of the implications of major loss for the individual's sense of identity, often necessitating deep revisions in his or her self-definition;
- increased appreciation of the possibility of life-enhancing "posttraumatic growth" as one integrates the lessons of loss; and
- a broadened focus not only on the experience of individual survivors but also on the patterns and processes by which loss is negotiated in families and wider social contexts.

A prominent theme in these newer models is their insistence that *symptoms have significance*, that the outward manifestations of distress associated with grieving can be understood only in terms of the struggle of bereaved people and their social domain to accommodate to a changed (inter)personal reality resulting from the loss. Viewed in its broadest terms, this suggests the gradual emergence of a new paradigm for grief theory, research, and practice, one founded on the postulate that *meaning reconstruction in response to a loss is the central process in grieving* (Neimeyer, 1998). Of course, sporadic attention to the problems of meaning making in bereavement is not without precedent; 25 years ago, Marris (1974) outlined a sophisticated view of grieving as the tension between conserving and relinquishing a world of meanings undercut by the loss of a defining attachment. What is new, however, is the rallying of cutting-edge researchers, scholars, and clinicians around the cluster of themes summarized above and the growing awareness that a meaning-making framework constitutes a potentially fresh point of departure for clinical practice. My goal in editing this book is to help consolidate these developments on the cutting edge of grief theory and to make them available for the first time to a broad scientific and applied readership. Thus, more scientifically oriented readers will find not only comprehensive discussions of some of the most progressive research programs in the area of trauma and loss, but also original data that extend the boundaries of what is known about these fields and their interface. Applied readers, on the other hand, will find both clinically informed (and informative) models to direct their practice and ample case descriptions to bridge the concepts with the lived world of real people suffering real losses. Above all, I hope that both sets of readers will encounter new paradigms for approaching loss and reconstruction in a respectful, revealing way that has equal relevance to our own lives as to those of our clients and research participants.

PLAN OF THE BOOK

Collecting exemplary work in any field into a thematically coherent volume presents the editor with a series of hard choices. How much space should be devoted to reviewing traditional work in the field, in order to provide a backdrop for the present project? To what extent should the contents present evaluative summaries of primary research, in a way that digests it for the first-time reader? Should the volume include original contributions to research and practice, or should it leave this task to professional journals? What balance should be achieved among conceptual, empirical, and applied contributions? Above all, how should the focus of the project be developed in a way that gives the project some definition but without imposing the risk of narrowness?

In undertaking the present project, I chose to focus on state-of-the-art contributions rather than exhaustive reviews of traditional theories that will be familiar to most readers. Thus, I have encouraged individual chapter authors to clarify their own positions by juxtaposing them with conventional grief theory when this served their purposes, leaving it to other recent handbooks (e.g., Stroebe, Stroebe, Hansson, & Schut, 2001) to provide authoritative coverage of other facets of the bereavement literature. Likewise, I have permitted contributors to write in their own style, sometimes reviewing conceptual developments within a given lineage of grief theory or research, sometimes offering fresh data illuminating the struggle for significance in different groups of mourners, and sometimes formulating clinical heuristics in keeping with a meaning-making perspective. The result, I hope, is a book that will speak to multiple audiences, promoting a respectful and mutually illuminating conversation among grief theorists, counselors, and researchers (in both the qualitative and quantitative traditions) about topics of central and shared relevance to them all.

Finally, the almost bewildering array of subjects that could be considered pertinent to loss required some judgment to be made about the topical scope of the book. At least in an expanded definition, *loss* could (and has been interpreted to) subsume a welter of human experiences, including bereavement, relationship dissolution, job loss, natural catastrophe, sexual assault, geographic displacement, physical illness, role redefinition, interpersonal violence, and political torture, to name just a few (Harvey, 1998). Rather than attempt a superficial coverage of each of these areas, I have chosen to focus primarily on what might be considered the prototypical form of loss—namely, the death of a loved one. I have, however, secondarily encouraged contributors to relate their work to other forms of trauma (e.g., sexual abuse, illness, vicarious traumatization) in order to suggest the permeable boundaries around a meaning-reconstruction approach to grief and its high relevance to practicing therapists. The decision to pay particular attention to the fertile but relatively neglected interface of grief and trauma stems from my conviction, shared by a growing number of researchers and scholars, that the conjunction of the two poses special challenges for both theorists and practitioners. Accordingly, traumatic grief (such as in the deaths of children) receives special attention, alongside a broad sampling of other losses, including those of friends, partners, parents, and other family members. I hope that this deep engagement with a range of selected loss experiences (especially those that have attracted the greatest research attention) will adequately suggest both the focal utility of a meaning-making model of bereavement and the promise of extending its application to other closely allied areas.

ORGANIZATION OF THE CHAPTERS

The three chapters of Part I begin this effort by "clearing a space" that makes possible a new approach to the old problem of grieving. Working within the psychoanalytic tradition, George Hagman (chapter 1) analyzes the almost hegemonic influence of Freud's early conceptualization of mourning and the remarkable degree to which it has been taken up in unquestioning fashion by generations of subsequent theorists and therapists. Integrating new data on the dynamics of grieving and observations grounded in clinical practice, he then calls into question the central tenets of this traditional view, especially its cornerstone assumption of the necessity to "decathect" or withdraw emotional energy from the deceased in order to invest in new relationships. Thomas Attig (chapter 2) then expands on this frame by considering how life is augmented, not reduced, by maintaining our web of connection to those we have loved and lost. He finds richly illustrative case material in the diary of C. S. Lewis, whose reflections on the intermingling of joy and suffering prompt Attig's own on the way in which we both discover and invent new meaning in the face of loss. Finally, Margaret Stroebe and Henk Schut (chapter 3) detail their recent dual process model of grieving and consider for the first time its relation to the task of meaning reconstruction. A strength of their model is its capacity to integrate much of the leading-edge research on the way in which bereaved people cope with their new status by oscillating between preoccupation with the grief itself and re-engagement in a world forever transformed by their loss.

Part II examines the delicate tacking between the personal and interpersonal domains that characterizes the negotiation of grief in a social context—a context that involves not only other living people, but also one's ongoing relationship to the deceased person. Dennis Klass (chapter 4) exemplifies this perspective by sharing the results of his long-term ethnographic study in a chapter on bereaved parents, tracing the gradual psycho–spiritual consolidation of their "inner representation" of the child and its validation by the community of others who have suffered similarly tragic losses. His chapter is also valuable in illustrating a theme implicit in many chapters—that meaning reconstruction is as much a social practice as it is a cognitive process. Janice Winchester Nadeau (chapter 5) extends this view in her study of interactive meaning making in families in response to the death of one of their members. Drawing on her extensive grounded theory analysis of scores of family conversations, she detects and distills patterns of meaning making that transcend purely individual perspectives. Elizabeth Moulton Milo (chapter 6) concludes this section with a discussion of her own qualitative research on the conjunction of two losses: the death of a child with developmental disability. Significantly, she finds that the life and death of these children, despite the considerable stress associated with them, are almost invariably embraced as treasured sources of wisdom, perspective, and love by their mothers.

Part III develops this theme of the positive legacy of loss with a set of research reviews and original contributions. Christopher G. Davis (chapter 7) begins by situating his research with Camille Wortman, Daniel Lehman, and others in the context of three general approaches to understanding stress reactions: focusing on individual differences, coping behaviors, and the unique psychosocial responses occasioned by loss. Although his research program draws on features of all three approaches, it concentrates primarily on elucidating meaning-attribution processes (such as counterfactual thinking, sense making, and benefit finding) that impede or facilitate adaptation. Lawrence G. Calhoun and Richard G. Tedeschi (chapter 8) follow with a wide-ranging review of the substantial empirical literature that provides evidence of personal growth resulting from a struggle with loss, for at least a sizable minority of those who suffer it. They go on to develop not only a research agenda for future investigators, but also some preliminary guidelines for practicing clinicians engaged with their clients in an effort after meaning. T. Anne Richards (chapter 9) then offers an in-depth view of the quest for spiritual meaning in a group of bereaved partners of gay men whose lives were cut short by AIDS. Her work is exemplary for its sophisticated integration of both quantitative and qualitative methods, demonstrating that clinically astute researchers need not sacrifice richness for rigor. Thomas T. Frantz, Megan M. Farrell, and Barbara C. Trolley (chapter 10) conclude the section with a brief overview of previous research on the positive outcomes of bereavement and then share the results of their study of nearly 400 adults who had lost a loved one approximately a year before. Conducting extensive content coding of their structured interviews, these authors capture the "silver lining" in the dark cloud of bereavement, as well as the life lessons, changed sense of self, and personal resources endorsed by survivors.

Part IV explicitly develops a constructivist theme that informs many of the preceding chapters, by viewing loss through the lens of narrative theory. Marla J. Arvay (chapter 11) opens with a stirring study of the personal stories of trauma counselors attempting to reconcile their own shattered beliefs in humanity with the hope of a more viable future. Her account is thorough in its reflexivity and persuasive in its argument that narrative inquiry is uniquely suited to illuminate the self-referential, relational, and dialogical processes by which a violated world of meaning is rebuilt. John H. Harvey,

Heather R. Carlson, Tamara M. Huff, and Melinda A. Green (chapter 12) then consider another aspect of self-narratives, namely, the construction and confiding of accounts of loss in an affirming interpersonal context. Illustrating their thesis with accounts of Holocaust survivorship, relationship breakdown, and social upheaval, they demonstrate that "storying" one's experience in the presence of a relevant audience has healing potential, on levels from the personal to cultural. Bronna D. Romanoff (chapter 13) then brings the section to a close by usefully blurring the dividing line between research and therapy, drawing particularly on the self-exploration of a client seeking to capture the vicissitudes of her life and illness in narrative form. This prompts Romanoff to reflect on the function of self-narratives—whether fully formed or in formation—in permitting people to attribute meaning to a life by "re-authoring" it in preferred directions.

Although rich insights and implications for practicing therapists are woven through nearly all of the foregoing chapters, the contributions constituting Part V are the most consistently focused on meaning reconstruction in the clinical context. I (chapter 14) begin the section by describing a constructivist framework for understanding grief and grief therapy, one that attends to the linguistic and relational nuances of the client's account in an attempt to articulate its constraints and facilitate its elaboration. I then anchor these principles in a detailed transcript of an actual session of grief therapy, elucidating the client's intentionality and my own as we reweave her connection to her deceased mother and place in sharper relief the implications of this loss for her ongoing life. Kenneth W. Sewell and Amy M. Williams (chapter 15) then provide a synoptic review of their program of research on the personal meaning systems of trauma survivors, which sheds light on the constructive bridge that links exposure to tragic loss with the sequelae of posttraumatic stress disorder. As they demonstrate, their conceptual model has wide applicability to traumatic events ranging from military combat to incest and offers an organizing frame for clinical intervention. Stephen J. Fleming and Sheri Kathleen Bélanger (chapter 16) extend this integrative perspective in their own cogent analysis of the correspondence between the struggles instigated by bereavement and sexual abuse. In particular, they argue that trauma mastery in such cases entails many aspects of the grief process, including reckoning with the devastation of one's assumptive world. Finally, Sandra A. Rigazio-DiGilio (chapter 17) provides a moving account of her use of videography with a family anticipating the death of a daughter, who assumes the role of director in recording scenes for and with her family. The creative use of this medium to "tell a story" and confer a sense of authorship makes it clear that narration is more than a metaphor and can transcend the written or spoken word.

I hope that the collection of chapters in this book—authored by more than two dozen leading contributors to grief theory, research, and therapy—

convey something of the depth and breadth of a meaning-reconstruction perspective. I trust that the contributing authors speak for themselves in articulating not only their views of grief theory and the empirical work supporting it, but also the import of their thinking for the practice of grief therapy. I hope that the reader will encounter in these pages a fund of fresh concepts, methods, and strategies for engaging, and perhaps facilitating, the reconstruction of meaning in the lives of people struggling with loss.

REFERENCES

Downe-Wambolt, B., & Tamlyn, D. (1997). An international survey of death education trends in faculties of nursing and medicine. *Death Studies, 21,* 177–188.

Feifel, H. (Ed.). (1959). *The meaning of death.* New York: McGraw-Hill.

Glaser, B. G., & Strauss, A. L. (Eds.). (1969). *Time for dying.* Chicago: Aldine.

Harvey, J. (Ed.). (1998). *Perspectives on loss: A sourcebook.* Philadelphia: Taylor & Francis.

Kübler-Ross, E. (1969). *On death and dying.* New York: Macmillan.

Marris, P. (1974). *Loss and change.* London: Routledge.

Neimeyer, R. A. (1998). *Lessons of loss: A guide to coping.* New York: McGraw-Hill.

Neimeyer, R. A., & Hogan, N. (2001). Quantitative or qualitative? Measurement issues in the study of grief. In M. Stroebe, W. Stroebe, H. Schut, & R. Hansson (Eds.), *Handbook of bereavement research: Consequences, coping, and care.* Washington, DC: American Psychological Association.

Neimeyer, R. A., & Mahoney, M. J. (1995). *Constructivism in psychotherapy.* Washington, DC: American Psychological Association.

Neimeyer, R. A., & Raskin, J. D. (Eds.). (2000). *Constructions of disorder: Meaning-Making frameworks for psychotherapy.* Washington, DC: American Psychological Association.

Shneidman, E., & Farberow, N. (Eds.). (1961). *The cry for help.* New York: McGraw-Hill.

Strack, S. (Ed.). (1997). *Death and the quest for meaning.* Northvale, NJ: Aronson.

Stroebe, M., Gergen, M., Gergen, K., & Stroebe, W. (1992). Broken hearts or broken bonds: Love and death in historical perspective. *American Psychologist, 47,* 1205–1212.

Stroebe, M., Stroebe, W., Hansson, R., & Schut, H. (2001). *Handbook of bereavement research: Consequences, coping, and care.* Washington, DC: American Psychological Association.

Wass, H., & Neimeyer, R. A. (Eds.). (1995). *Dying: Facing the facts* (3rd ed.). Philadelphia: Taylor & Francis.

I

Breaking Ground:
Toward a Fresh Theory of Grieving

1

BEYOND DECATHEXIS: TOWARD A NEW PSYCHOANALYTIC UNDERSTANDING AND TREATMENT OF MOURNING

GEORGE HAGMAN

This chapter is a contribution to the sea change that is occurring in our culture's view of bereavement and mourning. Across disciplines, clinicians and researchers are questioning many of the assumptions that have influenced our conceptualizations about mourning over the past 80 years. Given that psychoanalysis has played a central role in the development of modern mourning theory (Jacobs, 1993; Parkes, 1981; Rando, 1993), a review of the current status of analytic thinking in this area is needed. In this chapter I examine recent developments in psychoanalytic theory and treatment of bereavement, mourning, and grief. I show how some contemporary analysts have proposed changes in the psychoanalytic model of mourning, which echo many of the points made by other disciplines. I will begin with a brief overview of the standard psychoanalytic model of mourning, which was based primarily on Freud's early metapsychological theories and, more specifically, on his 1917 article "Mourning and Melancholia." I next discuss a number of recent critiques of the standard model as well as some proposals for its revision. These critiques target the asocial, intrapsychic nature of the standard model and its failure to address the full complexity of mourning reactions. I then suggest an outline of a new psychoanalytic model of mourning that appears to be emerging from the current debate. In closing, I discuss a case report that illustrates the implications of the new model of mourning for clinical practice.

LITERATURE REVIEW

In this section I examine the major writings that have contributed significantly to what has been referred to as the *standard psychoanalytic model of mourning* (Hagman, 1995b). I do not believe that the analytic mourning literature is homogenous and without valuable deviations from the norm. However, what seems to be the case is that there has been a model that has dominated psychoanalytic thinking and practice since Freud originally outlined the basic components of his mourning theory in 1915. We will be concerned with the origin and development of that standard model.

Freud's writings about mourning are few in number, as well as extremely brief, which is surprising when one considers the importance of the subject. They consist of several scattered references, most of which are notes included in papers devoted to other subjects. Freud's most sustained discussion of mourning was in his 1917 article "Mourning and Melancholia." It was there that Freud first delineated the framework of what would become the standard model of mourning. However, that is not to say that Freud intended to promulgate a standard model. Erna Furman (1974) argued that Freud's purpose might have been only to set up a model situation to explore the dynamics of narcissism and melancholia. Furman claimed that it was misleading to assume that Freud intended to portray "actual mourning processes in their full clinical complexity" (pp. 241–242). Nonetheless, analysts after Freud would grant truth status to Freud's speculations on mourning. Hence, the following quote became one of Freud's (1917/1958) best-known and most influential writings:

> Now in what consists the work which mourning performs? The testing of reality, having shown that the loved object no longer exists, requires forthwith that the libido shall be withdrawn from its attachment to the object. Against this demand a struggle of course arises—it may be universally observed that man never willingly abandons a libido-position, not even when a substitute is already beckoning to him. . . . The normal outcome is that deference for reality gains the day. Nevertheless its behest cannot be at once obeyed. The task is carried through bit by bit, under great expense of time and cathectic energy, while all the time the existence of the lost object is continued in the mind. Each single one of the memories and hopes which bound the libido to the object is brought

up and hyper-cathected, and the detachment of the libido from it is accomplished. . . . When the work of mourning is completed the ego becomes free and uninhibited again. (pp. 244–245)

In this passage Freud described a normal, even universal, intrapsychic process the main function of which is the incremental divestment of libido (decathexis) from memories of the lost object. It is by means of this painful process that psychological equilibrium is restored and motivation to love is renewed. With the successful completion of the work of mourning all ties to the lost object are relinquished and premorbid functioning restored.

In later writings Freud continued to view mourning in terms of the economy of psychic energy. For example, in his 1926 monograph *Inhibition, Symptoms, and Anxiety* he reconsidered an as-yet-unexplained characteristic of mourning—its extreme painfulness. His answer was basically a matter of hydraulics. He asserted that separation *should* be painful in view of "the high and unsatisfiable cathexis of longing which is concentrated on the object by the bereaved person during reproduction of the situations in which he must undo the ties that bind him" (p. 172). In other words, energy (libido) that had been discharged through interactions with an object cannot be released, because the object is gone. This energy still pressing for satisfaction builds up in the mind, resulting in emotional pain. Recovery, according to this view, follows the redirection of libido from the memory of the lost person to available survivors with whom discharge can occur (recathexis), thereby removing the cause of the pain and renewing opportunities for pleasure in life.

A later addition to the developing standard model was the role of identification with the lost object. Although not discussed in his 1915 article, Freud made significant, but once again brief, comments in later works that would influence the writings of major psychoanalytic thinkers such as Karl Abraham and others (Fenichel, 1945; Klein, 1940). For example, in *The Ego and the Id* (1923/1961), Freud stated, "It may be that this identification is the sole condition under which the Id can give up its objects" (p. 29). Abraham (1927/1960) developed this idea further, commenting that the bereaved person effects "a temporary introjection of the loved person. Its main purpose is to preserve the person's relation with the lost object" (p. 435). This notion of identification following object loss would become a central component of object relations theory and the typology of ego defenses. However, despite its importance, identification with the lost object would play only a peripheral role in the developing standard model. Analysts continued to emphasize decathexis over continuity, while identification was viewed as at best an indication of unresolved mourning or, at worst, a symptom of depression (Gaines, 1997).

Regarding the affective component of mourning, Helene Deutsch (1937) wrote a short article, "Absence of Grief," that has had an enduring impact. Deutsch argued that the absence of the expression of the affect of grief was indicative and/or predictive of psychopathological mourning:

Every unresolved grief is given expression in some form or other . . . the process of mourning, as a reaction to the real loss of a loved person *must be carried out to completion*. As long as the early libidinal or aggressive attachment persists, the painful affect continues to flourish, and vice versa, the attachments are unresolved as long as the affective process of mourning has not been accomplished. (pp. 16–17)

Influenced by Deutsch's article, analysts and nonanalysts alike have come to view the expression of grief as an essential component of successful mourning. In fact, the absence of grief expression in a bereaved person became for many the diagnostic hallmark of pathological mourning and, to this day, in order to be considered normal from the point of view of mourning theory, bereaved people must endure the additional stress of *having* to express sadness and grief. Many popular forms of bereavement counseling, influenced by analytic thinking (Volkan, 1981), prescribe that the therapist challenge bereaved patients' "resistance" to mourning, compelling them to express sadness, in the belief that the abreaction of suppressed affect is at the core of successful treatment.

In 1961 there was another important addition to the standard model: the idea that the mourning process, by then accepted as an indubitable reality, was a biologically based process characterized by specific, identifiable stages (Bowlby, 1961; Parkes, 1981; Pollock, 1961; Volkan, 1981). For years the central concern of bereavement theorists became the identification of the nature and quantity of these stages. Once again this idea was enormously influential. With the advent of Kübler-Ross's work on death and dying, the idea that mourning unfolded in predetermined phases became accepted as nothing short of the truth. No one seemed to raise a dissenting voice as the stage model began to dominate the Western cultural perspective on bereavement.

The best summary of the standard psychoanalytic model of mourning as it is held to today can be found in the most recent edition of *Psychoanalytic Terms and Concepts* (Moore & Fine, 1991), the standard reference of the American Psychoanalytic Association. It is interesting to see how little has changed since Freud's original discussion in 1915. The following quote covers most of the major components:

Mourning is . . . the mental process by which man's psychic equilibrium is restored following the loss of a meaningful love object . . . it is a normal process to any significant loss. The predominant mood of mourning is painful and is usually accompanied by loss of interest in the outside world, preoccupation with memories of the lost object, and diminished capacity to make new emotional investments. Uncomplicated mourning is not pathological and does not require treatment. With time the individual adapts to the loss and renews his or her capacity for pleasure in relationships.

Although reality testing is preserved and confirms that the loved object no longer exists, in the internal process of mourning the aggrieved person initially is unable to withdraw attachment from the lost object. Instead the mourner turns away from reality, through denial, and clings to the mental representation of the lost object. Thus the object loss is turned into an ego loss. Through the stages of the mourning process, this ego loss is gradually healed and psychic equilibrium is restored. The work of mourning includes three successive, interrelated phases; the success of each affecting the next: 1) understanding, accepting and coping with the loss and its circumstances; 2) the mourning proper, which involves withdrawal of attachment to and identification with the lost object (decathexis); and 3) resumption of emotional life in harmony with one's level of maturity, which frequently involves establishing new relationships (recathexis). (1915/1958, p. 122)

COMPONENTS OF THE STANDARD MODEL

There are a number of component assumptions that comprise the standard model. These assumptions have been tremendously influential in psychoanalytic circles as well as modern Western perspectives on grief more generally. In fact, several may appear so familiar and basic to us that they are beyond question. Therefore, to contrast new developments in psychoanalytic mourning theory I start with a discussion of the essential components of the traditional model of mourning.

- *There is an identifiable, normal psychological mourning process.* Before Freud's time, bereavement was understood as a commonplace experience, viewed primarily in social–behavioral terms rather than psychological ones. Freud was the first to articulate a perspective on mourning as a private, interior psychological process having specific characteristics and dynamics. This—the intrapsychic process model of mourning—is perhaps Freud's most significant contribution to bereavement studies.
- *The function of mourning is a conservative and restorative one rather than a transformative one.* Rather than leading toward change, the psychoanalytic model is a conservative process. Restoration of psychic equilibrium and the return to premorbid conditions are the goals of mourning. The notion of mourning as a creative and transformative process was articulated by psychoanalyst George Pollock (1989) but has not had a major impact on the standard model.
- *Mourning is a private, intrapsychic process rather than a social and relational one.* The model of the mind, on which the standard model was based, was of a closed psychological system with its own inherent tendencies toward organization and conflict. Freud's model was constructed to explain the

economics of energy distribution within the mind. Some analysts have argued that the mourning process is part of the mind's biologically grounded adaptive responses, having developed over time to ensure optimal survivability in the face of inevitable separations and losses (Pollock, 1989). This view of the mind as isolated and intrapsychic did not allow for the role of relationships and social factors in mourning (Hagman, 1996c). Even those recent authors who have given some consideration to social factors have viewed the environment as supporting only the private, individual work of mourning (Slochower, 1996).

- *The affect of grief arises spontaneously from within the individual, and denial or suppression of grief leads to pathological states.* In classical psychoanalysis affects were viewed as derivatives of the drives, possessing a powerful motivational role. Thus, they were seen as arising from the depths of the person's unconscious, the most private and primitive part of the mind. As noted earlier, Deutsch (1937) was the clearest proponent of this viewpoint. To Deutsch, grief was an internally arising force, which was undeniable, and the suppression of grief would lead to psychological illness. Thus, in the standard model grief has no communicative or relational function. Grief in the standard model is primarily a physical aspect of mourning, closer to a bodily function than to thought or language.

- *Mourning has normal, standardized characteristics, rather than being unique and personal.* Freud's speculations led almost ineluctably to the normalization of mourning in the stage models of Bowlby and Pollock. From that point on, mourning became increasingly regimented and standardized. Despite attempts by many stage-model theorists to argue for a flexible application of the model, in practice the more personal idiosyncratic reactions to loss became de-emphasized. According to the standard model, health and normalcy are determined by successful progression through a specific sequence of stages within which the bereaved person was expected to complete certain tasks. Some authors (Foote & Frank, 1999; Neimeyer, 1998; Walter, 1994) have argued that these expectations have been granted an almost dogmatic status as the personal and different is viewed as resistance, pathology, or both.

- *Mourning is painful and sad rather than involving a range of affects.* The standard model, following Freud, limits the consideration of affect to painful grieving and despondency. This has also led to the expectation that the expression of pain and grief is indicative of successful mourning. Other affects—such as humor, pleasure, and even joy—are viewed as aberrations or resistances to normal mourning.

- *The central task of mourning is detachment (decathexis) rather than continuity.* This is perhaps the central component of the standard model. The primary function of mourning is to relinquish one's attachment to the dead person. Even those who included identification as a component of the standard model saw identification as a strategy to give up the object rather than maintain continuity in a meaningful, vital sense. Given this, a continuing passionate attachment to the dead person is almost invariably viewed as pathological. To experience the dead person as a living presence, with which one maintains a dialogue, would be viewed as maladaptive from the perspective of the standard model.

- *The vicissitudes of psychic energy are the basis of the standard psychoanalytic model; the meanings associated with the loss are not emphasized.* The standard model stresses accommodation and the internal vicissitudes of psychic energy. The meanings of the mourning process are important only to the extent to which they assist or impede the work of mourning, but the notion of meaning does not in and of itself have a motivating function in the standard model.

- *The normal mourning process leads to a point of full resolution rather than being open and evolving.* Following Freud, the standard model postulates that normal mourning leads to resolution—after all, there must be a point at which all energy is withdrawn and reinvested. The attachment to the dead person is given up, painful mourning remits, and the bereaved person joyfully and productively invests himself or herself in new relationships. In addition, because normal mourning is viewed as having a typical and time-limited course, there is the additional expectation that the resolution of mourning occur within a certain time frame. For years this was reflected in the *Diagnostic and Statistical Manual of Mental Disorders* criteria, which indicated duration of mourning as diagnostic. People who continue to be sad, or who continue to maintain a sense of relatedness to the dead person, are viewed as suffering from unresolved mourning—or, worse, pathologic grief.

CRITIQUES OF THE STANDARD MODEL: CREATING A NEW PSYCHOANALYTIC MOURNING THEORY

Contemporary psychoanalysts, particularly those whose theory base is object relations, self psychology, and relational psychoanalysis, have largely abandoned Freud's psychological model of instinctual energy and isolated mental functioning. There has been a growing acceptance that psychological life is fundamentally embedded in relationships and interpersonally oriented meaning (Mitchell, 1993). Analysts, once empiricists studying the universal principles of psychodynamics, now view themselves as interpreters (perhaps even coauthors) of complex and ambiguous organizations of meaning and personal narratives. This realization that psychological life is neither so private nor so predictable has led to a reconsideration of many long-held beliefs (Stolorow & Atwood, 1992). Recently, in keeping with this "paradigm shift," a number of psychoanalytic writers have begun to question the standard model of mourning and some of its characteristics described above (Gaines, 1997; Hagman, 1993, 1995a, 1995b, 1996a, 1996b; Kaplan, 1995; Shane & Shane, 1990; Shapiro, 1996; Shelby, 1993, 1994). In the following review I will structure the discussion thematically roughly following the components of the standard model just discussed:

- *Freud's original depiction of mourning was not valid as a general mode.* The source of Freud's model of mourning, as delineated in "Mourning and Melancholia" (1917/1958), is unclear. Freud rhetorically delineated the "normal" mourning process as a baseline for his discussion of the psychodynamics of melancholia. However, the emphatic quality of his writing is striking. The mourning process is "universally observed." There is a clear and unquestioning presentation of the work of mourning. Freud seemed to believe that the description offered is proven and obvious; however, prior to the publication of "Mourning and Melancholia" there had never been a systematic study of mourning, and few if any serious writings on the subject had been done. Mourning had not as yet become an object of medical or psychiatric study—this would not happen for another 30 years. Hence, it remains unclear on what empirical basis Freud founded his model of mourning. Furman's (1974) argument, mentioned earlier, that Freud was not making an empirical assertion, seems weak when one considers the assertive language and tone of Freud's essay. This is how people mourn, he is obviously claiming.

  In "Mourning: A Review and Reconsideration" (Hagman, 1995b), I argued that Freud's model of mourning was based on views of mourning that were prevalent in Western society during his lifetime, specifically, that mourning is a state that is distinct and exceptional, that the bereaved is withdrawn and preoccupied with the lost person, that grief is extremely painful, and that despondency is characteristic. I cited the historical analysis of Aries (1974, 1981) and Schor (1994), who both discussed the ostentatious and extreme behaviors of mourners during the 19th century in Europe. Aries called this reaction "hysterical mourning," and Schor referred to the "deep mourning" characterized by ostentatious displays of prolonged grief. I claim that it appears that Freud's model, which became the basis for contemporary psychoanalytic mourning theory and has influenced virtually all other models as well as general social attitudes, may have been descriptive of a new type of dramatic and passionate mourning that developed in 19th-century Europe, thus limiting its usefulness as a general model of human bereavement. (The psychoanalyst Charles Brenner [1972] believed that Freud drew the wrong conclusion from his observations and mistook defensive reactions for normal mourning.)

- *A model of isolated mourning does not recognize the important role of others in mourning.* The standard model of mourning was developed within a theoretical paradigm that is currently under revision. The notion that the mind is a private, closed system that primarily functions to regulate its own inner world of energies and defenses is essentially defunct. Modern psychoanalysis has recognized that human psychological life is profoundly relational. In addition, interest in the importance of meaningful self-experience within the context of relatedness to others has been driving psychoanalytic thinking toward how our psychological life is socially embedded. A central feature of virtually all of the recent critiques of the standard model is that the intrapsychic focus does not convey the role of other people and the social milieu in facilitating or impeding recovery from bereavement (Hagman, 1996c; Shane & Shane, 1990; Shelby, 1994).

- *We must look beyond decathexis and relinquishment to the central goal of continuity in mourning.* In his article "Detachment and Continuity: The Two Tasks of Mourning," Robert Gaines (1997) stated,

> Emphasis on the need to detach from the lost object has obscured another aspect of the work of mourning, which is to repair the disruption to the inner self–other relationship caused by the actual loss. . . . This is the task I call "creating continuity." (p. 549)

Several of the new mourning theorists have echoed Gaines's critique. I (Hagman, 1995b), Kaplan (1995), and Shapiro (1996) have each argued that the emphasis on relinquishment has so dominated the psychoanalytic perspective that normal processes of preservation and continuity have been neglected, if not pathologized. Shapiro stated that "Grief is resolved through the creation of a loving, growing relationship with the dead that recognizes the new psychological or spiritual (rather than corporeal) dimensions of the relationship" (p. 552). A fundamental argument of the new psychoanalytic model of mourning is the need to preserve attachment to the lost person, and the importance of securing a sense of meaningful relationship, which transcends loss. Anton Kris (1992) pointed out that the painful process of alternation between wishing to hold onto the lost relationship and wishing to live on in the present and into the future cannot be resolved by choosing one or the other. Kaplan described the importance of the continuing dialogue with the dead, Gaines stressed the work of "creating continuity," Shapiro (1994) underscored the social factors in preserving the object tie, and I (Hagman, 1995a, 1995b) have emphasized the transformation and internal restructuralization of the attachment to the deceased person. More recently, Gilbert Rose (1999) stressed the importance of acknowledgment of loss in the context of continuity.

- *The psychic energy model is too concrete: Meaning and dialogue are at the heart of mourning.* Robert Stolorow and his associates (1992) in their recent work have made powerful arguments against the classical psychoanalytic model of the "isolated mind." A central part of their critique is the notion that our standard metapsychology concretizes subjectivity, as if human experience could be reduced to things, which can then be described and studied. The standard model of mourning is such a concretization and, to that extent, it reduces meaningful human experience to a mechanistic process. The new psychoanalytic mourning theory stresses the view of mourning as a crisis of meaning. In my chapter "Death of a Selfobject: Towards a Self Psychology of the Mourning Process" (Hagman, 1995a), I described how "the network of cognitive–affective schemata (self-organizing fantasies) sustained by and within the selfobject tie is traumatized, broken down, reworked and gradually transformed to maintain the integrity of self-experience and restore self-cohesion and vitality" (p. 194). Kaplan (1995) approached the problem more interpersonally: "The human experience of loss is about our ongoing and everlasting dialogue with the dead" (p. 16). Mourning dialogue is the means by which human beings maintain the vital meaning of the lost relationship in their psychological and social lives. The new model views mourning as most importantly a crisis of meaning both on an intrapsychic level, through the transformation of psychological structure, and dialogically, through the maintenance of meaningful human connections in reality and fantasy.
- *The classical view of pathological mourning does not capture the positive function of the attempt to preserve meaning in the face of*

disruption. The conceptualizations of pathological mourning associated with the standard model take several forms. Freud emphasized conflicts in the drives, specifically, the vicissitudes of aggressive feelings toward the lost person and the redirection of aggression inward. Deutsch emphasized the denial of affect. Pollock and Bowlby sought to identify the specific phase of mourning in which the bereaved found himself or herself fixated. The most common way of viewing pathology, given the predominance of the process (stage) model, has been the notion of an inhibited or derailed mourning process. Refusal to give oneself over to the inevitable mourning process has been viewed as the single biggest cause of pathological bereavements. Recently some have questioned this perspective, which they see as inaccurate and perhaps harmful. With the growing recognition that mourning is intersubjective, meaningful, and concerned with continuity of the tie with the deceased person, our assessments of pathologic mourning must now consider, among many factors, the following: (a) whether there has been a failure of the social surround to assist with mourning; (b) how the patient is attempting to maintain meaningful life experience in the face of loss; and (c) how the patient is attempting to hold onto the tie to the deceased person, thus preserving a threatened relationship.

■ *The standard model's perspective on grief as private does not capture the complexity and fundamentally communicative function of grief affects.* Freudian psychological theory holds that affects, such as grief, could be explained as arising from the somatic abreaction of instinctual drives that are denied their normal avenues of discharge. In the case of bereavement, the absence of the object of love results in the experience of psychological pain and the eruption of despondent longings and grief. On the other hand, depression follows from the loss of an object of ambivalence, as aggression is turned inward taking the self as its object. Recent analytic models have revised this endogenously based model of grief, and affects in general, and replaced it with a view of affect as relational and intersubjective. Beginning in the 1960s Bowlby (1961, 1980) argued that the expression of grief was not simply a private response to loss but an effort on the part of the bereaved to re-establish connection with the lost object and/or to obtain comfort from other survivors. More recently, analysts (Stolorow & Atwood, 1992) have stressed the importance of affect attunement and responsiveness to psychological development, the resolution of trauma, and the integrity of self-experience. As a consequence of this relational approach to affects, grief is viewed as communicative and meaningful, its primary function being the preservation or restoration of interpersonal connection. In clinical terms, this means that the analyst's attunement to the bereaved person's expression of grief and responsiveness to the need for comfort and protection is now viewed as of central importance to the facilitation of mourning.

- *The stage model of mourning does not recognize the complexity and uniqueness of each mourning experience.* In my article "Mourning: A Review and Reconsideration" (Hagman, 1995b), I argued that normal mourning processes should be judged within a broad context that includes multiple variables and acceptable outcomes. Gaines (1997) stated explicitly that "mourning is not something that can be finished" (p. 568). Once we move beyond decathexis, it becomes clear that there is no need to declare an expectable endpoint to mourning. From this new perspective a person may mourn for a lifetime. Most important, the new perspective links mourning with developmental stages and crises. An example is when a childhood loss is revitalized in middle age and when, during periods of new loss, old bereavements are revitalized. Rather than being resolved, the significance of a loss may be elaborated throughout life; most important, it is the unconscious meanings that we attach to bereavement, and the dynamic function of the internal relationship with the dead, that account for the ongoing open-ended work of mourning.

A NEW DEFINITION

Let me offer a definition of this new psychoanalytic model of mourning. It is offered tentatively, but I think it is worthwhile to attempt to bring together into a brief statement the changes proposed by recent analytic writers. In this spirit, I offer the following definition:

Mourning refers to a varied and diverse psychological response to the loss of an important other. Mourning involves the transformation of the meanings and affects associated with one's relationship to the lost person the goal of which is to permit one's survival without the other while at the same time ensuring a continuing experience of relationship with the deceased. The work of mourning is rarely done in isolation and may involve active engagement with fellow mourners and other survivors. An important aspect of mourning is the experience of disruption in self-organization due to the loss of the function of the relationship with the other in sustaining self-experience. Thus, mourning involves a reorganization of the survivor's sense of self as a key function of the process.

TREATMENT OF PATHOLOGICAL MOURNING

There are a number of implications for changes in clinical practice, which arise from the emerging psychoanalytic model of mourning. These changes are in striking contrast to the closed-system, isolated, stepwise model of treatment that arises from the standard model. To my mind the following are just several aspects of this new clinical perspective:

- *Each person's response to bereavement is unique, and what is normal and what is pathological must be considered in the context of the patient's specific personality, relationship to the deceased person, and his or her familial and cultural background.* Openness to psychological individuality and a willingness to explore the unique bereavement response of the patient is crucial.
- *What therapists call "pathological responses" may be unsuccessful strategies to maintain meaning and preserve the attachment to the lost object.* Treatment requires not relinquishment but an exploration of the continuing value of the attachment to the survivor, with a consequent reconstruction of the meaning of that person in the context of the survivor's ongoing life.
- *Bereavement results in a crisis in the meanings by which a person's life is given structure and substance.* Therefore, pathologic grief is meaningful, however disturbed and painful it appears.
- *Grief affects are not the external manifestations of private processes but are efforts to communicate.* Given this, pathologic mourning, traditionally viewed as regressive and asocial, must be assessed for its often-hidden communicative motive. No matter how withdrawn into grief a person appears to be, he or she is struggling to maintain relatedness, whether to the internal representation of the dead person or to the social surround.
- *Mourning is fundamentally an intersubjective process, and many problems arising from bereavement are due to the failure of other survivors to engage with the bereaved person in mourning together.*

In concluding this chapter I would like to illustrate the clinical implications of a new psychoanalytic model. To do this I discuss an article by E. K. Rynearson in which he illustrates how his work changed with a particular patient when he began to question some of the standard assumptions of traditional mourning theory. What I find valuable in this article is the way in which a therapist who approaches his patient with openness and a willingness to jettison unhelpful and constricting assumptions can become better able to understand the underlying meanings and strengths of so-called pathological states. Unfortunately, space constraints will not allow a full summary of the article, but I will present enough to illustrate some significant clinical points.

In "Psychotherapy of Pathologic Grief: Revisions and Limitations," Rynearson (1987) described the treatment of a woman who experienced a refractory, pathological bereavement after the death of her teenage son. He pointed out how every effort to encourage the final resolution of mourning failed. In spite of years of therapy and a generally good treatment relationship, the woman remained despondent and deeply attached to the memory of her dead son. The patient would even say how she found the treatment "helpful enough" but, she would add, despairingly, "it will never bring my son back." Despite all efforts, the patient remained determined to continue her vigil. "I began to wonder aloud," Rynearson wrote, "how her dying son might help in reviving our therapy" (p. 496). He asked the patient to compose a letter from her son. He noted, "It did not feel contrived or unnatural to seek some caring and strength from an internalized 'presence' that he needed so much from us" (p. 496). The patient composed a series of moving and beautiful letters as if from her son, an admiring and supportive tribute to her as a mother. In one of these she wrote,

> Dear Mom and Dr. Rynearson:
> I will try to help you. Mom you know I don't want you to stay so sad and hopeless and I don't think it's good for you to visit my grave so often. You've got to start living more for you and the family and start taking better care of yourself.
> Don't give up on my mom, Dr. Rynearson, she's real stubborn and she won't give up, so don't you.

Rynearson concluded,

> We now look to David (the son) as a part of her that is increasingly able to help us by becoming more alive and nurturant. David remains an obsession, but he also advises and guides as a mother would a child. I cannot say precisely what is changing in this dissociated, highly traumatized and tangled attachment, but my patient and I, and now David, are all working together. (p. 497)

It is curious that Rynearson offered few comments regarding such a radical change in technique. He seemed surprised by his changed vision and strategy. I would like to suggest that Rynearson's new approach is quite consistent with recent thinking in psychoanalysis and is a fine illustration of the technical changes that follow from the new model of mourning. From this perspective let me conclude with some comments regarding Rynearson's case report.

- *Rather than being simply a refusal to give up the attachment to the lost object, Rynearson looks for the positive function served by the continuing relationship.* He recognizes that his active encouragement of relinquishment of the patient's attachment to the son is at best ineffective and at worst traumatic. His sudden insight into the positive function of the attachment to the son allows him to become more empathic regarding the woman's experience and especially of the positive meaning associated with the relationship to David. Although understanding the meaning of David is important to the treatment, in terms of technique, Rynearson's willingness to ask the question is even more crucial.

- *Mourning is viewed as varied and unique.* Most of the treatment of the bereaved woman is based on assumptions derived from the standard model of mourning. The idea that the woman must be encouraged to engage in a normal process, which is expected to lead to relinquishment, is the basis of Rynearson's clinical assessment and treatment strategy. The application of these standards essentially misses the point and may even be said to violate the woman's primary need for continuity. Once Rynearson is willing to accept the woman on her own terms (i.e., as needing an ongoing relationship with her dead son in order to recover) and recognize and appreciate the uniqueness of her grief, he is able to join her from within, rather than outside, her subjective experience.

- *Rather than viewing the therapist as a catalyst of the mourning process, the therapist plays an active, even central role in facilitating mourning.* At first, Rynearson takes a position external to his patient's experience. He acts on her, challenging her to give up her lost son and "go on with living." The conceptualization of grief as an internal, private process driven by universal psychological principles leads to an approach to the bereaved person that is characterized by estrangement and, in the worst case, intersubjective disjunction (Stolorow & Atwood, 1992).

- *The affects of mourning extend beyond grief and include positive affects such as joy and pride.* The assumption that mourning is primarily a painful and sad experience is basic to the standard model derived from Freud. Rynearson also focuses at first on the woman's grief in terms of her distress, and this results in a failure to elaborate and explore other affective features of her grief. Eventually, his openness to the woman's experience leads to the expression of tremendously important positive affects— such as pride, and even joy—associated with her relationship with her dead son. From the perspective of the standard model these affects would have been viewed as defensive, if not pathological, but Rynearson eventually welcomes these feelings and, rather than discouraging the patient's positive affects in deference to painful grieving, he welcomes their full expression and exploration.

- *The therapist is interested in the meaning of the relationship to the deceased person.* The standard model's emphasis on relinquishment leads inevitably to a lack of interest in the continuing meaning of the relationship to the deceased person. In fact, one of the effects of the standard model has been a fear on the part of therapists that the exploration of the positive meaning of the relationship will get in the way of relinquishment. One of the most important aspects of Rynearson's revised approach is his final question about what it all means in terms of the woman's continuing internalized relationship with her dead son. He has moved beyond assumptions about mourning and has placed the question of meaning and the continuity of relatedness at the center of his clinical approach. Most important he has included himself in the equation. The issue is no longer just what David means to the bereaved woman, it is what the meaning is of this new relationship configuration, of which Rynearson is now a central part. Rynearson has moved into a clinical realm where meanings and subjectivities are no longer private and isolated but social and intersubjectively based.

■ *A key aspect of the experience of bereavement is the impact of the loss on the self-organization of the bereaved person.* Another of Rynearson's insights is the function that the relationship to David plays in the woman's self-experience. David is part of her self, and it is the nature of the selfobject function of David that Rynearson begins to emphasize. In "Death of a Selfobject: Towards a Self Psychology of the Mourning Process" (Hagman, 1995a), I wrote the following about Rynearson's cases:

He became aware of the "function" of the selfobject (David), as he explored with the patient the positive, self-sustaining, self-repairing, and self-regulating nature of the woman's "moribund" attachment to her son. Once he ceased to promote decathexis and began to explore the functions of the selfobject in the areas of affirmation, mirroring, and merger needs, he noted a change in the ambiance of the treatment and a revitalization of the treatment relationship. (p. 204)

In other words, it was Rynearson's recognition of the powerful role that the relationship to David played in his patient's self-experience that permitted the expanded exploration of the meanings of his patient's mourning. This leads to my next point.

■ *In terms of technique, rather than confronting the patient's resistance to mourning, the therapist's empathy and support create an opportunity for self-reorganization, with the therapy being a holding environment.* The standard model of mourning leads to a clinical approach, that can be coercive and unempathic. At worst the frequent use of confrontation to provoke mourning results in further trauma and defense, which may masquerade as im-

provement. The new clinical approaches that are being elaborated in psychoanalysis in general and in the psychoanalytic
treatment of mourning in particular emphasize the importance
of empathy and security. Slochower, in her excellent monograph *Holding and Psychoanalysis* (1996), showed us just how
important the maintenance of a secure holding environment is
to the mourning process. In her discussion of the holding function of the Jewish ritual of "sitting shiva" she wrote regarding
her own grief experience:

> How did Shiva help? It seems to me that Shiva facilitates mourning by
> establishing an emotionally protective setting—one reminiscent of the
> analytic holding environment. In Shiva the caller, like the analyst,
> brackets her subjectivity in order to provide a large emotional space for
> the mourner. (p. 132)

In his brief but evocative case report, Rynearson (1987) showed how
he created a facilitative context for his patient's mourning in which she
could securely engage with him in the exploration and elaboration of the
continuing meaning of her relationship with her dead son. What the ultimate outcome of the treatment was I do not know; however, the case report
shows how, whatever the outcome, it is clear that moving toward a more
open and intersubjective approach can liberate both patients and therapists
from the restrictions and distortions of traditional models of grief.

REFERENCES

Abraham, K. (1960). A short history of the development of the libido. In D. Bryan
& A. Strachey (Eds.), *Selected papers of Karl Abraham* (pp. 418–503). New
York: Brunner/Mazel. (Original work published 1927)

Aries, P. (1974). *Western attitudes towards death*. Baltimore: John Hopkins University Press.

Aries, P. (1981). *The hour of our death*. New York: Knopf.

Bowlby, J. (1961). The processes of mourning. *International Journal of Psychoanalysis*,
42, 317–340.

Bowlby, J. (1980). *Attachment and loss, Vol. 3. Loss: Sadness and depression*. New
York: Basic Books.

Brenner, C. (1972). Some observations on depression, on nosology, on affects, and
on mourning. *Journal of Geriatric Psychology*, 7, 6–20.

Deutsch, H. (1937). Absence of grief. *Psychoanalytic Quarterly*, 6, 12–22.

Fenichel, O. (1945). *The psychoanalytic theory of neurosis*. New York: Norton.

Foote, C., & Frank, A. (1999). Foucault and therapy: The disciplining of grief. In
A. Chambon (Ed.), *Reading Foucault for social work* (pp. 157–187). New York:
Columbia University Press.

Freud, S. (1958). Totem and taboo. In J. Strachey (Ed. and Trans.), *The standard edition of the complete psychological works of Sigmund Freud* (Vol. 13, pp. 1–163). London: Hogarth Press. (Original work published 1915)

Freud, S. (1957). Mourning and melancholia. In J. Strachey (Ed. and Trans.), *The standard edition of the complete psychological works of Sigmund Freud* (Vol. 14, pp. 237–259). London: Hogarth Press. (Original work published 1917)

Freud, S. (1961). The ego and the id. In J. Strachey (Ed. and Trans.), *The standard edition of the complete psychological works of Sigmund Freud* (Vol. 19, pp. 12–66). London: Hogarth Press. (Original work published 1923)

Freud, S. (1959). Inhibition, symptoms, and anxiety. In J. Strachey (Ed. and Trans.), *The standard edition of the complete psychological works of Sigmund Freud* (Vol. 20, pp. 77–175). London: Hogarth Press. (Original work published 1926)

Furman, E. (1974). *A child's parent dies: Studies in childhood bereavement*. New Haven, CT: Yale University Press.

Gaines, R. (1997). Detachment and continuity: The two tasks of mourning. *Contemporary Psychoanalysis, 33*, 549– 571.

Hagman, G. (1993, December). *The psychoanalytic understanding and treatment of double parent loss*. Paper presented at the fall meeting of the American Psychoanalytic Association, New York.

Hagman, G. (1995a). Death of a selfobject: Towards a self psychology of the mourning process. In A. Goldberg (Ed.), *Progress in self psychology* (Vol. 11, 189–205). Hillsdale, NJ: Analytic Press.

Hagman, G. (1995b). Mourning: A review and reconsideration. *International Journal of Psychoanalysis, 76*, 909–925.

Hagman, G. (1996a). Bereavement and neurosis. *Journal of American Academy of Psychoanalysis, 23*, 635–653.

Hagman, G, (1996b). Flight from the subjectivity of the other: Pathological adaptation to early parent loss. In A. Goldberg (Ed.), *Progress in self psychology* (Vol. 12, pp. 207–219). Hillsdale, NJ: Analytic Press.

Hagman, G. (1996c). The role of the other in mourning. *Psychoanalytic Quarterly, 65*, 327–352.

Jacobs, S. (1993). *Pathologic grief: Maladaptation to loss*. Washington, DC: American Psychiatric Press.

Kaplan, L. (1995). *No voice if wholly lost*. New York: Simon & Schuster.

Klein, M. (1940). Mourning and its relation to manic–depressive states. *International Journal of Psycho-Analysis, 21*, 125–153.

Kris, A. (1992). Interpretation and the method of free association. *Psychoanalytic Inquiry, 12*, 208–224.

Mitchell, S. (1993). *Hope and dread in psychoanalysis*. New York: Basic Books.

Moore, B. E., & Fine, B. D. (1991). *Psychoanalytic terms and concepts*. New Haven, CT: Yale University Press.

Neimeyer, R. A. (1998). *Lessons of loss: A guide to coping*. New York: McGraw-Hill.

Parkes, C. (1981). *Bereavement: Studies of grief in adult life*. Madison, CT: International Universities Press.

Pollock, G. (1961). Mourning and adaptation. *International Journal of Psycho-Analysis, 42,* 341–361.

Pollock, G. (1989). *The mourning–liberation process*. Madison, CT: International Universities Press.

Rando, T. (1993). *Treatment of complicated mourning*. Champlain, IL: Research Press.

Rose, G. (1999). Discussion of Donna Bassin's paper "Rituals/Memorials/Mourning," Institute for Psychoanalytic Training and Research, New York.

Rynearson, E. K. (1987). Psychotherapy of pathologic grief: Revisions and limitations. *Psychiatric Clinics of North America, 10,* 487–500.

Schor, E. (1994). *Bearing the dead: The British culture of mourning from the Enlightenment to Victoria*. Princeton, NJ: Princeton University Press.

Shane, M., & Shane, E. (1990). Object loss and selfobject loss: A contribution to understanding mourning and the failure to mourn. *The Annual of Psychoanalysis, 18,* 115–131.

Shapiro, E. (1994) *Grief as a family process: A developmental approach to clinical practice*. New York: Guilford Press.

Shapiro, E. (1996). Grief in Freud's life: Reconceptualizing bereavement in psychoanalytic theory. *Psychoanalytic Psychology, 13,* 547–566.

Shelby, D. (1993). Mourning theory reconsidered. In A. Goldberg (Ed.), *Progress in Self Psychology* (Vol. 9, pp. 169–190). Hillsdale, NJ: Analytic Press.

Shelby, D. (1994). Mourning within a culture of mourning. In S. A. Cadwell, R. A. Burnham, & M. Forstein (Eds.), *Therapists on the front line: Psychotherapy with gay men in the age of AIDS* (pp. 53–80). Washington, DC: American Psychiatric Press.

Slochower, J. A. (1996). *Holding and psychoanalysis*. Hillsdale, NJ: Analytic Press.

Stolorow, R., & Atwood, G. (1992). *Contexts of being: The intersubjective foundations of psychological life*. Hillsdale, NJ: Analytic Press.

Volkan, V. (1981). *Linking objects and linking phenomena*. New York: International Universities Press.

Walter, T. (1994). *The revival of death*. New York: Routledge.

2

RELEARNING THE WORLD: MAKING AND FINDING MEANINGS

THOMAS ATTIG

Grieving is nearly always complicated—"nearly" because sometimes we grieve moderately for someone who was not particularly close or whose life did not extensively interconnect with our own; nearly "always" because, ordinarily, grieving involves nothing less than relearning the world of our experience (Attig, 1996); and "complicated" in the straightforward, dictionary sense of the term. That is, grieving as relearning the world consists of "an intimate combination of parts or elements not easy to unravel or separate." It is "involved, intricate, confused, complex, compound, the opposite of simple" (*Oxford English Dictionary*, 1971, p. 729).

Grieving is ordinarily complicated in the following ways: It is what we do in response to the compound suffering that bereavement introduces into our lives. As we grieve, we relearn a complex world. Our relearning itself is multidimensional. It involves simultaneously finding and making meaning on many levels. We grieve individually and collectively in complex and interdependent interactions with others in our families and communities. As we grieve we engage with several of the great mysteries of life in the human condition. We make a multifaceted transition from loving in presence to loving in absence. And we reweave that lasting love into the larger, richly complex fabric of our lives.

In this chapter I examine all of these complications in typical grieving. As I do, I pay particular attention to aspects of what has been called, perhaps too casually, "meaning making" in grieving. *Making* in this expression strongly suggests that we are self-consciously active, take deliberate initiative, and bring new meanings into existence as we grieve. I agree that, as we grieve, we give meaning to our experiences and actions, and especially to our suffering. We often read new meanings into or off of our surroundings. We create unprecedented patterns of meaning in our daily lives. We venture forth on new—and, we hope, meaningful—life courses. We restructure and reinterpret aspects of our life narratives and the self-understandings based in them. And we re-evaluate and often modify our understandings of our place in the larger scheme of things.

But there is also a strong sense in which much of what we do is a matter of "meaning finding." *Finding* in this expression strongly suggests that at other times we are less self-conscious in what we do, are more passive or receptive, and return to or encounter something already established, and often not of our own doing, as we mourn. We unreflectively return to experiences and actions that hold familiar meanings. We become aware of and accept meanings that seem to arise spontaneously in our suffering. We find our way home within surroundings filled with well-established meanings. We learn to trust elements of our daily life patterns that remain viable. We find that some long-held hopes and aspirations still move us down familiar life paths. We recognize meaningful continuity in our life narratives and the characters we embody in them. And we often deepen our appreciation of familiar understandings of our place in the larger scheme of things.

I will show how the interplay of meaning making and meaning finding permeates the diverse processes of relearning the world. As a rich example of this, I tell the story of C. S. Lewis and his life with his wife, Joy Gresham, and his grief and life after her death. The net effect will be to highlight and promote appreciation of some of the rich and subtle complications of grieving.[1]

---

[1] The dictionary definition of *complicated* cited earlier implies nothing about pathology, and there is nothing pathological about the complications I discuss here. Sometimes we contend with additional "extraordinary" complications (i.e., additions to the mixture of what we ordinarily contend with) as we relearn the world. These complications derive from aspects of our relationships with those who die (including preoccupation with and fervent longing for their return, preoccupation with unfinished business, and dysfunctions in the relationship), our own life histories and characters (including poorly developed capacities to relearn or psychological disorders), or our life circumstances (including difficulties surrounding the death itself, especially trauma, and social circumstances). These complications present special challenges that compromise, inhibit, interfere with, undermine, or block the already quite complicated processes of relearning the world or finding and making meaning. I have discussed these extraordinary complications elsewhere (Attig, 1996, pp. 75–93).

THE STORY OF C. S. LEWIS AND JOY GRESHAM

The film *Shadowlands* (Attenborough & Eastman, 1993) tells the story of C. S. Lewis's and Joy Gresham's life together and affords us glimpses into his experience of grief. Lewis's journal, *A Grief Observed* (Lewis, 1976; in which he refers to Joy as "H"), complements the film and is one of the most revealing personal accounts of loss and grieving in the English language.

Lewis, a confirmed bachelor, was an Oxford theologian known for his writings on courtly love, Christianity and suffering and, perhaps more widely, for his children's stories and science fiction. Although his writings and speaking made Lewis a public figure, he lived a sheltered life in a small cottage with his brother Warnie. Joy Gresham was a prize-winning American poet. Before she met Lewis, she was married to an American and had a young son, Douglas, who was known affectionately as "Dougie."

Joy came to England and asked to meet Lewis, whom both she and her son admired as an author. When they first met, she immediately impressed Lewis with her powerful, independent mind; winning wit; and a knack for penetrating pretense and insisting that ideas be firmly grounded in experience. A deep friendship developed through a series of subsequent visits, including times when Joy brought Dougie to meet Lewis and Warnie.

Joy's troubled first marriage eventually came to an end. Eager to relocate to England, she called on her friend Lewis and subsequently asked him to marry her to facilitate her immigration with her son. Lewis consented to the formality of a civil ceremony to help his friend. After the ceremony, they went their separate ways, with Lewis preferring a distant but hospitable relationship.

Some time later, Joy became ill and collapsed while attempting to call Lewis for help. They soon learned that Joy had cancer and was not expected to live. Faced with this loss, Lewis suddenly realized that he loved Joy truly and deeply and asked her to marry him again in the full meaning of the sacrament, and "before God." With Warnie and Dougie as witnesses, they were wed in the hospital with no expectation that Joy would ever leave.

Miraculously, Joy experienced a long-lasting remission. She recovered her strength and was able to come home to live at the cottage with Lewis and Dougie. They found great happiness together as a couple and as a family. Joy became the love of Lewis's life. The unprecedented intimacy and rich interaction with Joy affected Lewis profoundly.

A few years later, Joy's cancer returned, and further treatment proved ineffective. She came home to live her dying days, and Lewis devoted all of his time to caring for her. Within a short time, she died.

BEREAVEMENT AND SUFFERING

When those we love die, we embark on a difficult journey of the heart. We begin by suffering bereavement. We "suffer" in the sense that we have been deprived of someone we love. *Bereavement* in its origin means "the state of being deprived." Bereavement deprives us of the living presence of someone we love or care about, presence that has inestimable and irreplaceable value.

Lewis had suppressed his suffering following his mother's death when he was a boy. Although his books and speeches are filled with talk about suffering, they do not draw on his firsthand experiences. His life with and loss of Joy brought love and the suffering it often entails out of the pages of books and into the vital center of Lewis's life. His experiences took his heart places where he had never been before.

In bereavement, we also "suffer" in the sense that, when we lose someone dear, we experience loss of our wholeness. It is as if each of us were a web of connections to the things, places, other people, experiences, activities, and projects we care about (Attig, 1996, pp. 134–143). By extension, it is as if our families, communities, and all of humankind are joined as webs of webs. Our life stories, and those of our families and communities, are filled with weaving and reweaving of webs of connection, patterns of caring within which we find and make meaning. Bereavement strikes a blow to those webs, to our personal, family, and community integrity. The weaves of our daily life patterns are in tatters. Much of the weaving that comprises our individual and collective life histories is undone. Lines of connection with larger life contexts within which we find and make meaning are broken or damaged.

Lewis had rewoven the web of his daily life and his world of meaning around Joy and, in the end, her illness. Life with her led him in unprecedented and unanticipated directions. Returning to life as it had been before her was unthinkable. How would or could he go on without her at the center of his life? Even his previously unshakeable religious faith seemed to desert him. His diary tells of his confusion and despair about God:

> Go to Him when your need is desperate, when all other help is vain, and what do you find? A door slammed in your face, and a sound of bolting and double bolting on the inside. After that, silence. (Lewis, 1976, p. 4)

We "suffer" in the sense that we feel helpless and powerless in the wake of forces and happenings we could not control. We feel deep pain and anguish as we experience our losses as irretrievable and irredeemable and fear our distress may never end. Languishing in despair, we may feel unmotivated or unable to act. Again, Lewis captured this agony and helplessness vividly in his journal:

> Aren't all these notes the senseless writhings of a man who won't accept the fact that there is nothing we can do with suffering except to suffer it? Who still thinks there is some device (if only he could find it) which will make pain not to be pain. It doesn't really matter whether you grip the arms of the dentist's chair or let your hands lie in your lap. The drill drills on. (Lewis, 1976, pp. 38–39)

We "suffer" heartbreak as we miss viscerally the physical presence of those we love. We meet their absence everywhere. Seeing others together, we are vividly reminded that we will never see, touch, hold, or kiss our lost one again. Neither will we ever be seen, touched, held or kissed by them. We can no longer talk, laugh, or cry with them; or walk and experience the world with them. Lewis's journal describes succinctly the poignancy of this loss of physical presence as he wrote, "The rough, sharp, cleansing tang of her otherness is gone" (Lewis, 1976, p. 22).

In our yearning, we long for their return. We are at a loss as to how to go on without them. We want desperately to love them still, but we do not know how. Lewis wondered whether loving them still might be like the continuation of a dance when the partners have separated:

> And then one or other dies. And we think of this as love cut short; like a dance stopped in mid-career or a flower with its head unluckily snapped off—something truncated and therefore, lacking its due shape. I wonder. If, as I can't help suspecting, the dead also feel the pains of separation . . . then for both lovers and for all pairs of lovers without exception, bereavement is a universal and integral part of our experience of love. It follows marriage as normally as marriage follows courtship or as autumn follows summer. It is not a truncation of the process but one of its phases; not the interruption of the dance, but the next figure. (Lewis, 1976, pp. 58–59)

But, following the analogy, we are at a loss as to what the steps in the next figure of the dance might be and whether we are capable of learning them.

Our suffering includes "soul pain." I use *soul* to refer to that within us that sinks roots into the world, makes itself at home in our surroundings, finds nourishment and sustenance in the here and now of everyday life. When we suffer soul pain, we feel uprooted. We feel homesick. We feel estranged within and alienated from surroundings transformed by the death and our pain and anguish. We sense that we cannot find our way home to life as it was before the death. Fearing that we can never find our way to feeling at home again, we find it difficult to care about anything at all. In his journal, Lewis aches for the earthy, daily nurturance and love he knew with Joy. He finds it difficult to care about even the most trivial details of everyday life: "I loathe the slightest effort. Not only writing but even reading a letter is too much. Even shaving. What does it matter now whether my cheek is rough or smooth?" (Lewis, 1976, pp. 3–4).

And our suffering includes "spiritual pain." I use *spirit* to refer to that within us that reaches beyond present circumstances, soars in extraordinary experiences, strives for excellence and a better life, struggles to overcome adversity, and searches for meaning and transcendent understanding. When we suffer spiritual pain, we lose that motivation. We feel dispirited, joyless, hopeless. Life seems drained of meaning. We wonder whether we have the courage and motivation to face the challenges of daily life, much less relearning the world we now experience. Where will we find the will to reshape our shattered lives and redirect our life stories, the faith and hope to sustain us? We doubt our capacities to find and make meaning in life without those who died. We are afraid.

Lewis was profoundly dispirited when Joy died. Beginning with its very first words, "No one ever told me that grief felt so like fear," (Lewis, 1976, p. 1), he filled his journal with his spiritual anguish.

FUNCTIONS OF GRIEVING

Grieving is what we do in response to what happens to us in bereavement. As we grieve, we respond in two principal and interrelated ways. On one hand, we struggle to put our lives back together in a process I call "relearning the world." As we relearn the worlds of our experience, we reweave the fabric of our lives and come to a new wholeness (Attig, 1996, pp. 146–156). We reshape and restore integrity to our daily lives. We redirect and once again experience continuity and meaning in our life narratives. And we reconnect with larger wholes in meaningful ways. Relearning the worlds of our experience in each of these ways is a blend of meaning finding and meaning making. We glimpse only the beginnings of these processes for Lewis in the film and his journal, most specifically in his struggles to reconnect with Dougie, whose suffering so poignantly mirrors his own.

On the other hand, we struggle to come to terms with the pain and anguish that accompany the devastation in our lives and the hard labor of grieving itself (Attig, 1996, pp. 143–146). We eventually dissipate or overcome some of our pain. We learn to carry some other of our pain. But, more important, we move from *being* our pain—being wholly absorbed in and preoccupied with it—to *having* our pain—to carrying residual sadness and heartache in our hearts. We carry it in a place alongside other places where we hold those who died in lasting love and where we love others, love ourselves, and hold the cares that give our lives meaning and bring us joy and fulfillment. We find and give meaning to our suffering.

These two functions of grieving are intimately interrelated. Coming to new wholeness in our lives tempers some of our pain and anguish and modifies the meanings of our suffering, especially when we weave lasting love for those who died into that new wholeness. Reciprocally, as we overcome some of our pain and anguish and learn to carry what remains, we become better able to contend with the challenges of relearning our worlds and coming to new wholeness in our lives.

THE WORLDS WE RELEARN

Lewis captured the global character of the challenge of relearning the world when he wrote

At first I was very afraid of going to places where H. and I had been happy—our favorite pub, our favorite wood. But I decided to do it at once—like sending a pilot up again as soon as possible after he's had a crash. Unexpectedly, it makes no difference. Her absence is no more emphatic in those places than anywhere else. It's not local at all. . . . The act of living is different all through. Her absence is like the sky, spread over everything. (Lewis, 1976, p. 11)

Still, we must relearn each aspect of our world. We relearn our physical surroundings. For example, we are challenged to come to terms with the things that those who died left behind—for example, their clothing and personal effects, journals and diaries, treasures, photos, mementos, things they used in work or play, household furnishings, vehicles, creations, gifts, books, music, or items from their spiritual lives. Everyday places—homes, rooms, yards, workplaces, schools, places of worship, and other public places—each must be encountered. We are challenged in special places—for example, where we were raised by, grew up with, or first met those who died; experienced turning points in our lives with them; delighted in their company alone or with others; lived together and perhaps knew intimacy; or always dreamed of going together.

And we are challenged by their absence during recurrent occasions and singular events that have special significance for us, for example, holidays, birthdays, anniversaries, festivals, graduations, weddings, births, performances, celebrations of accomplishment, and times of need.

Many such things, places, events, and occasions were valued by and had meaning in the lives of those who died. What meanings did they have for us or in our lives with them? What meanings do or can they have for us now? How will their absence affect the meanings of events and occasions we now experience without them? These are issues we must address while we grieve.

Lewis returned to a world filled with things, places, and times that he and Joy had filled with memories and invested with soulful and spiritual meanings. His home and bedroom seemed strangely empty after she died. The wardrobe in his attic was filled with history, including some of Lewis's mother's clothing. Once the real-life inspiration for the entry to magic and imagination in several of his well-known children's stories, Joy and Dougie had admired the stories and asked to see the wardrobe when they visited. Joy had sparked magic in Lewis's life that he had not known since his mother died. Toward the end of the film, after Joy's death, Lewis and Dougie sit before the wardrobe, talk about losing their mothers and the unfairness of it all, and weep together.

On Lewis's office wall there was an idyllic picture of "The Golden Valley" that once hung in his nursery. Joy asked about it when she first visited, and Lewis told her that he always wondered if it depicted a real place. He said it represented his idea of heaven. When Joy came into remission and they honeymooned, they sought and found the place in the picture in

Herefordshire, walked the valley, and experienced an exquisite happiness there. Lewis returned there with Dougie after Joy died and talked with him about that happiness.

When we grieve we must also relearn our social surroundings. We are challenged within our most intimate relationships with, for example, parents, spouses and companions, children, brothers and sisters, in-laws, other close relatives, and our closest friends. And we are challenged in less than intimate relationships with, for example, casual acquaintances, work colleagues and associates, teachers and classmates, service personnel, and new acquaintances. We confront people who ask ordinarily inoffensive questions we do not know how to answer or who in some way unexpectedly remind us of those who died.

Many of these people and relationships were also valued by and had meaning in the lives of those who died. What meanings did they have for us in the context of our lives with those who died? What meanings do or can the relationships have for us now? How might the meanings of new relationships be affected by our relationships with those who died? With whom will we continue to interact? About whom will we continue or come to care? With whom will we struggle, strive, aspire, or soar? And how?

Lewis was left to contend with Warnie, Dougie, friends, and his Oxford colleagues. He wrote of a common ambivalence toward the presence of others when he feels acute grief:

> I find it hard to take in what anyone says, or perhaps, hard to want to take it in. It is so uninteresting. Yet I want the others to be about me. I dread the moments when the house is empty. If only they would talk to one another and not to me. (Lewis, 1976, p. 1)

In grieving we must relearn our very selves, including our characters, histories and roles, and identities that we find in them. We must also relearn our self-confidence and self-esteem. Like Lewis, we wonder Who am I now? How am I different for knowing and loving her or him? What is to become of me without her or him? How were these aspects of our selves affected, shaped by, and perhaps dependent on those who died? How do or can we now understand or meaningfully embody these aspects of our selves? How might we change our characters and give new shape to the next chapters of our life stories in the absence of those we love?

Finally, in grieving we relearn our relationships with those who died. With Lewis, we wonder about the shape of the next figures of the dance in relation to those we still love. What meanings did we know in loving and caring about them when they were alive? How, if at all, can we sustain meaningful, and even loving, connection to them when they have died? What meanings are there, or can there be, in lasting love?

THE NATURE OF OUR RELEARNING

Relearning the world after someone we love has died is not a matter of taking in information or mastering ideas or theories. It is, rather, a matter of learning again *how to be and act in the world* without those we love by our sides.

Bereavement shatters our taken-for-granted life patterns and undermines many of our life assumptions. Talk about changing our "assumptive worlds" (Parkes, 1971, 1988) is potentially misleading insofar as it suggests that assumptions are readily accessible and primarily cognitive. Instead, it is best to think of them as deeply embedded and obscured in habitual life and operative automatically in all dimensions of our being, not merely in belief or cognition.

Grieving is something we do as the complicated whole persons we are. We respond organically, in all dimensions of our being at once. Analyzing our experience of loss and our response to it inevitably distorts them. It suggests that elements of a complicated mix can be unraveled, understood, and addressed in isolation from one another.

We relearn in all dimensions of our lives. As we do, we relearn ourselves. Emotionally, we temper the pain of our suffering. Psychologically, we renew our self-confidence, self-esteem, and self-identity. Lewis's journal reveals how this is on ongoing process:

> I thought I could describe a state; make a map of sorrow. Sorrow, however, turns out to be not a state but a process. It needs not a map but a history, and if I don't stop writing that history at some quite arbitrary point, there's no reason why I should ever stop. There is something new to be chronicled every day. (Lewis, 1976, pp. 68–69)

Behaviorally, we transform our habits, motivations, dispositions, ways of doing things. We change the variety and patterns of our activities and experiences. Lewis's journal tells of the pervasive need for change:

> Thought after thought, feeling after feeling, action after action, had H. for their object. Now their target is gone. I keep on through habit fitting an arrow to the string; then I remember and have to lay the bow down. (Lewis, 1976, p. 55)

Physically and biologically, we expend great energy meeting the challenges bereavement presents. We blend old and new ways of meeting our biological needs, especially our needs for closeness. Lewis reminds us of the special anguish of the loss of a spouse:

> There is one place where her absence comes locally home to me, and it is a place I can't avoid. I mean my own body. It had such a different

importance while it was the body of H.'s lover. Now it's like an empty house. (Lewis, 1976, p. 12)

Socially, we reconfigure our interactions with others. We return to life with fellow survivors, and we meet others on life's way. Lewis wishes, as so many do, that others were more effective in responding to him in his grief:

> An odd by-product of my loss is that I'm aware of being an embarrassment to everyone I meet. At work, at the club, in the street, I see people as they approach me, trying to make up their minds whether they'll "say something about it" or not. I hate it if they do, and if they don't. . . . To some I'm worse than an embarrassment. I am a death's head. Whenever I meet a happily married pair I can feel them both thinking, "One or other of us must some day be as he is now." (Lewis, 1976, pp. 10–11)

Intellectually, we question and seek answers and meanings. We change our understandings and interpretations. Spiritually, we seek peace and consolation. We modify our hopes and deepen or modify our faiths. Lewis's journal is one of the great documents we have of the anguish of someone struggling with eternal questions while in spiritual crisis. He tells us early precisely what troubled him about his belief in God:

> Not that I am (I think) in much danger of ceasing to believe in God. The real danger is of coming to believe such dreadful things about him. The conclusion I dread is not, "So there's no God after all," but, "So this is what God's really like. Deceive yourself no longer." (Lewis, 1976, p. 5)

Sometimes we self-consciously reflect on how some of our taken-for-granted ways of being in all of these dimensions are no longer viable because they require the presence of the one who died. We deliberately examine and experiment with alternatives. We actively make new meaning as we do. Sometimes we do this out of a well-developed disposition to self-reflection. Sometimes we become more self-reflective in bereavement. Sometimes we are helped by others, especially counselors and therapists, to become so.

Perhaps more commonly, we less self-consciously change the taken-for-granted patterns in the diverse dimensions of our lives. Without giving it much thought, aversion to the pain of persistence in our old ways moves us in new directions. We straightforwardly find and revert to old patterns that remain viable. With no systematic or deliberate sorting of alternatives to ways that are no longer viable, we spontaneously try alternative ways of being and acting and find that some work for us. We find new meaning in our daily lives and life stories tacitly, in passing, or so it seems after a significant amount of time has passed.

Some of us seem, by disposition, to be more facile and effective in straightforwardly adapting our ways. But sometimes we stumble and even flounder. We may sense that we are "stuck" without being able to articulate fully how or why. When we find ourselves in such difficulty, counselors or therapists may need to show us other paths through suggestive stories about how others have found their way through these transitions. Or, they may teach us to be more self-reflective and deliberate in making rather than simply discovering meaning as we change.

I have already intimated that as we relearn our worlds we move in two directions at once. In part, *we return to aspects of our lives that are still viable.* We find or recover what still sustains and nourishes us in our daily life patterns. We find our ways back home among familiar things, in our usual places, in familiar activities and experiences, with fellow survivors, in wider social contexts and in the greater scheme of things. We return to some familiar hopes, dreams, and expectations. We revive what "still works" in our selves, families, and communities. We continue to draw nourishment and support from roots already in place. We discover and recover in them meanings that still sustain us. In short, we move in a soulful direction.

In part, *we transform ourselves as we reshape and redirect our individual, family, and community lives.* Realizing that life *cannot* be what it was, we reach for new life even as we suffer. We establish something without precedent. We find new ways in day-to-day life. We discern possibilities and make new and fresh meanings in the next chapters of our individual, family, and community life stories; we give them new direction and purpose. We build new connections to larger wholes in our families, communities, and within the greater scheme of things. In short, we move in a spiritual direction.

We often find and make meaning in ways that may not have occurred had we not suffered loss. We had no choice about what happened, but we can, and often do, grow positively through the experience. We find new strength of character. We grow in self-understanding and self-esteem. We become more sensitive and responsive to others. We learn how much others mean to us and learn new ways to show appreciation and love. We gain new critical perspectives on our relationships, on reality, and on the human condition. Lewis's journal, as we shall see, is very much about personal transformation rooted in life with Joy and his bereavement.

WE RELEARN INTERDEPENDENTLY

We grieve with and under the influence of those from whom we learned how to grieve, including the deceased. From them we have acquired expectations and ways of behaving, expressing ourselves, interacting with others, remembering those who die, and interpreting events and lives. We may find that ways we have learned from them are helpful. Or we may need to make new ways that work for us.

Lewis was helped immeasurably in his grief by Joy. In the film, their honeymoon walk in the "Golden Valley" in Herefordshire is interrupted by rain. They retreat to shelter. Lewis speaks of the depth of his happiness in the moment. There is no place he would rather be but with Joy. Joy reminds him that it will not last, because the remission cannot hold indefinitely. Lewis will hear nothing of her death and insists that he will "manage" some-how when that time comes. But Joy urges that he can do better than simply managing. She says she wants to be with him in his grief and that that will be possible only if he realizes that "The pain then is part of the happiness now" (Attenborough & Eastman, 1993). She insists that the pain to come does not spoil the happiness; rather, it "makes it real." She seems to be say-ing that the happiness they have found and will enjoy for some time to come can and will have a different character when they both realize how precious it is for being fleeting. And Lewis can later experience his pain as a reflec-tion of the depth of that happiness and their love.

We are not alone as we relearn the worlds of our experience. Interac-tions with others profoundly affect our individual relearning. And, together with others, we reshape and redirect our family and community life patterns and life histories. That is, we grieve not only as individuals but also as fam-ilies and communities. Family and community relearning are themselves complicated, collective, interactive processes.

We grieve with fellow survivors. We receive and give support and com-fort. We depend on one another or make demands. We find and make mean-ing alongside others who are themselves struggling to find and make mean-ing. Often we must contend with their finding or making meanings that differ from, and even conflict with, those that we find or make. They may or may not tolerate or respect our individual needs and preferences. We may more or less tolerate or respect theirs. What they do or say affects what is possible for us, and vice versa. They, or we, may make decisions or take ac-tions that block paths that others would have chosen. They, or we, may or may not negotiate, compromise, or cooperate in joint efforts to reshape and redirect family or community life patterns and histories.

Lewis found that many of his friends and colleagues persistently disap-pointed him. By contrast, his brother Warnie remained quietly patient and understanding. And his relationship with Dougie grew as they reflected to-gether on the agonies of losing their mothers, discussed the unfairness of Joy's death, wept together before the wardrobe in the attic, and returned to walk the Golden Valley together.

We also grieve in interaction with those who enter our lives after the death. Some take peripheral places, some central. Some present new chal-lenges. Some prove to be sources of new support. They may or may not be welcome additions to our families or communities.

WE SEEK ACCOMMODATION TO MYSTERY

As we relearn the world, we come to new accommodation to the *great mysteries of life in the human condition*. When those we love die, we wonder about, and search for what may be called, our "spiritual place" within the greater scheme of things. We draw on, or seek, understandings, perspectives, and experiences that ground confidence that we are connected to something greater than ourselves; that we belong, and are at home, in this world; that it is a safe, orderly, and trustworthy world; that there is a point to going on day to day, pursuing purposes, caring, loving, hoping, and aspiring; that living a human life is ultimately meaningful and worthwhile; that there is a reason to continue to experience and act in the world, however elusive that reason may be.

We struggle to accept and come to terms with the great mysteries of finiteness, change, imperfection, uncertainty, and vulnerability. Is it OK that we are small and insignificant when compared with the vast expanses of space, time, and history that surround us? Is it OK that change and impermanence pervade our lives, and that we have little to no control over many of the things that happen in them? Is it OK that we are imperfect; that we fall far short of our highest aspirations? Is it OK that our knowledge is limited, our judgment is fallible, and certainty eludes us? Is it OK that we are vulnerable to suffering and death?

I call the greater scheme of things, finiteness, change, imperfection, uncertainty, and vulnerability *mysteries*, because they challenge us in ways that ordinary problems do not. They are constants in life, persistently provocative, and too important to ignore. They present themselves in ever-changing perspectives. They command our attention in some of the most difficult times of our lives. Fresh encounters with them challenge us to modify our previous, tentative understandings and responses to them. We cannot solve them once and for all, answer them definitively, control, manage, or master them.

In coming to terms with mystery, finding and making meaning are tentative at best. We find meanings already assigned to these mysteries within our own histories and in our surrounding cultures, families, and communities. Sometimes they satisfy us, sometimes not. When they do, their depth and resonance with our experience enable us to renew confidence in our spiritual place. When they do not, we may self-consciously examine our beliefs and assumptions about these mysteries and deliberately seek and make new meaning in response to them and thereby come to new confidence in our spiritual place.

Lewis was brought up short in his easy way of speaking of such mysteries, handling them on a purely intellectual plane, once he experienced Joy's death. He was humbled before them, plunged into deep self-reflection and exploration. His soul-searching journey led him to acknowledge how little he really knew of such things. And he came to praise the mysterious grace that brought Joy and her love into his life (Lewis, 1976, p. 72).

THE TRANSITION TO LASTING LOVE

As we grieve we seek and find ways of making a transition to lasting love (Attig, 2000). We do not want to stop loving those who die. We rightly resist those who say we must. We know that it matters too much to us and to those who died. We want to remember them and to continue to be affected by them. They wanted to be remembered and to make lasting differences in our lives. In our lasting love, we give them symbolic immortality.

The central challenge as we grieve is moving from a life where we loved them in presence to a new life where we love them in absence. Nothing is more difficult. Nothing is more important. Nothing is more rewarding.

We continue to hold those we love in our hearts in the place where we miss them. We learn to carry our hurt there. Missing them is itself a manifestation of our love for them. We will always hold them in a place of sadness.

Loving in absence is not strange to us. We spend most of our waking lives apart from those we love and cherish, not only those who live at great distances but also those closest to us on most average days. While we are apart, we include them in our thoughts and prayers, remember them, speak of them with others, shape our lives in terms of commitments to them, share their interests and concerns, model our actions and characters on theirs, think of and appreciate how our lives are different because of them, are motivated by and draw inspiration from them, share their hopes and dreams, laugh sometimes and cry others. All of these are ways of the heart we know well. We could hardly maintain any relationship if we did not. When those who are absent are alive, we can come together again. But we do not stop loving them even when we do not reunite.

When another dies, loving in absence is not so very different from loving in presence. Give and take need not end. We can still give them, for example, attention, interest, admiration, understanding, respect, acceptance, forgiveness, loyalty, affection, praise, and gratitude. We can sense that they reciprocate in the living energy of our memory of them. We can receive and still benefit from, for example, material assistance, advice and counsel, instruction, intellectual stimulation, perspective, direction, honesty and candor, moral and spiritual guidance and support, modeling of how to be and act, encouragement, expressions of confidence, enthusiasm, a sense of belonging, and inspiration. Some of us believe that they literally watch over or walk with us. Most of us sense that they are with us in spirit and remain our life's companions in our hearts.

To be sure, reciprocity changes. We continue to give and receive. They continue to give us their legacies. Sadly, we cannot contribute directly to their lives any longer, but we can still further their interests. And we can sense that they witness or support us as we give to others. We give them places in our hearts alongside the place where we miss them. There we can make the fruition of their lives our own just as we did when they were alive.

Ceremonies of separation, such as funerals and memorial services and other less formal rituals and gestures, help us to move toward lasting love. They support us as we let go of life in their presence. They help us to acknowledge and express our pain and anguish. They enable us to take beginning steps in remembering those who died. We begin to open other places in our hearts where we hold their legacies. We make ourselves receptive to what their lives still offer us.

Memory

Sadness is not their only legacy. We learn to hold their more positive legacies in other places in our hearts. Centrally, we hold and cherish them in memory. Lewis's journal tells us poignantly how dwelling in sadness sometimes masks the ways in which we hold them elsewhere.

> And suddenly at the very moment when, so far, I mourned H. least, I remembered her best. Indeed it was something (almost) better than memory; an instantaneous, unanswerable impression. To say it was like a meeting would be going too far. Yet there was that in it which tempts one to use those words. It was as if the lifting of the sorrow removed a barrier. (Lewis, 1976, pp. 51–52)

When we think of those who have died in our lives, we notice how an ongoing relationship with them in memory takes a place alongside our other relationships. Their legacy in memory consists of their lifetimes, remembered moments, episodes, periods, and stories, none of which is canceled by death.

Our memories are incomplete and partial. We can learn more about those who died through researching their lives, exploring diaries, letters, and other records they left behind, and the like. And we can extend and modify our individual memories through exchanging, discussing, and exploring memories with others. We give these legacies places in our memories and in our lives with family, friends, and community. Doing so, others often hold memories of times in the lives of those we love and aspects of their characters that we did not know well. Sometimes we find in their memories understandings and meanings that complement our own. Sometimes we come to new perspectives on their lives and make new sense of what we find in them.

Our memories are fragile and fleeting. At first, Lewis feared that he would not be able to hold Joy even in memory:

> We have seen the faces of those we know best so variously, from so many angles, in so many lights, with so many expressions—waking,

sleeping, laughing, crying, eating, talking, thinking—that all the impressions crowd into our memory together and cancel out into a mere blur. (Lewis, 1976, p. 17)

Slowly, quietly, like snow-flakes—like the small flakes that come when it is going to snow all night—little flakes of me, my impressions, my selections, are settling down on the image of her. The real shape will be quite hidden in the end. Ten minutes—ten seconds—of the real H. would correct all this. And yet, even if those ten seconds were allowed me, one second later the little flakes would begin to fall again. (Lewis, 1976, pp. 21–22)

We can hold memories more permanently by reverting to them often privately, reviving them through reference to photographs, tapes, diaries, and other records, returning to them deliberately or casually with others or recording them in writing or on tape.

Our memories are also rich and fertile in meaning. As we cherish memories, we return to freshen and deepen our understanding of those who died, attend to them again, bring them closer, embrace them in their absence, reconnect with some of the best in life, feel grateful, feel the warmth of our love for them, sense that they are grateful for our remembering, and feel the warmth of their love for us. In this vein, toward the end of his journal, Lewis reports that praising Joy revives and revitalizes his memories.

As we remember, we reconnect with the reality of their lives. Lewis succinctly refutes the view that we merely connect with an "inner representation" of the one who died when he writes, "It was H. I loved. As if I wanted to fall in love with my memory of her, an image in my own mind! It would be a sort of incest" (Lewis, 1976, p. 22). In memory, just as in perception, we connect, however fallibly, with the reality of their lives. Remembering is not a retreat to the past. Rather, memory brings aspects of the past into present awareness. We attend to and cherish their legacies here and now.

Memories are also the basis for deeper lasting love. They can help us see how we already hold those who died in other places: in practical life and in the lives of our souls and spirits. Memory is the ground for our opening ourselves further to the richness of their legacies in these other areas of our lives. We may find that they have already touched our lives and characters in meaningful ways. And we can make meaning through deepening these ties and allowing them to permeate further the fabric of our daily lives and the next chapters of our life narratives.

Practical Life

We hold those we love in our practical lives. Their practical legacies include material goods and practical wherewithal, advice and counsel, obligations owed to them because of promises we have made to them and covenants we have entered into with them, ways of doing things, vocations, and other practical interests and concerns.

We give them places in our practical lives as we use the material provisions they have left us, keep our promises and maintain our covenants, do things in ways they did or encouraged us to do them, follow in their footsteps, or make some of their interests and concerns our own. As we do these things, those who died continue to contribute to our individual, family, and community lives. Sometimes we find these influences are already in place. At other times we seek new opportunities to make further meaningful use of their practical legacies.

Although the film does not treat the matter explicitly, it is clear that Lewis made a commitment to Joy to look after her son Dougie following her death. And we see how Joy and her death have influenced his teaching at Oxford. He no longer approaches his students as an expert with all of the answers about love or suffering. Neither does he use his background knowledge and linguistic skills to take unfair advantage in arguments with them. Rather, he respects them as the inquiring and aspiring individuals they are, encourages them to speak from their own experiences, listens carefully to their offerings, and works with them in a spirit of joint inquiry after the ever-elusive answers to fundamental questions.

Life of the Soul

We hold those we love in our souls. They have touched our souls and are with us in our ways of living our everyday lives and inhabiting our life's surroundings. Their soulful legacies include the roots of our individual, family, and community traditions, histories, and characters. They have shown and taught us ways of caring about, and loving, things, places, food, music, ourselves, others, and our families and communities.

We give them places in the lives of our souls as we grow in understanding and appreciation of our roots in them. And we do so as we make ourselves at home again among the things, places, food, and music, within traditions and with the friends, families, and communities they have touched. Most commonly, we find soulful meanings as we return to familiar ways, sense abiding connection to those who died within them, and once again draw nourishment and sustenance from them. We make meaning when we deliberately cultivate traditions or soulful ways that we had abandoned, neglected, or failed to appreciate while they were alive and sense abiding connection to those who died as we do.

Lewis became far less a distant, intellectual observer and far more an engaged, grounded, participant in life with Joy. He changed his ways of inhabiting the world. He allowed himself to care more deeply for another than he had since his mother died. With Joy he invested his physical surroundings and aspects of daily living with soulful meanings. Lewis came to care differently and more deeply about others, including Dougie and his students, and about himself. As it was for Lewis, part of the challenge of grieving for any of us is reviving the motivation and trust that allow us to find soulful meanings that remain available to us.

Life of the Spirit

We hold those we love in our spirits. They have touched our spirits and are with us in our ways of transcending present circumstances, soaring, striving, overcoming, and searching. Their spiritual legacies include lessons about ways of soaring and finding joy in life, becoming the best we can be, overcoming adversity (including bereavement itself), and searching for meaning and transcendent understanding.

We give them places in our spirits as we grow in understanding and appreciation of how they have inspired us. We take inspiration from them as we revive our capacities for joy and laughter, live with enthusiasm, revive our motivation to strive to be our best, and renew our faith and hope for the future. And we do so as we follow them in our ways of coming to terms with the mysteries of death, suffering, and life itself; human limitation; change; imperfection; not knowing; and vulnerability. We find meanings as we return to spiritual ways we have learned from them. We make meanings by drawing on their inspiration as we face unprecedented challenges in life without them, add new elements to our daily life patterns, and strike out in new directions in our life histories.

Life with Joy revived Lewis's spirit. He found delight and laughter with her and opened himself to the wonder and celebration in the world around him. They struggled together, each with his and her own miseries, through the trials of her illness. Lewis wrote, "It is incredible how much happiness, even how much gaiety, we sometimes had together after all hope was gone. How long, how tranquilly, how nourishingly, we talked together that last night!" (Lewis, 1976, p. 13). Joy taught him a new way of coming to terms with suffering. When his mother died, Lewis swallowed his hurt and did his best to turn away from what had happened. When Joy died, he resolved to be open to the full range of his experience and to reach for whatever new life was possible. And Joy and her death brought Lewis's intellectual faith into contact with real life experiences of love and suffering. Reaching to and finding lasting love led him to praise God once again. He summed it up best when he wrote,

> There are two enormous gains. . . .Turned to God, my mind no longer meets that locked door; turned to H., it no longer meets that vacuum—nor all that fuss about my mental image of her. My jottings show something of the process, but not so much as I'd hoped. Perhaps both changes were really not observable. There was no sudden, striking, and emotional transition. Like the warming of a room or the coming of day-

light. When you first notice them they have already been going on for some time. (Lewis, 1976, p. 71)

LASTING LOVE AND MYSTERY

As we grieve and find our ways to lasting love, we respond to yet two more great mysteries: the person of the one we love and love itself. We never finish with, resolve, master, or control either of them. Both have a compelling presence in our lives. They regularly present new faces and new challenges. Both are deeper than we can fathom. We can give no ultimate accounting of the incredible grace or good fortune that brought them into our lives. We experience them as privileges of our existence. We stand before them in wonder and awe. Our appreciation of them can grow indefinitely. They were and remain unique and irreplaceable.

As we find and make our ways to lasting love, we find and make more comfortable places to rest in response to the other great mysteries I mentioned earlier. The greater scheme of things becomes more acceptable as we begin to see that our love for them does not die with them. Being small and insignificant becomes more acceptable as we realize that in lasting love we affirm the value of the meaningful differences those we love made in the corners of the world where we knew them. Change and impermanence become more acceptable as we realize that the meanings we embrace in their lives continue beyond their physical death. Imperfection becomes more acceptable as we forgive them their shortcomings, sense that they forgive ours, and find consolation in the lasting good we found in our imperfect love. Not knowing and uncertainty become more acceptable as we find ways of continuing in faith and hope even in their absence.

REWEAVING LASTING LOVE INTO LIFE'S FABRIC

The journey to lasting love brings us to a different place in our suffering. Missing those who died becomes more like missing them when they lived and we were separated. We fulfill our desire to continue loving them. We give them a new presence in our lives.

We find and accept their legacies and make them our own in several ways: We reweave threads of caring, first woven into the fabrics of our lives while they lived, into new daily life patterns. We blend what they have given, and continue to give, into the life histories we reshape and redirect. And we join our changed and enduring connections with them with modified connections with our family, friends, the larger community, and God. In these ways, we find and make ourselves whole again as individuals, families, and communities. We blend the found and the new into unprecedented life patterns and histories.

We see the beginnings of these movements at the end of *Shadowlands*. Lewis is walking the Golden Valley with Dougie. When he and Joy honeymooned there, Joy said she wanted to be with him when he was grieving. As he and Dougie are walking, we hear his voice reflecting on the difference between his suffering when his mother died and his present suffering. And he says about the earlier walk in the valley, "The happiness then is part of the pain now." As he utters these words we sense how Joy is still with him as he has made her legacy his own. And we sense how what he learned from her colors his continuing relationship with her son.

As we relearn the world, we give lasting love for those who died a place within the larger context of our lives. No matter how important those who died and our love for them have been, we did not, nor do we, give our hearts to them alone. Not only must we struggle to let go of their physical presence and longing for their return, but we also need to let go of any singular, sometimes preoccupying, focus on them and their absence. We need to let go of loving only them to the exclusion of any others.

Grieving is a journey of the heart that brings us to the fullness of life in the flesh and blood, here and now, and into the future with those who still share the earth with us. In this life, we still have places in our hearts for our families, friends, and communities. We can and often do make places for others who enter our lives later. And we have room in our hearts for self-love and the many cares that make us unique and distinct individuals.

Those who died wanted us to remember and to cherish the good that was in them and our lives with them. And they wanted us to return to, thrive, and prosper in the world they no longer inhabit, to cherish the life they no longer enjoy. Sometimes they told us explicitly before they died, as Joy did Lewis. Sometimes they told us indirectly in their concern that we not allow losing them to overwhelm us. Some of us have experiences after they die that powerfully suggest that they live on, not only in our hearts but also independently. Some of us have encounters so powerful that they are like meetings. Others are visited in dreams or visions. Still others sense in seeming coincidences or in their surroundings that those they love are signaling them.

We often experience such encounters as assuring us that they are in good places, they want us to hold them in our hearts, or they want us to live well in separation from them and to continue to take care of ourselves and love others. Those who died knew that it is truly a remarkable thing to draw breath, a royal thing to be alive. They wanted us to know this in our hearts even in separation from them.

We love those who died when we go on without them by our sides, with lasting love for them in our hearts and with our hearts open again to the wonders of life on earth.

REFERENCES

Attenborough, R. (Producer and Director), & Eastman, B. (Producer). (1993). *Shadowlands* [Film]. New York: Savoy Pictures.

Attig, T. (1996). *How we grieve: Relearning the world*. New York: Oxford University Press.

Attig, T. (2000). *The heart of grief: Death and the search for lasting love*. New York: Oxford University Press.

Lewis, C. S. (1976). *A grief observed*. New York: Bantam Books.

Oxford English Dictionary (Vol. 1). (1971). New York: Oxford University Press.

Parkes, C. M. (1971). Psycho-social transitions: A field for study. *Social Science and Medicine, 5,* 101–115.

Parkes, C. M. (1988). Bereavement as a psycho-social transition. *Journal of Social Issues, 44,* 53–65.

3

MEANING MAKING IN THE DUAL PROCESS MODEL OF COPING WITH BEREAVEMENT

MARGARET S. STROEBE AND HENK SCHUT

In the following passage from *War and Peace*, Tolstoy described reactions to the death of Prince Andrei:

> When the body, washed and clothed, lay in the coffin on the table everyone went to take leave of him, and everyone wept.
>
> Little Nikolai cried because his heart was torn with perplexity. The countess and Sonya cried from pity for Natasha and because he was no more. The old count cried because he felt that before long he too must step over the same terrible threshold.
>
> Natasha and Princess Maria wept too now, but they wept not because of their own personal grief: they wept from the emotion and awe which took possession of their souls before the simple and solemn mystery of death that had been accomplished before their eyes.

It is evident from this passage that reactions to the loss of the prince differed according to the specific meaning attached to the death by each of the bereaved people present: To say that everyone cried because they were grief stricken emerges as a gross oversimplification. Everyone cried, but for very different reasons.

How a person feels and reacts on becoming bereaved is dependent on the meaning that is assigned to the loss. Although this seems intuitively convincing—even a truism—and well demonstrated in such literary accounts, the problem remains that "meaning" is a nebulous concept. If it is so central, then to understand the phenomena associated with bereavement we need to define meaning in a scientifically useful way. Furthermore, we need to empirically operationalize and examine component parts of the concept.

Different scientific approaches reflecting differing theoretical positions have been adopted to elucidate "meaning" in research on bereavement. For example, attachment perspectives (e.g., Bowlby, 1980) have examined the nature (meaning) of the relationship with the deceased person. Family systems theorists (e.g., Nadeau, 1998) have examined processes of meaning making in families. The sociologist Tony Walter (1996) has addressed meaning-related themes in his "New model of grief," wherein the construction of biography about the deceased person becomes a central process in grieving. Social support theorizing (e.g., W. Stroebe & Stroebe, 1987) has analyzed the meaning of loss in terms of the deficits (emotional, companionship, instrumental, appraisal, etc.) created by the death of the significant person. Cognitive stress theorists (e.g., Folkman & Lazarus, 1980; Lazarus & Folkman, 1984) have focused on appraisal processes in dealing with stressors such as bereavement and the relation of these to coping and adjustment. The psychosocial transition model (Parkes, 1993) defined specific psychological and social aspects of loss and gain that are concomitant with bereavement. Similarly, Rubin's (1992) two-track model can be regarded as defining categories of meaning. Finally, cognitive therapists (e.g., Fleming & Robinson, 1991) have provided analyses in terms of attributions and cognitive processing.

None of these perspectives offers an analysis of the dynamics of cognitive processing within the framework of a bereavement-specific model of coping. We need to understand what types of cognitions bereaved people are going through and how these are regulated across the course of time: What categories of meaning are used, and how do these change to enable the bereaved person to progress through grief and come to terms with loss? The purpose of this chapter is to provide an exploration of such cognitive processes, using the framework of the dual process model of coping with bereavement (DPM; for a more detailed description of the basic model, see M. Stroebe & Schut, 1999). This analysis of the process of coping with bereavement focuses specifically on the aspect of confrontation and avoidance, the positive and negative valence of the emotion or situation being confronted or avoided, and its effects on coping with loss.

STRUCTURAL COMPONENTS OF THE DPM

The DPM provides an analytic framework for understanding how people adapt to the loss of a significant person in their lives. Earlier theoretical formulations and principles of intervention emphasized the centrality of grief work in this process (e.g., Bowlby, 1980; Freud, 1917/1957; Lindemann, 1944; Raphael & Nunn, 1988). The so-called "grief work hypothesis" that can be derived from these perspectives states that people need to confront their loss, to go over the events before and at the time of death, to focus on memories, and to work toward detachment from the deceased person. Fundamental is the view that one needs to bring the reality of loss into one's awareness as much as possible and that suppression is maladaptive. Recently, following questions raised at the theoretical level (e.g., Rosenblatt, 1983; Stroebe, 1992; Wortman & Silver, 1987) and failures to verify it empirically (e.g., M. Stroebe & Stroebe, 1991; Wortman & Silver, 1987, 1989), bereavement researchers have come to realize the potential limitations inherent in the grief work hypothesis. Although grief work is seen as an integral part of coming to terms with loss, other processes need consideration. Thus, although the DPM incorporates the grief work principle it extends conceptualization of the manner in which adaptation takes place in the following way.

The DPM specifies two types of stressors: loss orientation and restoration orientation. This specification is necessary because research has shown that bereaved people not only have to cope with the loss of the loved person himself or herself, but also have to make major adjustments in their lives that come about as secondary consequences of the death. Both of these aspects are potential sources of stress and anxiety. *Loss-oriented coping* thus refers to dealing with, concentrating on, and working through some aspect of the loss experience itself (e.g., crying about the death, yearning for the person, looking at his or her photograph). *Restoration-oriented coping*, on the other hand, includes mastering of the tasks that the bereaved person had undertaken, dealing with arrangements for reorganizing life, and developing new identities.

It is important to make this specification with respect to stressors, first, because it enables us to define *meaning* accordingly. For example, loss-oriented coping would involve dealing with such cognitions (meanings) as "I miss his presence every minute of the day," whereas an example of restoration-oriented meaning would be "I am a single person in a 'couple' society." Second, although the two types of stressor are interrelated, one cannot simultaneously attend to both: Coping at any one point in time is either loss or restoration oriented. The bereaved individual can, in fact, to some extent choose to ignore or to concentrate on the one or the other aspect of loss and change in their lives. Thus, it becomes necessary to introduce a regulatory process, which we have designated *oscillation*. Oscillation is a dynamic process, fundamental to adaptive coping, of alternation between loss- and restoration-oriented coping and alternation between coping with one of these two stressors and not coping at all (complete distraction, unrelated daily activities). Confrontation of loss is, then, interspersed, for example, with avoidance of memories or attendance to the additional stressors such as managing extra household chores or dealing with the changed finances. These basic components of the model are depicted in Figure 3.1.

COPING STRATEGIES IN THE DPM

The process of coming to terms with the loss of a loved person emerges as more complex than described in grief work formulations. Grief work is indeed part of grieving—at least within our own Western, industrialized culture. It does seem that one needs to focus on grief in order to assimilate the experience into pre-existing schemas or change the schemas to accommodate to the changed world (cf. Janoff-Bulman, 1992). Repetition, rumination or—arguably most important—sharing with others who would help change schemas would seem necessary. But this—following the DPM—is not enough. How can we define the more complex cognitive processes underlying the structure outlined in this model? What dimensions are relevant for the analysis of coping with bereavement, and how can we describe the mechanisms that influence the course of adjustment? Answers to these questions should bring us closer to describing ways to analyze meanings of loss and to examine the role that such cognitions may have in the process of adjustment to bereavement. Some leads can be found in the cognitive stress literature. Theorists in this field have identified major types of coping strategies, including emotion-focused versus problem-focused coping and the confrontation–avoidance dimension (e.g., Billings & Moos, 1981; Lazarus & Folkman, 1984; for a review, see de Ridder, 2000).

As discussed elsewhere (M. Stroebe & Schut, 1999), the emotion–problem-focused dimension is not equivalent to but cuts across loss- and restoration-oriented coping. For example, restoration-oriented coping differs from problem-focused coping, even though the former is defined in terms of secondary problems. It subsumes emotion-focused coping associated with managing the secondary life stressors, such as mastering the skills lost with the deceased person, which could be tackled either by trying out the task or by working on one's anxiety about accomplishing the skills (e.g., through distraction, avoidance, and emotional control). For such reasons, the problem–emotion-focused coping dimension is not considered useful for further analysis in this context.

A Dual Process Model of Coping With Bereavement

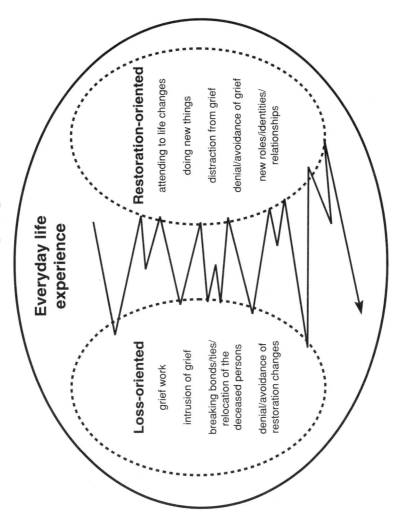

Everyday life experience

Loss-oriented

grief work

intrusion of grief

breaking bonds/ties/
relocation of the
deceased persons

denial/avoidance of
restoration changes

Restoration-oriented

attending to life changes

doing new things

distraction from grief

denial/avoidance of grief

new roles/identities/
relationships

Figure 3.1. A dual process model of coping with bereavement.

Confrontation–Avoidance Coping Dimension

By contrast, the confrontation–avoidance dimension is applicable. It is evident that, conceptually, grief work and confrontation overlap. It would be impossible to do grief work without confrontation. What the grief work concept does not incorporate, however, is an analysis of the dynamic processing of confrontation versus avoidance of specific aspects of loss, as stipulated in the DPM. Furthermore, the model describes the necessity of oscillation, that is, a regulatory process, for successful outcome rather than claiming that confrontation is adaptive and avoidance of grief is maladaptive. Furthermore, one can confront or avoid restoration tasks, too.

What evidence is there that the grieving process involves confrontation–avoidance? Studies of the regulatory process itself (oscillation) have not yet, to our knowledge, been undertaken. However, there is a growing body of empirical research in the areas of trauma and bereavement that provides evidence of the relation between confrontation on the one hand and avoidance on the other and on the beneficial versus detrimental effects of using one of these strategies. Given the centrality of confrontation–avoidance in the DPM, we review this literature in some detail next. Information comes from a broad spectrum of studies, which can be categorized in the following ways: First, the literature includes both self-disclosure and other-disclosure (intra- vs. interpersonal) investigations. These have examined the impact of informal social interactions and professional intervention. Second, the type of disclosure investigated varies from that occurring in natural settings to research manipulations and from written to spoken disclosures. Third, the nature of the cognitions that have been investigated in confrontation–avoidance range from negative to positive affect appraisal and reappraisal.

The literature testifies to both benefits and costs of confronting and avoiding stressors such as traumas and bereavements. Prominent among studies that have shown that confrontation is efficacious (cf. Smyth, 1998, for a recent review) is the body of research conducted by Pennebaker and colleagues. Much of this has centered on the anonymous written disclosure of (previously undisclosed) traumatic events. Many of the studies involve student samples, among whom disclosure was shown to improve academic performance (Pennebaker & Francis, 1996). Pennebaker also found that writing about stressful events reduced illness-related consultations with doctors (Pennebaker & Beall, 1986; Pennebaker, Kiecolt-Glaser, & Glaser, 1988) and boosted immune system resilience (Pennebaker et al., 1988; Petrie, Booth, Pennebaker, Davison, & Thomas, 1995). The effects of these manipulations were strong and consistent, leading Pennebaker to probe for causal mechanisms underlying the deleterious effects of emotional inhibition (Pennebaker, 1989). In the past few years, the focus has been on the role of language (through structuring, assimilating, imposing of meaning, etc.) in the disclosure process (Pennebaker, 1993; Pennebaker & Francis,

1996). Some replications and extensions of this type of research have been conducted by others. Greenberg and Stone (1992) showed the health benefits of writing about traumas, as did Murray, Lamnin, and Carver (1989), who found therapy—thus, verbal communication—even more helpful than writing.

Although the above-mentioned studies produced clear-cut results supportive of the grief work hypothesis, others have been far less so, suggesting that confrontation is not (always) efficacious. The early work of Wortman and Silver (1987, 1989) refuted the grief work hypothesis on the basis of their own empirical results and those of Parkes and Weiss (1983). An alternative interpretation to this analysis has been presented elsewhere (cf. Stroebe, 1992). In the meantime, other studies have provided support for the view that confrontation is not always beneficial. These come from a wide range of sources, including bereavement-specific intervention efficacy assessment (for reviews, see Kavanagh, 1990; Schut & Stroebe, 1997) and studies of debriefing efficacy (for reviews, see Deahl, Gillham, Thomas, Searle, & Srinivasan, 1994; Kenardy et al., 1996; Mitchell & Everly, 1995).

Illustrative are a number of our own studies (W. Stroebe, Stroebe, Schut, Zech, & van den Bout, 1997). We and our colleagues used the Pennebaker type of paradigm in an investigation of written diary disclosure following spousal bereavement but failed to identify beneficial effects of this type of confrontation. In a further study, in which respondents were asked about their way of going about grieving (confrontation vs. avoidance), M. Stroebe and Stroebe (1991) found that widowers who did grief work had better adjustment scores over an 18-month period than those who avoided confrontation of their loss. Widows who avoided confrontation did not differ in depressive symptomatology from those who worked through their loss. Thus, the beneficial effects were not as clear generally as would be concluded from the Pennebaker results.

In a longitudinal study of bereaved spouses conducted by Schut, van den Bout, de Keijser, and Stroebe (1996), the causal relation between the expression of emotions and health outcome (psychological/somatic symptomatology) was analyzed. The measure tapped emotional discharge as well as social sharing. Again in contrast to predictions from the grief work hypothesis, the results showed that the expression of emotions was almost entirely independent of outcome scores: Whether one did or did not express one's grief had little impact on recovery.

Along slightly different lines, Rimé and his colleagues in Louvain, Belgium, have concentrated on verbal disclosure—or *social sharing*, as they have termed it. Their studies have investigated patterns of sharing following a wide variety of situations through which nonclinical samples have gone, from giving birth, to bungee jumping, to watching a horror film, to bereavement (e.g., Rimé, Mesquita, Philippot, & Boca, 1991; Rimé, Philippot, Boca, & Mesquita, 1992; Rimé, Finkenauer, Luminet, Zech, & Philippot, 1998).

The sharing of highly emotional events is very frequent but, again in contrast to the Pennebaker findings, the amount of social sharing did not show a clear relation to recovery over time from the emotional impact of the event.

Other studies have examined the functions of avoidance. Bonanno, Keltner, Holen, and Horowitz (1995) provided evidence that avoidant strategies may be more functional than had previously been assumed in the bereavement literature. Using a longitudinal strategy, Bonanno et al. found a dissociation between physiologically measured arousal and indexes of psychological upset among bereaved men who were placed in an "empty chair" situation. High physiological arousal, but low psychological confrontation, were associated with good outcome (measured at a later time). Thus, whereas too complete a denial has frequently been associated with pathological forms of grieving (e.g., Jacobs, 1993), Bonanno et al.'s study suggests that some degree of avoidance may be healthy (see also Bonanno & Keltner, 1997).

Kelly and McKillop (1996) reviewed studies on the benefits of keeping secrets, ones in which the secret keeper was directly involved. Contrary to the large literature testifying to the advantages of revealing personal secrets, they provided evidence to show that choosing to reveal secrets is very complex and may have disturbing consequences (e.g., being rejected, alienated from the listener), including the emergence of a negative self-image. Not all secrets should be revealed, and not indiscriminately, to just anybody, it appears.

Kaminer and Lavie (1993) even showed the benefits of denial over confrontation among people who have endured extremely traumatic experiences. These researchers studied survivors of the Holocaust in Israel, who could be expected to have had multiple bereavements as well as the experience of lasting trauma. In order to study the survivors' long-term adaptation, Kaminer and Lavie focused on sleep and dreams, comparing difficulties and disturbances among well-adjusted versus less well-adjusted survivors. The higher the intrusion of Holocaust-related memories and complaints and distress in everyday life, the more disturbed was the sleep, and the higher the dream recall. Well-adjusted survivors had lower recall of dreams than non-Holocaust control survivors. Kaminer and Lavie argued that the massive repression of dream content is an adaptive mechanism. Assisting traumatized survivors to repress the terrors of the past may have more adaptive value than "working through" strategies.

Taken together, the results reported above appear discrepant, with some studies indicating beneficial effects, and others detrimental effects, of confrontation or of avoidance. How can these apparent discrepancies be explained? A range of stressors has been investigated. It must be recognized that the nature of the experiences associated with some traumas are different from some bereavements, such that disclosing or confronting has very different implications. For example, a trauma may not have been shared before because of secret, stigmatizing, inhibition-related or nonsharable aspects (e.g., one may not want to burden others with horrendous images).

Rimé et al. (1998) recently described a similar phenomenon in their "threshold for sharing" idea. Loss of an attachment figure, by contrast, is frequently not horrific or secret. Many of the studies induced confrontation or disclosure. In cases where a bereavement is not also traumatic it is also likely that there is occurrence of "natural" sharing, that is, that there has already been confrontation with, and cognitive processing of, the death (cf. Rimé et al., 1998). The manipulation would not be expected to have a significant impact in such cases. It is also possible that the manipulation is sometimes not strong enough to yield discernible consequences.

Analysis of Cognitions Related to Confrontation–Avoidance

It is evident that we need to define precisely what is being confronted or avoided. What cognitive expressions (meanings) versus nonexpressions are associated with good versus poor outcome? The key to understanding who will adjust well to bereavement and who will not lies in the analysis of cognitions associated with confrontation–avoidance.

Two lines of empirical research are useful in an analysis of cognitions. On the one hand, research has been conducted on the relation between the impact of (expression/confrontation of) negative affect and well-being; on the other hand, research has addressed the impact of positive feelings and well-being. First we describe the research findings. Then we examine pathways within the coping process. Finally, we relate this research to the DPM, providing a framework for incorporating "meaning" into the analysis of coping with bereavement.

Rumination in Confrontation With Loss

According to our analysis, studies that have shown confrontation to have detrimental effects on adjustment (e.g., Wortman & Silver, 1987, 1989) are those in which the confrontation is associated with negative affect. People whose style is to confront and talk about negative, distressing aspects of their loss a lot or who, in studies in which disclosure is forced, talk to investigators about distressing things to do with loss, *over time* do not do as well as those who refrain (more) from this type of disclosure. It is evident that disclosure versus nondisclosure has to be shown to be a predictor and not just a corollary of adjustment. A few studies have indeed controlled for the amount of distress at the outset of the evaluation and thus provide information on the potential impact of the disclosure on later recovery.

Nolen-Hoeksema, Parker, and Larson (1994) reported disadvantages of ruminative ways of going about coping with bereavement. They defined *ruminative coping* as thoughts and behaviors that focus attention on symptoms of distress and the meanings and consequences of these symptoms. It is also defined as repetitive and passive, not active, problem solving. Examples of self-focused responses to depressed mood are "I think 'Why do I react this way?'" and "I think back to other times I have been depressed," whereas symptom-focused responses would include such thoughts as "I think about how hard it is to concentrate." Possible consequences and causes of mood are illustrated in the following: "I think 'I won't be able to do my job if I don't snap out of this'" and "I go away by myself and think about why I feel this way."

People with a ruminative style early in bereavement were found to have higher depression levels 6 months later (when depression level at Time 1 was controlled for). Those with a more distractive style became less depressed over time. Bereaved women were found to ruminate more than did bereaved men.

Capps and Bonanno (in press) provided further evidence of such processes. They used a narrative analysis procedure—a carefully developed coding system to evaluate the type, valence, and intimacy of the narratives. How does this predict grief, distress, and somatic symptoms over time? Six-month measurements were compared with those taken at 14 months and 25 months. Disclosure of negatively valanced emotions predicted increased distress and somatic complaints.

Positive Feelings in Confrontation With Grief

Along similar lines, it has recently been shown that disclosing or otherwise confronting positive aspects associated with loss leads to recovery. Again, the same stringent methodological requirements, with baseline controls, and longitudinal designs as outlined for the studies on negative affect reviewed above, are necessary for an adequate test of the mediating role of positive affect in recovery.

Foremost in this research has been the work of Folkman and her colleagues. Folkman has conducted a large-scale prospective study of the effects of caregiving and bereavement among partners of men with AIDS. The study included self-report and clinical observation both during the time leading up to and following the death of a partner (see Folkman, Chesney, Collette, Boccellari, & Cooke, 1996; Folkman, Chesney, Cooke, Boccellari, & Collette, 1994). Despite harrowing and extremely exhausting circumstances, it was found that, in addition to negative emotional states, these men experienced positive emotions through their caregiving and bereavement.

Folkman also has examined types of coping that had to do with the search for and finding of positive meaning (positive reappraisal, goal-directed problem-focused coping, spiritual beliefs and practices, and the infusion of ordinary events with positive meaning). These were associated with positive psychological states during bereavement. She carried out quantitative analyses of longitudinal data. (For a review, see Folkman, in press.) Of importance here is the result that positive appraisal and problem-focused coping were significantly and independently associated with positive affect, when positive affect for the previous month and for the other seven types of coping on the Ways of Coping Checklist were controlled for (see Mosko-witz, Folkman, Collette, & Vittinghoff, 1996). In line with this, path analysis of the spiritual beliefs measure, positive reappraisal, and positive affect showed that spirituality facilitated positive reappraisal of the difficult situation and that the latter, in turn, helped support positive psychological states.

This suggests that being able to find positive meaning in bereavement-related stressful events brings about or enhances positive affect, that being able to interpret positively is effective in creating a positive state of mind and, presumably, in reducing distress. Positive psychological states emerge as part of the coping process. This study (Folkman, 1997) suggests the need to focus on these positive states of mind in addition to focusing, as in the past, on coping with distress.

Support for this pattern comes from studies conducted by Bonanno and colleagues. In the narrative analysis study described earlier (Capps & Bonanno, in press), more frequent disclosure of positive thoughts predicted decreased grief. In a further analysis of this data set, Keltner and Bonanno (1997) investigated laughter and smiling—similarly looking for predictors of good adjustment over time. Duchenne laughter (which involves the action of the orbicularis oculi muscle and is interpreted as a genuine smile) was found to be related to self-reports of reduced anger, increased enjoyment, dissociation of distress, and better social relations.

The implication of the above reasoning is that positive psychological states are integral to the coping process itself. In other words, positive emotions can actually help one to cope with bereavement; they are part of the grieving process. They are not just "off-setting" emotions that occur in relation to the cessation of an aversive condition (cf. Folkman, 1997). Not only does one "feel good while feeling bad" but one also "feels good to make one feel less bad"—even "feels less bad by feeling good" (cf. Folkman, 1997, in press). How does this analysis supersede previous understanding? It does so in two important ways: It states that it is not just that positive states coexist with depression (e.g., Wortman & Silver, 1992) or that blocking negative information and creating positive illusions enhances mental and physical health (Taylor, 1989). By designing a longitudinal study, and controlling for the level of distress and symptomatology at the first point of measurement, Folkman (1997) was able to show not only an association but also the predictive strength of positive thoughts, just as this was done with respect to negative thoughts in the research of Nolen-Hoeksema et al. (1994).

Pathways to (Mal)Adjustment

Following the above lines of research, we suggest that ruminating about a loss will worsen grief and depression, whereas positive appraisal of aspects associated with the loss experience will do the opposite, supporting the adjustment process. The next question to address, then, is how this comes about. How does rumination operate to lengthen and worsen grief and positive appraisal to ameliorate it?

With respect to rumination, Nolen-Hoeksema and Jackson (1996) argued that it first enhances the effects of depressed mood on thinking. Their research showed that people who engaged in ruminative coping when they were distressed would think more negatively about their current situation and their life in general. Second, it interferes with everyday instrumental behaviors. These people were less motivated to participate in everyday activities that raise feelings of well-being and give a sense of control. Third, it interferes with good problem solving. They were less effective in using interpersonal problem-solving skills. Nolen-Hoeksema's analysis of ruminative coping was applied to depressed mood in general. Her naturalistic studies included samples of bereaved people. It would seem fair to infer that these three pathways—the enhancing effect of negative mood on thinking, the interference with instrumental behavior, and the interference with effective problem solving—also apply more specifically to the lengthening and worsening of grief.

The pathways whereby Folkman (1997) integrated positive psychological states into a model of coping were threefold. First, meaning-based processes (e.g., positive reappraisals) lead to positive psychological states. Second, negative psychological states may motivate people to search for and create positive psychological states in order to gain relief (coping as a response to distress). Third, positive psychological states lead back to appraisal and coping, and coping efforts are sustained.

An example, taken from Chuang Tzu, China, third century B.C., illustrates the ways that positive affect and appraisal can lead to adjustment:

> When first she died, how could I not help being affected? But then, on examining the matter, I saw that in the Beginning she had originally been formless. And not only formless, but she had originally lacked all substance. During this first state of confused chaos, there came a change which resulted in substance. This substance changed to assume form. The form changed and became alive. And now it has changed again to reach death. In this it has been like the passing of the four seasons, spring, summer, autumn, and winter. And while she is thus lying asleep in the Great House (i.e. the Universe), for me to go about weeping and wailing, would be to show myself ignorant of Fate (ming). Therefore I refrain.

Finding existential meaning would be an example of the impact of positive reappraisal. The motivation to search, the second pathway, is also clearly illustrated and, with respect to the third, perhaps one could say that the positive affect created by the reappraisal was the next step in the chain to being able to cope with the loss of the loved one, enabling a continuation of refrainment from grief because of the peaceful state of mind that had been achieved.

Cognitive Mechanisms in the DPM

How do (a) confrontation versus avoidance of positive and negative states and (b) the pathways to enhancement versus amelioration of grief fit into the DPM? There are good reasons to argue the need for oscillation between positive and negative affect/(re)appraisal as an integral part of the coping process, just as was argued above for the fluctuation between attention to loss and restoration-oriented stressors. Persistent negative affect intensifies grief, yet working through grief, which includes rumination, is the essence of coming to terms with a bereavement. Positive reappraisals, on the other hand, sustain the coping effort, yet if positive psychological states are maintained relentlessly, grieving is neglected. Alternation between these psychological states emerges as essential.

Folkman (1997) recently integrated positive meaning states into a revision of stress-coping theory, which can be incorporated into the dual process formulation. In accordance with the line of argument above, also needed is integration of negative appraisals. This can be done by introducing pathways as shown in Figure 3.2. Oscillation between positive and negative affect and (re)appraisal facilitates and provides pathways whereby one can cope with the different dimensions of grieving.

To illustrate: Riches and Dawson (1998) explored the manner in which photographs can provide opportunities for parents to remember the life (as opposed to the death) of their deceased child. This may facilitate conversations and reminiscences about the living relationship and enable introduction of the deceased child to people who did not know him or her (this frequently occurred in our own interviews with bereaved parents). Photographs can assist the development of the ongoing narrative about the deceased child and can be searched for meaning, furthering the process of coming to terms with the fact of loss and the reality of the child's life. Riches and Dawson described an interview with a couple who lost their teenage daughter Vicki quite suddenly. Photograph albums were drawn out, as the conversation turned to her life, and Vicki's mother, who had not wanted to take active part in the interview before, became as involved in the conversation as her husband. In the authors' words,

> The tenor of the interview noticeably shifted from the story of their distress at Vicki's death and of their feelings immediately following it, to a growing expression of pride in her achievements and immense fondness for the life they had lived together. For a short while, photographs taken on school trips, family outings and holidays, stories that recalled her personal idiosyncrasies and her strength of character, and pieces of work she had written and drawn (especially the neatness of her geography folder with its meticulously drawn maps and perfect handwriting) allowed Sheila and Peter to "browse" through her life, celebrating the fact of her existence and identifying those features that best characterized

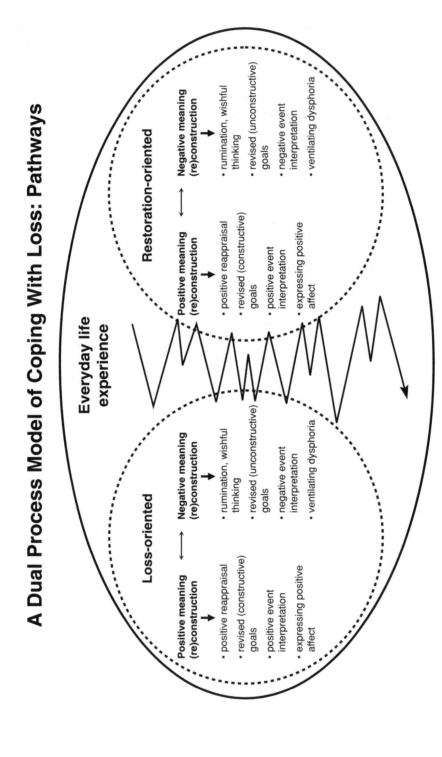

A Dual Process Model of Coping With Loss: Pathways

Everyday life experience

Loss-oriented

Positive meaning (re)construction ⟷ **Negative meaning (re)construction**

Positive meaning (re)construction →
- positive reappraisal
- revised (constructive) goals
- positive event interpretation
- expressing positive affect

Negative meaning (re)construction →
- rumination, wishful thinking
- revised (unconstructive) goals
- negative event interpretation
- ventilating dysphoria

Restoration-oriented

Positive meaning (re)construction ⟷ **Negative meaning (re)construction**

Positive meaning (re)construction →
- positive reappraisal
- revised (constructive) goals
- positive event interpretation
- expressing positive affect

Negative meaning (re)construction →
- rumination, wishful thinking
- revised (unconstructive) goals
- negative event interpretation
- ventilating dysphoria

Figure 3.2. A dual process model of coping with loss: Pathways. Jagged arrow represents oscillation.

her. By the end of the interview, I had come to "know" Vicki and had a sense of the presence which Sheila and Peter retained. (Riches & Dawson, 1998, pp. 133–134)

The shift from confrontation of negative affect associated with the shock of the death to positive ones relating to Vicki's life and achievements are evident, as are the implications for struggling on with the identity of bereaved parents. It is not hard to imagine how such photographic memories, sporadically dwelt on, help to regulate the cognitive processing of affect associated with loss and restoration tasks.

CONCLUSION

In the words of Robert Neimeyer (cf. the Introduction to this volume), needed in our field of study is an understanding of bereavement that recognizes the fundamental revision of assumptive worlds, meaning systems, or life narratives. The effort must be to move toward an appreciation of grieving as a process whereby we effortfully and idiosyncratically reconstruct a world of meaning and restore coherence to the narratives of our lives (cf. Neimeyer, Keesee, & Fortner, 2000). The analysis of loss and restoration orientation, the underlying negative and positive cognitions associated with each of these dimensions, and the process of oscillation between these components provide a framework for a systematic probing of assumptive worlds, meaning systems, and life narratives. Basic to the conceptualization of grief is that it is dynamic, fluctuating, and changing over time. It also lends itself to appreciation of idiosyncrasies (there is no single "correct" way to grieve).

The task now is to provide empirical verification for the DPM. Until this has been done we must, of course, be cautious in deriving practical implications from assumed regularities: Supportive evidence has been described for component parts of the model, demonstrating first the positive and negative consequences of confronting and of avoiding both loss and restoration tasks of grieving and, second, the impact of positive and negative psychological (re)appraisals and states of mind in confrontation–avoidance of the various aspects. What remains to be examined empirically is the process itself of oscillation between these components.

REFERENCES

Billings, A. G., & Moos, R. H. (1981). The role of coping responses and social resources in attenuating the stress of life events. *Journal of Behavioral Medicine, 4*, 139–157.

Bonanno, G. A., & Keltner, D. (1997). Facial expressions of emotion and the course of conjugal bereavement. *Journal of Abnormal Psychology, 106*, 126–137.

Bonanno, G. A., Keltner, D., Holen, A., & Horowitz, M. J. (1995). When avoiding unpleasant emotions may not be such a bad thing: Verbal–autonomic response dissociation and midlife conjugal bereavement. *Journal of Personality and Social Psychology, 69,* 975–989.

Bowlby, J. (1980). *Attachment and loss: Vol. 3. Loss: Sadness and depression.* London: Hogarth.

Capps, L., & Bonanno, G.A. (in press). Narrating bereavement: Thematic and grammatical predictors of adjustment to loss. *Discourse Processes, 30.*

Deahl, M. P., Gillham, A. B., Thomas, J., Searle, M. M., & Srinivasan, M. (1994). Psychological sequelae following the Gulf War: Factors associated with subsequent morbidity and the effectiveness of psychological debriefing. *British Journal of Psychiatry, 165,* 60–65.

de Ridder, D. (2000). Gender, stress, and coping: Do women handle stressful situations differently from men? In L. Sher & J. S. St. Lawrence (Eds.), *Women, health and the mind* (pp. 155–135). Chichester, UK: Wiley.

Fleming, S. J., & Robinson, P. (1991). The application of cognitive therapy to the bereaved. In M. Vallis, J. Howes, & P. C. Miller (Eds.), *The challenge of cognitive therapy: Applications to nontraditional populations* (pp. 135–158). New York: Plenum.

Folkman, S. (1997). Positive psychological states and coping with severe stress. *Social Science & Medicine, 45,* 1207–1221.

Folkman, S. (in press). Revised coping theory and the process of bereavement. In M. S. Stroebe, R. O. Hansson, W. Stroebe, & H. Schut (Eds.), *Handbook of bereavement research: Consequences, coping, and care.* Washington, DC: American Psychological Association.

Folkman, S., Chesney, M. A., Collette, L., Boccellari, A., & Cooke, M. (1996). Post bereavement depressive mood and its pre-bereavement predictors in HIV+ and HIV− gay men. *Journal of Personality and Social Psychology, 70,* 336–348.

Folkman, S., Chesney, M. A., Cook, M., Boccellari, A., & Collette, L. (1994). Caregiver burden in HIV+ and HIV− partners of men with AIDS. *Journal of Consulting and Clinical Psychology, 62,* 746–756.

Folkman, S., & Lazarus, R. S. (1980). An analysis of coping in a middle-aged community sample. *Journal of Health and Social Behavior, 21,* 219–239.

Freud, S. (1957). Mourning and melancholia. In J. Strachey (Ed. & Trans.), *The standard edition of the complete psychological works of Sigmund Freud* (Vol. 14, pp. 239–260). London: Hogarth Press. (Original work published 1917)

Greenberg, M. A., & Stone, A. A. (1992). Emotional disclosure about traumas and its relation to health: Effects of previous disclosure and trauma severity. *Journal of Personality and Social Psychology, 63,* 75–84.

Jacobs, S. (1993). *Pathologic grief: Maladaptation to loss.* Washington, DC: American Psychiatric Press.

Janoff-Bulman, R. (1992). *Shattered assumptions: Towards a new psychology of trauma.* New York: Free Press.

Kaminer, H., & Lavie, P. (1993). Sleep and dreams in well-adjusted and less adjusted Holocaust survivors. In M. Stroebe, W. Stroebe, & R. O. Hansson

(Eds.), *Handbook of bereavement: Theory, research and intervention* (pp. 331–345). New York: Cambridge University Press.

Kavanagh, D. G. (1990). Towards a cognitive–behavioral intervention for adult grief reactions. *British Journal of Psychiatry, 157*, 373–383.

Kelly, A. E., & McKillop, K. J. (1996). Consequences of revealing personal secrets. *Psychological Bulletin, 120*, 450–465.

Keltner, D., & Bonanno, G. A. (1997). A study of laughter and dissociation: Distinct correlates of laughter and smiling during bereavement. *Journal of Personality and Social Psychology, 73*, 687–702.

Kenardy, J. A., Webster, R. A., Lewin, T. J., Carr, V. J., Hazell, P. L., & Carter, G. L. (1996). Stress debriefing and patterns of recovery following a natural disaster. *Journal of Traumatic Stress, 9*, 37–49.

Lazarus, R., & Folkman, S. (1984). *Stress, appraisal and coping.* New York: Springer.

Lindemann, E. (1944). Symptomatology and management of acute grief. *American Journal of Psychiatry, 101*, 141–148.

Mitchell, J. T., & Everly, G. S. (1995). Critical incident stress debriefing (CISD) and the prevention of work-related traumatic stress among high risk occupational groups. In G. S. Everly & J. M. Lating (Eds.), *Psychotraumatology* (pp. 269–280). New York: Plenum.

Moskowitz, J., Folkman, S., Collette, L., & Vittinghoff, E. (1996). Coping and mood during AIDS-related caregiving and bereavement. *Annals of Behavioral Medicine, 18*, 49–57.

Murray, E. J., Lamnin, A. D., & Carver, C. (1989). Emotional expression in written essays and psychotherapy. *Journal of Social and Clinical Psychology, 8*, 414–429.

Nadeau, J. W. (1998). *Families making sense of death.* Thousand Oaks, CA: Sage.

Neimeyer, R., Keesee, N., & Fortner, B. (2000). Loss and meaning reconstruction: Propositions and procedures. In R. Malkinson, S. Rubin, & E. Witztum (Eds.), *Traumatic and non-traumatic bereavement.* Madison, CT: Psychosocial Press.

Nolen-Hoeksema, S., & Jackson, B. (1996, August). *Ruminative coping and the gender differences in depression.* Paper presented at the 104th Annual Convention of the American Psychological Association, Toronto, Ontario, Canada.

Nolen-Hoeksema, S., Parker, L. E., & Larson, J. (1994). Ruminative coping with depressed mood following loss. *Journal of Personality and Social Psychology, 67*, 92–104.

Parkes, C. M. (1993). Bereavement as a psychosocial transition: Processes of adaptation to change. In M. Stroebe, W. Stroebe, & R. O. Hansson (Eds.), *Handbook of bereavement: Theory, research and intervention* (pp. 91–101). New York: Cambridge University Press.

Parkes, C. M., & Weiss, R. (1983). *Recovery from bereavement.* New York: Basic Books.

Pennebaker, J. (1989). Confession, inhibition and disease. In L. Berkowitz (Ed.), *Advances in experimental social psychology* (Vol. 22, pp. 211–244). New York: Academic Press.

Pennebaker, J. (1993). Putting stress into words: Health, linguistic, and therapeutic implications. *Behavior Research and Therapy, 31*, 539–548.

Pennebaker, J., & Beall, S. (1986). Confronting a traumatic event: Toward an understanding of inhibition and disease. *Journal of Abnormal Psychology, 95,* 274–281.

Pennebaker, J., & Francis, M. (1996). Cognitive, emotional, and language processes in disclosure. *Cognition & Emotion, 10,* 601–626.

Pennebaker, J., Kiecolt-Glaser, J. K., & Glaser, R. (1988). Disclosure of traumas and immune function: Health implications for psychotherapy. *Journal of Consulting and Clinical Psychology, 56,* 239–245.

Petrie, J., Booth, R., Pennebaker, J., Davison, K., & Thomas, M. (1995). Disclosure of trauma and immune response to a hepatitis B vaccination program. *Journal of Consulting and Clinical Psychology, 65,* 789–792.

Raphael, B., & Nunn, K. (1988). Counseling the bereaved. *Journal of Social Issues, 44,* 191–206.

Riches, G., & Dawson, P. (1998). Lost children, living memories: The role of photographs in processes of grief and adjustment among bereaved parents. *Death Studies, 22,* 121–140.

Rimé, B., Finkenauer, C., Luminet, O., Zech, E., & Philippot, P. (1998). Social sharing of emotion: New evidence and new questions. In W. Stroebe & M. Hewstone (Eds.), *European review of social psychology* (Vol. 9). Chichester, England: Wiley.

Rimé, B., Mesquita, B., Philippot, P., & Boca, S. (1991). Beyond the emotional event: Six studies on the social sharing of emotion. *Cognition & Emotion, 5,* 435–465.

Rimé, B., Philippot, P., Boca, S., & Mesquita, B. (1992). Long-lasting cognitive and social consequences of emotion: Social sharing and rumination. In W. Stroebe & M. Hewstone (Eds.), *European review of social psychology* (Vol. 3, pp. 225–258). Chichester, England: Wiley.

Rosenblatt, P. (1983). *Bitter, bitter tears: Nineteenth century diarists and twentieth century grief theories.* Minneapolis: University of Minnesota Press.

Rubin, S. (1992). Adult child loss and the two-track model of bereavement. *Omega, 24,* 183–202.

Schut, H., & Stroebe, M. (1997, June). *Does help help?* Paper presented at the International Conference on Grief and Bereavement, Association for Death Education and Counseling, Washington, DC.

Schut, H., van den Bout, J., de Keijser, J., & Stroebe, M. (1996). Cross-modality grief therapy: Description and assessment of a new programme. *Journal of Clinical Psychology, 52,* 357–365.

Smyth, J. (1998). Written emotional expression: Effect sizes, outcome types, and moderating variables. *Journal of Consulting and Clinical Psychology, 66,* 174–184.

Stroebe, M. (1992). Coping with bereavement: A review of the grief work hypothesis. *Omega, 26,* 19–42.

Stroebe, M., & Schut, H. (1999). The dual process model of coping with bereavement: Rationale and description. *Death Studies, 23,* 197–224.

Stroebe, M., & Stroebe, W. (1991). Does "grief work" work? *Journal of Consulting and Clinical Psychology, 59,* 479–482.

Stroebe, W., & Stroebe, M. (1987). *Bereavement and health.* New York: Cambridge University Press.

Stroebe, W., Stroebe, M., Schut, H., Zech, E., & van den Bout, J. (1997, June). *Must we give sorrow words?* Paper presented at the Third International Conference on Grief and Bereavement in Contemporary Society, Washington, DC.

Taylor, S. E. (1989). *Positive illusions: Creative self perception and the healthy mind.* New York: Basic Books.

Walter, T. (1996). A new model of grief: Bereavement and biography. *Mortality, 1,* 7–25.

Wortman, C. B., & Silver, R. C. (1987). Coping with irrevocable loss. In G. R. VandenBos & B. K. Bryant (Eds.), *Cataclysms, crises and catastrophes: Psychology in action* (pp. 189–235). Washington, DC: American Psychological Association.

Wortman, C. B., & Silver, R. C. (1989). The myths of coping with loss. *Journal of Consulting and Clinical Psychology, 57,* 349–357.

Wortman, C. B., & Silver, R.C. (1992). Reconsidering assumptions about coping with loss: An overview of current research. In L. Montada, S. H. Filipp, & M. L. Lerner (Eds.), *Life crises and experiences of loss in adulthood* (pp. 341–365). Hillsdale, NJ: Erlbaum.

II

Re-Establishing Relationships:
Context and Connection

4

THE INNER REPRESENTATION OF THE DEAD CHILD IN THE PSYCHIC AND SOCIAL NARRATIVES OF BEREAVED PARENTS

DENNIS KLASS

The resolution of parental grief involves a series of transformations of the inner representation of the dead child in the parent's inner world and social world. As the reality of the child's death and of the parent's continuing bond with the child are made part of the socially shared reality, the inner representation of the child can be transformed in the parent's psychic life. The goal of grief is not to sever the bond with the dead child but to integrate the child into the parent's life and social networks in a different way than when the child was alive.

Adapted with permission of Taylor & Francis Inc., http:www.routledge-ny.com, from Klass, D. (1996), "The deceased child in the psychic and social worlds of bereaved parents during the resolution of grief," in D. Klass, P. R. Silverman, & S. Nickman (Eds), *Continuing Bonds: New Understandings of Grief* (pp. 199–215). Philadelphia: Brunner/Mazel.

This chapter is based in a long-term ethnographic study of a local chapter of Bereaved Parents,[1] a self-help group of parents whose children have died (Geertz, 1973; Glaser & Strauss, 1967; Hammersley & Atkinson, 1983; Klass, 1988, 1999; Powdermaker, 1966; Wax, 1971; Whyte, 1973). The study began in 1978 when I was asked to be the professional advisor of the chapter. There were many opportunities to gather material in ongoing conversations and open-ended interviews with members and in attending meetings in which members shared their grief and those at which they conducted business and planning. An especially valuable resource were chapter newsletters in which members wrote to share their pain, their progress, and their insights.

THE PURPOSE OF GRIEF

The purpose of grief has been defined for most of the 20th century as to break an attachment. In fact, however, the members of Bereaved Parents do not detach from their child and, it is now clear, neither do many others who survive the death of significant people in their lives (Klass, Silverman, & Nickman, 1996). They transform the bond in ways that enable them to keep the child an important element in their lives. The consensus that seems to be emerging among scholars and clinicians is that the purpose or goal of grief is the construction of a "durable biography" (Walter, 1996), a narrative story (Neimeyer & Stewart, 1996) that organizes and makes meaning of the survivor's life after the death as well as of the life of the person who died. The process by which this is achieved is active interaction within a community in which the death is recognized, the deceased person is mourned, and the continuing bond with the dead person is validated and shared.

In the modern, developed world it is difficult to find a term that adequately describes dead children who remain such living realities in parents' lives. *Ghost* and *spirit* have too many associations with 19th-century spiritualism (see Finucane, 1996, pp. 172–216; McDannell & Lang, 1988, pp. 228–306). The terms *living dead*, from many African cultures, and *ancestors*, from Asian cultures, do not translate well into contemporary thought forms. I have chosen the concept of "inner representation" because it seems to be a more neutral term. We can define *inner representation*, following Fairbairn (1952) and Kernberg (1976), as the part of the self actualized in the bond with the person, characterizations and thematic memories of the person, and the emotional states connected with the characterizations and memories.

---

[1]The group was formerly a chapter of the Compassionate Friends but has changed its affiliation to the Bereaved Parents of the USA. Except for the name change and the national affiliation, none of the dynamics by which the group operates has changed.

The word *inner* in *inner representation* may be somewhat misleading. Our psychic life is structured to a great extent by social bonds. A child, living or dead, plays roles within the family and psychic system. The role can be as simple as the child being the one who will live out the parent's ideal self or as complex as the child being the parent's surrogate parent (see Benedek, 1959, 1970, 1975). Phenomena that indicate interaction with the inner representation of the dead child are a sense of presence, hallucinations in any of the senses, belief in the child's continuing active influence on thoughts or events, or a conscious incorporation of the characteristics or virtues of the dead child into the self. These phenomena can be private or shared within the family and community. Thus, the various narrative stories surrounding the death add themes to the inner representation (i.e., the narrative stories about the child who died, about the individual bereaved parent, about the father's and mother's relationship, about the family to which the child belonged, and about the parent's and child's wider community). To a great extent, the degree to which parents in our study feel integrated into the social system and can find social support in their grief and, therefore, the ease with which they can resolve their grief, is the degree to which the inner representation of the child is integrated into their social world.

MARKERS ON THE JOURNEY THROUGH GRIEF

It seems reasonably well accepted today that there are no invariant stages in grief. Over the years, however, group members have evolved some terms by which they locate themselves and others in their journey: "newly bereaved," "into their grief," "well along in their grief," and "resolved as much as it will be." It is not a formal system; other terms may be used—for example, "into their grief" can also be "that first year," and at the end a parent may be "pretty much resolved." Because the system was developed by the participants in our study to explain their own experience, I am appropriating it as a way of organizing this chapter, but the scheme may not describe the experience of anyone except parents who find this self-help process a useful way to reach resolution. For each of these phases I discuss the representation of the child in the parent's inner world and in the communities of which the parent is a member. A summary of these transformations appears in Table 4.1.

The Newly Bereaved

The Parent's Inner World

For parents, their child's death is an awful truth that seems unreal. Kauffman (1994) noted that the initial response to traumatic death is dissociation, not denial. A Bereaved Parents newsletter article reads,

TABLE 4.1
Representation of the Deceased Child in the Inner and Social Worlds of Bereaved Parents at Different Phases of the Grief Process

Phase	Inner world	Social world
Newly bereaved	• Dissociation • Out of touch with the child • Anticipation of continuing bond with the child • Linking objects that evoke the presence of the child	• Isolation from usual social networks • Inadequate symbol systems by which to interpret the new reality
Into their grief	• Separate from the living child • Connect with child's pain • Deal with ambivalence in parent–child bond	• Share bond with the child in self-help group • "Being there" for each other • Share practical solutions • Validate interactions with dead child
Well along in their grief	• Exchange pain for positive bond with the child • Connect bond with the child to parent's own healing	• Stabilize continuing bond • Share continuing bond in ritual and customs • Helping other bereaved parents as expression of the continuing bond • Include continuing bond in other communities
Resolved as much as it will be	• Learn to live with sadness • Continuing bond guides the parent's better self	• Make child's life count • Reintegrate into wider communities • Accept non-ordinary phenomena as part of the everyday world

We awaken to the sun shining in our windows—a beautiful day. But wait, was I dreaming, or is something wrong. Why do I hesitate to become fully awake? No, it isn't a bad dream, it's reality. The room is empty.

He wasn't there when we went to bed, he isn't in his bed this morning. It can't be. . . . Our hearts are left with an empty room that will never be filled again.

As the shock of reality hits them, parents often have intimations of the future bond they will have with their child. In a newsletter poem a mother described a recurrent dream in which it seems "as though you were still there," but when she reaches out to touch, the child disappears. Her interpretation of this dream is that the child is sending a message that he has not yet gone and is still with her. One can see that the child and the parent are not separated as the poem shifts from the parent's dream to the child's dream. The mother feels herself in the child's dream just as the child is in hers.

> For in your dreams each night,
> God lets my love shine through.
> God sends you all the pictures,
> for in your mind to view,
> of all the precious times we had,
> and all the love we knew.

During this early grief, parents often establish a connection with the dead child through a *linking object* (Volkan, 1981) that will transmute over time but be long lasting. Three years after her 21-year-old daughter died a mother reported on the meaning of some dolls that E., her daughter, had stopped her from throwing away.

> Raggedy Ann and Andy still sit there, perched on top of a bookshelf in what used to be E's room. . . . Years ago I tried to throw the forgotten dolls away, and my then-teenaged daughter indignantly rescued them from the trash. "Not Ann and Andy!" she cried, settling them in her room. . . . E is gone now . . . her beautiful promising young life snuffed out by a drunk driver. . . . Our lives have been changed, and so has E's room. We use it primarily as a computer/word processor room now, but many of the reminders are still there—including Raggedy Ann and Andy.

The Parent's Social World

The dissociation parents feel in their inner life is also their experience in their social world. Newly bereaved parents care whether other people share the loss. Parents report whether people came to the funeral, whether a memorial was planned at the school, whether they see other people deeply affected by their child's death. But for many in the group it often seems to them that neither the child nor the child's death has social reality. They find that people will not mention the child's name in their presence, that inquiries about how they are doing imply that it doesn't hurt as bad as it does, that the child can be replaced by a new baby, or that God loves the child in heaven better than the parent could have loved the child here. The sense of isolation can be bitter.

Symbols of the mainline culture or of the parents' community affiliations are little help in making sense of parents' experience, because those symbols do not meld the reality that the child is dead with the reality that the parent is still bonded to the child. A continual theme in newsletter articles is an appeal to friends and family to understand and to accept the parents' feelings and behaviors. They are often written in first-person plural, for one of the early discoveries is that other bereaved parents are treated in a similar way.

> Please don't tell us to turn off our memories, to snap out of it, that he/she is dead and life has to go on. But our love for them doesn't end with death. . . . Yes, we fully realize that he/she is dead, gone forever, and that's what hurts.
>
> Please have patience with us. Try to understand why we are acting or feeling the way we are today. In a small word or gesture let us know it's all right with you for us to love, to cry, to remember. We aren't doing it to make you uncomfortable or to gain sympathy. We are just trying to cope.

A mother wrote about how differently her community responded to the news of her pregnancy than to the news of her child's death. When she was expecting, everyone told her that this was the most blessed of life's events and that her baby was a new person, a unique individual, different from anyone else. She was told that this new person would change her life forever.

> And yet when this most blessed and unique person dies, everybody acts like it's nothing. "Oh well, better luck next time." "It's better he died before you got to know him." "You'll have more babies". . . So parents who lose a baby will generally try to hide their feelings of grief from others for fear of ridicule, disapproval, or stern lectures about how lucky they are—to have other children or the ability to have new (and obviously improved) babies.

Into Their Grief

The Parent's Inner World

As parents "move into their grief," the complexity of their bond with the child becomes expressed in the complexity of their grief. The more the parent's daily psychic and social worlds involve the inner representation of the child, the more difficult for the parent to separate out the inner representation of the child. We see differences in the way the child is integrated into various parts of the parent's self and thus into the different social systems in which the parent participates. A crucial issue, for example, is how the child's death affects their work. For some parents, work is an island in a stormy sea. Tasks and relationships on the job seem "normal." Other parents find work difficult and their performance diminished. The difference seems to be the degree to which their selfhood at work involves the child. For those who can work, the transition from work to home is marked by a surge of emotion. A mid-level executive said she functioned well at work, although she was occasionally teary. During the drive home, however, she became overwhelmed by the thought that her son was gone forever. She had the same surge of thoughts and feelings returning to her hotel room when she was out of town.

Some difficulty in marriages grows out of this dynamic (see Gilbert, 1989). One salesman felt he had to control his grief severely, because he was expected to be his old self with clients. He was fired from one job because his grief impaired his production, and he had a hard time finding another. His wife kept her job but was moved to a position where little was expected of her. His wife could not understand how he could turn off feelings that were for her so uncontrollable. It seemed to her that he could not have loved the child as she did.

Some parents' self-functioning depends on the availability of the child (see Rynearson, 1987, and Horowitz, Wilner, Marmor, & Krupnick, 1980). In those cases, the inner representation of the child may be integrated early in the grief in a way that maintains the child in the same role the live child played. For example, a recovering alcoholic whose 15-year-old daughter, K., was shot as a bystander in a holdup was having trouble controlling his anger and maintaining sobriety in the painful months after her death. From her childhood, K. had been the one in the family who "could tell me off when I was being stupid. She would just say, 'Dad, cut the crap.' She loved me and didn't back off like the boys did. When she told me to stop it, I did." About 6 months after the death, he was standing at the grave when he heard a voice say "Dad, why are you acting this way? This is what you were like when you were drinking." Within a week K. was his constant inner companion, helping him control his rage and stay sober. A strong bond with other members of Bereaved Parents later allowed him to separate himself from the direct dependence on K. As he became active in the group, K. became more than just the voice telling him to control. She became part of his good self, which was expressing itself by helping other bereaved parents.

Before the inner representation can be established, as it will be in the parent's ongoing life, many parents must spend time separating from inner representations of the living child and separating conflicting inner representations of the child from each other. Many parents who begin to separate from the inner representation of the living child find that the first point of connection between them and their dead child is the pain of their grief and the pain the child knew. A woman whose 2-year-old daughter died after several months in the hospital said the child was often pained when blood was drawn. Shortly after the death, the mother went to the clinic for tests.

> As I went in, I found myself saying over and over, maybe even out loud, "Look at mommy, she can have them take blood, and she will be a big girl so it will not hurt. See, J., mommy is going to be a big girl." When they stuck me it really hurt. I have given blood a lot, and it never hurt like that—I mean, it never hurt before, but this time it really did. When I told my mother about it she said, "This may seem strange, but I think

that was J. who was hurt." I think she is right. I cried all the way back to work, and I knew what she had suffered. The next time I had blood drawn it was like always, just a little prick.

The child's pain can take many forms. A woman whose daughter had a degenerative disease said "I never let myself experience her pain," because the medical staff urged the mother to be the voice of hope and determination. When her daughter cried and wanted to give up, it was the mother who insisted she get up and try again. "Well," the mother said in an interview, "I know the pain now." Several parents whose children committed suicide use the phrase "Suicide is a way to pass the pain."

As parents come to terms with the inner representation of their child they often must come to terms with ambivalence in the parent–child bond. A parent's inner representation of a child, living or dead, may merge or interact with the parent's conscious or unconscious negative self-representations, or the parent may cast the child into the role another person played in the parent's past. Inner representations of the parent's less-than-good self or of extensions of negative figures in his or her history produce more difficult grief because of the multiple and difficult meanings the death might have that are due to the often-conflicting interrepresentations of the child in the parent's psychic life and the family system. Separating inner representations from each other can be simply a matter of purging the representation of stressful memories and holding the child in an idealized way. Most parents do this to some extent, for we typically find them describing the dead child in glowing terms.

In coming to terms with ambivalence, parents may need to find ways to work through guilt stemming from what the parent now sees as less-than-adequate parenting. If the bond with the child was very difficult, a parent may also renarrate both the parent's life and the child's life in quite complicated and thorough ways. Negative elements in the bond with the living child are not usually completely eliminated, so we find many parents living with regrets, some of which can play a major role in the parent's ongoing life story.

It is not unusual for severe marital conflict to grow from ambivalence and guilt about negative inner representations of the child. For example, the son of one couple in the group died while on drugs. His mother attributed his behavior to the father's strict discipline and distant emotional relationship to the boy. She blamed herself only for acquiescing to her husband's child-rearing ideas. The fault was her husband's, not her son's. The difficulty was resolved only after the mother, as part of her working through the anger she felt toward her husband, acted out a part of her own "bad" self by almost having an affair. In coming to terms with the resultant guilt, she was able to reconcile herself to her negative inner representation of her son. Like her son, she had a "bad" side, but that did not make him or her a bad person.

In the most difficult cases, the inner representation may be purged almost completely, only to return again unexpectedly. A sociopathic young man died in a holdup attempt. His mother had supported him, but to do so she repressed memories of his violence toward her. In the third year after he died, she went through 4 months of having vivid images of him repeatedly arise. She thought he was coming back to hurt her. She did not believe the body in "that box in the ground" was her son. One evening after work, as she was on her way to see her counselor, she went into a fugue state and found herself lying on the grave at the cemetery. After what seemed to be a long time, she sensed that the bad side of her son was in the box. Over the next weeks, she no longer saw him lurking around, and she began to feel safer. As she relaxed in her safer world, she turned her attention to helping her daughter, who had just moved back to town after a divorce. She developed an especially close bond with her 6-year-old grandson, who "just fills my heart." As she talked to the counselor about her grandson, she said it was much easier for her to be a grandmother than it had been to be a mother. The memories of her son, however, could not be erased, although they were less intrusive as time went by. In counseling sessions, when she recalled something that was connected with her son, she talked about it for awhile and then ended that part of the conversation by tightening her lips, shaking her head, and saying "Well, that's the past. There is nothing we can do about the past."

The Parent's Social World

As parents separate the living child from the self and come to terms with ambivalent bonds they had with the child, they are aided by integrating the inner representation into their social world. Many of the unique aspects of Bereaved Parents are expressions of the shared bond members have with each others' children. Thus, membership means membership as a bereaved parent, a person whose life is not as it was before. Membership means that the dead child is also included, that the child is valued, remembered, celebrated, and loved.

Sharing a bond with the child begins with sharing the pain brought by the death. Sharing pain is summed up by a phrase that recurs in members' accounts of what they need from people: "just being there." "Being there" means being with the parent in a way that acknowledges that the reality of the child's death and the reality of the pain are not the parent's alone. The phrase is turned somewhat differently when members describe how the group is helpful to them. They say the people who can really understand are other bereaved parents, for they have "been there."

Sharing the pain also means sharing ways to relieve some forms of the pain, especially in the parent's social world. Often the meeting time is devoted to practical issues—for example, how to include the child in celebrations of holidays. There are several ways these issues may be solved, but each answer is really a stance, a way of being-in-the-world. One mother made a holiday wreath for the front door with many colored ribbons, including a black one. "It is there," she said. "If they want to see it and mention it, they can. It is not me that didn't bring it up." Using a solution someone else has suggested proves that the pain is shared, because the same solutions work. These answers to practical problems help parents to find new stances in their families and communities. It is common for parents to report that they have to teach families and friends how to relate to them. Often what they teach is what they have learned in the group.

As the dead child is integrated into the social network, experiences by which parents maintain contact with their children can be socially validated. Seeing, hearing, and sensing the presence of dead children is not easily integrated into modern social reality, yet for many bereaved parents such experiences are part of their daily reality. Most of the members have linking objects. To validate linking objects, members may tell each other about them. Parents often report holding an item of clothing and smelling the child's scent. It is common at meetings for parents to tell about the solace they feel from their linking object and to have that experience mirrored as they hear about other parents' linking objects. Every year, one meeting is devoted to these experiences, and several members have become well read on the topic. At national and regional meetings, sessions on nonordinary experiences are well attended.

Well Along in Their Grief

The Parent's Inner World

Members eventually begin to find a new equilibrium in their lives; they find it in terms of the inner representations of their children. The movement is often cast in terms of letting go and holding on. One group's logo has a circle with a child figure distant from a pair of hands. In a newsletter, one mother reported that her 4-year-old asked why the child was so distant from the hands. She replied "because the kid has died and the hands are Mommy's or Daddy's reaching for the child." The 4-year-old disagreed: "I think you're wrong, Mom. I think the hands are letting him go." For the mother, the child's interpretation provided an impetus for new insights.

> She made me see that I was still reaching. It has been two years since B. was stillborn, but I continue to reach for something. Just what that something is, I don't know, but I'll know what it is when I find it. Perhaps then a part of me can let go.

The "something" for which the mother is reaching is a positive bond with the child. The idea that letting go of the pain in exchange for a clearer, comforting inner representation of the child is one of Bereaved Parents' central insights. Rather than identifying with the child's pain, the parent identifies with the energy and love that were in the living child. In a speech at a holiday candlelight service 5 years after her son's death, a mother reflected on her progress:

> I was afraid to let go. Afraid that I would forget the details of him, the peculiar color of his eyes, the shape of his nose, the sound of his voice. . . . In a strange way my pain was comforting, a way of loving him, familiar. . . . Finally I had to admit that his life meant more than pain, it also meant joy and happiness and fun—and living. The little voice in my heart was telling me that it was time for me to let go of him. . . . When we release pain we make room for happiness in our lives. My memories of S. became lighter and more spontaneous. Instead of hurtful, my memories brought comfort, even a chuckle. . . . I had sudden insights into what was happening to me, the pieces began to fit again, and I realized S. was still teaching me things.

One of the clichés of bereavement work is that grief is the price we pay for love. In a newsletter article a father worked through the balance: "If the price I pay for loving D. is the pain and sorrow I now have, I still think I got a bargain to have had him for 13 years."

The developing bond with the dead child is often quite explicitly linked with the parent's thoughts about his or her own healing. A father reported that when he began running, his 17-year-old daughter encouraged him to keep it up by registering both of them in a 5-km race. She was killed 2 weeks before the race. He wanted to quit running, but he did not, because he thought she would have been disappointed to think she had caused him to abandon running in general and the race in particular. He ran wearing her number. Soon, she became part of his running.

> Every time I ran, I took a few minutes to think about D. and how I was dealing with her death. I was alone with no distractions but the pounding of my feet, and I could focus on her and my feelings. I tried to coach myself a bit, inch myself toward the light. That done, I often moved on to report silently to her about what I'd been doing lately, about what I thought of the weather, how my conditioning was going, what her younger brothers were up to. Frequently, I sensed she was nearby, cruising at my elbow, listening.

The Parent's Social World

The socially shared inner representation stabilizes the inner representation in the parent's life. One mother whose living children had moved away reflected in the newsletter on how she keeps the bond with all her absent children, including the one who is dead. She finds she does it in similar ways but that although she can hold her living children on her own she needs the group meetings to hold the bond with the dead child. She wrote that in the group mentioning the child's name doesn't cause an "awkward gap."

You know, the kind that makes you feel somehow you shouldn't have said anything. How can anyone else know that your child is still real? That they were real and are real? I want to scream sometimes that my boys are real! See, he's here in my heart.

As the bond with the child is made part of the parent's group membership, the inner representation can be more fluid and thus can be transformed within the parent's inner world. We can see many self-help dynamics in a newsletter article written by the coordinator of the annual picnic. She says there will be good food and games but that

> our children lost are the heart and soul of our picnic. It is for and because of them that we have come, and it is for them that we have our cherished balloon release, a time set aside in our day to remember and include our special children. Helium filled balloons are passed out, along with markers, giving us all one more chance to tell our children the things we most long to say—mostly "I Love You." And then, oblivious to the world around us, we stand as one, but each involved in his own thoughts, prayer, and emotions as we release hundreds of balloons to the sky, and they disappear to a destiny we are certain they will reach.

The ritual provides a means by which the parent can both reach out to the dead child and feel the presence of the child within. They "stand as one, but each involved in his own thoughts, prayer, and emotions." Because the bond with the child is shared within the group, the parents can be in touch privately with the individual inner representation of their child. Because the group shares in the strong bond with the child, there is tremendous strength within the group. Because there is such strength within the group, the bond with the child feels surer. One balloon sent into the sky would seem a lonely and fragile message. Hundreds of balloons, each addressed to an individual child, are sure to get through.

In meetings the pain is shared and, in that sharing, the bond with the child is shared. In the ritual with which each meeting begins, each person attending introduces themself, giving their name and then their child's name and something about the child's death. Often parents add a sentence or two about how good or bad a month it has been or if there is a significant date such as a birthday or death anniversary near. At the end of the introductions, the cumulative effect of all those names and all that pain is a deep quiet punctuated by the soft sobs of some newly bereaved. Just to be able to say and hear the name is important. A father's poem concludes,

> He is real and shadow, was and is.
> Say O. to me and say O. again.
> He is my son and I love him as I always did.
> Say O.

Nearly every year, at a particular meeting, everyone brings and passes around pictures of their children and tells stories about the child. At national and regional meetings there are long lines of picture boards. Parents from around the country often begin talking as they stand looking at the pictures of the children. Cards and telephone calls come on the children's birthdays. The sense of oneness with other bereaved parents and the sense of oneness with the inner representation of the dead child can be seen in the Credo of The Compassionate Friends, the national organization with which the chapter was formerly affiliated.

> We reach out to each other with love, with understanding, and with hope. Our children have died at all ages and from many different causes, but our love for our children unites us. . . . Whatever pain we bring to this gathering of The Compassionate Friends, it is pain we will share just as we share with each other our love for our children.

As they learn to share the child in Bereaved Parents, members find ways to include the child in their other communities. One woman reported that 6 years after her daughter's death she decided she wanted the child included in the family Christmas gift exchange.

> Last year, 1991, I shocked my sister who usually organizes the name exchange. I called her ahead of that day and said, "I want J.'s name in the exchange too." Well, there was silence on the phone. So I began to explain—whoever gets J.'s name can make a donation to a charity in her name. Yes, her name was included, and for the first time since 1985, I felt she was part of things.

Resolved as Much as It Will Be

The Parent's Inner World

Members are adamant in their conclusion that "you don't get over your grief." They often add, "but it doesn't stay the same." The message to newly bereaved parents at their first meeting is unequivocal: "It will always hurt, but it will not hurt they way it does now." What, then, can resolution mean?

At an "alumni gathering" group members went around the room doing the ritual of introductions. There was a lot of humor. The fourth person, who had been a group facilitator a few years earlier, paused for a moment after she introduced her child and said, "Gosh it feels so good to say that and not cry. Look, we are doing this and we are sitting around laughing. Isn't that really nice to do." Several said they remembered their child regularly and that it was a good feeling. Occasionally they still cried, but that was OK, too. Their sadness was part of them, and they could recognize it and not be afraid of it.

In a newsletter, a mother wrote about "older grief":

Older grief is gentler
It's about sudden tears swept in by a strand of music.
It's about haunting echoes of first pain, at anniversaries.

It's about feeling his presence for an instant one day while I'm dusting his room.

It's about early pictures that invite me to fold him in my arms again.

It's about memories blown in on wisps of wood smoke and sea scents.

Older grief is about aching in gentler ways, rarer longing, less engulfing fire.

Older grief is about searing pain wrought into tenderness.

The bonds we have with our children are complex, and so transforming that the bond can be a long and exhausting task. Eventually, however, the parents are able to re-establish the inner representation of their dead child as part of their ongoing lives. Moving on with life has its own ambivalence for bereaved parents, but the ambivalence is somewhat tempered by the re-established inner representation of the child. Betty Johnson wrote a poem for the newsletter:

Time roars on, but I rear back,
Resisting, afraid to move on and leave you behind.
I was safe with you, unafraid in my own realm.
If I heal, will you be gone forever?
Your leaving opened new worlds.
I have time now and my days and energies no longer revolve around your needs.
I want you to come with me into the future.
Your youth protected my youth, but now new beginnings eclipse the past.
My eyes strain as they search my heart for distant memories.
But your face fades as I reach out to you.
All that remains are warm feelings, smiles, tears and
Glimpses of your love, left in the wake of your parting.
Will you forgive me if I go on?
If you can't make this earthly journey through time with me,
Will you then come along in my heart and wish me well?

The parents often tie the resolution of their grief to their bond with their child. The parent's newfound interest in life is often described in terms of the active inner representation. As the child comes along in their heart to wish them well, many report that the peace they have found in their resolution is what their child wishes or would have wished for them.

It was an unmistakable thrill
That moment I first noticed
I think more about his life now
Than about his death!
It's just what he would have wanted!

Dead children are often melded into the parent's better self in a way that makes the children seem like teachers of life's important lessons. The father of a child born with multiple congenital heart defects, but who lived "2,681 days," tied his present activity in the group to those lessons.

He not only taught me the importance of what really matters in life, but through his death, also how we can make even more use of his life.

Because of J. we make ourselves available to other bereaved parents who are at some point on death's desolation road. . . . So whenever people ask if I'm done grieving for my precious son, I answer with much conviction: "Most assuredly so. But I will never be done showing my appreciation for having been blessed with such a gift."

The Parent's Social World

Part of the resolution of grief is making the child's death and the experience of it count for something. In making their own life meaningful, parents make real the inner representation of the child. One of the ways parents' lives can count, and the child be real, is to help others. The organizational life of Bereaved Parents depends on some people staying and leading the group as a way of expressing the change in their lives that their child and their grief made. A man who led the committee that planned the candlelight ceremony wrote, "I wanted most to do it for J. All that I do now I do to honor his memory and his life." He continued, "Do something that illustrates the positive effect that your child had on you—even if you are the only one to see it."

Early in their membership, parents find they can be bonded with their child in their affiliation with the group. Over time, as their bond with their child becomes more secure in their lives, the bond with the group becomes less focused. In a meeting of a committee to rethink the organizational structure, a discussion centered around the idea that the group works best when there is a steady turnover of meeting facilitators. Two former facilitators said that they just knew when the time had come for them to move on from that job. A woman whose daughter had been dead 2-1/2 years and who had just taken on the task of facilitating a meeting said, "I don't understand. The time I give to Bereaved Parents is my A. time." She thought of the energy and care she gave the group as care and energy she would be giving to A. She said worriedly, "So, what does it mean to move on? Do I lose my child? Does that mean I won't have that anymore?" A veteran who no longer attended meetings replied, "No, you don't lose that. It has been 13 years for me. I was like you when I was facilitating the meeting. That was my connection with B. It was real direct." She then said, "He is there all the time. He is just there; he is part of me." She said she felt indebted to the group, that it gave her

> something important when I needed it, and I want to give something back. Sometimes it is good for me to be very involved, and other times it seems like I should pull back more. Right now I feel like getting more involved again. But that is because it feels right to be part of something good. B. is part of that, but B. is part of many things in my life.

The dynamic creates some moments of irony, as when a father was honored for extraordinary service to the organization. After a lengthy standing ovation, he said, "I just had a funny thought. I thought if T. were here wouldn't he be proud. But if he were here, this wouldn't be happening." But the irony is not often expressed. The interactions in the life of the group have an authentic feel. Members take long calls from newly bereaved, spend 2 days in a small group folding and labeling newsletters, or make calls all over the city to solicit donations for the picnic that includes the balloon release. Meeting facilitators prepare for several days and then spend hours debriefing each other as they try to keep abreast of members' progress and the complex interactions in the meetings. The organization has proved itself to these parents. In giving back to others, their bond with the child becomes part of their better selves.

Early in their grief, parents searched for a community in which they could keep their bond with the child. They were angry when their child was not included in their interactions with the family. An important element in transforming the bond was sharing with others their bond with the child. As they begin to resolve their grief, parents find that the bond with the child is a natural part of many of their social affiliations. A father whose son had been dead more than 10 years reported that, early in his grief, people seemed afraid to talk to him about his son, but now the boy becomes part of many spontaneous conversations. He said that at work he keeps a piece of metal from his son's welding class on his desk. He reported that even people who could not have known what the object was used to avoid asking about it.

> For a couple years there, you could just see them trying not to look at it, let alone mention it. Now someone will see it and ask, and when I tell them what it is and why I keep it there and what it means to me, they just accept it and seem comfortable with how I feel about my son.

And then the conversation moves on to business. Thus, the inner representation of the child is integrated into the parent's social world in similar ways the inner representation of a living child would be.

The phenomena that indicate active interaction with the inner representation of the dead child—a sense of presence, belief in the child's continuing active influence on thoughts or events, or a conscious incorporation of the characteristics or virtues of the child into the self—are no longer occasions for the parents' concern about their own sanity but are accepted as a positive part of everyday living.

CONCLUSION

The dynamics by which grief is resolved in Bereaved Parents are transformations of the inner representation of the dead child in the parent's inner world and social world. As the reality of the child's death, as well as the reality of the parent's continuing bond with the child, are made part of the socially shared narrative the inner representation of the child can be transformed in the parent's psychic life. The end of grief is not a severing of the bond with the dead child but an integration of the child into the parent's life in a different way than when the child was alive. The self-help group seems a temporary affiliation in members' lives in that the group is the social bond in which the pain can be shared and the bond with the child acknowledged and honored. When parents stop active participation in the group, however, it is not because they have moved away from their dead child. At the end of their time in Bereaved Parents, the child is part of their ongoing inner lives and of the social bonds in which they feel at home.

REFERENCES

Benedek, T. (1959). Parenthood as a developmental phase. *American Psychoanalytic Association Journal, 7,* 389–417.

Benedek, T. (1970). The family as a psychologic field. In E. J. Anthony & T. Benedek (Eds.), *Parenthood: Its psychology and psychopathology* (pp. 109–136). Boston: Little, Brown.

Benedek, T. (1975). Discussion of parenthood as a developmental phase. *Journal of the American Psychoanalytic Association, 23,* 154–165.

Fairbairn, W. D. (1952). *An object-relations theory of the personality.* New York: Basic Books.

Finucane, R. C. (1996). *Ghosts: Appearances of the dead and cultural transformation.* Amherst, NY: Prometheus Books.

Geertz, C. (1973). *The interpretation of cultures.* New York: Basic Books.

Gilbert, K .R. (1989). Interactive grief and coping in the marital dyad. *Death Studies, 13,* 605–626.

Glaser, B. G., & Strauss, A. L. (1967). *The discovery of grounded theory: Strategies for qualitative research.* Chicago: Aldine.

Hammersley, M., & Atkinson, P. (1983). *Ethnography: Principles in practice.* New York: Tavistock.

Horowitz, M., Wilner, N., Marmor, C., & Krupnick, J. (1980), Pathological grief and the activation of latent self-images. *American Journal of Psychiatry, 137,* 1157–1162.

Kauffman, J. (1994). Dissociative functions in the normal mourning process. *Omega, Journal of Death and Dying, 28,* 31–38.

Kernberg, O. F. (1976). *Object-relations theory and clinical psychoanalysis.* New York: Aronson.

Klass, D. (1988). *Parental grief: Resolution and solace.* New York: Springer.

Klass, D. (1999). *The spiritual lives of bereaved parents.* Philadelphia: Brunner/Mazel.

Klass, D., Silverman, P., & Nickman, S. (Eds.). (1996). *Continuing bonds: New understandings of grief*. Washington, DC: Taylor & Francis.

McDannell, C., & Lang, B. (1988). *Heaven, a history*. New Haven, CT: Yale University Press.

Neimeyer, R. A., & Stewart, A. E. (1996, June). Trauma, healing, and the narrative employment of loss. *Families in Society, 77*, 360–375.

Powdermaker, H. (1966). *Stranger and friend: The way of an anthropologist*. New York: Norton.

Rynearson, E. K. (1987). Psychotherapy of pathologic grief: Revisions and limitations. *Psychiatric Clinics of North America, 10*, 487–499.

Volkan, V. (1981). *Linking objects and linking phenomena: A study of the forms, symptoms, metapsychology, and therapy of complicated mourning*. New York: International Universities Press.

Walter, T. (1996). A new model of grief: Bereavement and biography. *Mortality, 1*(1), 7–25.

Wax, R. (1971). *Doing fieldwork: Warnings and advice*. Chicago: University of Chicago Press.

Whyte, W. F. (1973). *Street corner society: The structure of an Italian slum*. Chicago: University of Chicago Press.

5

FAMILY CONSTRUCTION OF MEANING

JANICE WINCHESTER NADEAU

Ronnie Primo changed his infant daughter's diaper and put her in her crib. Then he planted a kiss on his 3-year-old's forehead, kissed his wife, and left the house. Ronnie was going to fly with his friend, a new pilot who was taking passengers for the first time. They never returned. Their small plane crashed and burned. Ronnie's family was left to make sense of the tragedy. Family members agreed that, if Ronnie had to die, he would have wanted to make the front-page news. In a family discussion his father-in-law lamented, "I should have stopped him from getting in that plane." His mother-in-law replied, "He wouldn't have listened to you." His sister-in-law chimed in, "He never wanted to grow old." His brothers and brother-in-law argued that, although Ronnie had been a big risk taker, he did *not* want to die. His 3-year-old daughter said, "I miss my daddy taking me shopping." His young wife, while crying in her walk-in closet, felt her husband's hand grasping hers as she ran her fingers down the sleeve of his empty suit coat. From this experience she concluded, "In some way, he is still here with me."

Grief is a family affair. Family members struggle to make sense of their loss by talking to each other. In so doing they attach meaning to their losses.

The meanings they attach can be defined as their cognitive representations of reality. We know precious little about how families construct meanings. Most of what we do know is from an individual perspective, but individuals do not grieve in a vacuum. They make sense of their experience by interacting with others.

Furthermore, the meanings families attach to the loss of a loved one are critical to how their grieving will proceed. When, for instance, a family construes the death of a family member as preventable, much of their energy is consumed with how the death should have been prevented. Grieving the actual loss of the person may be delayed or postponed. By contrast, a family who construes the loss of a family member as a relief from unbearable suffering is less likely to dwell on the particulars of the death. They are more likely to spend their energy in grieving the loss of the person and learning to live in the world without him or her. Most, if not all, of what is important about family grief can be seen by examining how families construct the meaning of their loss and how their meanings affect their grief.

In this chapter I use my research and clinical examples to illustrate family construction of meaning. I call the process by which families make sense of their experience *family meaning making*. By studying family meaning making we can see critical dimensions of both meaning construction and of grief, dimensions that might otherwise be overlooked. Understanding grief from a family meaning-making perspective is critical to building grief theory, conducting family grief research, and developing appropriate interventions.

A STUDY OF MEANING MAKING IN FAMILY BEREAVEMENT

In a qualitative study of family bereavement (Nadeau, 1998), I studied patterns of meaning in 10 nonclinical, multigenerational families. The purpose was to investigate the process by which grieving families construct meanings and the nature of those meanings. Symbolic interactionism and family systems theory provided the conceptual underpinnings for the study. I conducted intensive interviews with 48 family members, both separately and in family groups, using a modified form of Milan circular questioning (Boscolo, Cecchin, Hoffman, & Penn, 1987). Interview data were transcribed verbatim and content analyzed with techniques greatly influenced by the methodology of grounded theory (Strauss & Corbin, 1990). Findings included specific strategies families used to make sense of the death, insights into the patterns of family meaning-making, and a typology of family meanings.

Background of the Study

As long ago as 1959 Hess and Handel coined the term *family worlds* to capture the notion of family as a finite province of meaning, having its own consistent logic of knowing that applies within the family world but not outside of it (Hess & Handel, 1959). Family researchers, studying a variety of family phenomena, refer to *shared meaning* or *family meanings*. Sometimes researchers assume that they have identified family meanings when only one member has been interviewed and very little effort has been made to collect systemic data.

My interest in family meanings grew out of my work with grieving families over a period of 25 years, as an intensive care nurse, as a hospice nurse and, in recent years, as a psychologist and family therapist. Over the years, I have noticed that, when families learned that someone in the family was expected to die, they started talking to each other immediately about the death and what it might mean. Adult siblings would say such things as "We couldn't wish Mother to go on living with all the pain she is having." Another sibling might chime in, "Yes, and you know, I think Mom has been trying to die ever since Dad passed away." And yet another sibling might disagree by saying, "I don't think Mom has been trying to die. She just has cancer; that's why she's dying."

By talking among themselves, family members seemed to be jointly evolving toward some sense of what the loss of their loved one meant. In some families, particularly if death had been expected for some time, the expressions of meaning sounded litany-like. Family members repeated the same phrases about the death over and over to each other. There seemed to be a shared family need to make sense of the experience, to create order out of the perceived chaos, and to gain some sense of control over the uncontrollable. Intrapsychic explanations of what I had observed in families did not seem to be adequate, because they did not capture the interactive nature of the process.

When a person dies, families have a story to tell about the events surrounding the death, and such stories are laden with meaning. Much has been written about how bereaved individuals search for meaning and purpose in life (Frankl, 1959) and, judging by my research, much of the meaning-making process related to a death goes on in family relationships.

Conceptualizing Family Meaning Making

Two theories that help us understand family meaning making are *symbolic interaction theory* and *family systems theory*. These two theories are useful in both family meaning-making research and family grief therapy approached from a meaning-making perspective. Symbolic interaction theory is useful because it provides a way of thinking about how meaning is jointly created. Symbolic interaction is a theoretical orientation that grew out of the philosophical writings of James (1890), Cooley (1902, 1909), Dewey (1922), and Mead (1932, 1934, 1936, 1938). This theory has been identified by family scholars as useful in understanding a variety of family phenomena because it emphasizes the relation between mental and social processes. Symbolic interactionism includes the assumption that humans live in a symbolic environment as well as a physical environment and that humans acquire complex sets of mental symbols (Rose, 1962). Symbolic interaction theory reflects Thomas's (1923) belief that, if people define situations as real, they are real in their consequences. If Thomas were correct, one could expect to find a connection between how a family construes a particular event—be it death, a divorce, chronic illness, or any other event—and how the family responds to the event.

In the prestudy interviews, one widow of 6 years said that her husband, who had had a massive stroke, should not have been taken off the breathing machine. Their son, a physician, had convinced the family that his father was "brain dead." The widow had lingering doubts. She had read about people coming out of comas after prolonged periods of unconsciousness. Her grief seemed acute and unresolved 6 years later. The family dialogue that might have helped her make sense of his death was inhibited by her fear that, if she expressed her doubts, she would be calling into question her son's professional judgment. She could not share these doubts with her other children. The matter of how her husband had died became a taboo subject in family discussions. Sharing was restricted, and the entire process of family meaning making was inhibited.

Interactionists posit that meanings of various phenomena vary from person to person and from situation to situation and are subject to historical time and culture (Burr, Leigh, Day, & Constantine, 1979). Rosenblatt and Fischer (1993) noted that "from a symbolic interactionists' perspective it is less important to know whether or not an event actually happened than whether or not people believe it happened, because all interaction emerges from the meanings with which people imbue events" (p. 168).

Berger and Luckmann's classic book *The Social Construction of Reality* (1966) is helpful in guiding thinking about the interactive processes by which individuals and families become able to integrate a "marginal reality" such as a death into their "paramount or every day reality." Berger and Luckmann suggested that one's everyday life could be viewed as the working of a conversational apparatus that ongoingly maintains, modifies, and reconstructs one's subjective reality. They contended that significant others are the most important players in reality construction and maintenance.

The widows referenced above are good examples. The young widow who felt her husband's hand at the end of his coat sleeve concluded that he was with her in some way and felt comfort. Her meaning came from her interaction with her husband as they had interacted in life. The widow of 6 years who thought her husband should not have been taken off the ventilator construed his death as preventable. Her interactions with family members were inhibited, and she could not find peace.

Family systems theory is the second conceptual framework that is useful for understanding family meaning making. A *system*, according to Hall and Fagan's (1956) most-quoted definition, is "a set of objects together with relationships between the objects and their attributes" (p. 18). Family systems theory is an adaptation of general systems theory as it is applied to the family as a system. Muxen (1991) described family systems theory as

> providing a view of the family as a set of intimately connected people who are mutually influential on each other in some way, and whose relationships evolve over time interactively with each other as well as with past, present, and anticipated future contexts. (p. 16)

There are a number of systems concepts and systems ways of thinking about families that are useful in describing family meaning-making processes and their interaction with family structure and family dynamics. The systems framework provides the concepts necessary for describing the structural changes that occur in the family following a death, namely, changes in roles, rules, and boundaries. Defining these concepts here will become useful in analyzing clinical material to follow.

Constantine (1986) defined *structure* as "the sum total of the interrelationships among elements of a system, including membership in the system and the boundary between the system and its environment" (p. 52).

Roles are the expectations attached to given positions within the family, such as mother, father, and child (Stryker, 1972). Family therapists commonly expand the notion of roles to include roles such as peacemaker, scapegoat, mascot, and so on. When a family member dies, the roles of the deceased, both positive and negative, are assumed by others in the family.

Rules are prescriptions for familial responses to a wide range of possible inputs (Broderick & Smith, 1979). Rules may be spoken but, more commonly, are less-than-conscious understandings within the family. Rules govern all of family life. A death in the family calls for the creation of new rules.

Boundaries delineate the elements belonging to the system in question and those belonging to its environment (Broderick & Smith, 1979). Family restructuring, in systems terms, means changing family roles, rules, and boundaries. Adding or subtracting even a single member of a family has dramatic implications for the structure of the family (Broderick & Smith, 1979). The meanings that families attach to the death may both influence, and be influenced by, structural changes in the family. Not only are there new meanings to be made related to the death, but there also are fewer members to make them.

An important consideration in family meaning making is the relation between family meaning making and family structure. A given family's openness or closedness to outside meanings or openness or closedness to each others' meanings is thought of in systems terms. *Openness* is construed as a willingness to engage in meaning making with others. In the meaning-making study, family systems thinking was useful in conceptualizing how a family's meaning-making process was influenced by the absence or presence of a particular member, including the one who had died.

Collecting Systemic Data

If one is to understand family meaning making, then the family system must be observed. Systemic data can be increased in two ways. One is to interview family members together as a family and then separately. In my study this made it possible to make comparisons among and between individual and family subsystems of meaning.

The second method of increasing systemic data is to interview families using an adaptation of the Milan method of circular questioning, which was originally developed as a systemic, meaning-focused, family therapy method by Selvini, Boscolo, Cecchin, and Prata (Boscolo et al., 1987). In family therapy the therapist asks one family member in the presence of other family members to say how he or she thinks another might respond to a given question. Family patterns are revealed. In the adaptation of the Milan method (Wright, 1990) the individual being interviewed is asked to speak for absent members of his or her family. Wright described it as "mind reading." In the study the method was further adapted to include reading the mind of the deceased family member.

Using the adapted form of circular questioning with individual family members includes a line of questioning such as "What beliefs do you hold that relate to ___'s death?" This is followed by "What beliefs do you think your sister holds?" and then "What beliefs do you think your father holds?" and so on through each of the absent members of the family, including how he or she thinks the deceased family member thought about his or her own death. Another use of circular questioning is to identify agreement patterns. On hearing a meaning such as "Charlie died because his number was up," the interviewer might ask who in the family would agree most with this explanation, who would agree least, and how the deceased family member would respond to this meaning.

Circular questioning has proven as useful in family grief therapy as it has in research. It tends to raise the family meanings in a nonthreatening way, and it provides a way to include the deceased in meaning-making interactions.

Study Findings

The study's findings included some general patterns of family meaning making, the specific strategies families used to make sense of their experience, and a typology of the meanings families made. I discuss general patterns first.

General Patterns

Meaning making occurs in families at all systems levels, from the individual level to full family groups. The meanings made and the processes revealed depend on who is present. Families settle on some meanings soon after the death, but others seem to evolve over time. The family meaning-making process appears to be quite fluid in nature, and there are certain factors that either enhance or inhibit how the process flows.

The presence of in-laws, for example, enhances the process of family meaning making. The *in-law effect*, as it was called in this study, refers to how in-laws fueled the family conversation by introducing elements that members who were more closely related did not. In-laws are not privy to some family information and so may ask naïve questions. They are also not subject to the family rules governing the avoidance of taboo subjects and may introduce material that otherwise would not be mentioned.

Other meaning-making enhancers include the family's willingness and ability to share meanings, the frequency of family contact, family rituals, tolerance for differences, and the nature of the death. Families who experienced the death of younger members or an unexpected death struggled more to make sense of their experience than did families who lost older members whose deaths were expected.

Factors that inhibit family meaning making include family secrets, fragile family ties, cutoffs (family members avoiding all contact with other family members), divergent beliefs, and family rules prohibiting sharing.

Here is an example of the inhibition of family meaning making. In a family with a history of alcohol abuse were a number of previous-generation cutoffs and restricted interaction in the present generation. Family members had formed coalitions based on the use or nonuse of alcohol. Family members' meanings were disparate. The sons thought that their mother had deliberately refused to call 911 when their father suffered a cardiac arrest. Other family members said that their mother had called but that paramedics had been tied up at a fire. Family members, rather than talking openly about the father's death, speculated about others' actions and motivations. This led to more misunderstanding. Several in-laws tried to help the family process by asking about things that only blood relatives knew. Unfortunately, the in-law effect was not sufficient to help make family meaning.

Strategies

Strategies is the term used for the "methods" that families used interactively to make sense of their loss. Family meaning-making strategies include storytelling, dreaming, comparison, "coincidancing," characterization, and "family speak." In my research, the most commonly used strategy was *storytelling*. Families began telling their story as soon as they were asked who in the family had died. Most meanings were embedded in the family story. Other meanings were found as family themes. The following example demonstrates thematic meanings.

Four members of the Buchanan family told the story of how their mother/grandmother, Florence, came to die at home. She had been in a nursing home in Wisconsin when her daughter-in-law, Coral, came to visit. Florence expressed her desire to die at home. The family conferred and agreed to try it. There were eight children, and they were economical. They put an easy chair in the family van and drove to the nursing home. They helped Florence into the chair, tied her in with a sheet, and brought her home to Minnesota. They called their trip "an escape from Wisconsin." (Wisconsin promotes tourism with the slogan "Escape *to* Wisconsin.") The family said that from the moment Florence was brought into her room to the moment of her death, she was happy. The theme of the family story was "We gave Grandma a good death." They found comfort in this family meaning.

Not all thematic meanings bring comfort; some bring distress. A family theme such as "She should not have died," expressed by a family who saw their loved one as a saint, caused a great deal of pain and anger. The family theme of "We could have prevented his death if we had. . . ," expressed by a family who thought they had failed to act, was accompanied by deep regret and remorse. Such negative themes indicate that the family is far from being at peace with the death, and their search for meanings that will bring them peace is likely to be prolonged.

Families used *dreams* to make sense of their loss. No direct questions about dreams were asked, but respondents talked about their dreams while responding to other questions. Most dreams included interactions with the deceased person. Meaning making through dreaming occurred on at least three levels: (a) when the dreamer had and interpreted his or her own dream, (b) when the dreamer shared the dream with the family, and (c) when family members responded to the dream.

In an interview with a family of eight, Sally, a sister-in-law and childhood friend of Ann, struggled with where Ann went after her death. Sally reported her dream in the following way:

> Ann came to me in a dream about two months after she died and she told me [pause]. The dream was on the front steps of my parents' home. . . . I was sitting on the steps . . . she walked over to me and we walked over towards this metal fence. . . . She was beautiful, and she had on, not what I would consider heavenly clothes or anything. She had a lot of layered clothing on that was real light and flowing. . . . But there was a white-haired man who I'd never seen before in my life and who I would never see again. Pure white hair, and she put her hand on my shoulder and . . . she said to him first that she's ready, and then she said, "I feel more at peace now than I ever have and it's undescribable. It's okay." And that was it, the dream ended [pause]. It's like prior to that I had woke up every night like three in the morning crying; after that I

was at ease with it. And it's like my idea is that she is present with whoever when whoever needs her [pause]. She's present and she is in completeness, a peace that none of us will understand until the time comes when we'll join her [pause]. Then you know. She's with the gods, and it's not necessarily the gods we all read about and have been taught about. That's where she is.

One could say that this represents a private meaning, but Sally's dream was about family member interaction. Grief is always about a minimum of two people: the one who is grieving and the one who is lost.

Sally's meanings included that Ann was available to anyone who ever needed her and that she was now complete and at peace with the gods. Sally made her meaning by dreaming a much-needed interaction with Ann and then discussing it with the family. Sally reported having denied that Ann was going to die right up until the time of her death. Sally's dream typified not only a way in which meaning is made but also the role that meanings may play in the grieving process. Sally was clear that having understood the meanings expressed in her dreams put her "at ease." When Sally shared her dream with the other seven family members, they began to recall their dreams and their meanings while those who had not had dreams expressed jealousy. Sally's account of her dream seemed to bring Ann into the room. The widower became teary but was quick to remind the group that Ann was not always saintly in that she was very skillful at getting her own way. What followed was a more realistic characterization of Ann, something that is believed by most grief theorists to be helpful in coming to terms with the loss.

The third strategy families used was *comparison*. Families compared the most recent loss of their loved one with the loss of others inside and outside the family and losses of things other than people. Families talked about whether their loss was more or less bearable than the losses of others. It was as if they were establishing their loss somewhere on the continuum of possible losses and finding their place within the reference group of grieving families. The following is from an interview with Jenny and her daughter Pam, an only child. Their husband and father, Rich, had died during cardiac bypass surgery. This passage exemplifies interactive comparison. The daughter speaks first:

Pam: We lost, and I'm not saying it's the same thing but, we lost how many dogs?
Jenny: Dogs are dogs, and as much as we love them . . .
Pam: Oh, bullshit!
Jenny: No! They were part of the family and felt just as bad but it isn't the same. There is no way I could even compare it. There is no way to compare it as far as I'm concerned.
Pam: They were like sisters and brothers to me.
Jenny: It still is a loss. It's a very definitely a loss and they were, any dog we had was a member of the family, and I don't deny that but it, it's not

the same, no way! It's just like, um, losing my mother I thought was, I said it before, I thought, I hurt as much then as I could possibly hurt and it's not the same at all. It's an entirely different loss.

Clearly, there is little consensus, but earlier in the interview Jenny and Pam had compared how coping with Rich's death had been easier than to cope with the brutal rape and murder of a child.

"*Coincidancing*," the fourth strategy families used to make sense of the loss of a family member, is the term I gave to the tendency families had for using seemingly coincidental events associated with the death to make meaning of the death. The *dancing* component of the word was used to capture the interactive nature of this strategy. The following excerpts capture the ways in which co-occurring events, so-called coincidences, became grist for the family meaning-making mill.

Rafi lost his wife to cancer when she was in her mid-40s. One of Rafi's rules was to avoid thinking magically about his wife's death. His in-laws, by contrast, readily made connections among the most remotely connected events. Rafi's role in the family system was to "hold the line" against some of their magical thinking. He did not allow himself to notice connections between his wife's death and other events that, if he had, might have been a comfort to him. He said,

> I'm not big on magical thinking. So, even though there are things that other people have thought of, coincidences like that. . . . For instance, I'm not sure exactly how my daughter thinks about this, but she got pregnant shortly before Ann died. And she has told me that if it's a girl she's going to name it after her mom. And I believe that she has some magical thinking about that. That somehow it's her mom's spirit going into the next generation.

Rafi was able to identify coincidences and report how others in the family used them in spite of his own reluctance to give coincidences special meaning. His doing so gives us clues as to how family dynamics play a role in the attachment of meanings. Rafi's response may have been simply a report of individual differences, but it seemed that he was reacting to the extremes of other family members.

Rafi was not entirely successful in his balancing act when he was interviewed alone. In this next excerpt we see that, although he had a personal rule against magical thinking, when pressed, he still had thoughts about what coincidences might mean.

> It's possible that something would happen and I would, against my better judgment, I would have a thought about oh, this is weird or this is, is what a coincidence, oh yeah, I take it back. . . . Right when she died, a whole bunch of stuff broke right at once. The garage door opener broke. The toaster broke. And one of the ovens went out. And the refrigerator broke. It was very strange. . . . Well, you know, because when

we had the shiva, that crossed my mind. It was pretty hard. You know the refrigerator wasn't working, and I couldn't get out of the garage. The toaster and the oven still hadn't been fixed, but those other things we got fixed right away. . . . The irrational part of me thinks oh well, it's just kind of like everything was like, all those mechanical things were in mourning (teary eyed). I just, you know, basically just, I think it was a coincidence. Except it was a pain in the ass. . . . I keep the magical part pretty well in check.

Rafi's interpretation that even the mechanical things were in mourning for Ann elicited great sadness for him, and he cried freely. Noticing so-called coincidences and giving them meaning allowed Rafi free expression of his sadness. Meanings of all types can be projected onto coincidences, and our paying attention to them reveals a great deal about a particular family's meaning making.

There is an important feature of family grief to recognize in this illustration of Rafi's reluctant coincidancing: the interaction of family structure, family dynamics, and family meaning making. Structurally, Rafi is an in-law. He is outside the related-by-blood family and, therefore, less bound by family rules. This allows him to hold more divergent meanings and to interact with family members differently. In terms of family dynamics he has taken on, and/or been assigned, the family role of being the rational member, balancing the extreme magical thinking of his wife's family. The meaning-making components are the meanings that emerge as products of the interactions.

The fifth strategy families used to make sense of their loss was *characterization*. Even though they were not asked directly, families talked about who the deceased was as a person, what he or she had accomplished in his or her life, and what had been important to him or her. It was as if, in order to make sense of their loved ones' deaths, they had to first make sense of their lives. Most of the people who had died were positively characterized. When negative characterizations were given, they were quickly followed by something positive or by an excuse for the deceased person's "bad" behavior in life.

Ronnie Primo, the young man killed in the airplane crash and described at the beginning of this chapter, was characterized extensively by his family. They struggled to make sense of why Ronnie, who had two young children, would have taken the risk of flying with an inexperienced pilot. They characterized Ronnie as "flashy" and vain, not ever wanting to grow old and as a taker of high risks. Their remarks culminated in the statement that if Ronnie had to die, he would have been pleased that his death got him a front-page spread. Attaching such a meaning to his tragic death seemed to help them.

The sixth strategy families used was *family speak*. This was the term given to the use of ordinary conversation to make sense of the death. Family speak included agreeing and disagreeing with one another, interrupting one another, echoing each other's meanings, elaborating on something someone said, and finishing each other's sentences. In the Primo family interview, the widow Rena and her parents Joyce and Dominic used family speak extensively to make sense of Ronnie's death. This is one example.

> Joyce: I remember hearing him say that particular phrase. "Oh, I don't think that I'm going to get old anyway. I'm probably going to die young."
> Dominic: No, I don't remember him talking like that with me.
> Joyce: He wasn't talking with me, he was saying it in general.
> Rena: Just in general.
> Joyce: To the crowd or whatever.
> Dominic: If he did say it I didn't . . .
> Rena: Didn't hear it.
> Dominic: Didn't hear it, or, you know, or it didn't register.

First, Dominic mildly disagreed with Joyce. Next, Rena echoed Joyce. Then, Rena interrupted Dominic to finish his sentence. By using these ordinary ways of communicating, families were able to weave together individual threads of meaning to form the fabric of the family meaning system. Such meanings could not be attributed to any one family member.

Typology of Meanings

Ten categories of meanings were formed from the hundreds of meaning statements families made. Grouping meanings as a typology highlights similarities and differences in ways that will help the clinician identify them in ongoing family conversations. Paying attention to the types of meaning being made helps the clinician track the family's progress in grieving and target certain meanings as the focus of treatment.

Categories or types were labeled as follows: what the death did *not* mean, that there is no sense to be made, that the death was unfair or unjust, the afterlife, religious meanings, philosophical meanings, the nature of the death, the attitude of the deceased person toward death, how the death changed the family, and lessons learned and truths realized.

To give a sense of the meaning typology two types are outlined here. The first is "what the death was *not*." In their struggle to make sense of the loss of a loved one, some families recite over and over what the death does not mean. Family members in the study repeated such things as, "I know it was *not* God's will," and "I know that it did *not* happen to teach us something." Saying what the death does not mean seems to be an important step along the path of identifying what the death *does* mean. Noticing this step could be helpful to the practitioner in validating both the family's current meaning and in developing respect for, and patience with, the family's ongoing process.

The second category is "the attitude of the deceased toward his or her own death." Families made sense of their loss by turning to the meaning that they believed death had to the family member who had died. The wife and sister-in-law of one man who had died in his sleep found comfort in finding a letter of instructions he left for his wife and some quotes about Heaven. The meaning they made was that, even though his death had come as a shock to them, he had been expecting it.

This concludes the description of the family meaning-making study. What follows is an application of the findings to a clinical family. The goal of presenting this family is to integrate some of the notions of family meaning making discussed above and to suggest ways of working with grieving families from a meaning-making perspective.

LAURA'S FAMILY

Laura, an 11-year-old girl, was jumping her horse in the show ring as her father Rich watched from the stands. She was no novice in spite of her youth. She was described as "riding lightly and confidently in the saddle." This particular day, as she came to a particular jump, her horse, Sweet Pea, became frightened, reared up on its heels, and fell backward, crushing Laura to death. Her father, who was trained as an emergency medical technician (EMT), leapt from the stands and rushed to her side. Recognizing in a few short seconds that nothing could be done to revive her, he held his daughter's limp body in his arms and tried to whisper comforting words in her ear.

The family's long struggle to make sense of this terrible tragedy began. Rich had to go home to tell his wife Linda and Laura's 8-year-old sister Kristin what had happened. They had to tell the extended family, friends, and members of their community.

Meanings began to emerge immediately. Rich, in a television interview, said that he had gone to the barn to bring Laura's horse some carrots, "Because that is what my daughter would want me to do. . . . She would not blame the horse for doing what was natural." Rich went to the school to talk to Laura's friends to explain what had happened and to comfort them. In several weeks the three remaining family members came for grief therapy. In telling their story, they relayed the intimate details again and again. Their litany-like telling was heart wrenching and laden with meanings.

The first meaning to emerge in Laura's family was that Laura would have wanted them not to blame Sweet Pea for doing what was natural for horses to do when they become frightened. The family had *characterized* Laura as a horse lover from the time she was a toddler playing with plastic toy horses. She would not want the horse destroyed, they said. This meaning guided them to find Sweet Pea a retirement home.

They *compared* Laura's death with that of Rich's mother's a few years before and described Laura's death as much harder to bear. Rich struggled with whether he had done the right thing at the time of the accident and whether Laura was okay after her death. Laura's mother, a pediatric nurse practitioner, needed to know the medical details. She struggled with the unwelcome identity of "bereaved parent." Mostly, she kept an eye on Rich and Kristin, postponing her own need to let down. Kristin found comfort in sleeping in Laura's sweatshirt and in Laura's bed. Kristin brought her child's way of making sense of Laura's death. She said "Laura's soul left her body before she touched the ground . . . it didn't hurt her." Linda and Rich frequently referred to Kristin's meaning. There was talk between Linda and Kristin of how Laura had become an angel. Kristin's meaning comforted Linda both because it was an explanation she might like to adopt for herself and because she saw how Kristin's meanings helped Kristin. Rich was comforted by Kristin's meaning, but he could not embrace it for himself. Their *"family speak"* was rich and filled with questioning and referencing each other. Rich began soul searching and reading whatever he could get his hands on about death. They kept talking.

The family *"coincidanced"* about how some woman saw their story in the newspaper and offered to retire Sweet Pea on her farm in honor of her daughter, who also had been killed. They coincidanced around how Rich had randomly picked up a helpful book in the airport. The book had the story of a horseback riding accident not unlike Laura's. Rich continued to agonize. One dark night found him lying on his back on a country road, far from home, pleading with the cosmos for answers.

Then came an extraordinary coincidence. Rich had resumed his EMT work. On the one-year anniversary of Laura's death Rich was called out in the wee hours of the morning to a serious car accident involving three young men. At the scene one youth lay dead on the highway. Rich was assigned to be with a second young man, who was in critical condition in the ambulance. On examination of the boy, he found no palpable pulses. The boy's restraints were undone, and shock trousers were applied. They rushed to the hospital. While transferring the boy from the ambulance to the emergency room, Rich noticed that one of the boy's hands had not been secured. As Rich caught his hand to secure it, he was shocked to feel the boy's hand closing around his in a firm grip. Thinking he was imagining things, Rich asked the boy to squeeze his hand again. He repeated the squeeze, although his vital signs indicated that he was too close to death to be doing so. The boy was taken to surgery, but his body was beyond repair. Rich later described the boy's grasp as "strong and intentional." Rich interpreted the boy's action to be a message to his parents that he was all right. Rich took this to mean that his daughter, too, had been all right in her traumatic passing. Rich described the experience as helping him to break through some kind of a wall that had been holding him back, keeping him from moving forward in his life. He had, as he put it, needed reassurance that Laura was all right. He had his answer. He told the story to Linda and Kristin, and they wove their threads of meaning into the cloth of the family story.

The story did not end with the boy's death. The next day Rich broke with EMT protocol and went to the home of the boy, whose name was Troy, and told Troy's family the story of Troy's last moments in the ambulance. They received Rich as if he were a messenger from Troy. They drew strength from Rich and comfort from knowing how peaceful Troy had been, that he had not suffered. Troy's family invited Rich to tell his story at the funeral. He agreed to do so. The two families made meaning, intricately weaving their stories together.

Troy's parents, his 21-year-old brother, and his 23-year-old sister came for family grief therapy. I had the honor of hearing them make sense of Troy's last moments and the story Rich had told. Unlike Rich, they construed Troy's reaching for Rich's hand as his reaching to God, asking not to live if he would have to live in a crippled body, in a wheelchair the rest of his life. Mostly, they were comforted by what Rich could tell them of Troy's last moments. They continue in the early stages of meaning making as I write this chapter.

GRIEF THERAPY FROM A MEANING-MAKING PERSPECTIVE

Working with grieving families consists, first of all, of hearing their stories in the most intricate detail. Help consists of listening for meanings, clarifying that which is not clear, and verifying meanings as one hears them. Support for emotional reactions needs to be congruent with what the death means to the family, not what it means to the helper. It is important to hear the story again and again over time, looking each time for subtle differences as the family modifies previously held meanings and evolves new meanings. Changes in meaning mark family progress.

From the start, it is important to work with family dynamics and family structure in terms of changing roles, rules, and boundaries. Doing so will assure that meaning-making processes are less inhibited. Problems that plagued the family before the loss are likely to be accentuated by the loss; therefore, any family therapy designed to address pre-existing problems will go a long way toward promoting healthy meaning making.

Helping families later in the grieving process may consist of keeping the family members interacting about their loss, even though there may be no new facts per se. On the basis of my study I have learned that it is important and helpful to have as many family members present as possible, remembering that the more peripheral members such as in-laws can energize the meaning-making process, because they are usually less bound to family rules. If one is working with a single family member, the system can be expanded simply by asking how other family members would make sense of what has occurred and how others' meanings compare with his or her own. It is important to help the family accept divergent meanings, develop tolerance for others who do not agree with them, and to help the family create rituals to make sense of what has occurred.

There was little need in the case of Laura's family to help stimulate rituals because, from the start, this family had been immersed in community life. Rich and Linda's involvement at Laura's school led to the building of a garden dedicated to Laura and other students who had died in the past. Laura's garden was dedicated 2 months after the anniversary of her death and drew more than 150 community members and children. Troy's family is still too much in shock at the present time to do more than process the funeral rituals.

Working with family dynamics and structural features of Laura's family turned out to be important. Linda needed encouragement to express her own pain and not hold back to protect Rich and Kristin. Kristin needed help in resisting the draw to fill the vacuum in the family created by Laura's absence and needed encouragement to stop taking care of her parents by being overly "good." Giving Kristin permission to take an occasional "brat day" became a way of making this dynamic overt and helping Kristin to feel less responsible.

CONCLUSION

Few events affect a family as powerfully as the death of a family member. How the family members construe the death is critical to how they will react, yet we know precious little about how this process of construing occurs within the family world.

The research and clinical examples presented in this chapter constitute a beginning. Researchers and clinicians need to look further. In the future such questions as how family meaning making changes over time in terms of both meanings and processes of meaning-making need to be studied. It will be important to study different types of death, including suicide, homicide, sudden infant death syndrome, and AIDS deaths. We need to know whether making sense of losses other than death proceeds in a similar manner. It will be important to investigate what outcomes tend to be associated with each type of meaning and to test the effectiveness of interventions.

Looking at families from a meaning-making perspective will provide a way of apprehending the broader system. It will open up new dimensions of grief and, thereby, enhance therapists' ability to reach out to grieving families with greater understanding, skill, and compassion.

REFERENCES

Berger, P. L., & Luckmann, T. (1966). *The social construction of reality*. New York: Doubleday.

Boscolo, L., Cecchin, G., Hoffman, L., & Penn, P. (1987). *Milan systemic family therapy*. New York: Basic Books.

Broderick, C., & Smith, J. (1979). General systems approach to the family. In W. Burr, R. Hill, F. I. Nye, & I. L. Reiss (Eds.), *Contemporary theories about the family* (Vol. 2, pp. 112–128). New York: Free Press.

Burr, W. R., Leigh, G. K., Day, R. D., & Constantine, J. (1979). Symbolic interaction in the family. In W. R. Burr, R. Hill, I. F. Nye, & I. L. Reiss (Eds.), *Contemporary theories about the family* (Vol. 2, pp. 42–111). New York: Free Press.

Constantine, L. L. (1986). *Family paradigms*. New York: Guilford Press.

Cooley, C. H. (1902). *Human nature and the social order*. New York: Scribner's.

Cooley, C. H. (1909). *Social organization*. New York: Scribner's.

Dewey, J. (1922). *Human nature and conduct*. New York: Scribner's.

Frankl, V. E. (1959). *Man's search for meaning*. New York: Washington Square Press.

Hall, A. D., & Fagan, R. E. (1956). Definition of systems. *General Systems I*, 18–28.

Hess, R. D., & Handel, G. (1959). *Family worlds: A psychological approach to family life*. Chicago: University of Chicago Press.

James, W. (1890). *Principles of psychology* (Vol. 2). New York: Holt.

Mead, G. H. (1932). *The philosophy of the present* (A. E. Murphy, Ed.) Chicago: Open Court.

Mead, G. H. (1934). *Mind, self and society*. Chicago: University of Chicago Press.

Mead, G. H. (1936). *Movements of thought in the nineteenth century*. Chicago: University of Chicago Press.

Mead, G. H. (1938). *The philosophy of the act*. Chicago: University of Chicago Press.

Muxen, M. (1991). *Making sense of sibling loss in adulthood: An experimental analysis*. Unpublished doctoral dissertation, University of Minnesota, St. Paul.

Nadeau, J. W. (1998). *Families making sense of death*. Thousand Oaks, CA: Sage.

Rose, A. M. (Ed.). (1962). *Behavior and social processes*. Boston: Houghton-Mifflin.

Rosenblatt, P. C., & Fischer, L. R. (1993). Qualitative family research. In P. B. Boss, W. J. Doherty, R. LaRossa, W. R. Schumm, & S. K. Steinmetz (Eds.), *Source book of family theories and methods: A contextual approach* (pp. 167–177). New York: Plenum.

Strauss, A., & Corbin, J. (1990). *Basics of qualitative research*. Thousand Oaks, CA: Sage.

Stryker, S. (1972). Symbolic interaction theory: A review and some suggestions for comparative family research. *Journal of Comparative Family Studies, 3*, 17–32.

Thomas, W. I. (1923). *The unadjusted girl*. Boston: Little, Brown.

Wright, S. (1990). *Adapting Milan style systemic therapy from family therapy to family research*. Unpublished manuscript.

6

THE DEATH OF A CHILD WITH A DEVELOPMENTAL DISABILITY

ELIZABETH MOULTON MILO

Several years ago I was invited, as a special education teacher and as a therapist, to lead a unique bereavement group. This group of mothers had parented and then lost children with severe developmental disabilities. They claimed, somewhat resentfully, that they felt out of place, isolated, and unheard in bereavement groups that they had previously joined. They were continually told that their children were not as valuable or that "it was better this way" and that they should be "over it by now"—sentiments that they found totally out of line with their experience. One mother said, "Our loss is different. There is nothing in the literature to help us. Please write our story." So I did.

This chapter focuses on the qualitative research project that grew out of my work with this bereavement group. The experience revealed to me was intense and gut-wrenchingly painful, but inspiring. Trained in the more traditional theories of loss and bereavement, I was unprepared for the stories I heard and the profound life changes that had occurred in these women. Out of what one would assume to be two tragic losses—first the loss of the dreamed-for child and then the loss of the actual child—emerged a greater sense of identity and of priorities, deeper relationships, greater faith, and an entirely different worldview. The experience of loss had been the catalyst for remarkable growth in these women.

In preparing for the group, I drew on my traditional training in loss and bereavement. It is generally accepted that loss of a child results in grief that is more intense, more painful, and more enduring than any other loss (Rando, 1983; Sanders, 1979). I did not know, however, what might be the experience of mothers when this loss followed on the heels of another profoundly challenging and shaking experience—parenting a child with a developmental disability. I suspected that it was somehow different, as the mothers insisted.

The literature on parenting a child with a developmental disability has portrayed different views over the years. Olshansky (1962) described the phenomenon of *chronic sorrow*, which is the term he used to describe the never-ending process of parental bereavement in response to life with a child who is disabled. In the 1980s Copley and Bodensteiner (1987) wrote that chronic sorrow was characterized by emotional highs and lows, fueled by the cycle of impact, hope, and denial, that keeps parents on an emotional roller coaster and prevents them from moving through the bereavement process. However, Copley and Bodensteiner found that some parents were able to move on to a phase of acceptance in which sadness periodically re-emerged. This sadness was sparked by anniversaries and significant events, but it had a less wrenching quality.

In the 1990s research and clinical experience have shown that many families do not experience chronic sorrow; they have found that parenting a child with a developmental disability, although unexpected and exhausting, becomes the single most defining experience of families' lives. Turnbull et al. (1993) found that families find meaning, power, and value in their experience of parenting children with disabilities.

As the mothers had told me, this literature, however, still did not address the interaction of parenting a child with a disability and then losing that child. Unlike a mother who has lost a normally developing child to disease or accidental death, the mothers in my group experienced two "deaths": the metaphoric death of their dreamed-for child and then, after months or years, the death of their actual child. It was clear that there was a gap in the research literature, a gap that I attempted to fill.

As I undertook this qualitative study, five specific questions came to mind. (a) What is the experience of mothers who have lost a child with a developmental disability, and how is it unique? (b) Do mothers who have parented a child with a developmental disability through emotionally challenging months or years, only to lose that child, manage to cope and make sense out of their experience, or do they experience a sense of devastation and hopelessness? (c) What strategies do mothers use to regain a sense of hope, mastery, and control in a world that has been challenged by the birth and then the death of their child who has a developmental disability?

(d) Were coping strategies used by all of the mothers, and what differences might be associated with mothers who did or did not use the strategies? (e) When the early death of a child with a developmental disability is inevitable, what can professionals who specialize in death and dying do to help families cope in an optimal way?

THE MOTHERS

I selected 8 mothers from a pool of about 20 referred by the local Association for Retarded Citizens. Four of the mothers had attended the Special Loss bereavement group that I facilitated. I recruited 4 more by letter or telephone from a list of those who had been invited to join the Special Loss Group but who declined to do so. Selections were made to reflect diversity in age (from 31 to 72), socioeconomic status (from women on welfare to women in the upper middle class), and current family structure (from divorced women to those who were married with several children) (see Table 6.1). The children ranged in age at time of death from 10 months to 37 years and had been diagnosed with severe chromosomal disorders, such as Miller–Diecher's

TABLE 6.1
Demographic Data for the Mothers and Their Children

Mother/Age	Deceased child	Current family structure	Deceased child's diagnosis	Age of child at time of death; time elapsed
Darby, 39	Kelly	Married; 2 daughters	Trisomy 18	12 years, 1 year
Patty, 40	Anna	Married; 2 daughters	Miller–Diecher's syndrome	17 months, 2 years
Hazel, 72	Margaret	Widowed; 2 daughters	Down's syndrome	37 years, 1 year
Casey, 31	Amber	Divorced; 1 son, 2 daughters	Heart defect, seizures	3 years, 1 year
Kerri, 39	Brian	Remarried; 2 sons	Cerebral palsy, seizures	16 years, 3 years
Tammy, 34	Annie	Married; 2 sons	Severe cerebral palsy	7 years, 2 years
Sarah, 51	Cindy	Married, 1 son	Multiple developmental delays	16 years, 4 years
Denise, 37	Ronnie	Married; 1 son, 1 daughter	Cerebral palsy, seizures	10 months, 7 years

Note. From "Maternal responses to the life and death of a child with a developmental disability: A story of hope," by E. M. Milo, 1997, *Death Studies, 21,* pp. 443–476. Copyright 1997 by Taylor & Francis, Inc., http://www.routledge-ny.com. Reprinted with permission.

or Down's syndrome, or with other disabilities, such as cerebral palsy, heart defects, seizure disorders, or profound mental retardation.

Measures

The nature of the experience I wished to explore led me to choose as assessment tools a semistructured open-ended interview in combination with the Grief Experience Inventory (GEI) (Sanders, Mauger & Strong, 1985). Much of the current research on parental loss of a child, adjustment to parenting a child with a disability, and the cognitive coping strategies one uses to do so has used interviews, which are later analyzed to determine common themes (Affleck & Tennen, 1991; Davies, 1987; Helmruth & Steinitz, 1978; Jost & Haase, 1989). I chose the GEI because it is a widely respected, standardized quantitative measure by which I could compare the mothers in my sample with each other and with other bereaved parents in different samples. The GEI is a 135-item self-report inventory that is used to assess an individual's grief experience through a 12-scale profile. The scales include Denial, Atypical Responses, and Social Desirability, which are used as validity scales, and Despair, Anger, Guilt, Social Isolation, Loss of Control, Rumination, Depersonalization, Somatization, and Death Anxiety, which comprise the Bereavement scale (Sanders, Mauger, & Strong, 1985). The GEI scales are expressed as standard T scores, with a mean of 50 and a standard deviation of 10. The larger the T score, the greater the intensity of the behavior measured by that scale.

Procedure

Each mother was interviewed formally one time, with follow-up questions conducted over the telephone when needed. The interviews, which were audiotaped and transcribed, lasted 1.5–2.5 hours and were conducted in the mother's home or in my office. Each interview began with an open-ended question, allowing the mothers to talk freely about the lives and deaths of their children and ended with more specific questions to fill in the gaps.

At the close of the interview each mother was given a GEI, which she was asked to complete and mail back. A mean composite score was computed for each of the 12 subscales of the GEI for the 7 mothers who returned the survey. These mean scores were compared with the mean scores of the reference group of bereaved parents (see Figure 6.1). In addition, the scores of 2 exceptional cases—mothers whose stories did not fit the more typical pattern—were compared with the mean scores of the other mothers in this study and the parents in the GEI reference group (see Figure 6.2). A score was determined to be noticeably different if it was ≥ 1 standard deviation from the mean for the mothers in my study or those in the parental reference group.

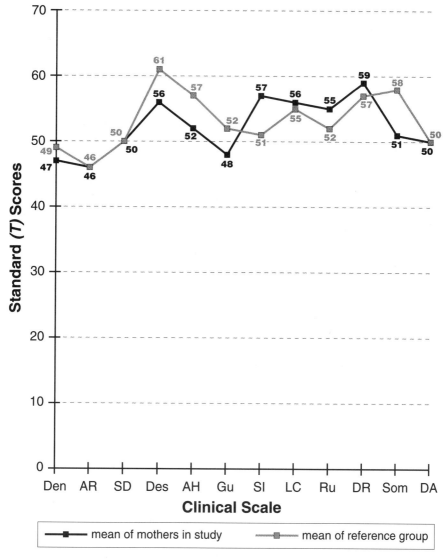

Figure 6.1. Comparison of mothers in the study to the reference group of bereaved parents on the Grief Experience Inventory. Den = Denial; AR = Atypical Responses; SD = Social Desirability; Des = Despair; AH = Anger; Gu = Guilt; SI = Social Isolation; LC = Loss of Control; Ru = Rumination; DR = Depersonalization; Som = Somatization; DA = Death Anxiety.

Note. From "Maternal responses to the life and death of a child with a developmental disability: A story of hope," by E. M. Milo, 1997, *Death Studies, 21*, pp. 443–476. Copyright 1997 by Taylor & Francis, Inc., http://www.routledge-ny.com. Reprinted with permission.

Data Analysis

The interviews were audiotaped, transcribed, and analyzed with constant comparative analysis (Glaser & Strauss, 1967) and a synthesis of other

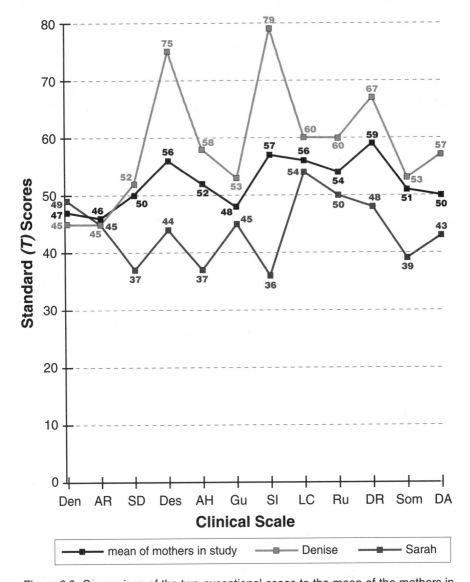

Figure 6.2. Comparison of the two exceptional cases to the mean of the mothers in the study on the Grief Experience Inventory. Den = Denial; AR = Atypical Responses; SD = Social Desirability; Des = Despair; AH = Anger; Gu = Guilt; SI = Social Isolation; LC = Loss of Control; Ru = Rumination; DR = Depersonalization; Som = Somatization; DA = Death Anxiety.

Note. From "Maternal responses to the life and death of a child with a developmental disability: A story of hope," by E. M. Milo, 1997, *Death Studies, 21,* pp. 443–476. Copyright 1997 by Taylor & Francis, Inc., http://www.routledge-ny.com. Reprinted with permission.

procedures outlined by Miles and Huberman (1984), Strauss and Corbin (1990), and Glesne and Peshkin (1992). I and a second coder, a professional who works with families of young children with developmental disabilities, developed and revised a coding system to categorize the transformations that the mothers revealed in areas such as identity, spirituality, relationships, worldview, and priorities and to categorize the coping strategies they used to deal with their children's lives and deaths. We coded the interviews by finding a theme for each 4- to 6-line "chunk" and then looked for overriding themes and relations between themes. We checked for both positive and negative instances and then formed some hypotheses that took into consideration all of the cases. Reliability in applying the coding system was assessed between me and the second coder, who was unfamiliar with the mothers. Interrater agreement was high, and disagreements were resolved through discussion.

RESULTS

The results surprised me, but they should not be unexpected to any reader who has progressed thus far in this volume. Out of the experience of profound loss, the mothers emerged with a sense of clarity, a sense of identity, and strengths that they had not imagined before. Their stories revealed the following themes:

- The mothers felt set apart because their love for the child and their loss were not validated by others.
- The mothers had to work through two difficult transitions.
- The mothers generally felt that although this was not an experience they would have expected or welcomed, all things considered it was one of the central defining experiences of their lives and had transformed them in many positive ways.
- The experience had profoundly shifted their sense of identity, worldview, relationships, spirituality, and priorities, sometimes not only with the birth and parenting experience but also after the loss of the child.
- The mothers were usually able to restore a sense that life is meaningful and predictable, both after the birth or diagnosis of their child with a developmental disability and again after the death of their "special child."
- The mothers used cognitive coping strategies of construing benefits or gains, finding meaning, re-establishing control, and using humor more than they used downward comparison (comparing their situation with the worst-case scenario) in order to restore their assumptive world.
- The mothers who used cognitive coping strategies early and extensively were better able to cope than those who delayed using them or who did not use them extensively.

Two mothers represented exceptional cases that did not fit the more typical pattern. One mother's assumptive world was not shattered as much by the experience as those of the other mothers, and she did little cognitive shifting.

Another mother is still struggling to find benefit and meaning and has not yet been able to see her worldview as benign and meaningful; instead, she continues to view the world as unpredictable and full of danger. As part of my analysis I began to realize that the mothers were using many cognitive coping strategies to transform their experience from one of pain to one of growth and meaning. In the next section I discuss these findings in detail, using quotes from the mothers.

Experiential Themes

Continual Justification: "Well, Don't You Think It Was for the Best?"

A common and painful theme that set these mothers' experience apart was feeling the continual need to justify to others their love for this "unlovable" child, both during the child's life and after his or her death. All of these mothers had affirmatively decided to take their children home and "just love them" and "enjoy every minute we had with them," but outsiders often questioned this decision. Darby, whose child had Trisomy 18 and died at the age of 12, said,

> You spend so much of your kid's life justifying why you're doing this, and why you love them. . . . If somebody else out there who had a normal kid, if they break their leg or are brain injured, they don't have to justify that. Because their child was normal, and might be normal again. But in a case like this, they never were and they never will be. And they say, "Certainly you can't have the same kind of love for that child as you do for your normal kid."

Mothers were often subjected to questions such as "How can you love somebody like that?" or "Wouldn't she be better off dead? Why don't you just stop feeding her?" Once the child died, well-meaning but insensitive condolences were offered, along the lines of "It's not as great a loss as it would have been if you lost one of your other kids"; "It shouldn't hurt as much, and you should be over it now"; or "Well, don't you think it was for the best?", to which the mothers responded with a resounding "No!" As Darby said, "You know I was blessed with 12 1/2 years, and if I had been given the option of 12 1/2 more, I wouldn't even have to think about it!" Yet even in bereavement groups these mothers felt set apart by the unspoken message that their child was less valuable, that their grief should be less, and that they should feel relief instead of sadness.

A Double Transition: "Who Am I Now?"

Unlike most mothers who lose normally developing children to disease or accident, these mothers were faced with two profoundly significant life experiences, one following the other. They were called on and succeeded in making sense of what others might define as "tragedy" twice: once to accommodate a child with a disability into their world and again to assimilate the death of that now-special child into their view of a world that has meaning and purpose.

The required cognitive shifts concern the loss of the mothers' dreamed-for child, acceptance of a life for which they had not wished, and then the giving up of that life. These shifts were not easy. Many of the mothers struggled with the double transition. The overwhelming needs of a child who requires feeding, positioning, help with swallowing, or constant vigilance create a very intense bond, especially between the child and the primary caretaker. Most of the mothers spoke of the special bond with their "wounded chick." Darby said,

> I think the bond is different, because somebody like Kelly will never be able to do for herself . . . so there's that kind of a bond, where you know she's not going to grow up and become an independent person, and she's got three strikes against her to begin with.

This child needed them more, was more vulnerable, and the care given was much more intensive. Thus, the "hole" that was left was felt to be bigger: "I will never again in my whole life be as loved as I was." Once the mothers grew to value a child whose life was considered a tragedy by others and grew accustomed to their new identity and roles, it was devastating to lose both the child and the new identity. Tammy, whose child had cerebral palsy and died at the age of 7, explained,

> After I lost Annie I was back to square one. Well, she's gone now so who am I? Am I still that person? Who, who, am I? I was very lonely and lost, lost, lost. I said, "What am I going to do now?"

The Paradox: "It Sounds Like a Contradiction, But to Me It's Not."

Parenting a child with a developmental disability can be a bittersweet time: wrenching grief mixed with joy, setbacks mixed with challenges to overcome, losses intertwined with benefits and gains. In the final analysis, however, when the joys and the sorrows, the losses and the gains, were balanced, 7 of the 8 mothers believed that parenting and losing a child with a developmental disability was an experience they would never give up. Patty, whose infant died of "smooth brain syndrome," confessed that

> I used to wish that she would die. I remember before I brought her home from the hospital thinking, God, I wish she would just die, and then I wouldn't have to bring her home and go through this and put the kids through this. And I just couldn't have been more wrong.

These mothers came to value children whom they would have aborted or who they wished had died in the hospital and were in awe of the process that they had been through. Kerri, whose child had severe mental retardation and also pica, cerebral palsy, and a sleep disorder and who lived until the age of 16, was frank:

If I were pregnant and knew the child were handicapped, I would not bring that child into this world . . . and for me that is not a conflict. I would not put a child through that, and I would not put myself through that . . . it's extremely painful. But having said that, I can't say I really regret it either, my life, or Brian. Brian brought me so much, brought everyone around him so much, so I don't know. It sounds like a contradiction, but to me it's not.

If one relied only on the 1960s view of chronic sorrow and disregarded the more current literature, one might expect the mothers in this study to be reeling from the double impact or to be experiencing a very complex bereavement, as predicted by Bourke (1984), who believed that an emotionally complicated predeath experience will lead to a similarly complicated postdeath experience. The results both from the interviews and from the GEI showed, however, that 7 of the 8 mothers had managed to emerge from potentially difficult and challenging years strengthened by this meaningful, powerfully transforming experience (see Figure 6.1).

Transforming Crises Into Opportunities: "That's the Greatest Gift She's Given."

As the interviews proceeded, and the themes remained generally positive and hopeful, I began to listen more closely to how the transition from crisis to hopefulness, from feelings of grief and loss to those of awe and wonder at the personal growth and learning, had been accomplished. How had these mothers coped so well?

The mothers described the ways in which parenting a child with a developmental disability was in many ways the most difficult challenge they had ever had to face. Yet, when all was said and done, the positives far outweighed the negatives. For 6 of the mothers it became clear that they had managed to shift what could have been considered a tragedy into the most significant and powerful experience of their lives. The mothers used cognitive coping strategies, detailed below, to help them restore their sense of well-being in the face of crisis (see Table 6.2). These strategies are similar to the ones outlined by Taylor (1983) and Affleck and Tennen (1991).

Coping Strategies

Construing Benefits or Gains: "She Made Me Who I Am Today."

All of the mothers said that they now liked themselves better and felt they had gained a better identity through their experience with their children, including confidence and the ability to speak up for themselves, to be empathic, to be nonjudgmental, to be assertive, to value diversity, and to be patient. Several expressed the belief that they simply were forced to know themselves better. Tammy, whose child had had cerebral palsy, said,

TABLE 6.2
Cognitive Coping Strategies Used by the Mothers

	Cognitive coping strategy				
Mother	Finding benefits	Using humor	Construing meaning	Making downward comparisons	Establishing control
Darby[a]	Priorities, relationship, identity, spirituality, worldview, great kid	She had the cutest smile	Personal, public		Took charge of medical care
Patty[a]	Identity, priorities, spirituality, worldview		Personal, extended personal	We were fortunate, had good insurance	Coordinated care, trust God
Hazel[a]	Identity, spirituality, worldview, great kid		Personal, public	She was high functioning	Treat as normal, trust God
Casey[a]	Identity, spirituality, priorities, great kid		Personal	She could have died at 11 days	Never out of sight, trust God
Kerri[a]	Relation-ships, identity, great kid	Created comedy out of tragedy	Personal		Never out of sight, trust respite care, trust karma
Tammy[a]	Identity, priorities, great kid		Personal, public	We knew the ropes	Became a warrior, trust God
Sarah[a]	Priorities		Public	It could have been a spouse	Work on legislation
Denise	Identity, priorities, relation-ships				Orchestrated death

[a]Able to restore her belief in the world as benevolent, purposeful, and meaningful.

Note. From "Maternal responses to the life and death of a child with a developmental disability: A story of hope," by E. M. Milo, 1997, Death Studies, 21, pp. 443–476. Copyright 1997 by Taylor & Francis, Inc., http://www.routledge-ny.com. Reprinted with permission.

Annie made me who I am today. She gave me the strength to stand up for myself and to realize the power I have as a person. I never had that before. I was not vocal, I was young, I was just married and in la-la-land. I never actually understood who I was as a person, and Annie made me grow.

Each mother reported that her sense of priorities was vastly changed, in a way she valued, because of her experience with her child who was developmentally delayed. What was important in life became simpler, more basic, and incredibly clear, and trivial things could no longer bother or interest them. Patty, who described her child as having "smooth brain syndrome," with a very short life expectancy, mused,

> They are telling you that life is very short. They give you your sense of mortality. . . . You're going to die, your children are going to die, everybody is going to die. . . . Sometimes when I get caught up I can tell myself, "I mean you are going to die, so what's this worth?" It's not what's important here because you're not going to take this with you . . . it's a constant reminder that we all have a certain amount of time, and you make your choices.

The mothers gained a simpler, more basic view of the world and why we are on earth through the experience of parenting and losing a child with a developmental disability. Darby concluded that "If you leave the world a better place than when you found it, if you've helped someone along the way or you've touched somebody along the way . . . what else is there?" In this way of viewing the world Darby's daughter had as much value as any other child. Patty echoed the simple sentiment, "Anna just told you, life is precious, life is short, we're all going to die. . . . It's not the big house and the nice vacations. It's the moments, the feeling, the love. And she taught that just so well."

Six of the mothers felt that their sense of spirituality had grown toward a greater trust in the plans or knowledge of a higher being and a more personal relationship with their god. Whereas many of the mothers had been part of a formal religion before the child was born, several had moved toward a more personal one. Darby, who was busy with the special needs of her daughter who had Trisomy 18, found little time to go to church, saying, "you can pray in the toilet, you can pray wherever you need to be." A few mothers, like Casey, challenged a god that could let such horrible things happen but ended up with a stronger faith in the end.

> When I see what I went through, what other people go through, I don't understand the reason why the child suffers and the parent agonizes . . . it amazes me that you can love so much and then it's taken away, it's kinda harsh. . . . I almost thought of giving up the faith, but it was all too real. . . . God was all I had, and I came to realize that God was all I really needed.

For the most part, the mothers came to the understanding that the meaning of the world is determined by a higher power, be it God or something like Karma, and that what happened to them in the past and would happen in the future has a purpose.

Relationships changed dramatically with the birth and death of the child with a disability. A huge part of the mothers' interviews was focused on relationships and how they shifted both with the birth and parenting and often once again after the child died.

Marital relationships that were solid and deep strengthened with the challenges, and marriages that were shaky fell apart. Tammy said,

> It's brought us closer together. You have to work as a team to be successful. To make her life successful, basically you had to. There had to be cohesion, and to make family life work it just had to be that way. I can't imagine trying to do it on my own!

Kerri's and Casey's marriages both ended when their husbands opted to leave. Kerri said that she did not regret the loss. "He chose to bail out, to decide it wasn't something he could handle . . . and so he did. He has a real problem with that he had a child with a handicap—but that's his problem!" Other couples were able to nurture each other and hold things together "during the heat of the battle," while their child was still alive. However, after the child's death they were unable to console each other, each being deep into his or her own grief. Darby reported that

> We always took it for granted that we would be together forever, in the same way we always were you know. And um, mourning Kelly has been so complex for both of us, that for the middle six months of the time that she was gone, we didn't have room for each other. We couldn't be there for each other . . . and we, we drifted apart.

Grandparents also distanced themselves in two of the cases, but although the rejection was painful the mothers decided that they were better off. Kerri cut off connections with her father, who rejected her son, Brian:

> I've severed my ties with my father because he does not accept Brian. . . . I realized the kind of person my father is, and he's not the kind of person I want in my children's lives or in my life. . . . And then, after Brian's death it was complicated. Because he really wanted me back, because Brian wasn't there. And that really fueled the fires of anger in me.

Mothers often changed their support groups, growing distant from friends who did not accept their child and gathering a group with similar values: parents of children with disabilities, doctors, teachers, therapists, and respite care workers. They cut out people who would not accept their child or those who were caught up in trivial matters. Darby explained,

> You lose a lot of people along the way because you don't want to spend time on a bunch of trivial crap . . . you don't have time to put up with someone else's prejudices, and you don't have the energy to give a damn about what bugs somebody else.

Respite care providers in particular became an immense source of support and often replaced the extended family, particularly when the family did not accept the child. The respite care providers accepted the child with unconditional love.

One of the biggest struggles the mothers encountered was balancing the needs of their special-needs child with those of their other children. Several of the mothers felt they had no option but to focus on their "wounded chick," who needed them more. Darby reported,

> They don't need me in the same way that Kelly needed me. And it really wasn't until we really ran into some problems with our oldest daughter that the lightbulb went on. . . . My oldest daughter had run away from home, and was drinking and doing all sorts of nasty things . . . and I think that's probably the one area I have the most regret in. As far as how my other girls had it during Kelly's life.

Casey, who reached a point of total exhaustion, which she described as a nervous breakdown, said, "It was scary. I didn't know what to do. I said, 'I can't fall apart . . . who will take care of my baby?'" She seriously considered putting her two other children in foster care, knowing that she was stretched far beyond her breaking point and not seeing any other solution.

And yet with the death of the special-needs child came the opportunity to re-establish sadly neglected relationships. Darby spoke with joy and sadness of her 17-year-old daughter:

> Yeah, that relationship hadn't been good for five years. There wasn't a lot of time, and there wasn't a lot of room to work on that relationship during the heat of the battle with Kelly. Now . . . it's hard to pull a 17-year-old woman onto your lap and hug her like you would a 4-year-old. But I do it anyway. Because it's something she went without for so long. I need it too you know. I lost a big chunk of her life, and I'd like some of it back.

Other mothers were able to incorporate the child with a disability into the routine of the entire family, feeling that they had achieved a balance. They talked about how much their other children had gained and felt that the birth of the child had enhanced rather than detracted from the siblings' lives. Tammy said, "I mean she touched anybody who met her. Incredibly. I'm sure she was an angel. I'm sure . . . the gifts she's given to her brothers, the sensitivity to human beings . . . that's the greatest gift that she's given."

In sum, every mother was able to describe several ways in which her life had become better or richer by dealing with the challenges of her child's life and death. This perspective helped the mothers to cope with several difficult challenges and loss. Some mothers were able to construe more benefits and gains than others, which was associated with better coping.

Finding Meaning: "I Just Don't Believe This Happened for No Point and No Reason."

Mothers searched for, and usually found, a special meaning in the lives and deaths of their children, something that helped them re-establish their belief in the benevolence and purposefulness of the world. Redefining the meaning of the children gave them a sense of serenity and peace. It helped end the struggle of fighting against the inevitable and made them feel honored to be part of the special child's life. A prerequisite for finding a special meaning in the child's life was first accepting the child as imperfect, giving up the dreamed-for child.

The special child's purpose was often believed to redeem the mother personally, as related by Casey: "For me personally, I think God allowed this in my life for my own salvation." Kerri said she believed that

> I feel like some way there's a plan here . . . there was a plan for Brian and I, we are interconnected in his life and his death. . . . Maybe if there is reincarnation, there is something we needed to work through, I needed him and he needed me. It was too good a match to be accidental. . . . I just don't believe that all this stuff happened for no point and for no reason.

Other mothers felt that their child was sent to accomplish a broader mission. Darby believes that Kelly, who had Trisomy 18, was here to teach: "You know the reason that Kelly lived as long as she did was because there needed to be a lot of changes in the way kids around here were treated . . . medically, out in society, educationally, all sorts of things." Cindy and Annie, who both had severe disabilities, were instrumental in changing legislation and education for people with disabilities. Margaret, who had a higher level of functioning, had shared her experience with medical students. Three of the mothers mentioned that they were sure their child was an angel. Hazel explained the purpose of Margaret's life as she lived until 37 with Down's syndrome:

> She taught the [medical] students that you have to challenge a person and build for them as far as they can go. She made a tremendous contribution to the future of our medical system. . . . I think she is one of those angels that we meet once in a while. She was sent to teach me a lot of things and to teach the community with which she came in contact about tolerance and how to care for each other. . . . And then God said, "Margaret, I think you have done a wonderful job on earth, and I think it's time for you to come home and rest."

It was interesting to see that the mothers coped with the death of their children, in part, by continuing the work that the children had begun. They either made a commitment to maintain their personal growth or continued to advocate for people with disabilities as a legacy to their children. Each of the mothers has continued on the path she began with her child as a way of honoring the child.

Gaining Control of the Uncontrollable: "It Was a Beautifully Orchestrated Death."

In a situation in which the mothers realized they had very little control, they nevertheless sought to gain control where they could. During the life of the child each of the mothers worked hard to advocate for medical treatment, education, and the rights of their children. Sarah, whose daughter was profoundly retarded yet lived until age 16, mused,

> that was a way of dealing with our grief, and it did give us more control over it. I think that is part of it. You don't feel so buffeted by this thing that just happened to us instead of somebody else.

When death was inevitable, mothers sought to control the way the child left the world. Denise received some comfort in a heartbreaking situation. "We went back into Ronnie's room, and if you could have a beautifully orchestrated death, that was it. I'm really grateful for that." When doctors told Denise and her husband that there was no more hope for Ronnie, they gathered family, friends, and minister, dressed Ronnie in his familiar pajamas, ripped off the mandatory face masks, made their apologies for what might have been different, and said their goodbyes. Denise conveyed that "I wanted him to go and be with the Lord. That we would see him again. He wouldn't have to deal with all of this." Several of the mothers felt that the children waited for permission to die and that they were able to grant it. Darby shared the following experience:

> I said, "Kelly you can go," and I took her mask off and she looked at me, I mean right into my soul, and then she died. And just that whole process of feeling the change in her body, it was just so much like it is giving birth. . . . You know, it was just incredible.

The mothers strived to ensure that the children's last moments were as comfortable and meaningful as possible. For Kerri, who had not been present at her child's death, there was a profound sense of loss: She had worked so hard during the child's life, and she felt robbed of the chance to offer comfort and say goodbye at the end. Kerri said,

> I feel like I was robbed of something very important. I wasn't able to say goodbye. I think it would have been so much easier if I could have, if they had called me. . . . It still hurts. It hurts a lot. Because I feel like I was just robbed of that closure.

Using Humor: "You Have a Way of Creating This Comedy."

Even though Kerri felt her life was like an "unending prison sentence" she took great delight in the antics of Brian. When Kerri found humor in the funeral home as she prepared for the burial of one child and went into labor with another, her friend said to her, "You know, you have a way of taking a situation that is so bad that you don't think you are going to survive it and turning it around and creating this comedy." I suspect that Kerri, who had experienced an emotionally abusive childhood, frequently used humor to see the bright side of very bleak situations. She had told me with obvious joy of many of Brian's antics, such as sneaking into the neighbor's house at midnight and jumping on his much-coveted waterbed, interrupting a very romantic first date. Many of the mothers took some delight in their child's sunny personality, funny smile, or humorous antics, which offered some comic relief in a difficult situation.

Downward Comparison: "At Least She Won't Outlive Me."

Taylor (1983) and Affleck and Tennen (1991) found that people sometimes can mitigate the meaning of a threatening event by comparing it with alternative circumstances. People rationalize that the event may not have been purposeful or beneficial, but it could have been worse. This strategy was not widely used by the mothers in my study in describing their children or the lives of their children. Hazel had the highest functioning child, Margaret, and was able to lessen her pain by finding that Margaret was almost normal, that Margaret was like her sisters—only slower. The other mothers never used this strategy in reference to their children; things were in reality very difficult. They did, however, compare themselves with less fortunate parents, saying that at least they knew how to work the system, knew how to advocate for their child's rights, or were fortunate enough to have good insurance.

After the child had died the mothers did use some downward comparison; for example, saying that in some ways things could have been worse if their child had lived. Most of the mothers expressed relief that the child was out of pain, that he or she would not be subjected to any more medical procedures, and that at least the child would not outlive the support and love of the mother.

Differential Use of Cognitive Coping Strategies and Relation to Outcome

Not all of the mothers used cognitive coping strategies equally to mitigate their feelings of loss and helplessness and to restore a sense of control and well-being in a world that is purposeful. Two mothers were noticeably different; I refer to them as the exceptional cases. With such a limited sample I can only speculate on the factors that may have influenced the use of cognitive coping strategies and differential outcome.

When children were diagnosed at birth and given a clear-cut, unambiguous prognosis the process of letting go of the dreamed-for child and accepting the actual child began. Darby, Patty, and Hazel each grieved intensely with the early diagnosis of her child but then were able to take the infant home to love. Hazel informed her husband, who wanted to institutionalize Margaret, "There's no way I can do anything but totally love her"—just the way she was. Darby accepted Kelly's disability quickly. She explained, "She came home at 11 days, and we just decided that whatever time we were going to have with this baby that we wanted every second of it." The mothers who were given an unambiguous diagnosis and prognosis at birth began to find meaning and construe benefit in the life of their actual child very early.

In contrast, the mothers of children who were pronounced normal at birth and then later revealed more and more troubles were the ones who experienced a more prolonged, continually wrenching process, cycling through hope and despair. Amber and Ronnie, children who had unclear diagnoses, went progressively downhill for their short lives, leaving the mothers in continual despair.

Denise, whose child Ronnie had no clear diagnosis yet did not develop on schedule despite her hope and valiant efforts, stands out as an exceptional case. Ronnie died earlier than the other children, which in conjunction with an unclear diagnosis left little time for anticipatory grief. Denise explained, "It was as if we were delaying the grieving process for his disabilities until we knew what we were dealing with." She kept hoping her baby would be normal, praying to God to save him, waking him up for therapy with someone who promised to cure him, bravely pushing on, ignoring the advice of friends and professionals who urged,

> "You've got to let go of the baby that you thought you were going to have. This is the baby you have, accept it, deal with it, grieve with it." And I'd look at this precious little gift, and I'd think, "How can I grieve over a brand new baby? This is a gift, and I'll be damned if I'm going to grieve over it!"

Denise's hope was high until the moment of Ronnie's death, at 10 months, and she had not let go of her dreamed-for child in order to accept her "special child" before he died. She did not, in the confusing 10 months, complete the process of finding a new meaning for Ronnie's limited life. When asked about his purpose she said, "I don't know," and when asked about benefits she named only a few: "I'm not sure it's positive, it's anything but positive!" Seven years after Ronnie's death Denise still has many regrets and sees the world as a "darker place." In contrast to the other mothers, who found meaning in their experience and have hope and trust, Denise reported,

> You don't have control, and I think it affects my life on a daily basis in that every day when I put Amy on that bus across the bridge, I don't necessarily expect that she'll arrive at school healthy. . . . I mean that sounds really dark, but that's the reality of living today. I think I am darker than other people because of that. I think it's probably harder to live that way. Whenever Rick leaves, he's on a business trip right now, I don't just necessarily expect him to come home . . . and then the panic ensues.

Denise's GEI profile is noticeably different than the mean profile for the other mothers or for the reference group (see Figure 6.2). She scored approximately 2 standard deviations above the mean of both groups on Desperation and Social Isolation. It is possible that Denise's process is still continuing. She cannot say with conviction that Ronnie's life and death were a positive experience, but she did say, with some hesitancy,

> I've grappled with that because I would never wish this on anyone, and I would never willingly wish to go through it. But if I liked myself more now than I did before and feel more capable and loveable, if you will, then I guess you do choose it, and that gives you back some of the control that you lost.

Sarah also stands out as an exceptional case, but for different reasons. It appears that mothers make major cognitive shifts and transformations with the life and death of a child with a disability when that child is sufficiently dissonant with the mother's assumptions of the world, but the mothers may not shift as much when the child can be accommodated into that world. Sarah, who was a civil rights activist in her younger days, apparently had already accepted that the world was not a perfect place, that "everyone has their pain and sorrow." When her daughter Cindy was diagnosed as profoundly retarded before her first birthday, Sarah grieved intensely but soon took her imperfect child in stride, believing that "everyone has their pain, whether it's alcoholism in the family or maybe abuse. Ours is just more visible." Cindy's disability had no cosmic meaning but, "was by random chance—this awful thing happened to us rather than somebody else." Sarah had always advocated for disadvantaged people, and she continued to do so. Just as Sarah helped others in need, she gathered support from her family and community to help share in the care of Cindy. Sarah became a full-time professional and spent time with her son and husband, sometimes away from Cindy. Perhaps other activities in Sarah's life formed a different kind of bond than that experienced by mothers who were full-time caretakers. Sarah reported only a few changes in her identity and a few in her worldview—she said she is more serious now and that she does not put so much emphasis on intelligence anymore. Sarah's GEI profile is below the mean for both the mothers in my sample and the reference group on every scale but one, indicating that her bereavement process may have been less intense (see Figure 6.2).

DISCUSSION

Although I had expected to hear about how difficult it was to raise a child with a developmental disability and how the experience left the mother exhausted, ambivalent, and at risk for experiencing a very complicated bereavement process once the child died, I did not expect to hear over and over how this group of mothers had found the whole experience a blessing in many ways and how it had completely transformed many aspects of their lives. It is clear from this study that the experience of parenting and then losing a child with a developmental disability has the power to shift profoundly one's sense of identity, worldview, relationships, spirituality, and priorities but that that transformation is in part determined by how dissonant the reality of the child is with one's original beliefs and one's ability to use cognitive coping strategies.

Helping Families to Cope Optimally

If family, friends, professionals, and support groups can facilitate the process of cognitive coping they can help parents to restore a worldview that is benevolent and purposeful. How might this process be facilitated? The experience of the mothers in this study may help to illuminate some helpful strategies.

- It appeared that giving as clear a diagnosis and prognosis as possible early on allowed parents to progress to the stage of accepting a child with severe disabilities. It was more harmful for a mother to hope for a recovery, only to have her hopes shattered, than to expect the worst and be continually delighted by the child's unexpected progress.
- Support groups of parents of children with developmental disabilities were essential both while the child was living and after the child's death, because they surrounded the parent with others who valued their child, who did not question how they possibly could love a child with such a severe disability, or offer consolation that "it was better this way" when the child died. The parents in support groups felt valued and validated and began to see more benefits and meaning in their common experiences.
- Allowing the mother some control in an uncontrollable situation was helpful. Mothers who actively advocated for their children felt that they had some control and were less buffeted about by fate. Mothers who were able to orchestrate their child's death found some peace and serenity in the worst possible scenario, often describing it as the most beautiful experience of their lives.
- Professionals and support systems were most helpful when they facilitated and encouraged, but did not push for, cognitive coping, by helping the parent find gains, benefits, and purpose in their experience.
- If parents were helped to accept the paradoxes of their experience they were less likely to see the world as a dangerous and

unpredictable place in spite of their personal tragedy. The mothers in my group who were best able to continue on with a positive worldview were the ones who could openly embrace the paradoxes so common to those who lose a child with a disability. They could accept the knowledge that their child was flawed yet precious, that they yearned for a break from the parenting yet longed for their child to come back, that they were relieved that their child was out of pain yet would have their child live for many more years, and that this was the worst and yet the most beautiful and powerful experience that they had ever been through.

- It was helpful when parents were allowed time for grieving, processing, and reflecting. Mothers needed some time and space away from the exhausting reality of parenting a child with a disability in order to grieve and reach the stage of acceptance necessary to move on to optimal coping. The mothers who had been allowed time to accept the reality of their child's disability were better able to cope with their child's untimely death.

CONCLUSION

I hope that this study, and the stories of these 8 women, will add to the knowledge of the transformative power of loss. Even today I continue to be inspired by these women, whom I feel very privileged to have known. Much to my surprise, 2 years and again 4 years after this study was completed the mothers requested and gathered for reunions. They, who once felt alone and unheard, have talked far into the night with a sense of awe about their common experience and their continued growth resulting from what most would see as a tragic double loss. They realize that the lives and deaths of their children with developmental disabilities have in large part made them who they are today. Four years after the original interviews they endorsed even more strongly the sentiments of one: "I would never have wished for this experience, but I would never give it up either."

This study is important, but it is only a first step. It would be important to replicate this project with mothers who are in more remote geographic areas, away from the expertise and support of a major children's hospital and an active association for retarded citizens. Future research might look at various ethnic and cultural groups for differences in coping with these experiences. Interviewing fathers, siblings, and grandparents who have lost children with developmental delays would add more depth and breadth to the understanding of what it is like to love and then lose a child with a developmental disability. These further studies would enrich the theoretical understanding of parenting children with developmental disabilities, the cognitive coping strategies that are involved, and bereavement following the loss of a special child.

REFERENCES

Affleck, G., & Tennen, H. (1991). Appraisal and coping predictors of mother and child outcomes after newborn intensive care. *Journal of Social and Clinical Psychology, 10,* 424–447.

Bourke, M. (1984). The continuum of pre- and post-bereavement grieving. *British Journal of Medical Psychology, 57,* 121–125.

Copley, M., & Bodensteiner, J. (1987). Chronic sorrow in families of disabled children. *Journal of Child Neurology, 2,* 67–70.

Davies, B. (1987). Family responses to the death of a child: The meaning of memories. *Journal of Palliative Care, 3*(1), 9–15.

Glaser, B., & Strauss, A. (1967). *The discovery of grounded theory.* Chicago: Aldine.

Glesne, C., & Peshkin, A. (1992). *Becoming qualitative researchers: An introduction.* White Plains, NY, Longman.

Helmruth, T., & Steinitz, E. (1978). Death of an infant: Parental grieving and the failure of social support. *The Journal of Family Practice, 6*(4), 785–790.

Jost, K., & Haase, J. (1989). At the time of death—Help for the child's parents. *Children's Health Care, 18*(3), 146–152.

Miles, M., & Huberman, A. (1984). *Qualitative data analysis: A sourcebook of new methods.* Newbury Park: Sage Publications.

Olshansky, S. (1962). Chronic sorrow: A response to having a mentally defective child. *Social Casework, 43,* 190–193.

Rando, T. (1983). An investigation of grief and adaptation in parents whose children have died from cancer. *Journal of Pediatric Psychology, 8,* 3–19.

Sanders, C. (1979). A comparison of adult bereavement in the death of a spouse, child and parent. *Omega, 12,* 227–241.

Sanders, C., Mauger, P., & Strong, P. (1985). *The Grief Experience Inventory, Loss Version.* Charlotte, NC: The Center for the Study of Separation and Loss.

Strauss, A., & Corbin, J. (1990). *Basics of qualitative research.* Newbury Park: Sage Publications.

Taylor, S. (1983). Adjustment to threatening events: A theory of cognitive adaptation. *American Psychologist, 38,* 624–630.

Turnbull, A., et al. (Eds.). (1993). *Cognitive coping: Families and disabilities.* Baltimore: Brookes.

III

Transcending Trauma:
Growth After Loss

7

THE TORMENTED AND THE TRANSFORMED: UNDERSTANDING RESPONSES TO LOSS AND TRAUMA

CHRISTOPHER G. DAVIS

Loss and trauma events often represent severe threats to how people perceive themselves and how they perceive the world. These events can shatter hopes, destroy confidence, and cast people into despair to last a lifetime. In fact, epidemiological studies suggest that people who experience loss or trauma are subsequently at higher risk for a range of psychiatric disorders relative to those who have not experienced such an event (e.g., Kessler, Davis, & Kendler, 1997; Turner & Lloyd, 1995). Other studies that have also used nontraumatized comparison samples indicate that those experiencing significant loss (e.g., of a spouse or child) or trauma (e.g., as a victim of serious crime) tend to report lower self-esteem, a greater sense of vulnerability, less interpersonal trust, more worry, poorer health, and lower levels of psychological well-being, even many years after the event's occurrence (e.g., deVries, Davis, Wortman, & Lehman, 1997; Gluhoski & Wortman, 1996; Lehman, Wortman, & Williams, 1987; Norris & Kaniasty, 1991).

I am grateful to Susan Nolen-Hoeksema for her comments on an earlier draft of this chapter.

Although there is clear evidence that trauma and loss can have profoundly negative consequences for people, the observed long-term effects of trauma and loss often are statistically of a small magnitude and highly variable. For example, using discrete time survival models to predict the first onset of each of 14 psychiatric disorders, Kessler et al. (1997) found that although the experience (prior to age 17) of virtually any 1 of 26 adversities (e.g., death of a parent, sexual assault, physical assault, victim of a natural disaster) was associated with the subsequent onset of at least one psychiatric disorder, odds ratios were typically of the order of 1.5, indicating that the experience of an adversity increased one's odds of developing a disorder by 50%. A reasonable interpretation of the data might be that some people suffer greatly and are scarred by these events, but many others are quite resilient.

At the same time, much has been made in the past decade of the finding that undesirable life events often have profoundly *positive* effects on people's lives (e.g., Antonovsky, 1987; Tedeschi, Park, & Calhoun, 1998). Individuals who have experienced trauma or loss often report that the experience has changed them for the better; for instance, by teaching them what is important in life or the value of friendship and family (e.g., Tedeschi & Calhoun, 1995, 1996; Updegraff & Taylor, in press). Indeed, some people consider their experience with trauma or loss to be the turning point in their lives, a watershed after which their sense of identity or purpose was transformed.

THREE APPROACHES TO UNDERSTANDING
STRESS REACTIONS

The question of why some people succumb to the negative effects of loss and trauma while others are quite resilient and are at times even transformed by them has been the focus of volumes of research. In general this research has taken one of three approaches to understanding the variation in stress response: a personality approach, a coping approach, and "psychological issues" approach.

The personality approach suggests that pre-existing individual differences on key traits play an important role in predicting people who are at greater risk for the negative sequelae of stress. For instance, diathesis–stress models propose that the negative effects of adversity are most severe among individuals with pre-existing vulnerability factors (e.g., Abramson, Metalsky, & Alloy, 1989; Metalsky, Abramson, Seligman, Semmel, & Peterson, 1982). These vulnerability factors are typically construed as dispositions, including a ruminative coping style (Nolen-Hoeksema, Larson, & Grayson, 1999; Nolen-Hoeksema & Morrow, 1991) or a pessimistic attributional style (Peterson & Seligman, 1984). Whereas diathesis–stress models have focused on personality characteristics that increase the risk of depression and other disorders, other research suggests that the possession of traits such as optimism and mastery increase the likelihood of positive outcomes following adversity (Carver, 1998). Several researchers have reported that these traits significantly predict growth and transformation (e.g., Park, Cohen, & Murch, 1996; Tedeschi & Calhoun, 1996; Updegraff & Taylor, in press). However, the personality approach is limited in its ability to illuminate the processes by which people adjust to loss and trauma because it does not address the issues about which individuals facing such events are concerned and how they respond to (cope with) these concerns.

A second approach to studying moderators of trauma and loss focuses on the specific coping behavior or coping activity of people who have experienced trauma or loss. Largely motivated by Lazarus and Folkman's (1984) transactional model of coping, hundreds of studies have investigated the efficacy of various coping behaviors as moderators of the stress process (e.g., Carver, Scheier, & Weintraub, 1989; Parker, Endler, & Bagby, 1993; Valentiner, Holahan, & Moos, 1994). For instance, much has been made of the stress-buffering role of social support in helping people cope with trauma (e.g., Cohen & Wills, 1985). However, such models mask the dynamic nature of social support: The nature and quantity of support needed, its provision, and its perceived helpfulness will vary greatly over time as one attempts to come to terms with traumatic experiences such as spousal loss, child loss, and natural disaster (Lepore, Silver, Wortman, & Wayment, 1996; Nolen-Hoeksema & Davis, 1999; Pennebaker, 1993). If, in context of a single loss event, one's social support (and presumably also coping) requirements ebb and flow, then our attention needs to be drawn to the specific issues that drive these changes in coping behavior. As long as an inordinate amount of researchers' attention is focused on coping, and not on the underlying and changing issues with which one is coping, their understanding of the coping process will remain conceptually fuzzy and incomplete, and findings are likely to continue to be inconsistent and ungeneralizable across studies (cf. Coyne & Gottlieb, 1996).

A third, more recent approach to understanding the variability in response to trauma and loss, and one that I have followed in much of my own research, focuses on understanding the psychological issues that trauma and loss often evoke. Research in this tradition explores some of the major psychological issues with which people coping with trauma and loss often wrestle. Recognizing that every person's experience with loss or trauma is unique, this research tradition nevertheless tries to distill the major issues or themes that tend to come up over and over. The question addressed here is not so much "how is one coping?" as much as it is "with what is one coping?" In this respect, it attempts to bridge narrative and qualitative accounts of people's experience of loss or trauma with the largely quantitative approach typical of the first two approaches cited above.

In this chapter I sketch two examples of psychological issues on which I have focused in my research. The first issue concerns the counterfactual[1] ("if only") thoughts that often torment people losing a loved one; the second issue concerns the powerful need for meaning that many experience. Research that my colleagues and I have conducted suggests that these are important issues that people coping with various types of loss (and trauma) face and often do not resolve, even after several years. For many, the counterfactual thoughts do not go away, and the need for meaning does not dissipate.

Most of this research comes from studies of people grieving the death of a family member (e.g., a spouse), including losses that were sudden and unexpected (e.g., Davis, Lehman, Wortman, Silver, & Thompson, 1995; Davis, Wortman, Lehman, & Silver, 2000), and losses that were somewhat more predictable, following a lengthy terminal illness (Davis, Nolen-Hoeksema, & Larson, 1998). Although the kinship ties to the deceased person varied across these studies, the underlying processes involved (to the extent that we understand them) remain very similar.

COPING WITH THOUGHTS OF WHAT MIGHT HAVE BEEN

One issue with which the bereaved person—and those who have survived other traumas—seem to struggle are thoughts of what one might have done to prevent the event from happening. Several clinical researchers have described poignant counterfactual thoughts that their clients and research participants have reported as particularly distressing (e.g., Pynoos et al., 1993; Tait & Silver, 1989; Weiss, 1988). For instance, a 40-year-old woman reported to my colleague in therapy that she was tormented by thoughts of what she had done or failed to do that contributed to the suicide of her husband, from whom she had been separated for several months:

> Since X died, I've been a total wreck. I just keep going back over what happened, and thinking, "If only I hadn't left him, he would never have ended it this way." I knew he was depressed, and I tried to get him to seek help, but I know I could have pushed harder. It's strange how I thought of going by and seeing him the morning he, he shot himself . . . but I didn't, and I blame myself for that. I just kind of rehearse it in my mind, like I'm trying to go back in time and reverse the situation, though I know I can't. I just can't shake the thoughts that, that I should have done something different. (R. A. Neimeyer, personal communication, January, 2000)

---

[1]In the social psychological literature, these "if only" or "what if" thoughts are termed *counterfactuals* because they take the form of mental replays of scenarios or situations where the outcome is altered to be counter to the fact.

In two samples of people who had experienced the sudden and unexpected loss of a family member, my colleagues and I demonstrated that such counterfactual thoughts were commonly reported, even several years after a sudden, unexpected loss (Davis et al., 1995). Moreover, despite the fact that our respondents in these studies were not causally implicated in the death of their loved one, we observed that in almost all cases the focus of counterfactuals was on their own (in)actions rather than on the behavior of others. For instance, many of the respondents in a motor vehicle accident study lost a loved one when another motorist, alleged to be speeding or drunk, collided with the car occupied by their loved one. Yet not one of our respondents reported thinking "if only the other guy wasn't drunk" or "if only the other guy had driven more carefully." Rather, they almost invariably offered counterfactuals that changed their own behavior (e.g., "If I had grounded him that night as I wanted to, it might not have happened"). It is not surprising that in both studies we found that such thoughts were significantly associated with prolonged emotional distress and feelings of guilt and personal responsibility (Davis et al., 1995; see also Davis, Lehman, Silver, Wortman, & Ellard, 1996). These data suggest that people who can easily imagine preventing or avoiding the event have extra issues with which they must cope relative to those for whom such counterfactual thoughts are less salient.

Several researchers have suggested that counterfactual thoughts are adaptive in that they lend a sense of future control (Boninger, Gleicher, & Strathman, 1994; Taylor & Schneider, 1989)—that is, the desire to avoid a similar situation in the future might lead one to think of ways that a tragic event might not have happened. This makes sense for events that have a potential for recurrence, but for many life events avoidance of a recurrence is not really an issue (e.g., for those coping with a spinal cord injury that has left them paralyzed; see Davis et al., 1996), yet counterfactual thoughts are still prevalent in these situations. Even among events that might recur (e.g., the loss of a loved one in a car crash), we have found that counterfactuals generally do not imply that future control was a motivating issue (Davis et al., 1995). For example, one respondent, who had lost her husband in a car crash that occurred on his way to work one morning, said, "If I had talked him into staying home that day—but there was no reason to. . . . He was very good about not missing work" (Davis et al., 1995, p. 114). A father whose son was hit and killed by a car while the son was delivering newspapers told us that he often thinks, "Why didn't I have the alertness to think about it that night! . . . I could have driven him around the route. Why did I have to get so wrapped up in the TV?" (Davis & Lehman, 1995, p. 360). These quotes suggest that the goal behind such thoughts is not likely to be one of prevention of a recurrence.

Counterfactual thoughts such as these have been linked with higher levels of emotional distress and have been known to persist for many years (Capps & Bonanno, in press; Davis et al., 1995; Tait & Silver, 1989), and it is for these reasons that my colleagues and I suggest that these thoughts represent a significant issue for coping. Recent data also suggest that dysphoric ruminative thought (of which counterfactual thoughts are likely one type) disrupts effective coping and shatters self-confidence and optimism (Lyubomirsky, Tucker, Caldwell, & Berg, 1999). Yet how one attempts to cope with such thoughts is a topic that has received virtually no attention in the literature. Do people attempt to convince themselves that the counterfactual possibilities are implausible, based on alternative actions that were unlikely or unforeseeable? Perhaps people tormented by such thoughts might be encouraged to put their thoughts "on trial" as a means of convincing themselves that one could not have foreseen the outcome. Nevertheless, the very ease with which one could have prevented the situation that one now faces is likely to haunt one for years. At this point it remains unclear what, if any, cognitive strategies might be used to block these thoughts (cf. Wegner & Schneider, 1989). As Wegner (1994) and others (e.g., Rachman, 1981) have noted, controlling one's own thoughts under stress is a particularly difficult task.

THE NEED FOR MEANING

A second issue that confronts many people coping with loss and trauma concerns the meaning of the event for their lives. Several writers have noted that people coping with loss and trauma often seem compelled to imbue the event with which they are coping with some meaning or purpose; they often have a persistent need to make some sense of it (e.g., Chodoff, Friedman, & Hamburg, 1964; Neimeyer, 2000; Parkes & Weiss, 1983; Silver, Boon, & Stones, 1983). For instance, in their study of women who were victims of incest, Silver et al. (1983) reported that, for 80% of the sample, finding some meaning in their experience was still important to them an average of 20 years after the termination of the incest. In fact, a persistent and urgent need for meaning has been noted by researchers studying reactions to a wide range of traumas, including natural disaster (e.g., Erikson, 1976), loss (particularly those losses that are untimely or unexpected; e.g., Cleiren, 1993; Nolen-Hoeksema & Davis, 1999; McIntosh, Silver, & Wortman, 1993; Parkes & Weiss, 1983), cancer (Taylor, Lichtman, & Wood, 1984), severe burns (Kiecolt-Glaser & Williams, 1987), stroke (Thompson, 1991), rape (Burgess & Holmstrom, 1979), and spinal cord injury (Bulman & Wortman, 1977; Silver, 1982). Such a comprehensive and varied list suggests that searching for meaning may be a general response to severe, unexpected negative life events.

Different Notions of Meaning

The need for meaning has been so frequently observed and so urgently pursued by individuals coping with such events that a number of theorists have suggested that finding meaning is critical for successful adjustment. For instance, Moos and Schaefer (1986) argued that "when a death occurs, the loss must be accepted intellectually and somehow explained. Victims of disaster must appraise their personal losses and try to imbue their experience . . . with an acceptable meaning" (p. 11). Likewise, Gilbert (1997) claimed that "attributing meaning to loss is essential to grief resolution" (p. 103). In fact, many descriptive articles in the clinical literature have suggested that therapists should assist the client in a search for meaning in the loss (e.g., Brown, 1993; Frankl, 1969; Romanoff, 1993).

One problem with this claim, however, is that meaning is not clearly and consistently defined. Different writers have different notions of what constitutes meaning, and some notions of meaning are not clearly articulated. Indeed, Viktor Frankl, a leading proponent of the therapeutic importance of meaning making, suggested that meaning is sometimes obtained at an emotional level (as when one feels at one with the universe; see, e.g., Frankl, 1969). Some theorists and researchers define *meaning* in terms of one's ability to develop new goals and purpose or to reconstruct a sense of self that incorporates the significance of the negative experience (e.g., Thompson & Janigian, 1988). From this perspective, people who have found meaning are those who report that they have grown in important ways as a result of their experience, have been transformed by the experience, or have revised (for the better) their philosophy and attitudes toward life (Edmonds & Hooker, 1992; Schaefer & Moos, 1992; Tedeschi & Calhoun, 1995). For instance, Taylor and her colleagues have suggested that people find meaning by considering the positive implications or benefits that have accrued from their experience with trauma or loss and that these positive meanings serve to mitigate the negative aspects of the experience and thus to maintain self-esteem (Taylor, 1983; Taylor et al., 1984; Updegraff & Taylor, in press).

It is surprising that numerous studies suggest that benefits are commonly reported following trauma and loss, with most studies indicating that between 75% and 90% of participants report such benefits (e.g., Collins, Taylor, & Skokan, 1990; Davis et al., 1998; Lehman et al., 1993; Park et al., 1996; Taylor et al., 1984). Clearly not all of these reported benefits represent "growth" or "transformation," and separating that which is "growth" from that which is not represents a significant task for researchers to address.

Other researchers have defined *meaning* in terms of the explanation that one comes up with for the event (Burgess & Holmstrom, 1979; Davis & Nolen-Hoeksema, in press; Davis et al., 2000; Janoff-Bulman, 1992; McIntosh et al., 1993; Tait & Silver, 1989). For instance, people sometimes report making sense of loss by attributing it to God's will, by perceiving the event as fated or as in some way predictable. In trying to make sense of the event one is trying to interpret it as being consistent (or at least not inconsistent) with one's worldview, or fundamental beliefs about how and why such events occur (Davis & Nolen-Hoeksema, in press; Janoff-Bulman, 1992; Parkes, 1975).

Studies that have asked respondents who are coping with loss or trauma whether they have been able to make sense of (or find meaning in) their event report that most people do not find meaning, even many years after the event (Davis et al., 2000; Silver et al., 1983; Thompson, 1991). Some studies also indicate that a persistent desire to find meaning is a sign of protracted distress (Davis et al., 2000; Nolen-Hoeksema, McBride, & Larson, 1997).

Processes of Meaning Making: Making Sense of Loss

In a study of caregivers who had lost a loved one following a long illness, my colleagues and I (Davis et al., 1998) were able to demonstrate that each of these two construals of meaning (i.e., meaning as finding benefits and meaning as making sense of the loss) uniquely predicted emotional adjustment to the loss both concurrently and prospectively. In this study caregivers were interviewed prior to their loss and then 6, 13, and 18 months after the loss. At each postloss interview, participants were asked if they had been able to make sense of the loss and if any benefits had accrued from the experience.

In this study (Davis et al., 1998), most of our participants had both made sense of the death and found some benefit from the experience by the 6-month postloss interview. Those who reported that they had made some sense of the death typically indicated that (a) the death had been predictable in some way (e.g., as a logical consequence to some set of behaviors or factors in the deceased person's life), (b) it was consistent with the caregiver's perspective on life, or (c) religious or spiritual (afterlife) beliefs provided meaning. When people indicated that they could not make sense of the loss they often indicated that the death seemed unfair, unjust, or random. For instance, one caregiver who could not make sense of her mother's death described her concern in the following terms:

> Here was [my mother] who spiritually had a God that she believed in very strongly; lived her life according to what she felt were good religious beliefs; was known as everybody's angel; always there for people. Why she suffered as she did, and why she had to experience death in a very slow, painful way was the thing I couldn't accept.

This example, and many others offered by the participants, suggests that people appear to make sense of their loss by considering the event in terms of existing worldviews. If the loss is consistent with these worldviews (such that it is perceived as predictable, the natural end to a long life, or consistent with deeply held religious or philosophical principles about life and death), then making sense does not appear to represent a significant coping issue for the caregiver. As one participant in our study said, "You never question God."

Respondents unable to make sense of the death by 6 months postloss were unlikely to do so subsequently, and those who did find meaning later in the process tended to report meanings that suggested that their worldviews were undergoing revision. When asked at 13 months postloss if she were able to make sense of her mother's death, one respondent told us,

> I think so. In some ways it seems it doesn't make sense, like there is no sense. But that is what life is all about—that people are here for just a short time, and you don't know how long people are going to be here. . . . It's not exactly fair. It doesn't seem like there's any sense to it, in a way. It just kind of is the way it is. And for whatever reason, she needed to die.

This quote, and others like it, suggest that respondents who are unable to incorporate the event into their prior worldview cope with this inconsistency by attempting to change their worldview to incorporate the event. In the case cited above, the caregiver appears to be acknowledging that events in this world need not make sense, that life is sometimes unfair and unjust. Coping with the inconsistency between the data of the event and one's view of the world by changing one's worldview may not be easy, and the data indicate that finding meaning for the first time at this later point in time is not significantly correlated with changes in emotional adjustment to the loss (Davis et al., 1998).

Processes of Meaning Making: Finding Benefits

In contrast to their explanations for making sense of the loss, participants' accounts of the benefits or positives that followed from the loss experience typically fell into three categories: that the event (a) led to a growth in character, (b) a gain in perspective, and (c) a strengthening of relationships. These quotes from our respondents (Davis et al., 1998; Nolen-Hoeksema & Larson, 1999) illustrate these three themes, respectively.

> I saw myself acting a role of competence, where I had to pull on all my resources just to get through sometimes. . . . So I came away with a feeling of competence and strength, and gratitude. The gratitude not for having to go through it—I would never have asked for it—but I can see how the experience was a real benefit to me. I was forced to grow.
>
> In that having your health and living life to its fullest is a real blessing. I appreciate my family, friends, nature, life in general. I see a goodness in people. . . . It made me more mature.
>
> I learned that when you love someone, the relationship is so important. It's enhanced my relationship with other people because I realize that time is so important, and you can waste so much effort on small, insignificant events and feelings. (See also Davis et al., 1998, p. 566; Nolen-Hoeksema & Larson, 1999, pp. 145–150.)

Consistent with other studies of benefit finding, we observed that between 70% and 80% of caregivers reported perceiving benefits at each wave (e.g., Calhoun & Tedeschi, 1990; Edmonds & Hooker, 1992; Lehman et al., 1993; Yalom & Lieberman, 1991). Moreover, the types of benefits that caregivers in our study (Davis et. al, 1998) reported were very similar to those reported not only in other bereavement studies (e.g., Lehman et al., 1993) but also in studies of people coping with other adversities (e.g., Collins et al., 1990; McMillen, Smith, & Fisher, 1997; Park et al., 1996; Taylor, Kemeny, Reed, & Aspinwall, 1991).

Whether the bereaved caregiver was able to find benefit in the loss was not significantly associated with his or her ability to make sense of it. Thus benefit finding is not merely the task of those who failed to make sense of the event, and it appears that making sense of the death does not seem to aid one in deriving benefit. Moreover, the factors that predict being able to make sense of the loss do not predict one's ability to find some benefit (Davis et al., 1998). Finding benefit in adversity seems to reflect a different set of processes.

Unlike the process of making sense of loss, finding benefit appears to have little to do with the event itself, aside from the event serving as the catalyst for the process. For instance, regardless of the precipitating event (e.g., loss vs. diagnosis of a life-threatening illness), the benefits that people report, although uniquely expressed, typically fall into one of three categories: (a) growth in character; (b) change in life perspective, or (c) strengthened relationships or an increased sense of connectedness with others (see, e.g., McMillen et al., 1997; Park et al., 1996; Schaefer & Moos, 1992; Tedeschi & Calhoun, 1996; Updegraff & Taylor, in press). That the same categories of response come up more or less consistently regardless of the event type suggests that the perceived benefits have more to do with one's experience with adversity or suffering in general than with the particular characteristics of the adversity.

The data also suggest that whereas the relation of making sense to changes in emotional adjustment weakened with time since the loss, the relation of finding benefit to changes in emotional adjustment strengthened with time since the loss (see Davis & Nolen-Hoeksema, in press)—that is, with regard to making sense of the death, only those who reported making sense within the first 6 months of the loss evidenced significant improvement in adjustment over the first year of the loss. On the other hand, the effect for finding benefit grew stronger with time (Davis et al., 1998).

These data support the argument that sense making and benefit finding represent two distinct processes in the meaning-making process and suggest that they represent two distinguishable psychological issues for the bereaved person. Whereas making sense of loss involves the task of maintaining or rebuilding threatened worldviews, finding benefit seems to involve the task of maintaining or rebuilding a threatened sense of self. In many cases, the loss has forced people to redefine key aspects of their sense of self. As a widow in our study put it,

> I think that when you lose a loved one, it's a rebirth for yourself. You can't always dwell on the loss of the loved one. You have to look forward to what you are going to do with your life now—who you are as a single person, which is very disturbing. . . . And it's a whole new experience, learning who you are, knowing who you are as a single person. That's one of the hard parts about being a widow or widower. A lot of people don't have time to think of who they are, because they're always attached to someone. (Nolen-Hoeksema & Larson, 1999, p. 149)

Whether the benefit that people report involves a change in identity, a change in how one perceives one's abilities (e.g., as able to cope with an event as significant as this), or a change in the importance or value one attributes to positive relationships, the focus tends to be on the sense of self. People in our study unable to find positive aspects to the event sometimes seemed to suggest that they were unwilling to give up the aspect of the self that has been lost. As one widower said,

> I frankly can find no good has come out of her death. My situation has improved over what it would have been were she alive. . . . I wouldn't own a house, I wouldn't have $50,000 in the bank. . . . Honestly, I'd prefer not to have that and to have her alive. (Nolen-Hoeksema & Larson, 1999, p. 157)

Linking the Two Meaning-Making Processes

Although making sense of loss and finding benefit in the experience are not statistically related, it is nevertheless conceivable that the two issues are conceptually related. Specifically, I suspect that when people are unable to make sense of their loss some are able to compensate somewhat for the senselessness by reinterpreting the event as being in some ways positive. Focusing on what good has come of the experience may not help one make sense of the loss as much as it distracts one from it. Learning something new about oneself, or about the value of relationships, for instance, does not explain why the loss happened or what purpose was served by it. But such lessons learned may take some of the pain of suffering away from not understanding why.

In fact, research on the meaning-making efforts of parents coping with the loss of their baby to sudden infant death syndrome suggests that it is not so much making sense of the loss that alleviates distress as it is becoming less interested in the issue (Davis et al., 2000). In this 18-month longitudinal study we found that over the length of the study, less than half of the parents reported being able to make any sense of their baby's death, with most of those finding meaning reporting so in the first interview, approximately

3 weeks postloss. Whereas making some sense of the death by the first interview was associated with lower levels of emotional distress (relative to those searching for meaning but unable to find any at this time), finding meaning for the first time subsequently was not significantly associated with decrements in emotional distress. However, one factor that consistently predicted emotional adjustment over the length of the study was the extent to which parents were searching to make sense of the loss: The more parents searched to make some sense of their loss, the greater was their level of distress.

It is significant that making sense of the baby's death at the first interview did not put the issue to rest among these parents. Those who reported finding meaning early on were just as likely to be still searching for meaning at 18 months postloss as were those who searched but were unable to find meaning at the first interview. Thus it is not the case that people generally find meaning and then move on to other issues; many continue to search for meaning for years afterward (see, e.g., Silver et al., 1983; Tait & Silver, 1989). Those reporting the least emotional distress over the course of this study were those least interested in making sense of the death.

Although thus far there are no data to demonstrate this, one factor that may lead people to be less concerned with the need for meaning is their ability to find a redeeming feature or benefit in the experience with the loss. Whether such perceived benefits serve primarily to distract one from the meaninglessness of the event or serve a compensatory function remains to be determined. Having learned something important about oneself, or about what is important in life, may compensate for or ease the need to make sense of a senseless event (cf. Janoff-Bulman & Frantz, 1997). Also, to the extent that finding benefits might be a precursor of growth and adjustment, a persistent and hopelessly unsatisfied need for meaning may prevent people from constructing and elaborating on new perspectives, new goals, and new identities. Thus, excessive focus on a lack of meaning may inhibit growth and healing.

CONCLUSION

One of the main goals of my research has been to understand some of the common psychological issues that people face when they experience undesirable life events. The two issues that I have described here—counterfactual thoughts and the need for meaning—may or may not be among the most important issues that people face. I do not mean to suggest that all people coping with loss struggle with these issues. Indeed, for some these are not issues at all (see, e.g., Davis et al., 2000). For many, however, the haunting counterfactual thoughts and a pervading sense of meaningless are perceived as major issues and impediments to the healing process. Although much of my research so far has been oriented toward identifying and understanding these issues, future research will need to focus on how people attempt to come to terms with them.

Understanding how people come to terms with these issues is obviously a matter of clinical importance, but it also has significant implications for theory in social and personality psychology. How people resolve these issues not only helps one to understand some of the variation in emotional adjustment and resilience in the face of loss and trauma, but it also illuminates an understanding of the dynamics of coping and personality development (Miller & C'deBaca, 1994). For instance, by understanding the processes by which people come to grow from their trauma and loss experience one stands to learn much about the motivation for and function of narrative reconstructions of self and the world (cf. McAdams, 1996; Neimeyer, 2000). McAdams (1996) argued, for instance, that one's conception of one's identity is largely based on making a coherent story of one's past experiences, present situation, and future goals (see also Baumeister, 1989; Thompson & Janigian, 1988). Because trauma and loss tend to figure prominently in these narratives, and because such events often lead to significant changes in how people see themselves and the world in which they live, understanding meaning-making processes are likely to inform (and be informed by) theory and research on personality development.

Our study of distressingly persistent counterfactual thoughts similarly draws from and has implications for broader theory. Elsewhere, my colleagues and I have described counterfactuals as a special type of ruminative thought (Davis et al., 1995). Such thoughts have unique emotional consequences and perhaps, at times, a unique function (see Taylor & Schneider, 1989). Recent developments in our knowledge of ruminative thought may illuminate the processes behind counterfactual thoughts and, perhaps more important, may lead to methods of curbing them (e.g., Koole, Smeets, van Knippenberg, & Dijksterhuis, 1999; Lyubomirsky et al., 1999).

The issues that I have described are no doubt part of what others have referred to as *working through* (Horowitz, 1976) or *cognitive processing* (e.g., Creamer, Burgess, & Pattison, 1992; Lepore et al., 1996). One might also argue that these issues fall under the rubric of "grief." My colleagues and I have shown elsewhere that counterfactual thoughts and concern with issues of meaning are not merely symptoms of depression or emotional distress (Davis et al., 1995, 1998). Still, one might ask if anything is gained by pulling out these issues and putting them under the microscope. That these issues in particular stand out in clinical reports, as well as in people's own accounts of their trauma and loss experience, suggests that they have special importance.

By studying these issues in isolation one takes the risk of decontextualizing them and losing sight of the complex dynamics among grief processes. Indeed, my own approach to these issues has largely ignored the social environment. However, as we gradually turn our attention from a description of these issues to the ways people cope with them we are apt to find ourselves reintegrating them into the intrapersonal and interpersonal dynamics of the larger processes of healing, and it is in this process of reintegration that much more will be learned about the dynamic interactions among these personal issues, coping behavior, and personality processes.

REFERENCES

Abramson, L. Y., Metalsky, G. I., & Alloy, L. B. (1989). Hopelessness theory: A theory-based subtype of depression. *Psychological Review, 96*, 358–372.

Antonovsky, A. (1987). *Unraveling the mystery of health.* San Francisco: Jossey-Bass.

Baumeister, R. F. (1989). The problem of life's meaning. In D. M. Buss & N. Cantor (Eds.), *Personality psychology: Recent trends and emerging directions* (pp. 138–148). New York: Springer-Verlag.

Boninger, D. S., Gleicher, F., & Strathman, A. (1994). Counterfactual thinking: From what might have been to what may be. *Journal of Personality and Social Psychology, 67*, 297–307.

Brown, Y. (1993). Perinatal loss: A framework for practice. *Health Care for Women International, 15*, 469–479.

Bulman, R. J., & Wortman, C. B. (1977). Attributions of blame and coping in the "real world": Severe accident victims react to their lot. *Journal of Personality and Social Psychology, 35*, 351–363.

Burgess, A. W., & Holmstrom, L. L. (1979). Adaptive strategies and recovery from rape. *American Journal of Psychiatry, 136*, 1278–1282.

Calhoun, L. G., & Tedeschi, R. G. (1990). Positive aspects of critical life problems: Recollections of grief. *Omega, 20*, 265–272.

Capps, L., & Bonanno, G. A. (in press). Narrating bereavement: Thematic and grammatical predictors of adjustment to loss. *Discourse Processes.*

Carver, C. S. (1998). Resilience and thriving: Issues, models, and linkages. *Journal of Social Issues, 54*, 245–266.

Carver, C. S., Scheier, M. F., & Weintraub, J. K. (1989). Assessing coping strategies: A theoretically based approach. *Journal of Personality and Social Psychology, 56*, 267–283.

Chodoff, P., Friedman, S. B., & Hamburg, D. A. (1964). Stress, defenses and coping behavior: Observations in parents of children with malignant disease. *American Journal of Psychiatry, 120*, 743–749.

Cleiren, M. P. H. D. (1993). *Bereavement and adaptation: A comparative study of the aftermath of death.* Washington, DC: Hemisphere.

Cohen, S., & Wills, T. A. (1985). Stress, social support, and the buffering hypothesis. *Psychological Bulletin, 98*, 310–357.

Collins, R. L., Taylor, S. E., & Skokan, L. A. (1990). A better world or a shattered vision? Changes in life perspective following victimization. *Social Cognition, 8,* 263–285.

Coyne, J. C., & Gottlieb, B. H. (1996). The mismeasure of coping by checklist. *Journal of Personality, 64,* 959–991.

Creamer, M., Burgess, P., & Pattison, P. (1992). Reaction to trauma: A cognitive processing model. *Journal of Abnormal Psychology, 101,* 452–459.

Davis, C. G., & Lehman, D. R. (1995). Counterfactual thinking and coping with traumatic life events. In N. J. Roese & J. M. Olson (Eds.), *What might have been: The social psychology of counterfactual thinking* (pp. 353–374). Mahwah, NJ: Erlbaum.

Davis, C. G., Lehman, D. R., Silver, R. C., Wortman, C. B., & Ellard, J. H. (1996). Self-blame following a traumatic life event: The role of perceived avoidability. *Personality and Social Psychology Bulletin, 22,* 557–567.

Davis, C. G., Lehman, D. R., Wortman, C. B., Silver, R. C., & Thompson, S. C. (1995). The undoing of traumatic life events. *Personality and Social Psychology Bulletin, 21,* 109–124.

Davis, C. G., & Nolen-Hoeksema, S. (in press). Loss and meaning: How do people make sense of loss? *American Behavioral Scientist.*

Davis, C. G., Nolen-Hoeksema, S., & Larson, J. (1998). Making sense of loss and benefiting from the experience: Two construals of meaning. *Journal of Personality and Social Psychology, 75,* 561–574.

Davis, C. G., Wortman, C. B., Lehman, D. R., & Silver, R. C. (2000). Searching for meaning in loss: Are clinical assumptions correct? *Death Studies, 24,* 497–540.

de Vries, B., Davis, C. G., Wortman, C. B., & Lehman, D. R. (1997). Long-term psychological and somatic consequences of later life parental bereavement. *Omega, 35,* 97–117.

Edmonds, S., & Hooker, K. (1992). Perceived changes in life meaning following bereavement. *Omega, 25,* 307–318.

Erikson, K. T. (1976). *Everything in its path: Destruction of a community in the Buffalo Creek flood.* New York: Simon & Schuster.

Frankl, V. E. (1969). *The will to meaning: Foundations and applications of logotherapy.* New York: New American Library.

Gilbert, K. R. (1997). Couple coping with death of a child. In C. R. Figley & B. E. Bride (Eds.), *The traumatology of grieving* (pp. 101–121). Washington, DC: Taylor & Francis.

Gluhoski, V. L., & Wortman, C. B. (1996). The impact of trauma on world views. *Journal of Social and Clinical Psychology, 15,* 417–429.

Horowitz, M. J. (1976). *Stress response syndromes.* New York: Aronson.

Janoff-Bulman, R. (1992). *Shattered assumptions: Towards a new psychology of trauma.* New York: Free Press.

Janoff-Bulman, R., & Frantz, C. M. (1997). The impact of trauma on meaning: From meaningless world to meaningful life. In M. Power & C. R. Brewin (Eds.),

The transformation of meaning in psychological therapies (pp. 91–106). New York: Wiley.

Kessler, R. C., Davis, C. G., & Kendler, K. S. (1997). Childhood adversity and adult psychiatric disorder in the U.S. National Comorbidity Survey. *Psychological Medicine, 27,* 1101–1119.

Kiecolt-Glaser, J. K., & Williams, D. A. (1987). Self-blame, compliance, and distress among burn patients. *Journal of Personality and Social Psychology, 53,* 187–193.

Koole, S. L., Smeets, K., van Knippenberg, A., & Dijksterhuis, A. (1999). The cessation of rumination through self-affirmation. *Journal of Personality and Social Psychology, 77,* 111–125.

Lazarus, R. S., & Folkman, S. (1984). *Stress, appraisal, and coping.* New York: Springer.

Lehman, D. R., Davis, C. G., DeLongis, A., Wortman, C. B., Bluck, S., Mandel, D., & Ellard, J. H. (1993). Positive and negative life changes following bereavement and their relations to adjustment. *Journal of Social and Clinical Psychology, 12,* 90–112.

Lehman, D. R., Wortman, C. B., & Williams, A. F. (1987). Long-term effects of losing a spouse or child in a motor vehicle crash. *Journal of Personality and Social Psychology, 52,* 218–231.

Lepore, S. J., Silver, R. C., Wortman, C. B., & Wayment, H. A. (1996). Social constraints, intrusive thoughts, and depressive symptoms among bereaved mothers. *Journal of Personality and Social Psychology, 70,* 271–282.

Lyubomirsky, S., Tucker, K. L., Caldwell, N. D., & Berg, K. (1999). Why ruminators are poor problem solvers: Clues from the phenomenology of dysphoric rumination. *Journal of Personality and Social Psychology, 77,* 1041–1060.

McAdams, D. P. (1996). Personality, modernity, and the storied self: A contemporary framework for studying persons. *Psychological Inquiry, 7,* 295–321.

McIntosh, D. N., Silver, R. C., & Wortman, C. B. (1993). Religion's role in adjustment to a negative life event: Coping with the loss of a child. *Journal of Personality and Social Psychology, 65,* 812–821.

McMillen, J. C., Smith, E. M., & Fisher, R. H. (1997). Perceived benefit and mental health after three types of disaster. *Journal of Consulting and Clinical Psychology, 65,* 733–739.

Metalsky, G. I., Abramson, L. Y., Seligman, M. E. P., Semmel, A., & Peterson, C. (1982). Vulnerability to depressive mood reactions: Toward a more powerful test of the diathesis–stress and causal mediation components of the reformulated theory of depression. *Journal of Personality and Social Psychology, 52,* 386–393.

Miller, W. R., & C'deBaca, J. (1994). Quantum change: Toward a psychology of transformation. In T. F. Heatherton & J. L. Weinberger (Eds.), *Can personality change?* (pp. 253–280). Washington, DC: American Psychological Association.

Moos, R. H., & Schaefer, J. A. (1986). Life transitions and crises: A conceptual overview. In R. H. Moos (Ed.), *Coping with life crises: An integrated approach* (pp. 3–28). New York: Plenum.

Neimeyer, R. A. (2000). Narrative disruptions in the construction of self. In R. A. Neimeyer & J. Raskin (Eds.), *Constructions of disorder* (pp. 207–242). Washington, DC: American Psychological Association.

Neimeyer, R. A. (2000). Searching for the meaning of meaning: Grief therapy and the process of reconstruction. *Death Studies, 24,* 541–558.

Nolen-Hoeksema, S., & Davis, C. G. (1999). "Thanks for sharing that": Ruminators and their social support networks. *Journal of Personality and Social Psychology, 77,* 801–814.

Nolen-Hoeksema, S., & Larson, J. (1999). *Coping with loss.* Mahwah, NJ: Erlbaum.

Nolen-Hoeksema, S., Larson, J., & Grayson, C. (1999). Explaining gender differences in depressive symptoms. *Journal of Personality and Social Psychology, 77,* 1061–1072.

Nolen-Hoeksema, S., McBride, A., & Larson, J. (1997). Rumination and psychological distress among bereaved partners. *Journal of Personality and Social Psychology, 72,* 855–862.

Nolen-Hoeksema, S., & Morrow, J. (1991). A prospective study of depression and posttraumatic stress symptoms after a natural disaster: The 1989 Loma Prieta earthquake. *Journal of Personality and Social Psychology, 61,* 115–121.

Norris, F. H., & Kaniasty, K. (1991). The psychological experience of crime: A test of the mediating role of beliefs in explaining the distress of victims. *Journal of Social and Clinical Psychology, 10,* 239–261.

Park, C. L., Cohen, L. H., & Murch, R. L. (1996). Assessment and prediction of stress-related growth. *Journal of Personality, 64,* 71–105.

Parker, J. D., Endler, N. S., & Bagby, R. M. (1993). If it changes it might be unstable: Examining the factor structure of the Ways of Coping Questionnaire. *Psychological Assessment, 5,* 361–368.

Parkes, C. M. (1975). What becomes of redundant world models? A contribution to the study of adaptation to change. *British Journal of Medical Psychology, 48,* 131–137.

Parkes, C. M., & Weiss, R. S. (1983). *Recovery from bereavement.* New York: Basic Books.

Pennebaker, J. W. (1993). Social mechanisms of constraint. In D. M. Wegner & J. W. Pennebaker (Eds.), *Handbook of mental control* (pp. 200–219). Englewood Cliffs, NJ: Prentice Hall.

Peterson, C., & Seligman, M. E. P. (1984). Causal explanations as a risk factor for depression: Theory and evidence. *Psychological Review, 91,* 347–374.

Pynoos, R. S., Goenjian, A., Tashjian, M., Karakashian, M., Manjikian, R., Manoukian, G., Steinberg, A. M., & Fairbancks, L. A. (1993). Post-traumatic stress reactions in children after the Armenian earthquake. *British Journal of Psychiatry, 163,* 239–247.

Rachman, S. J. (1981). Unwanted intrusive cognitions. *Advances in Behavioral Research and Therapy, 3,* 89–99.

Romanoff, B. D. (1993). When a child dies: Special considerations for providing mental health counseling for bereaved parents. *Journal of Mental Health Counseling, 15,* 384–393.

Schaefer, J. A., & Moos, R. H. (1992). Life crisis and personal growth. In B. N.

Carpenter (Ed.), *Personal coping: Theory, research, and application* (pp. 149–170). Westport, CT: Praeger.

Silver, R. L. (1982). *Coping with an undesirable life event: A study of early reactions to physical disability.* Unpublished doctoral dissertation. Northwestern University.

Silver, R. L., Boon, C., & Stones, M. H. (1983). Searching for meaning in misfortune: Making sense of incest. *Journal of Social Issues, 39,* 81–102.

Tait, R., & Silver, R. C. (1989). Coming to terms with major negative life events. In J. S. Uleman & J. A. Bargh (Eds.), *Unintended thought* (pp. 351–381). New York: Guilford Press.

Taylor, S. E. (1983). Adjusting to threatening events: A theory of cognitive adaptation. *American Psychologist, 38,* 1161–1173.

Taylor, S. E., Kemeny, M. E., Reed, G. M., & Aspinwall, L. G. (1991). Assault on the self: Positive illusions and adjustment to threatening events. In J. Strauss & G. R. Goethals (Eds.), *The self: Interdisciplinary approaches* (pp. 239–254). New York: Springer-Verlag.

Taylor, S. E., Lichtman, R. R., & Wood, J. V. (1984). Attributions, beliefs about control, and adjustment to breast cancer. *Journal of Personality and Social Psychology, 46,* 489–502.

Taylor, S. E., & Schneider, S. K. (1989). Coping and the simulation of events. *Social Cognition, 7,* 174–194.

Tedeschi, R. G., & Calhoun, L. G. (1995). Trauma and transformation: *Growing in the aftermath of suffering.* Thousand Oaks, CA: Sage.

Tedeschi, R. G., & Calhoun, L. G. (1996). The Posttraumatic Growth Inventory: Measuring the positive legacy of trauma. *Journal of Traumatic Stress, 9,* 455–471.

Tedeschi, R. G., Park, C. L., & Calhoun, L. G. (1998). Posttraumatic growth: Conceptual issues. In R. G. Tedeschi, C. L. Parks, & L. G. Calhoun (Eds.), *Posttraumatic growth: Positive changes in the aftermath of crisis* (pp. 1–22). Mahwah, NJ: Erlbaum.

Thompson, S. C. (1991). The search for meaning following a stroke. *Basic and Applied Social Psychology, 12,* 81–96.

Thompson, S. C., & Janigian, A. S. (1988). Life schemes: A framework for understanding the search for meaning. *Journal of Social and Clinical Psychology, 7,* 260–280.

Turner, R. J., & Lloyd, D. A. (1995). Lifetime traumas and mental health: The significance of cumulative adversity. *Journal of Health and Social Behavior, 36,* 360–376.

Updegraff, J. A., & Taylor, S. E. (in press). From vulnerability to growth: Positive and negative effects of stressful life events. In J. Harvey & E. Miller (Eds.), *Handbook of loss and trauma.* New York: Brunner/Mazel.

Valentiner, D. P., Holahan, C. J., & Moos, R. H. (1994). Social support, appraisals of event controllability, and coping: An integrative model. *Journal of Personality and Social Psychology, 66,* 1094–1102.

Wegner, D. M. (1994). Ironic processes of mental control. *Psychological Review, 101,* 34–52.

Wegner, D. M., & Schneider, D. J. (1989). Mental control: The war of ghosts in the machine. In J. S. Uleman & J. A. Bargh (Eds.), *Unintended thought* (pp. 287–305). New York: Guilford Press.

Weiss, R. S. (1988). Loss and recovery. *Journal of Social Issues, 44*(3), 37–52.

Yalom, I. D., & Lieberman, M. A. (1991). Bereavement and heightened existential awareness. *Psychiatry, 54,* 334–345.

8

POSTTRAUMATIC GROWTH: THE POSITIVE LESSONS OF LOSS

LAWRENCE G. CALHOUN AND RICHARD G. TEDESCHI

In response to a question about how a motor vehicle accident had affected him, the man indicated that the accident, which led to his paralysis, "was probably the best thing that ever happened to me" (Tedeschi & Calhoun, 1995, p. 1). He regarded his struggle with the aftermath of the accident as a process that changed him and that had made him grow in ways that would not otherwise have been possible. The experience of the man, whom we have called "Jerry," of recognizing major gains from a major loss is not unique; neither is it a recently identified phenomenon.

Religious, philosophical, and folk traditions have for thousands of years recognized the possibility that the struggle with major losses in life can be the source of enhanced meaning in life and the impetus for positive change. In some traditional religious accounts—for example, the story of Job in the Christian Old Testament—suffering is paradoxically a result of special favor in the eye of God. In some Islamic traditions, suffering is viewed as instrumental for the purposes of God. The suffering of Jesus on the cross is interpreted in Christian tradition as the means by which believers are spared the eternal punishment and suffering they justly deserve.

Systematic interest by behavioral scientists and clinicians in this phenomenon is considerably more recent. In articulating the fundamentals of crisis intervention theory, Gerald Caplan (1964) described how life crises could upset the individual's psychological equilibrium. In the process of trying to regain homeostasis, if the individual could be assisted in successfully coping with the crisis, there was the possibility that he or she could actually benefit from the difficulty by developing new and better adaptive strategies. Finkel (1974) examined life events that produced positive changes and found that some of those events were actually negative. It has been only in the past few years, however, that systematic attempts have been made to examine the positive changes resulting from the struggle with major losses (Aldwin, 1994; O'Leary & Ickovics, 1995; Tedeschi & Calhoun, 1995, 1996).

We refer to gains that can result from the struggle with loss as *posttraumatic growth*, positive change that the individual experiences as a result of the struggle with a major loss or trauma. In this chapter we first provide a broad picture of the domains of posttraumatic growth and a brief overview of the process by which posttraumatic growth occurs. We then discuss some of the questions that research might profitably address, and we discuss some implications for clinicians interested in the process of posttraumatic growth in their clients. For more comprehensive reviews of posttraumatic growth, we refer our readers to Calhoun and Tedeschi (1999), Tedeschi and Calhoun (1995), and Tedeschi, Park, and Calhoun (1998).

POSTTRAUMATIC GROWTH

Before we begin the description of the ways in which individuals can be positively changed by their struggle with loss, an obvious but necessary reminder is needed. Major life trauma and loss can produce high levels of psychological distress; can lead to significant impairment in adjustment; and, for some people, can increase the risk of serious psychiatric symptomatology and of physical problems and complaints (Hodgkinson & Stewart, 1991). For many people, however, loss can also lead to significant gain, along with the experience of distress.

The phenomenon of posttraumatic growth has been observed at least in a significant minority (Silver, Boon, & Stones, 1983), and sometimes in the vast majority (Calhoun &Tedeschi, 1989–1990), of people who have experienced a variety of different kinds of loss. Posttraumatic growth has been reported by significant numbers of people who have encountered life challenges as diverse as the death of a child, the death of a spouse or parent, breast cancer, intense military combat, motor vehicle accidents, house fires, floods, terminal illness, heart attacks, chronic illness, divorce, sexual assault, and job loss (Tedeschi & Calhoun, 1995). The growth experienced tends to fall into three broad domains: changed sense of self, changed relationships, and changed philosophy of life.

Changed Sense of Self

The growth reported in this domain is paradoxical. Individuals who have experienced major losses tend to have an increased sense of their vulnerability to subsequent loss (Janoff-Bulman, 1992), but there can be a concomitant increase in the degree to which individuals view themselves as stronger and more capable (Tedeschi & Calhoun, 1995). The increased sense of vulnerability has been viewed as a negative change, and for most people it seems likely to be. However, for some individuals—for example, young men who routinely engage in highly dangerous actions simply for the sport of it—the enhanced estimate that harm can befall them may serve as an adaptive corrective device.

Closely connected to an increased perception of vulnerability can be an increased sense that life is fragile and hence very precious. "I appreciate each day much more now. I am so lucky just to be alive" is a common response in people who have experienced significant loss. It is in the general area of greater perceived self-competence, however, that survivors of loss articulate a changed sense of self.

A large majority of a group of widows who were interviewed several months after their husbands' deaths reported that an increased sense of independence and self-confidence had resulted from having to deal with the situation with which they had been forced to struggle (Calhoun & Tedeschi, 1989–1990). One of the respondents who was in her 60s, for example, proudly reported that she had learned how to drive and no longer relied on others for transportation. Other studies suggest that older widows tend to report increases in self-efficacy, self-reliance, and a stronger self-image compared to when their husbands were still living (Lopata, 1973; Tedeschi, 1999; Thomas, DiGiulio, & Sheehan, 1991).

Studies of people coping with other losses and traumas have reported similar patterns of findings. Not all, but a substantial percentage, of people who have faced a major loss view themselves as stronger simply because they have been able to go on, to continue in spite of the loss (Aldwin, Levenson, & Spiro, 1994; Andreasen & Norris, 1972). People who have survived the aftermath of floods, divorce, combat, sexual assault, death of a loved one, or any other major loss may well increase their estimates of their strength and resilience. The perception is that if they can survive "that," then they can survive just about anything that life can send their way.

Changed Relationships

Survivors of loss often report that their experience has led them to feel an increased connectedness with others and a deepened sense of empathy and the ability to connect emotionally with other people (Tedeschi & Calhoun, 1995). For example, some people report an increase in closeness in family relationships in the struggle to cope with a death in the family (Lehman et al., 1993). This is not a universal experience—some individuals report a worsening or breaking of social bonds in the struggle with loss.

An experienced change in one's ability to empathize and sympathize with other people, particularly with those who also experience loss, has also been reported by people who have faced traumatic circumstances. Although data are only suggestive, it is possible that this increased sense of compassion for others who suffer may reveal itself in a greater probability of engaging in altruistic behavior (Wuthnow, 1991).

An increase in the ability to express emotions and engage in self-disclosure is also found among people who have experienced loss. Self-disclosure tends to correlate positively with general indexes of well-being (Pennebaker, 1995), but reactions by others to self-disclosure can vary and are sometimes neither helpful nor positive (Dakof & Taylor, 1990). Nevertheless, individuals who report this increased freedom to express themselves tend to regard it as a positive change, and self-disclosure can provide an opportunity for an individual to try out new behaviors with appropriate people in his or her support system (Calhoun & Tedeschi, 1989–1990). The new expressive behaviors, in turn, can provide the chance for greater intimacy with others, enhancing the perception of greater interpersonal closeness.

Loss typically produces significant distress for most people, and the greater facility in self-disclosure, coupled with a desire to share one's own experience, can lead to a kind of "empathy training" (Tedeschi, 1999), allowing survivors of loss a chance to become more closely connected to significant others.

Existential and Spiritual Growth

For some people the experience of loss is so devastating and incomprehensible that their response is to feel the "bitterness of being forsaken by God" (Herman, 1997, p. 94). Some may experience an increase in cynicism and a loss of religious commitment (Schwartzberg & Janoff-Bulman, 1991), and others may experience no change in religious beliefs in the aftermath of loss (Overcash, Calhoun, Tedeschi, & Cann, 1996).

Some people, however, experience the struggle with loss as one in which their worldviews are challenged, severely shaken, or destroyed. The process of rebuilding the "shattered assumptions" (Janoff-Bulman, 1992), however, leads to an enhanced sense of meaning in life. For many people who are coping with major loss, the forced confrontation with the fundamental existential questions leads to an enhanced "existential awareness" (Yalom & Lieberman, 1991), and that existential awareness—for many North Americans, at least—leads to enhanced spiritual or religious life. The enhanced sense of the importance of one's spirituality may well come about after periods of struggle and doubt, but a significant proportion of people who experience loss report that their spiritual or religious lives are a more important and meaningful component of their assumptive worlds (Calhoun, Tedeschi, & Lincourt, 1992).

The transformative nature of loss, then, can be viewed as a process whereby the lives of some people are imbued with an enhanced sense of meaning and purpose. For highly salient and traumatic losses, the individual's life narrative can become divided into "before" and "after." The life after the loss, in the midst of the struggle to cope and adapt, can become a life in which the individual experiences either a new or a renewed sense that life is worthwhile and purposeful.

Posttraumatic Growth: Some Cautions

The picture of posttraumatic growth that emerges from the data is that at least some proportion of people who experience all kinds of difficult circumstances report at least some growth as a result of their struggle with the consequences of loss. It is important to remember several things about these findings, however. First, growth can manifest itself in many ways, and even people who do report growth do not necessarily experience it in all areas. Also, some people may not experience any growth at all in the aftermath of major loss. Second, the presence of growth does not mean the absence of pain and distress. Although measures of growth have been found in some studies to be positively related to measures of psychological adjustment, other studies have reported no such relation (Calhoun & Tedeschi, 1998; Park, 1998). Finally, it must be made clear that the findings on growth must not imply a rose-tinted Pollyanna view of major loss. People who experience posttraumatic growth tend to acknowledge both the positive and negative aspects of their experience. Even though some may view their loss as "the best thing that ever happened to me," it cannot be concluded that in general tragedy and loss are desirable—or necessary for development—for any human being.

POSTTRAUMATIC GROWTH FROM THE PERSPECTIVE OF RESEARCH

Researchers who adopt either a quantitative or a qualitative framework have much to examine in the area of growth following loss. In this section we offer a brief look at some promising areas for additional work (Calhoun & Tedeschi, 1998, and Tennen & Affleck, 1998, also offered a broad review of areas for investigation of posttraumatic growth).

Magnitude of Trauma

Our general assumption has been that posttraumatic growth is more likely when the loss involves a major disruption in the individual's worldview (Calhoun & Tedeschi, 1998). The data clearly show that major loss and trauma do consistently lead to significant posttraumatic growth for some people (Tedeschi & Calhoun, 1995). Is loss of traumatic proportion necessary for growth to be set in motion, however, or can relatively minor life disruptions produce similar effects? An unanswered question in the relation between the struggle with loss and the experience of growth is the magnitude of loss and trauma that is required for growth to be set in motion. What is the minimum amount of loss an individual must undergo for significant growth to occur? Certainly growth occurs in the absence of major loss, but some evidence suggests that, compared to people who report no trauma, people who have experienced major trauma experience significantly more growth (Tedeschi & Calhoun, 1996).

It seems likely that the relation between experienced growth and magnitude of loss is not linear, but the precise shape of the relation between magnitude of loss and amount of positive change is not yet clear. Do individuals who experience greater degrees of loss experience commensurately greater amounts of posttraumatic growth? One possibility is that once the minimal threshold of loss is crossed, additional degree or intensity of loss will not increase the likelihood of growth. For example, being exposed to major destruction in a war zone "a lot" may produce no more reported self-strengthening than being exposed to destruction "a little," but being exposed to destruction in any form may produce more growth than no exposure at all (Britt, Adler, & Bartone, 1998).

Another possibility, which also suggests a nonlinear relation, is that the extent of loss and the amount of growth are positively related, but only up to a point. After a certain degree of trauma and loss has occurred, additional loss and pain may no longer be related to degree of growth. Perhaps a reduced amount of growth may be reported as the level of loss becomes extreme. As the losses become more overwhelming, the ability to adapt and cope may simply be overwhelmed, and the possibility of growth may actually diminish or disappear.

Individual Differences

There also appear to be individual differences that affect the likelihood that growth will result from the struggle with loss. A variety of personal characteristics, including personality traits, gender, and characteristic adaptation strategies, appear to be related to growth outcomes (Tedeschi & Calhoun, 1996; Tennen & Affleck, 1998).

Personality

Individuals who are extraverted, open to their own subjective experiences, and who have complex belief systems may be more able to successfully cope with loss and to experience growth resulting from their struggle with it (Tedeschi & Calhoun, 1995, 1996). The nature of the relation between these kinds of personality factors and amount of posttraumatic growth still needs considerable clarification, however. Some individuals may simply be too strong, resilient, or adaptive and able successfully to negotiate even the most profound losses. One would expect that such people would have little to gain from struggling with loss, primarily because there would not be sufficient disruption or challenge for them. People at the other end of the continuum, who lack coping ability and who have little or no resilient qualities, could be overwhelmed with the loss, being unable to experience anything more than minimal growth. It would seem that those with the most to gain from the struggle with loss would be people who have sufficient resources to successfully adapt to most aspects of the loss but who, in a sense, still have room to grow. This again suggests a possible curvilinear relation, with the greater likelihood of posttraumatic growth occurring for people with moderate amounts of perceived control, extraversion, openness to experience, and similar personal qualities (Tedeschi & Calhoun, 1995; Tennen & Affleck, 1998).

Gender

The current pattern of results indicates that where differences between men and women are found following loss and trauma, women tend to report higher levels of growth than men (Britt et al., 1998; Park, Cohen, & Murch, 1996; Tedeschi & Calhoun, 1996). These findings, however, are based on highly selective, geographically and culturally restricted samples, and it is still not clear how ecologically valid these findings of gender differences are (Tennen & Affleck, 1998). Additional investigations of gender differences are needed to determine the degree to which this pattern of findings occurs for different kinds of people, dealing with different kinds of problems, in different contexts.

A related area for investigation involves the reason for such gender differences. One possibility is that in cultural contexts where women have been socialized into dependent social roles, some kinds of losses may act as a means to remove social constraints to growth and independence. For women in these social contexts, loss may in some ways be liberating. In our studies of bereaved adults this suggestion seems to fit the obtained data well. A significant number of older widows reported an increased amount of independence and self-reliance emerging from their struggle with their husband's death (Calhoun & Tedeschi, 1989–1990). Another possibility is that women and men can differ in coping styles and that those differences may be reflected in the experience of growth. It is not clear, however, whether gender differences in coping are sufficiently strong to account for the findings on growth (Tennen & Affleck, 1998). It may be that for women some of the elements of posttraumatic growth—for example, the quality and complexity of intimate social exchanges—may be more salient or accessible than they typically are for men (Tedeschi & Calhoun, 1996).

Age

An additional area in which work seems desirable is the developmental aspect of posttraumatic growth. Growth in the struggle with loss has been found in adults of all ages, including those of traditional college age and adolescents (L. A. Horowitz, Loos, & Putnam, 1997; Tedeschi, Park, & Calhoun, 1998). To what extent, if at all, does the struggle with loss lead to growth at early stages of development? Is it possible for children to experience it, or is there a minimum stage of psychological development that must be reached before the process of posttraumatic growth is possible?

Adjustment and Well-Being

A final general research question is one that we have mentioned briefly already: What is the general pattern of relations between psychological distress and psychological well-being on the one hand and posttraumatic growth on the other? No clear pattern of results has yet emerged, but there is no evidence that an increase in posttraumatic growth is detrimental to psychological adjustment. Our clinical experience with people dealing with a variety of different kinds of loss suggests that, for growth to be maintained over time, some degree of psychological discomfort must remain. Much like a pebble in one's shoe that occasionally and painfully reminds us of its presence, yet does not necessarily incapacitate us, perhaps the maintenance of posttraumatic growth requires an occasional experience of loss-related pain or distress. Sometimes the reminders are strong, overpowering, and very distressing. As the salience of loss fades, however, and as good coping mechanisms reduce psychological pain, we might expect the experience of growth to become less salient, too. When the pain persists, growth arising from the struggle with loss may be more likely to last. An important and broad question that is still in need of investigation is "How long does posttraumatic growth last, and what is necessary for it to be maintained (Park, 1998)?"

Growth Processes

The losses that can ultimately result in posttraumatic growth initially generate great emotional distress and rumination; reductions in coping mechanisms; and shifts in personal identity. Cognitive processing of loss and trauma has often been seen as quite useful or even necessary in bereavement (Stroebe, van den Bout, & Schut, 1994). Constructive cognitive processing seems to involve finding meaning in the trauma and its aftermath and noticing changes in the self. This processing first involves a recognition that important goals have been blocked because of the trauma and that beliefs about how the world functions and the meaning of life no longer seem so clear (M. J. Horowitz, 1986). For posttraumatic growth to occur, something has to replace the goals and beliefs from which a survivor of trauma and loss has necessarily disengaged. Sometimes this has been described as "grief work," and it happens not only in bereavement but also after many other types of traumas, because there is often a sense of loss of something precious, if intangible, including a goal, a view of the world, or part of one's identity. We have described (Tedeschi & Calhoun, 1995) how, after initial coping success, the real posttraumatic growth can emerge, and more attention can be paid to growth-oriented grief work (Stroebe & Schut, 1996). Posttraumatic growth may be most likely when there is an initial automatic ruminative process followed later by a more deliberative one that produces new worldviews (Calhoun & Tedeschi, 1998; Tedeschi, 1999). The various domains of posttraumatic growth may coalesce into a revised life narrative that divides things into "the old me" and "the new me" or "my life before" and "my life since." The trauma comes to have meaning as a catalyst for the creation of a new identity, being both the split and the glue between past and present. This integration plays a crucial role in renewal after trauma (Neimeyer & Stewart, 1996).

POSTTRAUMATIC GROWTH IN CLINICAL PERSPECTIVE

Although the focus of this chapter is on posttraumatic growth, we must point out that clients who have experienced major loss are typically suffering greatly. There is a high level of emotional distress characterized by sadness and yearning for what or who has been lost. Typically there is also a reduction in the individual's facility in meeting the demands of everyday life (Hodgkinson & Stewart, 1991; Raphael, 1986). In cases in which the loss has involved high levels of personal danger, there is a need to experience safety and security (Herman, 1997). In the early stages of loss the clinician's task should be to address these issues, focusing on assisting the client in experiencing what relief is possible.

Some clients early on have articulated how their struggle with loss is changing them in positive ways, but it is important for the clinician not to rush the client. The early stages of loss typically are not the time for the clinician to reinforce or identify posttraumatic growth. For many clients, opportunities to work on articulating aspects of posttraumatic growth that has occurred will come later in therapy.

Reconstructing the Shattered Life: The Clinician's Role

Helping the client identify, find, or achieve posttraumatic growth is not something that is amenable to a set of specific techniques. Also, enhancing posttraumatic growth in one's clients should probably not be the main focus or single goal of psychological intervention. The possibilities of posttraumatic growth should remain salient to the clinician, however, so that he or she can focus on aspects of it as they emerge in particular sessions. It is probably inappropriate to set out to look for posttraumatic growth in the client, but it is desirable to properly attend to the possibility of it when it is there.

A metaphor that we have previously used to describe trauma and loss is that of seismic activity (Calhoun & Tedeschi, 1998). Like an earthquake's effects on physical structures, loss can shake, severely damage, or destroy the fundamental components of an individual's worldview and life narrative. Although posttraumatic growth can manifest itself in overt changes of behavior (Park et al., 1996; Wuthnow, 1991), for the individual who experiences it the most noticeable changes are likely to be phenomenological. A primary task of the clinician working with people who have experienced significant loss is to assist in the process of rebuilding the damaged or shattered worldview, to help the client develop a new life narrative that incorporates the loss in a helpful way and, for some people, to articulate and experience more meaningfully the spiritual elements of the assumptive world. As the clinician assists in this process, one element to consider is the degree to which the changes move the client not only in the direction of greater well-being and reduced distress but also in the direction of greater personal growth. What might the clinician do to enhance this possibility?

Growth Work and Clinician Behavior

We have worked with beginning clinicians for some years now, and a general frustration is expressed by at least some students in every newly admitted class: "Tell me what I should do when the client. . . ." Our response is almost always "it depends." This reluctance to make specific prescriptions for how to deal with particular events in a session with a client is never greater than when the issue is growth arising from the struggle with loss. We have addressed clinical matters in greater detail elsewhere (Calhoun & Tedeschi, 1999), and although these are not suggested techniques, there are some aspects of clinician behavior that may enhance the possibility of posttraumatic growth in clients who are coping with significant loss.

Use Respectful Language

In this chapter, both the focus and the word usage have concerned growth coming from the *struggle with loss* rather than the direct effect of loss.

From the client's perspective, talking about good coming from the loss can be highly offensive, perhaps even blasphemous. Think of the parents of a toddler who has been killed in a freak backyard accident. The child fell, hit his head on the sharp edge of a pecan shell, and died of brain trauma. It is easy to imagine how hurt or angry those parents would be if a clinician talked about how their child's death had led them to be better people. When raising matters related to posttraumatic growth with clients, it is important that words be chosen very carefully. The focus should be on how the individual's *struggle* with the loss—not the loss itself—may have been a catalyst for change.

Even with careful word choices, the very idea that anything that was in any way positive could have emerged from the loss may be repellent to some people. When the loss is the death of a loved one, the very consideration of that possibility can be viewed as a betrayal of the loved one. Furthermore, a focus on growth arising from struggle implies respect for the hard work clients do in coping with loss and that their growth is in large degree from their efforts.

Work With Clients' Worldviews

Another important way for clinicians to demonstrate respect for clients is by exploring with them their worldviews. This includes how the client used to think about things, his or her current uncertainties, and what he or she may be thinking since the loss. Much therapy related to posttraumatic growth involves discussion of existential questions, life meaning, and how to express revised beliefs in everyday life.

For some people posttraumatic growth is more clearly experienced in spiritual or religious matters. Although the likelihood that clients will articulate this experience in very traditional religious terms may well vary with social context, this manifestation of posttraumatic growth tends to occur in a broad range of people (Park, 1998; Tedeschi & Calhoun, 1995). Clinicians who work with people who have experienced significant trauma and loss, if they are to be most effective in nurturing posttraumatic growth in their clients, need to be comfortable working with clients who raise existential and spiritual issues. A useful way of increasing this possibility is to read widely about the spiritual and religious views that are representative of those held by one's clients.

Be a Fully Present Listener

Although being a fully present listener applies to therapy in general, it is crucial in working with trauma survivors to listen closely and as comfortably as possible to horrific stories. Although it may be tempting to try to comfort, solve, or be quite sympathetic, it is important to support clients in the struggle, not to short circuit the constructive processing of trauma and loss. The therapist can encourage the client to engage in an examination of the effects of trauma on fundamental beliefs and of how the client perceives the self and the world, rather than focusing purely on distress relief. Furthermore, therapists will be most effective when they listen in a way that allows them to be changed by their clients' experience rather than being intent on promoting certain changes in the client.

Notice Growth as the Client Approaches It

We have found that the client's struggle to understand what losses have done to him or her, how life can be in the aftermath of loss, and the distress of not believing or even understanding things are usually indications that the client is on the kind of search—engaging in constructive cognitive processing—that ultimately yields posttraumatic growth. This is not merely the distressing outcome of trauma but a precursor to growth. It would be premature for a clinician to mention this until the client begins to articulate changes. Then the clinician can mention and reinforce the reasonable positive interpretations of growth that the client offers. The clinician must not respond with platitudes, however, although sometimes what might seem like a platitude at one point is a clearly acceptable response at another. Therefore, the clinician must be sensitive enough to the client to make sure that responses that bring growth into focus for the client are timed well.

Vicarious Growth

The process of being fully present with clients who suffer traumatic loss can be taxing for clinicians. Those who work with people who have been exposed to major loss and tragedy can themselves be vicariously affected by their clinical work in negative ways (Figley & Kleber, 1995; Pearlman & Saakvitne, 1995). It may also be possible, although the data are still tentative (Calhoun & Tedeschi, 1999; Saakvitne, 1997; Schauben & Frazier, 1995), that clinicians may undergo vicarious growth in their work with people who have experienced major loss.

Working with clients who have experienced significant loss can lead the clinician more fully to appreciate the paradoxical dialectic that many clients learn. We as human beings are more vulnerable to loss than we had hoped, but we are also stronger than we had imagined possible. As the client's struggle with loss unfolds, the reality that loss is an integral part of life can become more salient for the clinician. As clients cope, survive, and perhaps grow as they face their struggles, however, the clinician may also derive from the client's story an increased sense of the strength that can be developed in the struggle with loss.

Listening to the personal tragedies of clients can also provide a significant challenge to the clinician's worldview and philosophy of life. Just as for the clients who directly have experienced the loss, existential and spiritual issues can be raised vicariously for the clinician. This indirect confrontation with fundamental existential matters is not necessarily a psychologically pleasant one. Confronting these issues seems necessary, however, and to the extent that the clinician can address them honestly then the confrontation can enhance the likelihood of growth in the clinician's own philosophy of life.

One way in which this seems to occur is that the client's loss leads the clinician to rethink his or her own life priorities and perhaps to make conscious choices to change how to live one's life. As clinicians work with bereaved clients, for example, they may become more aware of the degree to which their own loved ones are important to them, leading to a choice to make them more of a priority in the conflict of commitments that is typical in modern life. A frequently reported finding is for individuals to report an increased appreciation for domains of life that have not been lost, that are still available (Tedeschi & Calhoun, 1995). People who have experienced a loss of health because of major, life-threatening illnesses often report that simple things, such as a bright day with sunshine, are now appreciated much more than before. Clinicians working with such people may experience a similar but vicarious change whereby they become more clearly aware of how the things they still have, but which the client may have already lost, are precious to them.

CONCLUSION

We hope that this chapter will encourage further study of the phenomenon of posttraumatic growth, prompting the reader to examine more detailed references mentioned here. Some readers may be encouraged to tackle the many research questions that this perspective on trauma and loss opens. We hope that heightened awareness on the part of clinicians will result in more careful attention being paid to clients' attempts to imbue their experiences of loss with meaning. As one of our clients told us, "this hurts too bad for something good not to come of it."

REFERENCES

Aldwin, C. M. (1994). *Stress, coping, and development.* New York: Guilford Press.

Aldwin, C. M., Levenson, M. R., & Spiro, A. (1994). Vulnerability and resilience to combat exposure: Can stress have life-long effects? *Psychology and Aging, 9,* 34–44.

Andreasen, N. L., & Norris, A. S. (1972). Long-term adjustment and adaptation mechanisms in severely burned adults. *Journal of Nervous and Mental Disease, 154,* 352–362.

Britt, T. W., Adler, A. B., & Bartone, P. T. (1998). *The meaning and impact of stressful events: Lessons from the Bosnia peacekeeping operation.* Manuscript submitted for publication.

Calhoun, L. G., & Tedeschi, R. G. (1989–1990). Positive aspects of critical life problems: Recollections of grief. *Omega, 20,* 265–272.

Calhoun, L. G., & Tedeschi, R. G. (1998). Posttraumatic growth: Future directions. In R. G. Tedeschi, C. L. Park, & L. G. Calhoun (Eds.), *Posttraumatic growth: Positive change in the aftermath of crisis* (pp. 215–238). Mahwah, NJ: Erlbaum.

Calhoun, L. G., & Tedeschi, R. G. (1999). *Facilitating posttraumatic growth: A clinician's guide.* Mahwah, NJ: Erlbaum.

Calhoun, L. G., Tedeschi, R. G., & Lincourt, A. (1992, August). *Life crises and religious beliefs: Changed beliefs or assimilated events?* Paper presented at the 100th Annual Convention of the American Psychological Association, Washington, DC.

Caplan, G. (1964). *Principles of preventive psychiatry.* New York: Basic Books.

Dakof, G. A., & Taylor, S. E. (1990). Victims' perceptions of social support: What is helpful from whom? *Journal of Personality and Social Psychology, 58,* 80–89.

Figley. C. R., & Kleber, R. J. (Eds.). (1995). *Beyond trauma: Cultural and societal dynamics.* New York: Plenum Press.

Finkel, N. J. (1974). Strens and traumas: An attempt at categorization. *American Journal of Community Psychology, 2,* 265–273.

Herman, J. (1997). *Trauma and recovery.* New York: Basic Books.

Hodgkinson, P. E., & Stewart, M. (1991). *Coping with catastrophe.* London: Routledge.

Horowitz, L. A., Loos, M. E., & Putnam, F. W. (1997, November). *"Perceived benefits" of traumatic experiences in adolescent girls.* Poster presented at the meeting of the International Society for Traumatic Stress Studies, Montreal, Quebec, Canada.

Horowitz, M. J. (1986). *Stress response syndromes* (2nd ed.). Northvale, NJ: Aronson.

Janoff-Bulman, R. (1992). *Shattered assumptions.* New York: Free Press.

Lehman, D. R., Davis, C. G., DeLongis, A., Wortman, C., Bluck, S., Mandel, D. R., & Ellard, J. H. (1993). Positive and negative life changes following bereavement and their relations to adjustment. *Journal of Social and Clinical Psychology, 12,* 90–112.

Lopata, H. Z. (1973). Self-identity in marriage and widowhood. *Sociological Quarterly, 14,* 407–418.

Neimeyer, R. A., & Stewart, A. E. (1996). Trauma, healing, and the narrative emplotment of loss. *Families in Society: The Journal of Contemporary Human Services, 77,* 360–374.

O'Leary, V. E., & Ickovics, J. R. (1995). Resilience and thriving in response to a challenge: An opportunity for a paradigm shift in women's health. *Women's Health: Research on Gender, Behavior, and Policy, 1,* 121–142.

Overcash, W. S., Calhoun, L. G., Tedeschi, R. G., & Cann, A. (1996). Coping with crises: An examination of the impact of traumatic events on personal belief systems. *Journal of Genetic Psychology, 157,* 455–464.

Park, C. L. (1998). Implication of posttraumatic growth for individuals. In R. G. Tedeschi, C. L. Park, & L. G. Calhoun (Eds.), *Posttraumatic growth: Positive change in the aftermath of crisis* (pp. 153–177). Mahwah, NJ: Erlbaum.

Park, C. L., Cohen, L., & Murch, R. (1996). Assessment and prediction of stress-related growth. *Journal of Personality, 64,* 645–658.

Pearlman, L. A., & Saakvitne, K. W. (1995). *Trauma and the therapist: Countertransference and vicarious traumatization in psychotherapy with incest survivors.* New York: Norton.

Pennebaker, J. W. (1995). *Emotion, disclosure, and health.* Washington, DC: American Psychological Association.

Raphael, B. (1986). *When disaster strikes.* New York: Basic Books.

Saakvitne, K. W. (1997, November). The rewards of trauma therapy for the therapist. In R. G. Tedeschi (Chair), *Posttraumatic growth in survivors, therapists, researchers, and communities.* Symposium conducted at the meeting of the International Society for Traumatic Stress Studies, Montreal, Quebec, Canada.

Schauben, L. J., & Frazier, P. A. (1995). Vicarious trauma: The effects on female counselors of working with sexual violence survivors. *Psychology of Women Quarterly, 19,* 49–64.

Schwartzberg, S. S., & Janoff-Bulman, R. (1991). Grief and the search for meaning: Exploring the assumptive worlds of bereaved college students. *Journal of Social and Clinical Psychology, 10,* 270–288.

Silver, R. C., Boon, C., & Stones, M. H. (1983). Searching for meaning in misfortune: Making sense of incest. *Journal of Social Issues, 39,* 81–102.

Stroebe, M., & Schut, H. (1996, August). The dual process model of coping with loss. In L. G. Calhoun (Chair), *New perspectives on interventions and growth following traumatic loss.* Symposium conducted at the 104th Annual Convention of the American Psychological Association, Toronto, Ontario, Canada.

Stroebe, M., van den Bout, J., & Schut, H. (1994). Myths and misconceptions about bereavement: The opening of a debate. *Omega, 29,* 187–203.

Tedeschi, R. G. (1999). Violence transformed: Posttraumatic growth in survivors and their societies. *Aggression and Violent Behavior: A Review Journal.*

Tedeschi, R. G., & Calhoun, L. G. (1995). *Trauma and transformation: Growing in the aftermath of suffering.* Thousand Oaks, CA: Sage.

Tedeschi, R. G., & Calhoun, L. G. (1996). The Posttraumatic Growth Inventory: Measuring the positive legacy of trauma. *Journal of Traumatic Stress, 9,* 455–471.

Tedeschi, R. G., Park, C. L., & Calhoun, L. G. (Eds.). (1998). *Posttraumatic growth: Positive change in the aftermath of crisis.* Mahwah, NJ: Erlbaum.

Tennen, H., & Affleck, G. (1998). Personality and transformation in the face of adversity. In R. G. Tedeschi, C. L. Park, & L. G. Calhoun (Eds.), *Posttraumatic growth: Positive change in the aftermath of crisis* (pp. 65–98). Mahwah, NJ: Erlbaum.

Thomas, L. E., DiGiulio, R. C., &, Sheehan, N. W. (1991). Identifying loss and psychological crisis in widowhood. *International Journal of Aging and Human Development, 26,* 279–295.

Wuthnow, R. (1991). *Acts of compassion: Caring for others and helping ourselves.* Princeton, NJ: Princeton University Press.

Yalom, I. D., & Lieberman, M. A. (1991). Bereavement and heightened existential awareness. *Psychiatry, 54,* 334–345.

9

SPIRITUAL RESOURCES FOLLOWING A PARTNER'S DEATH FROM AIDS

T. ANNE RICHARDS

Providing care to a dying person, witnessing death, losing a loved one—all can open us to existential issues and spiritual experiences that refocus our lives. The hospice movement has brought to light the integral role that spirituality plays for dying people and their family members during palliative care (Millison & Dudley, 1992). The emergence of spiritual awareness at bereavement is recognized as a part of normal grief. Spiritual beliefs and practices function in both the cognitive and emotional assimilation of loss (Bowlby, 1980; Parkes, 1972; Parkes & Weiss, 1983; Shuchter & Zisook, 1993). In this chapter I examine the place of spirituality in the lives of bereaved partners of men with AIDS who live in the San Francisco gay community. Narrative accounts of bereaved partners lead the reader through the men's experience of their partners' dying process and time of death, the first month of bereavement, and their transition and growth 3–4 years following bereavement. The final narrative accounts also provide insight as to how spirituality interacts with other life perspectives and values.

This work was supported by Grants MH44045, MH49985, and MH52517 from the National Institute of Mental Health. I am indebted to Susan Folkman, Principal Investigator, and my colleagues Judith Wrubel, Michael Acree, and Judy Moskowitz for their encouragement and support of this work.

THE SPIRITUAL SELF AND MEANING

Grief and the Spiritual Self

Death is both natural and mysterious. The death of a loved one can activate a complexity of emotions, thoughts, behaviors, and changes like no other experience in life. After the death of a loved one we grieve our loss, try to make sense of it, and find it necessary to reorder our private worlds and their meanings in a whole new way. Meaning making is an operative part of the individual's assumptive world (i.e., the individual's internal mapping system through which he or she filters, organizes, and interprets life). This mapping system includes beliefs about the nature of reality, causality, the nature of knowledge, and codes of ethics (Crocker, Fiske, & Taylor, 1984; Frank, 1977; Parkes, 1971; Walsh & Charalambides, 1989).

Experiences and their meanings can never be fully articulated in language (Shafranske, 1998). However, the effort to describe experiences and their meanings shapes the cognitive mapping system that interprets self, environment, and relationship. Experiences of loss sometimes provoke experiences of transcendence, of self larger than previously conceived and of self in relationship to other. These experiences are then conceptualized, interpreted within an individual's private framework (i.e., assumptive world), and generate new notions of self and relationship.

Development of the Spiritual Self

A spiritual dimension of self guides our recognition and comprehension of the connectedness of life and of ultimate reality. As this dimension of self emerges, our experience of the sacredness and the divinity of life expands. The spiritual self can develop through several types of engagement. Involvement with religion, art, or music; spending time in nature; experiences of great suffering; or altruistic acts can potentiate the activation of the spiritual self. As this facet of the self grows, new resources become available for defining one's personage, one's relationships with others and one's environment, and how one goes about conducting one's life. In this sense, spirituality is part of the guiding system that allows one to interpret one's experience and generate personal meaning and purpose in life. Others have provided similar and overlapping definitions (Fowler, 1981; Frankl, 1963; Klass, 1995; Pargament, 1990; Prest & Keller, 1993; Tillich, 1963).

THE SAN FRANCISCO GAY COMMUNITY

Culture provides us with common symbols for expressing our individual meanings. Therefore, it is useful to understand some of the cultural history of the San Francisco gay community in order to contextualize the findings presented in this chapter (see also Christopher-Richards, 1993; Fortunato, 1987; Katz, 1997; Paul, Hays, & Coates, 1995; Shilts, 1987). In the early 1970s San Francisco became a center for gay men seeking to escape repression and stigmatization. Thousands of gay men from all over the country came to establish new lives and identities. The era had a political focus of gay liberation that pushed for sexual openness and experimentation. Although coming out as a gay man often precipitated estrangement from formal religions that rejected homosexuality, some gay men sought to maintain a religious identity. The Metropolitan Community Church was established in 1970 to serve gay Christians, and the Temple Sha'ar Zahav served gay Jews. Others sought less traditional sources of spirituality, through Pagan practices, metaphysics, or New Age philosophies and practices. However, the guiding principles of the community were those of gay liberation and sexual freedom, and they generated the values of the time.

It was in the early 1980s, when the AIDS epidemic struck, that the spiritual needs of the gay community more fully emerged. The spiritual needs of dying and bereaved people in the community were diverse and complex, requiring less dogmatic approaches in spiritual counseling, practices, and rituals. Spiritual care often became a part of psychological counseling and medical practices, embracing Buddhist practices and beliefs, New Age conceptions, and alternative health therapies based on spiritual principles.

The death toll and the experiences of caregiving overwhelmed the gay community. From the onset of the epidemic in 1981 through 1997, there were 16,999 reported deaths from AIDS in San Francisco, of which 90% were gay men (San Francisco Department of Public Health, 1997). The epidemic shifted the worldview of the entire community as well as the private worlds of the community's individual members.

THE STUDY

The University of California, San Francisco (UCSF) Coping Project was a longitudinal study of caregiving and bereavement among partners of men with AIDS (e.g., Folkman, Chesney, & Christopher-Richards, 1994; Folkman, Chesney, Collette, Boccellari, & Cooke, 1996; Folkman, Chesney, Cooke, Boccellari, & Collette, 1994; T. A. Richards, Acree, & Folkman, 1999; T. A. Richards & Folkman, 1997; Weiss & Richards, 1997). The study participants were gay men from the San Francisco Bay area who were in a committed relationship with a partner diagnosed with AIDS. They were their partner's primary caregiver, and one third of the participants themselves were infected with HIV. Each participant was followed for 2 years, at which point he was given the option of leaving the study or continuing for an additional 3 years. Two hundred fifty-three caregiving partners enrolled in the study between April 1990 and June 1992. One hundred fifty participants were bereaved during the first 2 years of the study. One hundred ninety-five participants enrolled for an additional 3 years, and 145 completed the second portion of the study. Thirty-seven participants were bereaved during the last 3 years of the study. Qualitative and quantitative data were collected bimonthly and biannually. Data collection concluded in May 1997.

This chapter draws on data collected at two time points: the month following the participants' bereavement and their exit from the study 3–4 years later. Open-ended interviews were conducted approximately 2 and 4 weeks post-bereavement. In the first interview participants were asked "Tell me what happened." In the second interview participants were asked "Tell me what has happened since I saw you last." The two interviews together provided an account of what occurred from the final stage of caregiving through approximately 1 month following the death of the partner. Interviews of 125 participants were used for analysis at Time 1. In addition, measures of psychological well-being, coping, physical health symptoms, and demographics, collected at the same time, were analyzed.

The second time point was 3–4 years post-bereavement, when participants exited the study. In the final interview, the Exit Interview, participants were asked the following questions: "What have you learned from this period of your life?", "How has it changed you?", "What's important to you now?", "What are your thoughts at this time about your deceased partner?", and "What do you see happening in your future?" In addition, the same measures administered at Time 1 were administered again at exit. Seventy of the original 125 participants completed the Exit Interview and comprise the source of data for Time 2.

All interviews were tape recorded and transcribed verbatim. The coding scheme for the bereavement interviews emerged from a review of the data conducted by two coders. This scheme was then used as the foundation for coding the Exit Interviews. As the exit narratives were analyzed, the coding scheme was reorganized in response to the data. The Ethnograph (Seidel, Friese, & Leonard, 1995), a software program for qualitative analysis, was used for all analyses. All names used in the narrative examples in this chapter are pseudonyms.

FINDINGS

Time of Death and First Month of Bereavement

The narrative accounts of bereaved partners describe experiences that began in the final stage of the dying partner's life and continued through the first month of bereavement. Sixty-eight of the 125 bereaved participants spontaneously described spiritual phenomena of this time. The spiritual focus was not on themselves but rather on the dying or deceased partner. Spirituality was revealed through the expression of beliefs, experiences, and ritual practices. The nature and function of these phenomena varied according to their placement in the processes of caregiving, death, and grief.

Spiritual Role and Rituals at the Time of Death

The initial concern was for a passage into death that was free of struggle and pain. Caregiving partners assumed a spiritual role through the final stage of the lives of their partners. Vigils were consciously conducted to honor the final stage of life and help create a peaceful atmosphere for dying. Vigils could include the caregiving partner, the immediate social circle of friends, hospice support, kin of the dying or kin of the caregiving partner, clergy, and pets. Establishing vigils required the recognition and acceptance that the person with AIDS was indeed dying. No attempts were made to resuscitate the dying partner. Music, candles, and pictures of the dying partner were used to enhance the atmosphere of vigil. When the time of death approached, the caregiving partners would often give the dying partner permission to let go into death. The intention behind giving permission to die was to ease the passing of the spirit. This required an attunement with the dying partner and the subtle shifts of the dying process. Language and imagery most meaningful to the dying partner were used by the caregiving partner to convey acceptance of letting go. For example,

> I started to notice that his body temperature was cooling down and his breathing was changing. At that point, I told him again that it's okay and don't worry about me crying. I also told him that he would be with his dad. I helped him the best I could and whispered prayers into his ears. I kept watching him and talking to him. I told him that I loved him. At one point, I thought it was finished, but he was still breathing very slightly. I called the nurse. At 12:05 he died.

It was common for a bereaved partner to enact rituals immediately following the death of a partner, prior to contacting mortuary services. Rituals at the time of death involved grooming and preparing the body, ceremonies of transition, and visitations with the deceased partner. These rituals provided physical engagements, and ways of being with the immediate circumstances of loss of life and the presence of the remains, while taking in the transition that had just occurred. Grooming the body of the loved one, visitations, and ceremonies slowed the pace of events, making this delicate and confusing time more exacting and purposeful. As a result, the events at the time of death were more easily remembered when the bereaved partner later made efforts to reconstruct what occurred.

> He wanted to have a service at home with his body being present immediately after he died. So we called people. We only could reach four actual people. All the rest, we left messages. His mom and I got him

ready. We got him cleaned, and his kids (students) had given him a red sweatshirt for Christmas. It had a big Christmas tree on it, and they had signed all their names and said "We love you." He had written the service, and he wanted to be on an oriental carpet in the living room. At a quarter past ten all these people started coming. Calling and saying, "I just got home. I want to come—can you wait?" So we waited until the last person came. We didn't get started until midnight. Part of the service was that everyone should have new white socks to put on when they arrived at the door. John had bought all these new white socks, and so they left their shoes at the door, and they put on new white socks. Everyone formed a circle around his body. The service he had written was wonderful. Ellen conducted it—his best friend. She burned wild sage and blew the smoke all over us. Blessed the circle with water from a crystal bowl and read some poetry. Then we sang some chants. Each person was told to bring a gift that reminded them of John. And they knew that ahead of time. So the water was passed, and you blessed your gift, and you put it in the basket. Then you talked to John and told him good-bye and why you had brought this gift and what he meant to you in your life. Fifteen people including myself and the family had come. It took three hours. We weren't over till 3:00 a.m. It was just such a wonderful thing, and it helped all of us. It helped me tremendously. Beforehand, I was thinking, "I can't believe John's asking me to do this, and how will I call these people after he's died? How will I get him ready?" But it was the right thing to do.

Spiritual Beliefs and Experiences in the First Month of Bereavement

The experience of a partner's death activated spiritual beliefs that were used in constructing an acceptable and meaningful account of the location of the deceased partner. Bereaved partners were compelled to know, in some way, that their deceased partners were safe. The prevailing belief at the time of bereavement was in spiritualism, which essentially holds that a spirit inhabits the body and leaves the body at death to go on to another existence. Communication with the spirit is possible. The spirit is the true self, and it is a privilege to witness its passing. When the spirit passes from the body it is greeted by other spirits, by a higher power, or by God. Most frequently it was thought that a friend or relative would greet the spirit at passing. A variation of this view was that the deceased person's spirit merged into the essence of life, still remaining part of the whole of things, only in a different way.

> When we all go we become spirit. And pure spirit can join with other spirits, which means you can become part of me and God and everybody else living or dead. You can just join it like a glass of water is an individual entity, but pour it into the ocean and it's just simply water.

A construct that helped in stabilizing the bereaved partner's emotional response to the loss was a belief in the existence of a universal higher order that governed daily events and provided the bereaved partner with a connection to the whole of life. One could interact with this higher order by responding to its guidance and thus make life choices that were aligned with a greater purpose, plan, or power. Attunement with this higher order was often attained in a state of heightened awareness of one's self and one's environment. This belief provided a rightness and orderliness to events unexplainable and beyond the control of the bereaved partner.

> We truly believe the universe provides and that if you put the questions out there the answers will come back to you in one fashion or another. Sometimes they come from within and other times they come from outside.

Experiences of a higher order came about through conscious efforts, such as prayer or meditation, or unexpectedly, through shifts of consciousness related to perceptions of perfection, continuity, or a meaningful relationship between seemingly unconnected events. Some who believed in the existence of a higher order did so without a validating experience of its existence, and some who had direct experiences of higher order did so without holding prior beliefs. The description of many of these experiences bore striking resemblances to Jung's (1955) description of *syncronicity*. For example, in the following account there is a description of parallel events that are not causally linked but are explained as meaningfully and symbolically reflective of each other in their simultaneous occurrence:

> All night long there had been thunder and lightning outside, and Richard loved thunder and lightning. He had gone on a trip with Jeff a few years ago all over the Midwest, and they had chased thunder and lightning storms. They found out where one was going to be over there, and they drove after it. He wanted crash, boom, bang. And that night we had an incredible thunder and lightning storm. I mean the hospital was shaking, and the lightning bolts were right outside the window. But at 3:00 in the morning it was real peaceful and calm. It was like, he just went to sleep, and he just finally relaxed and stopped fighting.

A great deal of solace was found in the belief that the relationship with the deceased partner continued in some way. This belief held the possibilities that the deceased partner could communicate his safety and continue to be active in the bereaved partner's life. It was felt that the relationship was dynamic and could grow and change. The most common configuration of the new relationship placed the deceased partner in the position of mentor or guide.

> Around 10:00 I went into the kitchen and felt the weight leave me. This terrible burden left my body. It pushed out. I know that Robert, in his way, was whispering in my ear that everything was okay, and he was in a good place. Although I was still sad, this event made bearing it much easier for me.

The sense of the presence of the deceased partner, or communications with him, were perceived as natural and real. For the most part, these experiences were gratefully accepted and appraised as a useful part of coping with the loss. Sensing the deceased partner's presence, or communicating with him, sometimes occurred in dreams but primarily occurred when the bereaved partner was in a state of relaxation, that is, alone in a quiet room, during or following a massage, or just before falling asleep.

> I was almost asleep—kind of on that consciousness edge between sleep and awakeness. A voice came at me from my right, which is near the window, Jarod's side of the bed, but it wasn't Jarod. I was falling asleep thinking of him and saying, kind of thinking, I need to know you're okay. I need you to tell me, and I heard a voice and I don't know what the words were. It might not even have been words, but it was an awareness of a voice. It was my friend Gene who died last year. Then I heard another voice from my right, and it was my old boyfriend Darek, who died this year. I can't tell you what they said. It was just an awareness that they were somehow there. Then all of a sudden I felt Jarod, and he was on my left as if he were kneeling next to the bed. He was down low with his face near my face. He didn't say anything, but I felt it. I didn't see it with my eyes, but I felt the image.

Rituals in the First Months of Bereavement

Most rituals were distinctively reflective of gay culture and, in many respects, vastly different from the traditions of death rites in the mainstream culture in the United States. Death rites symbolize cultural meanings of existence. Rituals for a deceased partner honored and celebrated him as a gay man, recognized the relationship between partners, and acted to solidify "gay family" as well as kin of the deceased and the bereaved partners. To these ends, rituals of death were symbolic of gay liberation principles established prior to the AIDS epidemic.

Cremation was chosen as a means of disposition by an overwhelming majority of the partners with AIDS. This choice influenced the nature and the number of memorial services. Most often, cremains were privately dispersed without the assistance of formal mortuary services. Cremains were also divided among family and friends for multiple-site distributions. The locations for dispersion of cremains were chosen because of the meanings they held for the deceased and the bereaved partners.

> I'm going to be cremated, and when my ashes are spread, I want the remains of his to be spread with mine. I sent some of his ashes to his mom, and I'm going to spread some in his garden. I'm going to save some because he wanted some spread in the AIDS memorial garden, which won't be done for a year. He asked what I wanted, and I said I wanted to spread his ashes in Yosemite because that's where we both wanted to go

together. He was diagnosed with CMV (Cytomegalovirus) the week we were planning to go. He said he liked that idea. He liked to camp out.

Multiple memorials were held at various locations locally and nationally and served to extend ritualized mourning and the period of social cohesion and support. Three types of memorial services were conducted: (a) formal religious services involving clergy; (b) informal religious services created and conducted by bereaved partners; and (c) secular memorials involving a spectrum of activities, including dances, parties, dinners, day-long outings, and a quilting bee. In addition to these memorials one or more private or shared rites were enacted, such as construction of an AIDS Quilt panel, creation of a home altar, or writing poems or letters to the deceased person. As many as seven rites were conducted over a 2-month period by some bereaved partners.

The recognition of gay identity was a prevalent theme in enacting rituals. The need to recognize the deceased partner as a gay man and to honor the relationship between the two partners shaped the content and meaning of public rituals. When present, family estrangement due to gay or AIDS-related stigma interfered with the ritual process by delaying or disrupting the commissions of the deceased partner. Family estrangement and its sequelae cause additional distress for the bereaved partner during his grieving period. More often than not, family members honored the deceased person and his relationship with his partner, and the bond of family was reinforced (see T. A. Richards, Wrubel, & Folkman, 1999).

> The service lasted about an hour and a half. I was able to stand there in front of 55 or 60 people, many who were involved, straight, religious people—Roger [deceased partner] helped me to do this—and I was able to stand there and say that Roger and I loved each other very much. I felt very comfortable and confident saying that. Roger had selected all the music and his friend Andy sang "Empty Chairs, Empty Tables." It was just wonderful. He left notes. It was planned by the pastor and me. We then had a cortege, a funeral procession. We went to the grave and had quite a number of cars. Roger was a retired major in the army reserves and wanted a military service. They sent a team of nine men who shot three times and played taps. They folded the American flag while the pastors folded the gay freedom flag. They gave the American flag to Roger's mom and the pastor gave the gay flag to me. One of the final things that happened at the cemetery was the exchange of the flags. After all this, his mom wanted just her and I to stay at the cemetery until the casket was lowered.

Quantitative Comparisons

The qualitative findings resulted from an analysis of accounts from 68 participants who spontaneously discussed spiritual phenomena in their bereavement interviews. Fifty-seven participants did not make references to spiritual beliefs, practices, or experiences. These groups were compared, using t tests, on coping, mood, and physical health symptoms; chi-square tests were used for HIV-status comparisons. The t test comparisons were based on an average score for each variable from the combined bereavement interviews taken 2 and 4 weeks following bereavement. Only a descriptive summary of results is provided in this chapter. For quantitative details and a full report see T. A. Richards and Folkman's (1997) article.

The groups were compared on the eight kinds of coping assessed with the Ways of Coping Scale (Folkman & Lazarus, 1988). The group referencing spiritual phenomena used more positive reappraisal, more planful problem solving, and more confrontive coping than the group without spiritual references. The use of these forms of coping indicate an active and deliberate engagement with the circumstances of loss.

The groups also differed in depressive symptomatology (Center for Epidemiologic Studies—Depression Scale; Radloff, 1977), anxiety (Spielberger, 1988), and positive states of mind (Horowitz, Wilner, & Alvarez, 1979). The group with spiritual references had higher scores on both depression and anxiety and lower scores on positive states of mind—that is, functioning—than the group without spiritual references. There were no differences between the groups on anger (Spielberger, 1988) or positive morale (Bradburn, 1969).

Groups were also compared on HIV status and the presence of physical symptoms. The groups did not differ in terms of the proportion of HIV-positive participants. The group with spiritual references reported significantly more symptoms than the group without spiritual references.

Spiritual beliefs, experiences, and practices of newly bereaved caregiving partners were a part of coping adaptively with high levels of distress and physical health symptoms. Spiritual beliefs are sometimes thought to correlate with better mental health (P. S. Richards & Bergin, 1997). In our investigation the group reporting spiritual phenomena scored higher in depression and anxiety than the group that did not. However, of primary interest, from a coping perspective, is that those who reported spiritual phenomena sustained levels of positive morale comparable to the alternate group in the face of significantly greater distress. Sustaining positive morale while experiencing high levels of distress can quite possibly be attributed to the meaning created through spiritual experiences, newly formed spiritual constructs, and extensive ritual practices.

Spiritual phenomena were appraised in the narrative accounts as helpful in coping with the circumstances of loss. Spirituality functioned as an organizing principle when personal worldviews were most fragmented by the experience of loss. Spiritual phenomena helped bereaved partners interpret the events of the dying process, defined the location of the deceased partner and his safety, honored the life and death of the individual, and provided solidarity among living family and friends. Furthermore, experiences of a higher order of events, the presence of the deceased person, and communications from the deceased person moved individuals from a normative sense of reality that was defined socially and culturally into an expanded, transcendent reality. These experiences, and the construction of beliefs that ensued, were part of the foundation of changed worldviews of the bereaved partners 3–4 years later.

Three to Four Years Following Bereavement

Of the 125 participants involved in the study at the time of bereavement, 70 remained to complete the Exit Interviews conducted 3–4 years following bereavement. The remaining cohort consisted of 37 participants who made spiritual references at the time of bereavement and 33 who did not. However, 3–4 years later there was a profound shift in the area of spiritual development: Seventy-seven percent of the participants discussed spiritual emergence or growth that took place over the course of their recovery from grief. Because of the change in group sizes of those who discussed their spiritual life and those who did not, quantitative comparisons showed little differences between groups (T. A. Richards, Acree, & Folkman, 1999).

Conceptions of Spirituality

The narrative accounts given 3–4 years following bereavement revealed a very different picture of the participants of the study, largely because of the presence of spiritual development. Only one person came to question his prior spiritual beliefs as a result of his experiences of caregiving and bereavement. Overall, bereaved partners felt a deepening of their spirituality. As distress and grief diminished over time, spirituality became more of a source of personal purpose, direction, and meaning rather than a resource for interpreting loss. It became, more clearly, a means of defining self-identity, providing a sense of place and connection in life's larger scheme.

> I think that I'm understanding a little more the purpose of spirituality—the place of spirituality. Where we are in relationship to that. How we fit into the larger scheme of things and what it is that feeds and fuels us. You know, like sunshine and water and food—it's something else that people need to go on.

Many participants developed personal relationships with God or some other conception of ultimate power or order. Relationships with the sacred were active and participatory. There was a sense of connection to ultimacy that influenced values and direction in the life of the individual. The experience of a spiritual dimension of self also provided a strengthened capacity for living that resulted from a sense of connectedness to other persons, places, and things in the environment. This participant stated his views quite eloquently:

> Security, self-esteem, fulfillment, purpose in life, all really come from some spiritual source. The spiritual things become part of my life, then they attract or enable, or sometimes even create the people, places and things that seem to be the sources. But they're really not. They're the results. So I kind of look at something like God as like the wind. If we're in a sailboat, the idea is to set our sails the best we can. To understand where the wind is coming from. And then to rightly relate the sails to the wind so that the power comes from the wind that propels us across.

Continued Relationships

A continuing bond with the deceased partner remained a part of spiritual reality. Seventy percent of the cohort maintained a new form of relationship with their deceased partners. Some relationships, similar to bonds expressed at the time of bereavement, were maintained through experiential communications with the deceased partner, experiences of the presence of the deceased partner, and through the deceased partner acting as a guide or mentor. In addition, relationships were maintained in the form of active living memory or through a sense that the deceased partner was a part of the living partner's self. Relationships were experienced as evolving and growing. This was a belief stated within the first month of bereavement, now validated through personal experience. A continuing bond with the deceased partner was maintained as part of a reorganized present in which the deceased partner assumed a new position in the living partner's world scheme. This closeness persisted while participants changed the circumstances of their lives with new jobs or careers, primary relationships, and living situations. In the words of some of the men,

> I feel very close to him still. I feel like there is still a part of him that lives in me that was responsible for bringing me to the place where I'm at today.
>
> My remembrance of him is a prime factor of my being. It is one of my essential elements. There is a portion of my brain that is devoted to his memories. There is certainly a large portion of my heart that is devoted to the same thing. I will be eternally grateful for the relationship he gave me. In a certain sense, he will live as long as I do.
>
> This feeling that I needed to put some distance between me and Mark to move on with my life—I realize now you don't have to do that. You just move on with your life. It is just there. I miss him. I don't have the material things that reminded me of him. But I have him inside.

Persisting ties to the deceased person have been found in a number of other studies, including work by Stroebe and Stroebe (1989, 1991) with a sample of widows and widowers; Zisook and Shuchter (1986), also with a sample of widows and widowers; Klass (1995), with a group of bereaved parents; and Silverman and Worden (1992), with a sample of bereaved children. These studies support the theory that a continued relationship with a deceased loved one is an adaptive component of the grief process.

Intersection With Life Values

Three to four years following bereavement the men in this study viewed themselves, their relationships, and the world in which they live in newfound ways. The experience and conception of a spiritual self extended into other areas of growth and change. Maslow's (1964, 1971) theory of development provides a framework for viewing the transition from coping with the intensity of caregiving, the intimate experience with death and grief, to a resolution of self and other as a result of personal growth. For many caregivers experiences of loss provoked transcendent experiences of self and other. In this way, caregiving and bereavement elicited peak experiences that were transformational in nature. As grief abated, the self emerged, transformed beyond previous sensibilities. With new sensibilities, the position of self in relation to other was redirected.

> This whole five years has made me think a little bit different of the way I was raised and the way people do things and the way I did things. Things that were passed down to me from my father that I'm passing down to my son that I like or don't like. And either stopping that trend of passing the baggage, or passing the things that are good. And I don't think, if I hadn't gone through this whole situation, I don't think I would've looked at this. I just would've gone blindly along.

Acceptance of Death

One way that perceptions of self and private world were reorganized was through a recognition and acceptance of the fact of death for every living being. A series of contextual factors must be remembered in relation to this altered view. AIDS requires a lengthy caregiving process that involves a series of losses through the disease progression. Most of the deaths occurred at home, with the caregiving partner present in the intimacy of the dying process. The average age of the men in this study, at bereavement, was slightly higher than 38 years. Last, most of the men experienced multiple losses of friends as well as of partners over the course of the epidemic. In some cases, men lost their entire social circles. In a very vivid way, death became a part of life in the bereaved partners' worldviews. The following quote represents, explicitly and implicitly, the many voices of the way death came to be accepted.

> In some ways I have more inner strength. I think I have a better concept of what life is really about. I think that I was in denial. I think that

our culture is in denial. It doesn't deal with death. Life is a struggle, it is a battle. And, I've realized people are by and large in the same battle. That is my conclusion. After having dealt with all of this, I think that we deal with the same basic issues. Ultimately, being born means that you're going to die. And so that means everything will be taken away from us in one way or another. So that is a given. We spend a lot of our lives avoiding that because I think, first, people live a lot longer. We have a lot of distractions and so forth. I think that intensifies the pain of loss. You think it is unjust, unfair, and it shouldn't happen to us. But the fact is, it happens to everyone. It is the way it is. And to me, that doesn't mean that there isn't a God. I mean, to me it has inspired in me more awe for God, that God is so unknowable, his ways are so un-knowable. It is like—well, this doesn't make sense to me. But I'll bet there is sense here somewhere.

Relationships With Family

One aspect of the changed worldviews of the men in the study was a renewal of confidence in family ties. The meaning of family was enhanced. *Family* was defined as kin of the bereaved and deceased partners and as gay family, that is, an extended family of gay friends. It became apparent to many of the men that they were a valuable part of their family system and that the family system was vital to their own well-being. Some developed new priorities to care for aging parents or to participate in raising children of the family. Some went on to care for other gay friends or to volunteer in community-based AIDS service organizations. There was a feeling of having gained a better understanding of family members and of a stronger connec-tion to them. The quality of relationships with family members was highly valued. For example,

> My father had to take care of my mother during her last year. She had cancer. I found myself in the role of talking to him as the experienced caregiver. He knew what I went through with that, and let us connect around that in a very beautiful way, so that we feel we have shared something in terms of a loss, in terms of caring. My relationship with my partner was much shorter than his with my mother. But still, sharing around a loss that was difficult was also beautiful. So, out of all this stuff always comes a balance of things.

Another participant talked of his relationship with his brother:

> I wrote to my brother not too long ago, that we've become friends and how important that was. I sent him a birthday card, and I wrote that, in view of all these losses, that we—the people and the relationships—are most important.

Self-view

Finally, there was an overarching sense of self-worth shaped by the total set of experiences. There were discoveries that redefined personage. Each of the following phrases is from a different participant of the UCSF Coping Project. Together, they provide a communal voice that gives the flavor of this sense of self-worth and discovery.

Maturation

- "I've grown up."
- "I'm a stronger, better person."
- "I learned about trust."
- "I'm more giving and more loving."

Self-esteem

- "I gained a lot of competence and respect about myself."
- "I feel I can do anything."
- "I have a lot more capacity than I ever thought."

Achievement

- "I never worked so hard, never so focused."
- "I'm stronger than I've ever seen myself, more fortitude, more determination, more discipline."

Character

- "I did the right thing."
- "It was a testing ground for character."
- "I am enabled to help others."
- "I've never before found that kind of purity of my own intentions."
- "I will hang in there."
- "I can count on myself."
- "I've learned a level of commitment that I can make. It reflects my character, what I'm able to do."

CONCLUSION

The reconstruction of meaning is a vital part of grief recovery and reorientation following bereavement. Many participants in this study developed spiritually, maintained continuing relationships with deceased partners, came to include death as a natural process in their own lives, gained a new understanding of the value of family, and came to a strengthened sense of self and personal capacity. The interplay of experiences and resolutions, and the creation of new meanings, acted as creative dynamics in the reorganization of worldviews and personal meanings of existence. The process of spiritual discovery through circumstances of loss enabled an opening of lives toward self-realization rather than a closing down of growth and a collapse of the human spirit. Loss is normal, continuous, and has a formative impact on our evolving consciousness. It is necessary to recognize and understand the essential force that spiritual growth has in the maturation process and how it intertwines with situations of challenge and loss. Although spiritual phenomena may be thematic within a culture or a particular group of people, it is also idiosyncratic to the individual's assumptive world. Work with the grieving necessitates a recognition of the cultural keys as well as the individual framework of the spiritual in order to fully utilize the spiritual aspects of the self in the meaning-reconstruction process.

REFERENCES

Bowlby, J. (1980). *Attachment and loss: Vol. 3. Loss, sadness and depression.* New York: Basic Books.

Bradburn, N. M. (1969). *The structure of psychological well-being.* Chicago: Aldine.

Christopher-Richards, T. A. (1993). *The interrelationship of AIDS and spirituality in the San Francisco gay community.* Unpublished master's thesis, San Francisco State University.

Crocker, J., Fiske, S. T., & Taylor, S. E. (1984). Schematic bases of belief change. In J. R. Eiser (Ed.), *Attitudinal judgment* (pp. 197–226). New York: Springer-Verlag.

Folkman, S., Chesney M. A., & Christopher-Richards, T. A. (1994). Stress and coping in caregiving partners of men with AIDS. *Psychiatric Clinics of North America, 17*, 35–55.

Folkman, S., Chesney, M. A., Collette, L., Boccellari, A., & Cooke, M. (1996). Postbereavement depressive mood and its prebereavement predictors in HIV+ and HIV− gay men. *Journal of Personality and Social Psychology, 70*, 336–348.

Folkman, S., Chesney, M. A., Cooke, M., Boccellari, A., & Collette, L. (1994). Caregiver burden in HIV+ and HIV− partners of men with AIDS. *Journal of Consulting and Clinical Psychology, 62*, 746–756.

Folkman, S., & Lazarus, R. S. (1988). The relationship between coping and emotion: Implications for theory and research. *Social Science and Medicine, 26*, 309–317.

Fortunato, J. E. (1987). *AIDS: The spiritual dilemma.* San Francisco: Harper & Row.

Fowler, J. W. (1981). Stages of faith. New York: Harper-Collins Publishers.

Frank, J. D. (1977). Nature and function of belief systems, humanism and transcendental religion. *American Psychologist, 32*, 555–559.

Frankl, V. (1963). *Man's search for meaning.* New York: Washington Square Press.

Horowitz, M., Wilner, N., & Alvarez, W. (1979). Impact of Event Scale: A measure of subjective stress. *Psychosomatic Medicine, 41*, 209–218.

Jung, C. G. (1955). Syncronicity: An acausal connecting principle. In C. G. Jung & W. Pauli (Eds.), *The interpretation of nature and the psyche* (pp. 1–146). New York: Pantheon.

Katz, M. H. (1997). AIDS epidemic in San Francisco among men who report sex with men: Successes and challenges of HIV prevention. *Journal of Acquired Immune Deficiency Syndromes and Human Retrovirology, 14*(Suppl. 2), S38–S46.

Klass, D. (1995). Spiritual aspects of the resolution of grief. In H. Wass & R. A. Neimeyer (Eds.), *Dying: Facing the facts* (pp. 243–268). Washington, DC: Taylor & Francis.

Maslow, A. (1964). *Religions, values, and peak-experiences.* Columbus: Ohio State University Press.

Maslow, A. (1971). *The farther reaches of human nature.* New York: Viking.

Millison, M., & Dudley, J. R. (1992). Providing spiritual support: A job for all hospice professionals. *The Hospice Journal, 8*(4), 49–66.

Pargament, K. (1990). God help me: Toward a theoretical framework of coping for the psychology of religion. *Research in the Social Scientific Study of Religion, 2*, 195–224.

Parkes, C. M. (1971). Psycho-social transitions: A field for study. *Social Science and Medicine, 5*, 101–115.

Parkes, C. M. (1972). *Bereavement: Studies of grief in adult life.* New York: International Universities Press.

Parkes, C. M., & Weiss, R. (1983). *Recovery from bereavement.* New York: Basic Books.

Paul, J. P., Hays, R. B., & Coates, T. J. (1995). The impact of the HIV epidemic on U.S. gay male communities. In A. R. D'Augelli & C. Patterson (Eds.), *Lesbian, gay, and bisexual identities over the lifespan: Psychological perspectives* (pp. 347–397). New York: Oxford University Press.

Prest, L. A., & Keller, J. F. (1993). Spirituality and family therapy: Spiritual beliefs, myths and metaphors. *Journal of Marital and Family Therapy, 19*, 137–148.

Radloff, L. S. (1977). The CES–D Scale: A self-report depression scale for research in the general population. *Applied Psychological Measurement, 1*, 385–401.

Richards, P. S., & Bergin, A. E. (1997). *A spiritual strategy for counseling and psychotherapy.* Washington, DC: American Psychological Association.

Richards T. A., Acree, M., & Folkman, S. (1999). Spiritual aspects of loss among partners of men with AIDS: Postbereavement follow-up. *Death Studies, 23*, 105–127.

Richards T. A., & Folkman, S. (1997). Spiritual aspects of loss at the time of a partner's death from AIDS. *Death Studies, 21*, 527–552.

Richards, T. A., Wrubel, J., & Folkman, S. (1999). Death rites in the San Francisco gay community: Cultural developments of the AIDS epidemic. *Omega, 40*, 313–329.

San Francisco Department of Public Health. (1997, December). *AIDS surveillance report*. San Francisco: Department of Public Health.

Seidel, J., Friese, S., & Leonard, D. C. (1995). *The Ethnograph V4.0: A user's guide*. Amherst, MA: Qualis Research Associates.

Shafranske, E. P. (1998, August). *Representation in religion and psychoanalysis*. Paper presented at the 106th Annual Convention of the American Psychological Association, San Francisco.

Shilts, R. (1987). *And the band played on*. New York: Penguin.

Shuchter, S. R., & Zisook, S. (1993). The course of normal grief. In M. S. Stroebe, W. Stroebe, & R. O. Hansson (Eds.), *Handbook of bereavement* (pp. 23–43). New York: Cambridge University Press.

Silverman, P. R., & Worden, J. W. (1992). Children's reactions to the death of a parent in the early months after the death. *American Journal of Orthopsychiatry, 62*, 93–104.

Spielberger, C. D. (1988). *State–Trait Anger Expression Inventory*. Lutz, FL: Psychological Assessment Resources.

Stroebe, M., & Stroebe, W. (1989). Who participates in bereavement research? A review and empirical study. *Omega, 20*, 1–29.

Stroebe, M., & Stroebe, W. (1991). Does "grief work" work? *Journal of Consulting and Clinical Psychology, 59*, 57–65.

Tillich, P. (1963). *Systematic theology*. Chicago: University of Chicago Press.

Walsh, J., & Charalambides, L. (1989). Individual and social origins of belief structure change. *Journal of Social Psychology, 130*, 517–532.

Weiss, R., & Richards, T. A. (1997). A scale for predicting quality of recovery following the death of a partner. *Journal of Personality and Social Psychology, 72*, 885–891.

Zisook, S., & Shuchter, S. R. (1986). The first four years of widowhood. *Psychiatric Annals, 16*, 288–294.

10

POSITIVE OUTCOMES OF LOSING A LOVED ONE

THOMAS T. FRANTZ, MEGAN M. FARRELL, AND
BARBARA C. TROLLEY

Most people would never willingly seek or want to go through the pain associated with the death of a loved one. Bereaved parents, for example, routinely say that their child's death was the worst thing that ever happened to them. M. Stroebe, Stroebe, and Hansson (1988), in a review of bereavement research, highlighted the negative impact of loss on mental and physical health, social relationships, financial security, and basic beliefs about the world. Most bereavement research has focused on identifying the variables that affect the grief process, such as social support, quality of the premorbid relationship, coping style, and additional life stressors (Gass & Chang, 1989; Herth, 1990; Moss, Moss, Rubenstein, & Resch, 1993; Norris & Murrell, 1990; Yancey, Greger, & Coburn, 1990). There is little argument about the pain, hardship, and negative effects of losing a loved one. What has been largely overlooked, however, is the seemingly paradoxical observation that grief leaves in its wake many positive outcomes. Indeed, attempts to cast death in a positive light, such as "God never gives us more than we can handle" or "time heals all wounds" are, especially soon after a death, usually dismissed as unhelpful, irritating, and a sign of not understanding.

Yet most often the passage of time—sometimes years, for those who have lost children or loved ones to murder or suicide—does bring with it a psychological healing and an ability to love and laugh again. In fact, there is an increasing amount of research identifying a sizeable array of benefits that eventually become clear to many grieving people. These positive aspects of bereavement do not contradict or diminish the painful and frequently nightmarish effects of death; rather, they slowly and usually unexpectedly emerge as the dawn of healing replaces the lonely darkness of grief.

IN THE WAKE OF DEATH, SOME GOOD THINGS COME

Camus (1990), in an essay on death, observed that so many things are susceptible to being loved that surely no loss can be fatal. Attig (1996) saw those who grieve as beginning anew, as having washed up on the shore after having nearly drowned. Finding themselves no longer at sea, they recover and find wholeness as part of larger wholes as they reconnect with family, friends old and new, community, and God.

Death sometimes comes as a relief from the continuing stress of caregiving toward the end of a loved one's life. Norris and Murrell (1987) found that family stress for older adults decreased following the death of a loved one. If family members are ill for awhile, they remain the focus of time and attention, and normal routines take a back seat to caretaking. The death of the loved one may represent a burden of strain being lifted and a resumption of living for a family.

Social Bonds

Social supports and friendships may become strengthened or newly established through the grieving process (Krause, 1986; Zimpfer, 1991). Although not everyone can reach out to others in times of crises, those who do may find their friendships strengthened through the sharing. Taylor, Lichtman, and Wood (1984) and Collins, Taylor, and Skokan (1990) found that people dealing with life traumas, such as cancer, found more pleasure in their relationships with others and were more compassionate following their experience with this illness. Similarly, Lehman et al. (1993) found that the bereaved person had an increased openness to and concern for others as well as an increased emphasis on family. Social supports may become a lifeline and take a more central focus, especially when elderly people lose someone close to them. Lund, Caserta, Van Pelt, and Gass (1990) found that widowers' primary and secondary social networks steadily increased in size over the 2 years following the death of a spouse. Baring one's soul through the common pain of grief is the cement for many friendships.

Seven couples interviewed 4–8 months following their infants' deaths (Helmrath & Steinitz, 1978) said their relationships with each other and their other children had deepened and improved. In a study of bereaved parents, Miles and Crandall (1983) observed that as time passed, parents mentioned more positive than negative outcomes, including becoming more grateful, compassionate, and appreciative of the importance of loved ones. Calhoun and Tedeschi (1990) found that 83% of the 52 bereaved adults they interviewed said they had come to see that they had friends and family on whom they could really count.

In studying adolescent bereavement, Oltjenbruns (1996) found that nearly all of her sample reported caring more for other people, stronger emotional bonds, and increased empathy once some time had passed following the deaths of their loved ones. Closer relationships with select people seem to be a relatively common result of losing a loved one.

Spirituality

Although one's spirituality and beliefs about God and the universe are often upset by the betrayal of death, the altered belief system that emerges from bereavement is frequently stronger. Chen (1997) argued that grief has enormous potential to advance spiritual growth as the emotional trauma transcends everyday experiences and awakens or deepens spirituality. Calhoun and Tedeschi (1990) reported that 67% of their sample said their loved ones' deaths had strengthened their religious beliefs, and both African American and White widows interviewed by Salahu-Din (1996) said their spirituality was further developed and refined as a result of their spouse's deaths.

Tarockova (1996) argued that life's most painful losses can present an opportunity for personal growth and reviewed the literature on loss from 1973–1995 to support her claim of the positive growth that results from transcending life's losses.

Over 80% of the approximately 300 adults who had suffered the death of a loved one said that their religious and spiritual beliefs helped them during their grief, a strengthened belief in an afterlife being a significant benefit of their experience (Frantz, Trolley, & Johll, 1996). Those who have lost a loved one may have a greater appreciation of life and an increased focus on the present (Kallenberg & Soderfeldt, 1992; Lehman et al., 1993). Spiritual beliefs, whether in the form of a structured religion or a generalized belief system, may be strengthened because there is no other source of reason or solace. Balk (1991) and Gilbert (1992) found that religion was a source of renewed meaning and comfort for some of the teenage and adult participants in their studies.

The loss of a loved one may be associated with a higher existential meaning and positive change in life goals (Edmonds & Hooker, 1992). Folkman (1997) found that the coping process associated with positive psychological states during bereavement all had their roots in a common theme: searching for and finding meaning in a changed life. After investigating the effects of a child's death, Cook and Wimberly (1983), Talbot (1996), and Milo (1997) all reported that many of the bereaved parents they studied underwent a personal transformation that was often described as one of the defining experiences of their lives, leaving them with more positive, deeply held values and beliefs.

Lifestyle

Of course, changes in beliefs may spur or accompany changes in behavior or lifestyle. Salahu-Din (1996); Hogan, Morse, and Tason (1996); Humphrey and Zimpfer (1996); and Bernard and Schneider (1996) all concluded that personal growth often results from going through a grieving process. Feelings of self-confidence, ability to cope, and self-reliance may steadily increase (Lehman et al., 1993). Grieving people may gradually become aware of internal resources that were unknown to them prior to the death. The diagnosis of a serious illness, similar to loss by death, may be associated with a reaffirmation of self-esteem and self-worth, causing the individual to make positive life changes (Taylor & Brown, 1988; Taylor, Collins, Skokan, & Aspinwall, 1989).

Perhaps the most frequently cited and, to bereaved people, surprising change is a sense of independence and competence. Initially this is an unwanted independence forced on them by the vacuum of their loved one's death but, as grief begins to wane, the subtly acquired skills and competencies surface and spawn renewed self-esteem. After conducting a case study, Hainer (1990) concluded that widowhood can increase self-esteem as a widow works through the loss of her husband. Most of the bereaved adults interviewed by Calhoun and Tedeschi (1990) said they had developed new skills, done things they had never done before, were thankful that they no longer had to rely so much on other people, felt more mature, and were now better able to face a crisis if one emerged. Salahu-Din's (1996) widows reported increased self-confidence and ability to function independently, which was reflected in traveling alone, returning to college, and being seen as strong by their families and friends.

Emotion

The death of a loved one forces many grieving people to face head on the sadness, guilt, anger, or fear that follows a loss. They become familiar with emotion and its expression and learn mentally healthy ways to deal with emotion (Raphael & Nunn, 1988; Schwartz-Borden, 1986). The development of humor as an ally in the grieving process sometimes occurs (Stevenson, 1993). A majority of the 52 adult mourners interviewed by Calhoun and Tedeschi (1990) said they were now more expressive of their emotions, thoughts, and feelings; some said they had lost the fear of saying what they truly felt. In a study of individuals whose friends had died, Oltjenbruns (1996) reported that many developed more emotional strength and deeper emotional bonds than they had experienced before their friend died.

From this sample of research findings we see that for some people benefits do eventually arise from a loved one's death. A few researchers have addressed the issue of what enhances the possibility that something positive might result from a loved one's death.

Factors Leading to Positive Outcomes

The ability to accomplish simple daily tasks has been found to be indicative of positive outcomes. Lund, Caserta, Dimond, and Shaffer (1989) concluded that the ability to complete the numerous tasks of daily life was clearly associated with favorable bereavement outcomes. Rubenstein (1983) found that filling days with meaningful activities was essential to healthy bereavement, and Sanders (1981) reported that grieving people felt more competent when they were able to accomplish simple tasks.

Attig (1996) developed the idea that positive aspects of grief come about as a result of a process of relearning and reconnecting in a new way with family, old friends, and new friends; reconnecting with one's community through work; volunteering; social, creative, and recreational activities; and reconnecting with God and a reconstructed belief system about the universe. Folkman (1997), as mentioned earlier, sees that positive grief outcomes are most likely to come about when a grieving person actively searches for new meaning in ordinary daily events, in problems that arise, in spiritual beliefs, and in situations that could produce stress.

Neimeyer, Keesee, and Fortner (2000) posited that the experience of grieving may be full of choices (e.g., to attend to the distress caused by the loss or to focus on adapting to a changed external reality) and that certain choices may lead to more positive outcomes than others.

Finally, a specific philosophical belief was cited by both Braun and Berg (1994) and Wortman, Silver, and Kessler (1993) as a predictor of positive grief outcomes; that is, people whose belief system includes the possibility that their loved one might die will likely suffer a less negative impact when death comes than people whose belief system cannot accommodate such a calamity.

It seems safe to conclude that the aftermath of grief may hold some benefits for some bereaved people. Such benefits may not be initially apparent. It is difficult to predict with certainty the impact of death on survivors.

Variables that influence the grief process, such as the bereaved person's model of the world, the mode of death, the relationship of the survivor to the deceased person, unfinished business, and intellectual versus emotional responses, need to be considered (DeSpelder & Strickland, 1992). In no way can the pain of death be avoided, but the survivor is left undeniably different, and different does not necessarily mean devastated, or completely vulnerable, or a vesicle of unending pain. Certainly grief does not affect all people equally (Hansson, Stroebe, & Stroebe, 1988), but death can challenge bereaved persons to slow the pace of life, examine the core of their beings, and gradually become aware of growth and strengths that have emerged since the death.

PURPOSE OF THE STUDY

Armed with the general hypothesis that there may be some positive aspects of grief, we analyzed a series of structured interviews collected over an 8-year period to see, as our primary purpose, if people who had lost a loved one felt that anything good had happened as a result of the death and to identify what those positive experiences were. A secondary purpose of our analysis was to determine what grieving people themselves did that led to a positive outcome.

METHOD

Participants

Participants in this study were 397 adults whose loved ones had died approximately 1 year prior to the time they were interviewed to collect data for this research (mean time since death: 13 months). Each participant was interviewed with a structured questionnaire. Interviews lasted from 25 min to 3 hours (average time of interview was 1 hour 20 min) and were usually conducted in the bereaved person's home or, occasionally, at his or her office. Participants were not randomly sampled. In a few cases participants were known to their interviewers; in most cases they were not.

The data collection format for this study was somewhat unusual in that each participant was interviewed by a different interviewer. Data were collected over an 8-year period, from 1989 to 1996, by graduate students taking a grief counseling course. Each year each student had to select a person whose loved one had died about a year earlier and interview him or her with a set of questions provided by the instructor. Thus the only criteria for a person's participation in the study were experiencing a death a year prior and a willingness to talk about it with a student interviewer. Interviewers were all master's or doctoral students in counseling or counseling-related programs.

The timing of the interview (at a year past death) was chosen so that (a) most participants would be out of shock and able to view their grief with some perspective, yet (b) their grief would be fresh enough for its intensity to be felt and communicated. Each interviewer interviewed one bereaved person. Interviewers were given explicit instructions in two different class sessions on how to arrange for, conduct, and close the interview. Nonetheless, the unusual method of collecting creates a clear limitation on the interpretation of the findings.

At the time of the interview, participants were told that they would be recontacted by the interviewer in a couple of months to see how they were doing and to give feedback to the student about whether the interview had affected them in either a positive or negative way. No formal data were collected in the follow-up interview. Participant feedback from these follow-up sessions was overwhelmingly positive. Although in some instances participants said the interview had had little effect on them, most of the bereaved people interviewed said they were glad to have had the chance to talk about their loved one, appreciated that someone was interested enough to listen and, in some cases, felt the session had led to a successful resolution to key aspects of their grief.

As is often the case in bereavement studies, the sample was largely female—73% women and 27% men. Their average age was between 40 and 41 years. Although data on exact cause of death were not gathered, the loved ones of 39% of the sample had died suddenly and unexpectedly, whereas 61% had died a lingering death. A majority of the deaths (55%) had occurred in hospitals, 26% had occurred at home, and 19% had occurred elsewhere. Thirty-eight percent of the sample had lost a parent, 17% had lost a spouse, 13% had lost a grandparent, 7% had lost a child, 7% had lost a sibling, and 19% had lost some other relative or friend. Data on race were not recorded. Assuming that students interviewed people of their own race, the sample would be about 9% African American and 90% White, and mostly of the middle, and lower middle classes.

Questions and Analyses

In addition to the questions that were asked to gather the background information reported above, each participant was asked the following four open-ended questions, the responses to which were recorded in writing by the interviewer: (a) Despite the tragedy of death, is there anything positive or good that has come about as a result of the death? (b) What is the main thing you've learned so far from this experience? (c) Are there any ways in which you are now a different person than you were before the death? (d) Since your loved one died, what have you done for yourself that has helped the most?

Each response was read by Thomas T. Frantz and Barbara Trolley and synopsized into a phrase summarizing the content—for example, the response "I have learned to appreciate my husband more now that I compare my life to what our life was like when he was alive" to Question 1 (Did anything good happen?) was summarized "appreciated deceased more." A number of responses contained more than one element of content; in these cases more than one summary phrase was written. For example, the response "My relationship with my father has gotten a lot stronger. We do things together and spend a lot more time with each other since my mother died. I also decided to donate platelets realizing how much other people's blood helped Mom" yielded the summary phrases "spent more time with family" and "tried to help others."

For each question, Frantz and Trolley then separately classified the summary phrases into categories as each perceived them to emerge from the recorded responses. Then they each generated approximately 60 response categories to the first three questions and more than 100 to the fourth. There was over 90% agreement between them on the most prolific categories. Where there was disparity between Frantz and Trolley, especially on categories endorsed by 5 or fewer participants, they met to discuss and reach agreement about whether such categories could be subsumed under larger ones, combined, or eliminated. A functional list of response categories to each question was thus generated into which each participant's responses were sorted. Armed with these categories Megan M. Farrell, who had not been involved in the categorizing up to this point, then read each participant's response to each question and sorted it into a category, resulting in a little over 94% agreement between her sorting and that of Frantz and Trolley. Disparities were resolved through discussion.

RESULTS

The findings emerging from each question are presented consecutively. The number of response categories, together with the total number of discrete responses received to each question, are listed at the beginning of each paragraph.

Question 1: Did Anything Good Result From the Death?

Fifty-six response categories emerged out of 438 reported responses. Only 16% of the grieving people who were interviewed said that nothing good came about as a result of the death of their loved one; 84% indicated that, indeed, something positive had resulted. Positive outcomes mentioned by at least 10 participants in the study are summarized in Table 10.1. One third of the sample mentioned that the death had strengthened their rela-

TABLE 10.1
Responses to Question 1: Did Anything Good Come From the Death?

Response	% endorsing
1. Brought family closer together, improved communication, strengthened relationships with family and friends	33
2. I appreciate life more now, I live more fully, I've a better outlook on life, got my priorities in order	20
3. Had to rely on myself, I'm stronger, more independent	14
4. Loved one is no longer suffering, in good place	9
5. I'm more patient, understanding, accepting, compassionate	8
6. My burden of care has been lifted	6
7. I'm less afraid of death now	3
8. I've strengthened my religious beliefs	3
9. Nothing good came of it	16

Note. N = 397. Percentages do not add to 100 because some participants gave more than one response. From "Positive aspects of grief" by T. Frantz, 1998, *Pastoral Psychology, 47*, p. 8. Copyright 1998 by Kluwer Academic Publishers. Reprinted with permission.

tionship with family and friends and brought them closer together. Examples are "since my husband died my children call on me more often," "we're back in touch with relatives we seldom saw before," and "I'm now much closer with my stepmother." Closer relationships with family was clearly the major positive outcome of death found in this study.

The positive outcome that was mentioned second most often was a greater appreciation for life and for living more fully in the moment, which was mentioned by almost 20% of our sample. Examples include "I find I'm less willing to postpone things," "I'm less affected by things I used to think were important but really aren't," and "I tell my father I love him every time I see him now." A theme running through these respondents was that their loved ones' deaths had forced them to reflect on life and re-evaluate things they had been taking for granted.

Fourteen percent of our participants said they had become more self-reliant and independent since their loved ones' death. Many were quite surprised to find that they were capable of stepping in and handling things that they previously thought only the deceased person could handle. Examples include

> It forced me to differentiate from my family and become more independent.
> Now that my mother has died I realize I'm stronger than I thought I was.
> I do more things by myself and find I'm not afraid to take chances.
> The power of love—and to live for today—some things just aren't as important as I thought before. Set priorities.
> You have to cope. You could ruin your family if you don't.

Other positive outcomes of the grieving process mentioned by at least 10 of our participants were that (a) they had become more understanding, accepting, and compassionate toward others and that they were in less of a hurry and less easily upset (one man related that he'd been doing the laundry for his wife when the washer overflowed all over the floor: "Before my daughter died I'd have been totally bent out of shape, but now, with everything that's happened, it was no big deal."); (b) that they were less afraid of death; and (c) that they had grown stronger and more secure in their spiritual and religious beliefs.

Finally, one of the good things that happened was a different sort of outcome than those listed above, namely, a relief regarding the death itself either because their loved one was no longer suffering and was in a better place or because the burden of caring for their dying loved one had finally been lifted.

Question 2: What Have You Learned From These Experiences?

Fifty-five response categories emerged out of 477 separate responses. Ninety-eight percent of our sample said that they had learned something as a result of experiencing the death and the grief that followed. The 10 most frequently cited summary categories of what they learned are presented in Table 10.2. A majority (about two thirds) of the responses to this question were positive and encouraging; the most frequently mentioned one (endorsed by 35% of our sample) was that the person had learned to smell the roses along the way, to not take loved ones for granted, to be more thankful for small things, and generally to find new meaning in life. Significant numbers of participants said they had learned that they were stronger and coped better than they thought they would; that they became more compassionate and empathic; and that it was helpful to be able to cry, grieve, and talk about the deceased person.

TABLE 10.2
Responses to Question 2: What Have You Learned From This Death?

Response	% endorsing
1. To smell the roses, tell people you love them, live in the moment	35
2. Death can strike at any time, life is short, we're all going to die	22
3. I'm stronger, more independent, cope better	13
4. How devastating grief can be	9
5. That life goes on, put it behind you, just have to accept it	8
6. I'm more compassionate, understanding, considerate	6
7. That it's important to cry, share feelings, grieve	5
8. I'm less afraid of death	3
9. Stronger belief in God, more spiritual	2

Note. N = 397. Percentages do not add to 100 because some participants gave more than one response. From "Positive aspects of grief" by T. Frantz, 1998, *Pastoral Psychology, 47,* p. 9. Copyright 1998 by Kluwer Academic Publishers. Reprinted with permission.

Comments of some about what they learned follow:

Material things aren't important; looks, age, weight, etc. are superficial and not worth worrying about.
I learned not to take things for granted and that having a child is a gift!
Tell people you love them before it's too late.
Each day is special. If I wake up mad at the world—don't take it out on people.

One woman, whose 94-year-old mother had died, said what she learned was "not to hang on to a lot of junk."

It is interesting that nearly 40% of our sample indicated that what they had learned was not necessarily positive. More than 21% said they had learned that life is short, that death can come at any time, and that we are all going to die sometime. Coupled with the 8% who said that life goes on, that there's no point in worrying about it, you just have to accept it, put it behind you, and move on, this yields a sizeable minority of grieving people who have become somewhat fatalistic and resigned. For some of these participants what they have learned, although tinged with fatalism, seems to have brought a kind of freedom on the order of "If we're going to die anyway, why not do it my way while I can?" For others, this fatalism seems to have led them into a victim role where they feel they are cogs in some impersonal machine over which they have no control.

Finally, 8% of our interviewees frankly said that the main thing they learned was how devastating grief can be and that they did not see how life would ever be okay again. Some of their comments include

Parents aren't immortal. You think they'll always be there. You're wrong.
I didn't think it was possible to hurt this bad. I've never felt this much pain in my whole life. I wouldn't wish this on my worst enemy!
I didn't learn anything. What could I learn? The thought of it is still a nightmare.

Question 3: In What Ways Are You Different?

Sixty-four response categories emerged out of 521 separate responses. Most of the grieving people interviewed, 85%, said that they had changed as a result of experiencing their loved one's death. The most common ways in which they felt different are summarized in Table 10.3. The effects of the death and its aftermath were positive for more than three fourths of our sample but were negative for about one fourth. The most frequently mentioned changes (by 32% of the sample) were being stronger and more independent, self-reliant, and capable than they had been prior to their loved ones' deaths. Another 17% said they have come to live in the moment and

TABLE 10.3
Responses to Question 3: In What Ways Are You Different?

Response	% endorsing
1. More mature, self-confident, independent, stronger	32
2. Live in the present, appreciate life	17
3. More compassionate and understanding, tell people I love them	14
4. Closer to friends and family, new role in family	11
5. Lonelier, sadder, part of you dies	10
6. More afraid of death, cancer, more fragile	5
7. Bitter, hardened, nastier, tougher	5
8. Can't leave home, can't make decisions, more cautious	3
9. Become more spiritual	3
10. I'm not different	15

Note. N = 397. Percentages do not add to 100 because some participants gave more than one response. From "Positive aspects of grief" by T. Frantz, 1998, *Pastoral Psychology, 47,* p. 11. Copyright 1998 by Kluwer Academic Publishers. Reprinted with permission.

appreciate life more than before the death, whereas 14% felt more compassionate and said they now are more likely to express love to their family and friends. A sample of responses include

> I feel more competent, more in control of my life, like I can handle whatever comes.
> I'm more mature now. I've settled down a lot. Dad's death has made me grow up.
> I'm more willing to take risks. I've switched jobs and moved into my own apartment.
> I'm a lot more assertive, a lot stronger, less willing to allow people to tell me how to feel or what to think.
> It's made me more relaxed, though certainly not thrilled, about death. I understand death better, I'm more secure about it. I realize that some pains can be healed, but some can remain, and it's all right.

On the other hand, death left a number of our interviewees feeling lonelier, sadder, more cautious, indecisive, and afraid of death than before. Still others had become bitter, hardened, and angry at the injustice and capriciousness they felt death represented and at the difficult circumstances in which the death left them. In their words,

> I'm lonelier, I'm sexually frustrated, and I shaved my beard.
> I'll never be the same person. Part of me died. I think, feel and look differently. I feel like I'm 80 years old. (age is 47)
> I've become protective of my husband and son. I'm afraid they'll leave me as my father did. I have to protect them so they won't disappear.
> I'm stronger than I ever thought, but I'm angry. Life doesn't give me any pleasure. I don't like to leave home, and I've distanced myself from most of my family and friends.

Question 4: What Did You Do to Help Yourself?

One hundred and five response categories emerged out of 654 separate responses. There was a wider variety of answers to Question 4 than to any other question, and it took twice the number of categories than what emerged from the other questions to summarize the breadth of responses (see Table 10.4). What is so encouraging about these responses is that 381 (96% of the people interviewed) said that they had done something to help themselves; that is, despite their grief, they had not succumbed to the victim role in any consistent way.

Clearly the main thing that grieving people did to help themselves was keep busy, especially by going to work or school or by taking care of household duties or family members, particularly children. Many mentioned that having a routine to fall back into and not having to make decisions made grief a little easier.

TABLE 10.4
Responses to Question 4: What Did You Do to Help Yourself?

Response	% endorsing
1. Went to work, school; kept busy, followed routine, cared for family	25
2. Talked, cried, grieved, got feelings out	17
3. Became closer to family	16
4. Kept memory alive, thought of good times, looked at pictures, talked with deceased's friends	12
5. Became more independent, decisive, assertive, self-confident, new priorities	8
6. Increased faith, spirituality, went to church, prayed	8
7. Traveled, took vacation	6
8. Exercised, lost weight, ate healthier	6
9. Sought counseling	5
10. Went to support group, talked with others in same boat	4
11. Did things the deceased would have liked	4
12. Bought things for myself—clothes, boat, house	4
13. Dreamed of deceased, talked with deceased, believe he/she is with me	4
14. Helped others	3
15. Kept diary; wrote a song, poem, letter, made collage	3
16. Did volunteer work, joined club, took a class	3
17. Read	3
18. Nothing	4
19. Denied, avoided	3
20. Visited grave	2

Note. $N = 397$. Percentages do not add to 100 because some participants gave more than one response. From "Positive aspects of grief" by T. Frantz, 1998, *Pastoral Psychology, 47*, p. 12. Copyright 1998 by Kluwer Academic Publishers. Reprinted with permission.

It is interesting that about half of the things people did for themselves that helped were things that took their minds off their grief and provided some respite or escape from focusing on loss and grief; for example, working, traveling, exercising, reading, doing volunteer work, shopping for clothes, remodeling, and so on.

Conversely, roughly half of what grieving people did to help themselves dealt directly with the deceased person and grief; for example, going to a support group, visiting the grave, crying, talking about the deceased person, dreaming about the deceased person, keeping a diary, reminiscing, looking at pictures, going through possessions, reading the autopsy report, and so on.

Because half of the things people did to help themselves involved facing loss and grief directly, whereas the other half were focused away from death and on other aspects of life, it seems we must conclude that neither facing nor avoiding grief is alone the answer but rather both in combination.

DISCUSSION AND CONCLUSION

From years of counseling grieving people and leading bereavement support groups we know that mentioning to a grieving person that something positive is likely to come about as a result of his or her loved one's death is not only unhelpful but also brings on anger and shocked wonder at how we could be so stupid. Yet we have often noticed that for some people the death of a loved one does bring some good things into their life—a conclusion supported by a growing array of research studies.

Our study bears witness that significant positive things do result from death for an overwhelming majority of grieving people. In asking people who had lost a loved one to death approximately a year earlier—what good has come out of it, what they have learned as a result, and how are they different now—five major findings stand out.

First, many bereaved people say that they have learned to appreciate the value of life more than they ever did before. They have learned that life is special and precious and that it has to be lived in the moment as much as possible. They say they have re-examined their priorities and place greater importance on spending time with family and loved ones. They now try to take more time to smell the roses during even their average days.

Second, they report becoming stronger as a result of surviving the pain of the death and stepping forward to handle things that previously were done by the deceased person. Many say that they are more independent, mature, self-reliant, and self-confident now and often express surprise at their newfound and unexpected strength. Of course, this is not true for everyone, or even for a majority of our sample, but it was indicated by one fourth to one third of those interviewed.

Third, the cliché that "tragedy brings people together" seemed to be true for significant numbers of our sample, who found themselves much closer to their loved ones and family than before the death. Many reported that they no longer took loved ones for granted and were more apt to tell people they loved them and to stay in contact with family than previously.

Fourth, there were, nonetheless, a relatively small but noticeable minority of those interviewed whom the death had left significantly worse off than before. They felt devastated by their loss and lonelier, more sad, less full of life, and more resigned than prior to their loved ones' deaths. They expressed feeling powerless in the face of death, and many said it left them feeling hard and cold. Such reactions are not unusual in the early and middle phases of grief, and they often diminish with time, but not for everyone.

Fifth, it was heartening to see that 96% of the people said that they had done things to help themselves that worked and made at least some positive difference in coping with their loss. It is especially interesting to recognize that the two general types of efforts they made to help themselves were paradoxical. On the one hand, they faced their grief, felt it, expressed it, cried about it, and strove to keep their loved one's memory alive; on the other hand, they avoided it, throwing themselves into work, school, child care, travel, exercise, shopping, and volunteer work, hoping to push it to the back of their minds, at least for short periods. We might observe that those for whom grief turns out to be the hardest are those who only immerse themselves in it or who only avoid it. The ones who best cope with death may be those who both embrace and avoid grief, at times feeling the pain and at other times finding ways not to.

It is interesting that this finding is similar to that of Gallagher, Lovett, Hanley-Dunn, and Thompson (1989) who, in a study of 211 adult grievers, found that "good copers may be persons who can permit themselves to experience sadness and emotional upset caused by grief while still maintaining a variety of cognitive and emotional skills in their daily repertories" (p. 118). More important, our results seem to support the dual process model of grief proposed by Stroebe and her colleagues (M. Stroebe, Schut, & Stroebe, 1998; W. Stroebe & Stroebe, 1994), who have argued that both the emotional experience of grieving and the attempt to pull oneself together and carry on are necessary components of a healthy bereavement process—that is, the balance between tearful, emotive, falling-apart grief work and suppression of feelings, coping, and reinvesting in work or activity may be a barometer of how well a bereaved person will come through the process.

Counselors sometimes see people who are "stuck" in their grief (a) as a result of avoiding it by escaping into work or other activity, (b) as a result of immersing themselves in it to the exclusion of active living, or (c) as a result of doing neither. Our results indicate that, when working with such a person, we may need to help him or her find a balance between escape and immersion, realizing that each is healthy but only in conjunction with the other. To put it poetically, as Kahlil Gibran did in *The Prophet* (1923),

> Reason, ruling alone, is a force confining; and passion, unattended, is a flame that burns its own destruction. Therefore let your soul exalt your reason to the height of passion, that it may sing; and let it direct your passion with reason, that your passion may live through its own daily resurrection, and like the phoenix rise above its own ashes. (p. 50)

Finally, it is joyful to note that, for two of our interviewees, the death of their loved ones resulted in a minor miracle wherein they were united with family members they had never seen. In one case, a woman's father, whom she had never met, read the obituary and contacted her, and they were reunited after 32 years. The other case was similar in that the half-brother and half-sister, who our 23-year-old participant did not even know she had, saw the death notice and called her, resulting in her finding two new siblings.

As we step back and reflect on the course that bereavement writing and research has taken since Elizabeth Kübler-Ross brought death and dying out of the closet with her 1969 book, we may be witnessing a relatively new component in our understanding of grief's effects. As the research began to build in the late 1970s and especially the 1980s, it emphasized the tremendous toll bereavement takes on survivors and the need to grieve and face the pain with catharsis and support. Now we are seeing a shift away from a sole emphasis on grief's devastation toward a realization that grief's consequences are not necessarily all bad and an awareness, perhaps reluctantly arrived at, that the quality of some people's lives is in some ways better following their loved one's death than it was before.

REFERENCES

Attig, T. (1996). *How we grieve*. New York: Oxford University Press.

Balk, D. (1991). Sibling death, adolescent bereavement, and religion. *Death Studies, 15*, 1–20.

Bernard, J. S., & Schneider, M. (1996). *The true work of dying: A practical and compassionate guide to easing the dying process*. New York: Avon.

Braun, M. J., & Berg, D. H. (1994). Meaning reconstruction in the experience of parental bereavement. *Death Studies, 18*, 105–129.

Calhoun, L. G., & Tedeschi, R. G. (1990). Positive aspects of critical life problems: Recollections of grief. *Omega, 20*, 265–272.

Camus, A. (1990). *Youthful writings*. New York: Paragon House.

Chen, L. (1997). Grief as a transcendent function and teacher of spiritual growth. *Pastoral Psychology, 46*(2), 79–84.

Collins, R., Taylor, S., & Skokan, L. (1990). A better world or a shattered vision? Changes in life perspectives following victimization. *Social Cognition, 8,* 263–285.

Cook, J. A., and Wimberly, D. W. (1983). If I should die before I wake: Religious commitment and adjustment to the death of a child. *Journal of the Scientific Study of Religion, 22,* 222–238.

DeSpelder, L., & Strickland, A. (1992). *The last dance.* Mountain View, CA: Mayfield.

Edmonds, S., & Hooker, K. (1992). Perceived changes in life meaning following bereavement. *Omega, 25,* 307–318.

Folkman, S. (1997). Positive psychological states and coping with severe stress. *Social Science Medicine, 45,* 1207–1221.

Frantz, T. T., Trolley, B. C., & Johll, M. P. (1996). Religious aspects of bereavement. *Pastoral Psychology, 44*(3), 151–163.

Gallagher, D., Lovett, S., Hanley-Dunn, P., & Thompson, L. W. (1989). Use of select coping strategies during late-life spousal bereavement. In D. A. Lund (Ed.), *Older bereaved spouses* (pp. 111–121). New York: Hemisphere.

Gass, K., & Chang, A. (1989). Appraisals of bereavement, coping, resources, and psychosocial health dysfunction in widows and widowers. *Nursing Research, 38,* 31–36.

Gibran, K. (1923). *The prophet.* New York: Knopf.

Gilbert, K. (1992). Religion as a resource for bereaved parents. *Journal of Religion and Health, 31,* 19–31.

Hainer, J. (1990). Widowhood as a time for growth and development. *The Psychotherapy Patient, 6,* 147–155.

Hansson, R., Stroebe, M., & Stroebe, W. (1988). In conclusion: Current themes in bereavement and widowhood research. *Journal of Social Issues, 44,* 207–216.

Helmrath, T. A., & Steinitz, E. M. (1978). Death of an infant: Parental grieving and the failure of social support. *Journal of Family Practice, 6,* 785–790.

Herth, K. (1990). Relationship of hope, coping styles, concurrent losses, and setting to grief resolution in the elderly widow(er). *Research in Nursing and Health, 13,* 109–117.

Hogan, N., Morse, J. M., & Tason, M. C. (1996). Toward an experiential theory of bereavement. *Omega, 33,* 43–65.

Humphrey, G. M., & Zimpfer, D. G. (1996). *Counseling for grief and bereavement.* London: Sage.

Kallenberg, K., & Soderfeldt, B. (1992). Three years later: Grief, view of life, and personal crisis after death of a family member. *Journal of Palliative Care, 8,* 13–19.

Krause, N. (1986). Social support, stress and well-being among older adults. *Journal of Gerontology, 41,* 512–519.

Kübler-Ross, E. (1969). *On death and dying.* New York: Macmillan.

Lehman, D., Davis, C., DeLongis, A., Wortman, C., Blieck, S., Mandel, D., & Ellard, J. (1993). Positive and negative life changes following bereavement and their relations to adjustment. *Journal of Social and Clinical Psychology, 12*, 90–112.

Lund, D. A., Caserta, M. S., Dimond, M. F., & Shaffer, S. K. (1989). Competencies, tasks of daily living, and adjustments to spousal bereavement in later life. In D. A. Lund (Ed.), *Older bereaved spouses* (pp. 135–151). New York: Hemisphere.

Lund, D. A., Caserta, M., Van Pelt, J., & Gass, K. (1990). Stability of social support networks after later-life spousal bereavement. *Death Studies, 14*, 53–73.

Miles, M. S., & Crandall, E. K. B. (1983). The search for meaning and its potential for affecting growth in bereaved parents. *Health Values, 7*, 19–23.

Milo, E. M. (1997). Maternal responses to the life and death of a child with a developmental disability: A story of hope. *Death Studies, 21*, 443–476.

Moss, M., Moss, S., Rubenstein, R., & Resch, N. (1993). Impact of elderly mother's death on middle age daughters. *International Journal of Dying and Human Development, 37*, 1–22.

Neimeyer, R. A., Keesee, N. J., & Fortner, B. V. (2000). Loss and meaning reconstruction: Propositions and procedures. In R. Malkinson, S. Rubin, & F. Witztum (Eds.), *Traumatic and non-traumatic loss and bereavement* (pp. 197–230). Madison, CT: Psychosocial Press.

Norris, F., & Murrell, S. (1987). Older adult family stress and adaptation before and after bereavement. *Journal of Gerontology, 42*, 606–612.

Norris, F., & Murrell, S. (1990). Social support, life events, and stress as modifiers of adjustment to bereavement by older adults. *Psychology and Aging, 5*, 429–436.

Oltjenbruns, K. A. (1996). Death of a friend during adolescence: Issues and impacts. In C. A. Corr & D. Balk (Eds.), *Handbook of adolescent death and bereavement* (pp. 196–215). New York: Springer.

Raphael, B., & Nunn, K. (1988). Counseling the bereaved. *Journal of Social Issues, 44*, 191–206.

Rubenstein, R. L. (1983). *The construction of a day by elderly widowers.* Paper presented at the 36th Annual Scientific Meeting of the Gerontological Society of America, San Francisco.

Salahu-Din, S. N. (1996). A comparison of coping strategies of African-American and Caucasian widows. *Omega, 33*, 103–120.

Sanders, C. M. (1981). Comparison of younger and older spouses in bereavement outcome. *Omega, 11*, 217–232.

Schwartz-Borden, G. (1986). Grief work: Prevention and intervention. *Social Casework, 67*, 499–505.

Stevenson, R. (1993). We laugh to keep from crying: Coping through humor. *Loss, Grief, and Care, 7*, 173–179.

Stroebe, M., Schut, H., & Stroebe, W. (1998). Trauma and grief: A comparative analysis. In J. Harvey (Ed.), *Perspectives on loss: A sourcebook* (pp. 81–96). Washington, DC: Taylor & Francis.

Stroebe, M., Stroebe, W., & Hansson, R. (1988). Bereavement research: An historical introduction. *Journal of Social Issues, 44*, 1–18.

Stroebe, W., & Stroebe, M. (1994). Is grief universal? Cultural variations in the emotional reaction to loss. In R. Fulton & R. Bendiksen (Eds.), *Death and identity* (3rd ed., pp. 177–209). Philadelphia: Charles Press.

Talbot, K. (1996). Transcending a devastating loss: The life attitude of mothers who have experienced the death of their only child. *The Hospice Journal, 11*(4), 67–82.

Tarockova, T. (1996). Positive aspects of life losses. *Studia Psychologica, 38*, 277–286.

Taylor, S., & Brown, J. (1988). Illusion and well-being: A social psychological perspective on mental health. *Psychological Bulletin, 103*, 193–210.

Taylor, S., Collins, R., Skokan, L., & Aspinwall, L. (1989). Maintaining positive illusions in the face of negative information: Getting the facts without letting them get to you. *Journal of Social and Clinical Psychology, 8*, 114–129.

Taylor, S., Lichtman, R., & Wood, J. (1984). Attributions, beliefs about control, and adjustment to breast cancer. *Journal of Personality and Social Psychology, 46*, 489–502.

Wortman, C. B., Silver, R. C., & Kessler, R. C. (1993). The meaning of loss and adjustment to bereavement. In M. S. Stroebe, W. Stroebe, & R. Hansson (Eds.), *Handbook of bereavement* (pp. 349–366). New York: Cambridge University Press.

Yancey, D., Greger, H., & Coburn, P. (1990). Determinants of grief resolution in cancer death. *Journal of Palliative Care, 6*(4), 24–31.

Zimpfer, D. (1991). Groups for grief and survivorship after bereavement: A review. *Journal for Specialists in Group Work, 16*, 46–55.

IV

Healing Stories:
Research and Reflexivity

11

SHATTERED BELIEFS: RECONSTITUTING THE SELF OF THE TRAUMA COUNSELOR

MARLA J. ARVAY

We are sitting at Carol's dining room table, trying to make sense of my struggle. I am crying and my words tumble out between sobs. "For me, it comes down to not knowing how to proceed when most of my beliefs about the world and who I am have been broken . . . they are like shards of glass . . . too scattered to make any sense." Carol says, "Ruby, you've talked and talked about being a constructivist. Doesn't that mean that you can build a new belief system—one that is more real, more honest." I am stunned by her words. Yes, theoretically I am a constructivist, but how do I reconstitute myself when my feet are straddled between two paradoxical worlds—one foot stands in my past with all its illusions of stability and the other gropes for ground in an uncertain future. Right now being a constructivist just doesn't help. Constructivists don't show you how to do it—how to build bridges between beliefs, and all I know is that I am still stuck in this present hell.

This introductory passage from Ruby's journal in May 1996 highlights the struggle examined within this chapter, the struggle individuals experience when core assumptions about self and the world have been shattered through traumatic loss. Ruby was a participant in a narrative study investigating the impact of secondary traumatic stress on trauma counselors who work with survivors of traumatic life events. One aspect of that research study revealed the narrative constructions created by trauma counselors as they struggled to reconcile shifting core beliefs and the multiple ways in which these counselors reconstituted their lives in order to maintain psychological and physical well-being. The purpose of this chapter is threefold: (a) to present the narrative accounts of two trauma counselors as an illustration of the multiple and embodied ways individuals narratively construct meaning out of chaos, (b) to examine how they narratively reconstituted their lives in the process of telling their stories, and (c) to explore the ways in which individuals reconcile traumatic disruptions to their assumptive worlds.

In structuring the format of this chapter a few theoretical definitions need to be offered, and links need to be made, before the narrative reconstruction of shattered beliefs is discussed. First, I describe the various definitions of secondary traumatic stress in order to locate it within the discourse on trauma; second, I provide a discussion of the theoretical nexus between constructivism as an epistemology and narrative as a form of inquiry; and third, I explain how the self is narratively configured and provide a brief description of the reflexive narrative method used in this study. After this theoretical prologue, the narrative accounts of two trauma counselors will be presented followed by a discussion on how the self is reconstituted through traumatic loss.

A THEORETICAL PREFACE

Defining Secondary Traumatic Stress

Secondary traumatic stress has been described in the trauma literature as "traumatic countertransference" by Herman (1992); as "contact victimization" by Courtois (1988), who warned that posttraumatic stress disorder (PTSD) could be contagious; and as "compassion fatigue" by Figley (1995). Mollica (1988) suggested that counselors become "infected" with their clients' hopelessness, and Danieli (1984) reported in a study on countertransference that counselors treating Holocaust survivors shared the nightmares of the survivors whom they were treating.

Stamm (1995) claimed that secondary traumatic stress is a disorder because its definition can be found within the description of PTSD in the *Diagnostic and Statistical Manual of Mental Disorders* (4th ed., DSM–IV; American Psychiatric Association [APA], 1994). The essential feature of the disorder is the development of characteristic symptoms following exposure to or witness of an event that involves death, injury, or a threat to the physical integrity of another person or learning about unexpected or violent death, serious injury, or threat of death or injury experienced by a family member or other close associates (p. 424). The significant other in the case of the trauma counselor is the client. Stamm (1995) concluded that "if the care giver reacts with intense fear, helplessness or horror—then the possibility of care giving as an etiology of pathology exists" (p. xvii).

There is also a debate in the trauma literature concerning the difference between the terms *secondary traumatic stress* and *vicarious traumatization*. The former is subsumed under the diagnostic criteria in the *DSM–IV* (APA, 1994), and the latter is a construct based on McCann and Pearlman's (1990) constructivist self-development theory. Pearlman and Saakvitne (1995) did not endorse the practice of reducing this phenomenon to a set of symptoms; neither did they advocate conceptualizations of this experience as a pathology. They emphasized the adaptive nature of this experience and the role of individual meaning making. They defined *vicarious traumatization* as

> the transformation in the inner experience of the therapist that comes about as a result of empathic engagement with clients' traumatic material . . . it is our strong reactions of grief and rage and outrage which grow over time as we hear repeatedly about the torture, humiliation, and betrayal people perpetrate against others, and also our sorrow, our numbing, and our deep sense of loss which follows those reactions. . . . It is an occupational hazard and reflects neither pathology in the therapist nor intentionality on the part of the traumatized client. (p. 151)

The experience of secondary traumatic stress (or vicarious trauma) needs to be rescued from traditional Western models of psychotherapy and reconceptualized within a constructivist framework (Arvay & Uhlemann, 1996). Currently, there is a preoccupation with "disorder" in traumatology and, as Mahoney and Moes (1997) stated, "the disorder is not the dragon" (p. 188). As Sampson (1985) suggested, we need to reframe our theories that contend that psychopathology resides within the individual by broadening our perspectives to include cultural and political explanations of human suffering. A constructivist framework acknowledges the contextual nature of stress and the constancy of the flux. The current tendency among traumatologists (i.e., Figley, 1995; Stamm, 1995) is to frame this phenomenon within a disease metaphor. With the exception of Pearlman and Saakvitne (1995), who acknowledged the transformative possibilities in this work, the stress responses of trauma counselors are not usually treated as relational or socially driven constructs. A narrative approach to the study of secondary traumatic stress holds promise for revealing the social constructions of this "disorder."

A Nexus Between Constructivism and Narrative

From a constructivist perspective, there is no "single truth" or "reality" that can be known. Constructivists maintain that knowledge and truth are not discovered but are created or invented (Anderson, 1995; Schwandt, 1994). The nature of reality is formulated in both individual and collective constructions. Constructions are local and specific, emerging from our personal experiences. Kelly (1955) instructed that understanding or meaning making is proactive and purposive. Furthermore, meaning is constructed through contrasting differences, and "languaging," a form of social activity, is the path to meaning construction. Gonçalves (1997) stated:

> It is in language that meaning is constructed. . . . The hermeneutic and meaning nature of language results, above all, from the process by which words are combined with one another in the establishment of a narrative plot or matrix. It is within this narrative matrix that the individual proactively and creatively constructs a reality of meaning. (pp. xiv–xv)

Given these premises—that meaning is self-referential, relational, and dialogical—narrative as a form of inquiry is a good fit for human scientists researching the construction of meaning. Leading constructivists (Cox & Lyddon, 1997; Gonçalves, 1997; Hermans, 1995; Mahoney & Moes, 1997; Neimeyer & Stewart, 1996; Neimeyer, Keesee, & Fortner, 2000) are advocating a narrative turn in constructivist research and praxis.

The Narrative Nature of Self-Construction

> We are in the middle of our stories and cannot be sure how they will end; we are constantly having to revise the plot as new events are added to our lives. Self, then, is not a static thing nor a substance, but a configuring of personal events into a historical unity which includes not only what one has been but also anticipations of what one will be. (Polkinghorne, 1988, p. 150)

Polkinghorne offered a view of the self as a process, in particular, a narrative process. However, this has not been the traditional view of the self offered by those who use formal scientific methods. Until very recently, traditional theorists conceptualized the self as a unitary, core, and cohesive entity (Kohut, 1977) and, although we interact with the environment and are affected by our relationships and culture, each of us has an essence, or core being, that is dependable, stable, and fixed over the life span. Postmodern-constructivist writers (Anderson, 1995; Gibson, 1996; Hermans, Rijks, & Kempen, 1993; Hoskins & Leseho, 1996; Peavy, 1993; Sampson, 1996) have critiqued this view of the unitary self and claimed that the traditional Western concept of a "core self" is culturally biased. They propose a theory of the self that is multifaceted, dynamic, and narrative in nature. Polkinghorne claimed that the study of the self has "reemerged in research programs in the human disciplines, a 'rediscovery' due largely to the inability of formal science research to account for the unexplained variability in human behavior that has shown up in research using experimental designs" (p. 149).

Reconstituting the Self Through Narrative Research

Narrative as a form of inquiry is a dynamic process, and self in narrative research is construed through language. Attending not only to what is told, but also to how it is told—that is, the interaction between participant and researcher—is an essential focus in narrative research. It is in the activity of telling that narrative meaning is constructed. It is in the telling that the story is rendered meaningful to the participant and the researcher. Therefore, narrative is not only a product of the research process, but it also is an emergent mode of knowing for both parties in the research relationship (Josselson, 1995; Ochberg, 1995; Polkinghorne, 1988). Each telling will differ; each reading will render new interpretations. The plot is context bound and, because the contexts of our lives are always changing, research narratives are continually being rewritten or reconstructed. The implications for research are that our findings will always be contingent, given the ever-changing nature of narrative construction.

Constructing a Reflexive, Narrative Method

A collaborative, reflexive narrative method was created to coconstruct the following narrative accounts. The women in this study individually told their stories, and the interactions between storyteller and researcher were recorded and transcribed. The narrative accounts were analyzed at three levels of interpretation: (a) a textual interpretation of the research interview; (b) an interactional analysis of the researcher–participant interaction; and (c) four separate, collaborative, interpretive readings of the narrative account that involved reading for the context, reading for the self of the narrator, reading for the struggle with secondary trauma, and reading for power and gender issues.

A narrative account cannot re-present actual life, because the telling of a story is after the event; it is a remembrance fashioned by both the storyteller's and researcher's desire, context, and personal interests. The interaction between the storyteller and researcher are interwoven into the text. In this way, the narrative accounts presented here are blended texts: a construction of multiple voices, interwoven interpretations, and reflexive analyses. I wrote these narratives as first-person accounts, which means that I appropriated the voices of Donna and Anna. Their narrative accounts are my own constructions, carefully crafted through a reflexive and collaborative research process. Unlike traditional psychological research, in which the author of the text is concealed and the lives of the participants are objectified by writing in the third person, I did not want to reduce my participants' experiences to a chart or table listing common themes or categories. Instead, I am presenting the research findings as stories. I am conveying an embodied text by writing in the first-person point of view and by including emotionality into the text. It is an attempt to show instead of tell (Richardson, 1997).

The following two narrative accounts bear my authorial inscription. Acknowledging that we, academic authors, are always present in our writing no matter how hard we try to hide this fact (Richardson, 1997), I write this introduction to the narrative accounts as a way of "coming clean." My desire is to engage the reader and bring to life the multiple interpretations that inform the creation of these stories. Each participant's narrative account has been entitled "Lessons," because they are teaching stories full of instructions about the meaning of struggling with shattered beliefs through the participants' work as trauma counselors. They are not modernist tales in the sense of having a plot, a sequential ordering of events leading to a critical point or crisis and ending with a resolution. They are postmodern tales. They present issues that are left unresolved, in a chaotic bombardment for the reader to disentangle. Some of the accounts are contradictory and ambiguous, like "real" life, life in process, a chapter not yet finished.

DONNA: LESSONS ON MIRRORS AND MASKS

Donna is in her mid-50s and has recently separated from her husband. She has been counseling for 10 years and has been working at a center for women who have been physically and emotionally abused for about 2 years. Many of her female clients are survivors of childhood sexual abuse, and she also counsels her clients' children. In her first story Donna describes her struggle with being a trauma counselor. She alludes to the shattered assumptions that have influenced her belief system.

> It is probably very hard to understand my experiences unless you have been a trauma counselor. I am burdened by all the trauma stories and all the tormented lives that I have to embrace, day after day. All of my clients' trauma stories enter my being. I am left holding their pain. I ask myself, "Why do these people have to suffer?" I am left depleted because there is no answer. Often I am flooded with the images and emotions that their stories leave behind, and I am frustrated by wanting to fix it and make it all better. I want to rescue my clients, yet I know that I cannot fix their problems—that is not how healing works. It takes courage to witness these trauma stories week after week, knowing that I am being impacted and realizing that even though I get clinical supervision, the long-term effects are still going to be there.
>
> Doing trauma work has challenged a few of my fundamental beliefs about the world. The one that I struggle with the most is my sense of safety in the world—not just for myself but for everyone. I keep asking myself why it is that so many people have to suffer? Why isn't the world safer? Why do we allow abuse to happen? I struggle with what I yearn for—a safe world to live in. I also struggle with the masks that people

wear. I have learned that people are not always who they present themselves to be. So I also struggle with trust issues—wanting to believe that with certain "givens" I can trust the safety of my world. But some masks are very good.

I am confronted daily with the evil in the world, and often I am left speechless in the face of it. My fear is that the ever-present evil is increasing. I think I have a primitive kind of fear about evil. If I don't name it, I don't give it power. I have to keep reminding myself that the slice of pie I see every day is not the whole pie. As a society we need to learn to control our shadow side, because increasingly our individual barriers to evil seem to be breaking down. It is the collectivity of this breaking down of barriers that I fear the most. This is the evil that I fear.

Perhaps linked to the evil I fear out there is the shadow side of myself that I fear as well. My shadow side is about my potential for anger and rage. I carry a lot of rage inside that has to do with the amount of injustice in the world, and I am afraid if I vent it or unleash it I might be destroyed in the process. I am able to deal with some of this rage in clinical supervision, but only a portion of it gets released. Containing it and living with it I know is the source of the despair that I feel. What is under all the anger is my frustration and sadness around my belief that nothing will change.

The central paradox for me in doing this work is the fact that I need to have hope in order to continue in this field. You simply cannot do this work unless you have hope, and I am constantly struggling to find it. I am afraid that I will become cynical and fall forever into despair. It is like pushing a huge boulder up a mountainside. The task is almost impossible, yet you keep trying. It is crazy making. You ask yourself: "Where is the goodness in the world?" and you just can't find it. I have learned that I need to stop intellectualizing about it because it just doesn't help. I have learned that you just have to say to yourself, "There is no solution. There is no answer. It just is."

Donna tells a story within a story. After spending 3 hours narrating her experiences of being secondarily traumatized from her work with female survivors of spousal abuse, we ended the interview, and over a cup of tea Donna asked, "Now do you want to hear the real story?" Donna removed her mask and shared with me her recent personal trauma story—a story of physical and emotional spousal abuse. Donna was in her second marriage, a partnership of 14 years. She described her relationship with her husband as "very loving" and "respectful." Her spouse was the minister of the Protestant church in their rural community. She had a grown son from a previous marriage who no longer lived at home. The events of this narrative took place 6 months prior to this interview. Donna's personal trauma story is a parallel to her secondary-trauma story. The effects of secondary traumatic stress, which she had been experiencing for over a year in her work at the transition house, were intensified with the advent of this personal crisis.

Those first few weeks seemed totally surreal. I was scared, confused, and alone with no one to tell. I believed no one could help me. I also believed that no one would believe me because he was a clergyman. No one would be able to see this side of him—even I was having a hard time believing it. I started to think that maybe I was going insane. My whole world was shattering in front of my eyes, and I was helpless to stop it. I was completely numbed. I felt like I was walking and talking and doing my job, but it was a shell of my former self doing all these things. The struggle at this point was just staying alive. I did not want to live, but I did not have the courage to do anything about it. I just struggled with continuing to do the trauma work when I was hardly there for myself.

Eventually, after a few weeks, I told a colleague at work. She helped me name what happened. I was stunned when she said, "Donna, you have been abused. This is abuse." I know it sounds simplistic, but I had not been able to label the experience up until that moment. Her words hit me hard. I realized that I could no longer live with him. I struggled with the realization that in that single night, my marriage had been shattered. I felt that my life was over. I went into a depression. All my beliefs about what my life had meant to me, what my reality had been, and my own identity were shattered. I kept asking myself—how can I believe in anything anymore? How can I ever feel safe again? How can I trust myself? Why didn't I see the abusive side of my husband before this incident? My goodness, I dealt with abuse on a daily basis in my job; how could I have missed the signals?

Finally, with the support of my colleagues, I went into therapy. I took antidepressants for a short while and worked on my personal trauma with my therapist. It is a long process, but I am starting to heal. I learned a lot about trauma from my personal experience. My sense of self, my ability to trust my own judgments, my self-esteem, and my understanding of my own reality were all shattered that night. It was like my soul has been "punched-bagged." My husband ripped me and my world apart. Coming out of those therapy sessions, I felt like a piece of shredded steak that had one of those hammers mincing it. I thought I was going to feel that raw and bloody forever. It was chaotic. I was fragmented, and I did not know how to put my life back together. I did not have a framework for moving forward. I felt like I would never be able to feel happiness again. I was trying to learn how to be in the world while ripped to shreds.

Donna uses the mirror and mask metaphors to bridge secondary-trauma experiences with her personal trauma experiences. Like her traumatized clients, Donna experienced firsthand the aftermath of physical violence. Before and during her own trauma, Donna struggled in her work with changing beliefs about the world. As a trauma counselor she struggled with the discrepancies between concepts such as good versus evil, safety versus vulnerability, and trust versus mistrust. She saw important parallels between her clients' traumatic experiences and her own. She began to see that the same dynamics that perpetrators use to silence their victims were being enacted in her own life. There were also parallels between the grief and loss that she felt in losing her husband after 14 years of marriage and the grief and loss that parallel her clients' experiences in the breakups of their families. She and her clients shared the struggle of attempting to reconceptualize the former loved one as an abuser. Donna asked,

> What does it take to learn this in my soul? I could see more than just an abuser—he was a friend, a lover, a father to my children. Where did this split between his actual self and his portrayed self come from? Why hadn't I been able to see the masks that he wears? And, more important, how am I suppose to move on?

Here Donna alludes to the fundamental question: How does a person construct meaning from traumatic experience when one has no framework or grounding from which to build new beliefs? How does one step out of the quagmire (Hoskins & Arvay, 1999)?

ANNA: LESSONS ON SELF CARE

Anna, single and 40, was employed for many years as a sexual assault counselor but for the past 5 years has been an administrator, clinical supervisor, and part-time counselor at a center for survivors of political violence and torture.

> About a year and a half ago, I "hit the wall." Like a marathon race, the wall was that place, that moment in time, when both my mind and my body collapsed. Hitting the wall was a frightening, painful, and disorienting experience. The events leading up to this crash tell the story of an out-of-control, workaholic trauma counselor running a marathon toward her own self-destruction. I realize as I approach the next part of this writing that I am starting to get flooded physically, remembering that large, black stain on my life. I also realize that this written account cannot possibly capture this complex experience as I struggle to articulate it.
>
> For quite a long time I had been working anywhere from 12- to 15-hour workdays at the center. I was dealing with a lot of heavy cases at that time, many survivors from Bosnia and South America, as well as acting as clinical supervisor, which meant that I was continually debriefing my colleagues on their secondary trauma. My strategy at that time was to work myself to the point of exhaustion each day as a means of keeping the dogs at bay. I had put on weight, I was not getting any exercise or hardly any sleep, and I started to isolate myself socially. There were many nights when I did not want to go home. I wished I could sleep in my office. I just could not face the drive home. I was conscious

that my behavior was insane. I knew that I was becoming a workaholic, and I knew why.

Going home I would start to feel "it." It was like a large, heavy cloak slipping over me, weighing me down, and I became draped in despair. I felt gray, empty, and hopeless. Life felt hollow and meaningless. I could not find joy anywhere. I could not read or watch television, or converse with a friend. Driving toward my house, I would feel the energy going out of my feet. It was a very physical and intense feeling, like I had been beaten up. And no matter what I did I could not shake it off. If I tried going for walks, I would feel like weeping. Moving my body was exhausting, like I was dragging it along behind me. I just could not see the point of being in the world if this was how people could be treated. Images of their tortured bodies would flash before my eyes. These feelings threatened to immobilize me and engulf me. I was starting to lose control. My only salvation was going to work and staying there for as long as I could each workday.

In my counseling sessions with traumatized clients, I would sometimes get swept up in feelings of helplessness. I would flip into a desperate state where I would feel that there was nothing I could do to help the client in front of me. And I just could not stop myself from going into that state. I would suddenly be transported back to the same place that I had felt as a young child: There is nothing I can do; I am stuck. I have been screwed over by my family and by my sexual abuse, and now, by listening to all these trauma stories. Here I am. My life is going to pieces. So I started dissociating more and more. I was cut off from the neck down. I just lived in my head. I would fall into a numb depressing state. I plunged into my work, trying to fill the void, hoping to find a distraction—a way to stay away from my feelings, my body, and this overwhelming despair.

The crisis erupted one day as I was on my way to a conference at which I was supposed to speak about debriefing strategies. I knew I was not well. I had this blinding headache that I could not get rid of, but it was too late to cancel. Getting off the airplane, I collapsed. My body completely gave way; the pain in my head and face were excruciating. It was like somebody had hit me across the face with a two-by-four. Half of my face went into paralysis, and my body was like a limp rag. It was like I got the wind punched out of me. They called an ambulance and took me to the hospital. I was tested several times over the next two weeks by various doctors, but they could not figure out what it was. In the final diagnosis they claimed that I had some strange virus. They did not know where it came from, whether or not I would get worse, or how long it would last. They just sent me home. I felt completely numb.

Recovery took a very long time. My body had virtually collapsed. At first, I could not get out of bed. My face hurt so much that listening to someone speak or hearing people laugh would cause the pain to spike. My headaches were so excruciating that I could not see straight. I could not read or write for about a week. I could not listen, and I could not talk. All of my senses were screaming, "Shut it off!" No one could help me, and I was afraid that I would never get better.

Over 3 or 4 months I started to regain my energy. The paralysis and facial pain very gradually subsided. During this recovery period I struggled with recognizing the seriousness of my illness. Unbelievably, I made plans during the first week of my illness to return to work. My head kept playing the same old tape: "You're making it up. You're a wimp, and you should be back at work." My coping strategy of workaholism was no longer an option.

So I went to therapy. My therapist and I spent many sessions working on the metaphor of my physical illness—being slapped across the face. My body was saying, "Smarten up!" I realized that hitting the wall was an accumulation of three crises: (a) being physically ill, (b) being secondarily traumatized from my work, and (c) having a professional identity crisis. I had been living according to a formula that I had devised in my head. I had allowed the impact of my job to eat away at my whole being and, inevitably, I got ill. I had to ask myself: Why am I doing it? Why am I listening to people's trauma stories over and over and over for years to the point of risking my own health? How would I ever be able to adequately protect myself when hearing and witnessing the atrocities of mankind? How would I ever be able to continue to do the work? And, finally, why did I want to?

I realized the problem was complex. It was layered within the dynamics of work and intertwined with my own abuse history. Work was a double-edged sword. On one side there was the mission, a purpose in my life, something beyond myself that gave life meaning. On the opposite side I was working through my own trauma story, identifying with other survivors and trying to make a difference in their lives. It cuts both ways: The mission side of the sword was cutting me to shreds while I was bleeding to death from overidentifying with my clients.

After 8 months I returned to work—healthier and wiser. I no longer use workaholism as a coping strategy. My illness was a transformative experience. I learned that I was not invincible. The real lesson that I learned was that trauma work can be life threatening. If you don't have a self-care plan in place, this work can kill you! So I learned that self-care is not theoretical. Just thinking about self-care or talking about it isn't enough. You have to have a concrete plan—something you do regularly—and you need to have people around who "get it," who are not offended by your assertiveness and protectiveness in your self-care management. Playing the self-care game theoretically is like playing with fire—eventually, you get burnt.

Through Donna's and Anna's narratives we learn how one's assumptive world can be vicariously shattered. In the trauma literature, Janoff-Bulman (1992) posited that "our fundamental assumptions are the bedrock of our conceptual system; they are the assumptions that we are least aware of and least likely to challenge" (p. 5). She further claimed that one's core assumptions (the world is benevolent, the world is meaningful, and the self is worthy) are shattered by traumatic stress. Similarly, Pearlman and Saakvitne (1995) suggested that one's frame of reference—which includes one's world-view, one's identity, and one's spirituality—are disrupted through traumatic loss. Donna's and Anna's narrative constructions provide evidence that support both these theories regarding the traumatic impact on one's assumptive world. By reviewing the dominant metaphors in their narrative accounts we can comprehend the ways in which secondary traumatic stress has disrupted their worldviews and their senses of self.

METAPHORS OF STRUGGLE

If human science researchers attend to the metaphors used in their studies, what forms of understanding emerge? Lakoff and Johnson (1980) claimed that metaphors are constitutive of understanding. They further claimed that image schemas underlie the metaphors we construct and are themselves grounded in bodily experiences in the world. Metaphors, then, are viewed as constructive mappings from one domain of human experience to another, and this conception of metaphor, as an act of meaning making, plays an important role in human understanding. Metaphors build bridges between embodied knowledge and abstractions. Within Donna's and Anna's narratives we can see how metaphors work in their attempts to reconstruct past experiences. The construction of metaphors and imagery enables them to construe the complexity of their lives and aids them in describing elusive, intangible experiences yet to be named. It is not only an attempt to name the abyss; it is also an act of self-understanding.

Donna's narrative is a story within a story. In her first story we find examples of how her worldview has been affected by her work (secondary or vicarious trauma); in her second story Donna reveals how her worldview and sense of self have been altered by her personal trauma (primary trauma). Her stress is a combination of both secondary and primary traumatic stress. Given that 1 in 4 women experience sexual abuse (Russell, 1984) and that 80% of trauma counselors are female (Pope & Feldman-Summers, 1992), Donna's situation of dealing with two sources of stress simultaneously may not be an extraordinary experience among women working in the field of trauma.

In articulating her struggle with shattered worldviews, Donna predominantly constructs metaphors of violence and victimization. Her metaphors of mirrors and masks allude to an underworld, the shadow side of human nature. She creates imagery that resonates with the abuse experience.

> It's like being run over by a truck.
> It's like having your innocence raped.
> It was like my soul had been "punched-bagged."

I felt like a piece of shredded steak that had one of those hammers mincing it.
I was trying to learn how to be in the world while ripped to shreds.

One particular statement sums up her experience of having her assumptive world shattered: "All my beliefs about what my life had meant to me, what my reality had been, and my own identity were shattered. . . . How can I believe in anything anymore? How can I ever feel safe again? How can I trust myself?" These fundamental beliefs—identity, meaningfulness, safety, trust—were altered by her trauma experiences. She had to reconstitute herself from "wife" to "victim" and reframe all the losses that this changed identity entailed. She also became more aware of her own shadow side and her capacity for rage.

Donna's metaphoric use of mirrors and masks enables her to make sense of the struggles in her personal life and her work life. Through the metaphoric construction of mirrors, she construes parallels between her own trauma experience and those of her clients. These parallels include recognition of the multiple losses to self and one's relationships with others. She examined her professional identity and wondered whether she had "grown enough." Moving internally between her counselor self and victim self in her sessions with her clients became an extraordinary balancing act.

The mask metaphors illuminate the shattering of trust and Donna's sense of loss of personal safety in the world. She stated that it is difficult to have trust because "some masks are very good." Donna is overwhelmed by despair and hopelessness. She seems to be in the midst of her struggle and has not yet construed a way out of the abyss. She felt depleted at the time of this telling because there were no answers—"It just is."

Anna begins her narrative by stating that the written account cannot possibly capture the complex experience as she struggles to articulate it. She then uses metaphor to bridge this conceptual gap. In describing her physical struggle with secondary trauma, she stated:

I hit the wall. Like a marathon race, the wall was that place, that moment in time, when both my mind and body collapsed.
Moving my body was exhausting, like I was dragging it along behind me.
I started dissociating more and more. I was cut off from the neck down.
It was like somebody had hit me across the face with a two-by-four.
It was a very physical and intense feeling, like I had been beaten up.

In contrast to Donna, Anna stated that she did not experience a major disruption to her worldview through her work as a trauma counselor. Her early abuse history prepared her for a more "realistic" worldview. She stated during one of the interviews that her innocence had not been shattered through her work with trauma survivors. She entered the field knowing that bad things happen to people and that life is unpredictable. Yet several metaphors in her narrative confirm her struggle with an altered, negative worldview:

> It was like a large, heavy cloak slipping over me, weighing me down, and I became draped in despair.
> Life felt hollow and meaningless. I could not find joy anywhere.
> I just could not see the point of being in the world if this was how people could be treated.

Other metaphors in Anna's story point to her struggle with the ambiguities she experienced from having a mission in life that was life threatening. She stated that she knew her behavior was insane, yet she continued to use workaholism as a coping strategy. Several of these metaphors denote a battling or fighting motif:

> Work was a double-edged sword . . . . The mission side of the sword was cutting me to shreds while I was bleeding to death from overidentifying with my clients.
> I had allowed the impact of my job to eat away at my whole being.
> My strategy at that time was to work myself to the point of exhaustion each day as a means of keeping the dogs at bay.

Anna's metaphors also connote a struggle with an identity crisis. Because Anna's professional identity seemed to be a major component in her overall sense of self, the experience of having this professional self fractured was profoundly disruptive. She understood how her avoidance strategies, such as isolating herself socially, numbing out in sessions with clients, and dissociating from self and others, were self-destructive. She struggled to reconstitute a professional identity that is self-confirming. Her strategy was to learn from her past and plan for her future. She reaffirmed her sense of self as someone who was in control of her life. She felt confident that a vigilant self-care plan would keep her from falling into the abyss.

ATTEMPTING A JAILBREAK

> Suffering exposes the vulnerability of human existence, its lack of defense against the play of flux . . . our lives are conducted along a narrow line on either side of which lies the chaos. (J. D. Caputo, 1987, p. 278)

How do we escape the flux? How do we find stability in an unpredictable world? Narrative reconstruction, as illustrated through Anna's and Donna's narratives, is one way of dealing with the flux is an attempt to reconstitute a sense of stability. We construe any number of means to cope with crises in our lives. But there is no real escape—the flux is always there. As Caputo (1987) warned, "there is no escape out of the back door of flux." Mahoney and Moes (1997) concurred human beings live not only poised at the edge of chaos, but they work very hard 24 hours each day to maintain that dynamic poise. Oversimplifying as it is, this means that human lives are a potentially infinite number of ever-changing centers of uniquely personal storms. (p. 188)

If the flux is all there is, then perhaps what we need to do is learn to surrender to it. In the act of surrendering, a new self, tentative and transitory, may have an opportunity to emerge.

> Breaking down gives way to breaking open, so long as we take the occasion to let ourselves be instructed by the abyss, to let the abyss be, to let it play itself out, not in a possessive gesture of surrender to destruction, but in the sense of what Heidegger calls openness to the mystery. . . . We do what we can to construe the darkness, to follow the sequence of shadows across the cave, to cope with the flux. (Caputo, 1987, p. 278)

If we reconstrue acts of reconciling one's assumptive world in terms of surrendering, what forms of surrendering emerge? If we use surrendering as our guiding metaphor for how one might reconcile shattered beliefs, what shape does surrendering take? Within the narrative reconstructions offered in this chapter surrendering can be framed in three different ways: (a) passive surrendering, (b) no surrendering, and (c) active surrendering.

Donna illustrates passive surrendering. For Donna, the way out of the flux is to surrender it to a higher power: "I just give it to God to take care of." Relying on spirituality as a way out of the flux means that one does not have to reconstruct order out of chaos. God has a divine plan and, therefore, Donna does not need to come to terms with "why" abuse happens, or how to "fix it—it's simply God's will." She can accept this and move on.

For Anna, there is no surrender. She will never surrender to the abyss. Instead, she takes a proactive, warrior's stance, asserting that trauma counselors must stay vigilant about self-care management. By gaining the upper hand and maintaining control over her own life, she can keep the secondary-trauma "dogs at bay." Anna needs to have the belief that we can directly control what happens in our lives, even though random acts of violence occur every day. She does not reconcile this ambiguity but chooses to ignore it. Within her strategy rests the belief that principles of justice and control guarantee a sense of order.

Coming full circle, I reintroduce Ruby, who wrote the journal entry in the introduction to this chapter, as an example of the third way to surrender to the flux. Ruby takes an active surrendering stance. She acknowledges and accepts the ambiguity of living with the flux. She knows that she cannot change the fact that random acts of violence, and unpredictability, are a part of life, yet she needs to act in the world "as if" the flux is under control. Although she does not know how to rebuild new beliefs, she acts "as if" these beliefs were in place. She actively engages in her life holding a dual consciousness—that beliefs are transitory yet essential. Her "as if" philosophy

(Neimeyer & Mahoney, 1995) allows her to continue to act in the world and, eventually, new beliefs will take root. She knows that in the future her stress will have moved, transformation will have taken place, and she trusts in this cycle of human development. She actively surrenders to the abyss because she trusts the wisdom that unfolds from living in flux.

CONCLUSION

I have tried to show the unique and idiosyncratic ways in which individual trauma counselors reconstruct and attempt to reconcile shattered beliefs. Given that we live in these postmodern times, constructivism as an epistemology shows great promise for researching the meaning construction of individuals living with the constancy of the flux. Narrative as a form of inquiry is complementary to a constructivist approach to human understanding, because narrative is a dynamic process that recognizes that meanings are self-referential, relational, and dialogical.

In terms of the meaning of loss, narrative reconstruction of individual experiences offers "thick descriptions" (Denzin, 1997), rich in meaning. My hope is that the narrative reconstructions presented in this chapter resonate with other trauma counselors as teaching stories.

REFERENCES

American Psychiatric Association. (1994). *Diagnostic and statistical manual of mental disorders* (4th ed.). Washington, DC: Author.

Anderson, W. T. (Ed.). (1995). *The truth about the truth: De-confusing and reconstructing the postmodern world.* New York: Putnam's.

Arvay, M. J., & Uhlemann, M. R. (1996). Counsellor stress and impairment in the field of trauma. *Canadian Journal of Counselling, 30,* 193–210.

Caputo, J. D. (1987). *Radical hermeneutics: Repetition, deconstruction, and the hermeneutic project.* Indianapolis: Indiana University Press.

Courtois, C. A. (1988). *Healing the incest wound: Adult survivors in therapy.* New York: Basic Books.

Cox, L. M., & Lyddon, W. J. (1997). Constructivist conceptions of self: A discussion of emerging identity constructs. *Journal of Constructivist Psychology, 10,* 201–219.

Danieli, Y. (1984). Psychotherapists' participation in the conspiracy of silence about the Holocaust. *Psychoanalytic Psychology, 1,* 23–42.

Denzin, N. K. (1997). *Interpretive ethnography: Ethnographic practices for the 21st century.* Thousand Oaks, CA: Sage.

Figley, C. R. (Ed.). (1995). *Compassion fatigue: Coping with secondary traumatic stress disorder in those who treat the traumatized.* New York: Brunner/Mazel.

Gibson, A. (1996). *Towards a postmodern theory of narrative.* Edinburgh, Scotland: Edinburgh University Press.

Gonçalves, O. F. (1997). Foreword. In T. L. Sexton & B. L. Griffin (Eds.), *Constructivist thinking in counseling practice, research, and training* (pp. xi–xvii). New York: Teachers College Press.

Herman, J. L. (1992). *Trauma and recovery: The aftermath of violence—From domestic abuse to political terror.* New York: Basic Books.

Hermans, H. J. M. (1995). From assessment to change: The personal meaning of clinical problems in the context of the self-narrative. In R. A. Neimeyer & M. J. Mahoney (Eds.), *Constructivism in psychotherapy* (pp. 247–272). Washington, DC: American Psychological Association.

Hermans, H. J. M., Rijks, T. I., & Kempen, H. J. (1993). Imaginal dialogues in the self: Theory and method. *Journal of Personality, 61,* 207–236.

Hoskins, M., & Arvay, M. J. (1999). The quagmire of researching the postmodern self: Implications for constructivism. *Constructivism in the Human Sciences, 4*(2), 16–28.

Hoskins, M., & Leseho, J. (1996). Changing metaphors of the self: Implications for counseling. *Journal of Counseling and Development, 74,* 243–252.

Janoff-Bulman, R. (1992). *Shattered assumptions: Toward a new psychology of trauma.* New York: Free Press.

Josselson, R. (1995). Imagining the real: Empathy, narrative, and the dialogic self. In R. Josselson & A. Lieblich (Eds.), *Interpreting experience: The narrative study of lives* (Vol. 3, pp. 27–44). Thousand Oaks, CA: Sage.

Kelly, G. A. (1955). *The psychology of personal constructs.* New York: Norton.

Kohut, H. (1977). *The restoration of the self.* New York: International Universities Press.

Lakoff, G., & Johnson, M. (1980). *Metaphors we live by.* Chicago: University of Chicago Press.

Mahoney, M. J., & Moes, A. J. (1997). Complexity and psychotherapy: Promising dialogues and practical issues. In F. Masterpasqua & P. A. Perna (Eds.), *The psychological meaning of chaos* (pp. 177–198). Washington, DC: American Psychological Association.

McCann, I. L., & Pearlman, L. A. (1990). *Psychological trauma and the adult survivor: Theory, therapy, and transformation.* New York: Brunner/Mazel.

Mollica, R. F. (1988). The trauma story: The psychiatric care of refugee survivors of violence and torture. In F. M. Ochberg (Ed.), *Posttraumatic therapy and victims of violence* (pp. 295–314). New York: Brunner/Mazel.

Neimeyer, R. A., Keesee, N. J., & Fortner, B. V. (2000). Loss and meaning reconstruction: Propositions and procedures. In R. Malkinson, S. Rubin, & E. Witztum (Eds.), *Traumatic and non-traumatic bereavement* (pp. 197–230). Madison, CT: Psychosocial Press.

Neimeyer, R. A., & Mahoney, M. J. (Eds.). (1995). *Constructivism in psychotherapy.* Washington, DC: American Psychological Association.

Neimeyer, R. A., & Stewart, A. E. (1996). Trauma, healing, and the narrative emplotment of loss. *Families in Society: The Journal of Contemporary Human Services, 77,* 360–375.

Ochberg, R. (1995). Life stories and storied lives. In A. Lieblich & R. Josselson (Eds.), *Exploring identity and gender: The narrative study of lives* (Vol. 2, pp. 113–144). Thousand Oaks, CA: Sage.

Pearlman, L. A., & Saakvitne, K. W. (1995). Treating therapists with vicarious traumatization and secondary traumatic stress disorder. In C. R. Figley (Ed.), *Compassion fatigue: Coping with secondary traumatic stress disorder in those who treat the traumatized* (pp. 150–177). New York: Brunner/Mazel.

Peavy, R. V. (1993, October). *Envisioning the future: Sociodynamic counseling.* Paper presented at the International Association for Education and Vocational Guidance, International Conference on Unemployment and Counseling, Budapest, Hungary.

Polkinghorne, D. E. (1988). *Narrative knowing and the human sciences.* Albany: State University of New York Press.

Pope, K. S., & Feldman-Summers, S. (1992). National survey of psychologists' sexual and physical abuse history and their evaluation of training and competence in these areas. *Professional Psychology: Research and Practice, 23,* 353–361.

Richardson, L. (1997). *Fields of play: Constructing an academic life.* New Brunswick, NJ: Rutgers University Press.

Russell, D. E. H. (1984). *Sexual exploitation, rape, child abuse, and sexual harassment.* Beverly Hills, CA: Sage.

Sampson, E. E. (1996). Establishing embodiment in psychology. *Theory and Psychology, 6*(4), 601–624.

Sampson, E. E. (1985). The decentralization of identity: Toward a revised concept of personal and social order. *American Psychologist, 40,* 1203–1211.

Schwandt, T. A. (1994). Constructivist, interpretivist approaches to human inquiry. In N. K. Denzin & Y. S. Lincoln (Eds.), *Handbook of qualitative research* (pp. 118–137). Thousand Oaks, CA: Sage.

Stamm, B. H. (Ed.). (1995). *Secondary traumatic stress: Self-care issues for clinicians, researchers, and educators.* Lutherville, MD: Sidran Press.

12

EMBRACING THEIR MEMORY: THE CONSTRUCTION OF ACCOUNTS OF LOSS AND HOPE

JOHN H. HARVEY, HEATHER R. CARLSON, TAMARA M. HUFF, AND MELINDA A. GREEN

"Remembering a Rememberer"

Eugen Zuckermann died on November 24 [1997], the cancer finally accomplished what the Nazis did not. . . . He was a tailor by trade and a scholar by inclination. Neither wealth nor fame ever came his way. He never married. He was short, almost elfin, and his trousers, held high by suspenders, seemed to swallow his body up to his chest. His smile could be magically disarming, but his head was crowded with ghosts and his eyes were pools of sadness. His mother, his sister and a brother had left the world as smoke in the air above [Auschwitz]. (Bearak, 1997, p. A19)

In this chapter we report on a perspective on loss that supports the way Eugen Zuckermann lived his life, remembering and telling one's story. We

---

Part of the research reported in this chapter was supported by a Fulbright Research Award for the study of loss among Romanian women to John H. Harvey.

231

analyze and report illustrative evidence about the value of remembering and translation of memory into stories in dealing with the spectrum of life's hardships and dilemmas. As Barry Bearak reported, Zuckermann's early years in Nazi death camps were filled with the horror of frequent loss of family and friends, hunger, beatings, and death marches over frozen soil. Somehow Zuckermann survived. Bearak said that Zuckermann credited his survival to a combination of luck, kismet (or fate), and presence of mind when a fateful situation arose. Zuckermann also knew that people stronger and more clever than he died in multitudes.

Zuckermann's life bears great witness to the empowering value of "telling one's story." Bearak (1997) quoted him, "I'm afraid it is all too terrible. . . these are not things people will want to know. The extent of killing is beyond grasp. It will become sanitized and remote. People will not want to know" (p. A19).

Bearak (1997) wrote that when Zuckermann came to New York in 1949, friends and relatives told him to forget the war and the Nazi death camps—they were history, and it would be tiresome to Americans to listen to him go on about the camps. Nonetheless, Zuckermann devoted himself to being a "rememberer." He became a Holocaust expert, with relevant volumes filling his sagging bookshelves. He felt it was the duty of a survivor to tell and of others to listen—especially in the 1990s, with survivors now entering their 70s or older and dying off like so many "burned-out light bulbs." Bearak reported that after the war there were only an estimated 500,000 Holocaust survivors, and 60,000 of the 140,000 who immigrated to the United States are now dead.

Zuckermann spoke to others about his experiences at every opportunity. He recited his story so many times to a devoted following of diverse young people and to oral history projects that "each retelling held to the same anecdotes, the same asides, even the same adjectives. He could recount his history in versions of one hour, three or five—whichever suited the listener's time" (Bearak, 1997, p. A19).

Zuckermann's devotion to telling his story is consistent with the theme of a 1996 book by John H. Harvey, *Embracing Their Memory: Loss and the Social Psychology of Story-Telling*. The book was devoted to presenting some of the literature from scholarly and popular sources on different loss phenomena. It presented an argument about how people often cope with major personal loss by means of what has been referred to as accounts (see also Harvey, Orbuch, & Weber, 1990; Harvey, Weber, & Orbuch, 1990). In this chapter we elaborate on the theme of storytelling about major loss events and in the process address the broader thesis of this volume about how people use social constructive processes in grieving and adapting to loss and trauma. We also report representative case study evidence from a study of coping with major loss among women at mid-life in the United States and in Romania.

COPING WITH HAUNTING LOSS

Before detailing our theoretical conception of accounts and their empowering role in our lives we will describe the source of the phrase "embracing their memory" and how the idea of embracing a memory relates to haunting loss. A definition of *haunting loss* is a loss (by death, dissolution of a relationship, or other major loss event) that intrudes into a survivor's thoughts and that often is associated with dysfunction such as acute and paralyzing depression (Rando, 1993). The lyrics of a country and western tune that was popular in the early 1990s—"held captive by her memory"—are highly evocative of this state. We contend in this chapter that actively embracing the memory of the lost one is the antidote to such a state of paralysis and that confiding to others about the loss is key in this constructive process, which ultimately frees the captive from the bondage of unresolved loss and restores hope.

Harvey, Barnes, Carlson, and Haig (1995) reported data indicating that indeed many people at the time of mid-life and beyond felt as if they were "held captive" by the memories of close others who had died in recent months or years. They were haunted incessantly by their losses and what those losses meant for their present and future. They often felt that they could not go on and find new partners or establish new networks of friends because of the "weight" of their loss and their sense of being burdened by it. They often tried to preserve parts of their homes or their physical worlds in exactly the same way they were when the beloved was still alive, in part because of a sense of devotion (that sometimes bordered on bondagelike commitment) to their memory of the lost other.

An example of haunting loss for a nondeath event is found in a letter to a section of the *Chicago Tribune* entitled "Tales From the Front," edited by Cheryl Lavin. This letter, titled "Haunted by the Ghost of the One That Got Away," tells a story of being haunted by former love. The writer described how she and a man developed a strong romantic relationship during college, but he was 2 years older, and she still wanted to continue to date other people after he graduated. They grew apart and married other people. Now it is 10 years later, and the writer is 30, with two wonderful children and a doting husband. But the memory of her college flame spoils it all and haunts her:

> The only fly in the ointment of my life is the ghost of the perfect man that haunts me. I still think of Sam with longing and have off and on for the 10 years that we've been apart. I never considered getting back together with him. We live five hours apart and that part of our life is over. In my youthful stupidity, I thought I'd meet another Sam, thought there were a multitude of true loves out there for me. I am now beginning to realize that there was only one, and I let him get away. (*Chicago Tribune*, November 1, 1997, p. B2)

Harvey et al. (1995) suggested that an antidote to the haunting experienced by those who had lost close others to death or dissolution was to reframe the sense of bondage and make it a sense of embracing the memory of the lost other. This reframing involves a commitment to telling and retelling a story of loss and recognition of the value of "owning one's losses" as significant parts of one's regularly changing identities. It is a recognition that everyone has a story of loss to tell and a recognition that departed people's lives and contributions are enhanced as those who remain behind confide in others and share their stories. However, the telling process involves an active strategy of going on with one's life—a step that also honors the lost other. *USA Today* writer Jill Lawrence described such an active approach in Mary Bono's running for the congressional seat held by her late husband Sonny, who died 2 months earlier in a skiing accident:

> Mary Bono tells the story of the tragedy three, four, five times a day: Bringing Sonny's body down the mountain was "the most difficult task of my life, the longest walk of my life. . . . I had to be strong for my children. (April 6, 1998, p. 1A)

As Robert Coles (1989) suggested, the rock bottom human capacity of every person is the universal gift of a story—the power to own and tell a personal story. Thus, when death leads to a haunting-type experience, we believe that "embracing their memory" by account making is a constructive step toward accommodation to the loss and empowerment of one's work and contributions at the same time.

The haunting expressed by individuals who have left love relationships and then have lived to regret their decision may require a different type of coping process. These individuals may have to deal with regret and guilt over decisions and actions for which they view themselves as responsible. However, if the decisions are irrevocable, as they appear to be in the foregoing story, the individuals will have to try to reach the point of forgiving themselves. The "embracing their memory" metaphor also may play a role in this process. Reinhold Niebuhr's "Serenity Prayer" is suggestive of the courage and discernment they will need in their search for serenity: "God, give us grace to accept with serenity the things that cannot be changed, courage to change the things which should be changed, and the wisdom to distinguish the one from the other" (p. 75).

A THEORETICAL PERSPECTIVE THAT EMPHASIZES ACCOUNT MAKING

For more than 20 years, we have been working on a storytelling or account-making model of how people cope with severe stressors in their lives. The initial work on this model (Harvey, Weber, Galvin, Huszti, & Garnick,

1986; Harvey, Wells, & Alvarez, 1978) emerged out of a history of research on attribution theory in social psychology. In this work it was discovered that in referring to real events in their lives, such as the breakdown of their close relationships, people often try to "explain" what happened in storylike terms rather than by using unrelated internal and external attributions. This storylike construction was defined as an *account*. We view accounts as involving interpretive comments, description, and various other material, as are found in most stories. Our analysis extended work in sociology by Weiss (1975), who used an account analysis to understand marital separation. Orbuch (1997) provided an up-to-date review of work on the account concept in sociology and related fields.

The account-making and confiding model posits that not only in personal, private work on one's story, but also in public social interaction, the individual will need to confide part of his or her story to close others over time in order to assimilate different major stressors and losses. This social interaction part of the model is as crucial as the act of creating and working on a story. We have shown that if the confiding experience is discouraging for the storyteller, it may impede adaptation to the stressor (Harvey, Orbuch, Chwalisz, & Garwood, 1991).

We view account making as a lifelong process. Indeed, we do not believe that people "get over" major losses, as is implied in many stage models of grief. Rather, similar to Zuckermann's experience, described earlier, those losses become part of who we are. Our identities, like our stories, are changing from birth to death (Mead, 1934). As we argue in this chapter, using data from respondents, major losses have profound effects on people's identities. We argue that account making and confiding about losses help people understand their new identities and accommodate to the changed circumstances of their lives that accompany major loss.

Constructive Work Toward Finding New Meaning, Hope, and Generativity

The account-making and confiding model posits that people work in their accounts and confiding to find or create new meanings out of losses. It suggests that this effort often is associated with hope and broader goals for themselves, including giving back to others. Such reasoning is similar to Erikson's (1963) concept of *generativity*. Erikson suggested that, in the normal course of aging, there will be a point at which the individual will have the choice between (a) retreat and despair over imminent personal death or (b) generativity, acts of contributing to later generations of people. We believe that account making and confiding often represent generative acts regarding our personal and interpersonal losses. As described earlier, Zuckermann's accounts and confiding acts are reflective of this idea of generativity.

The logic of the account-making and confiding model parallels the argument presented by Neimeyer, Keesee, and Fortner (2000) about the limits of stage models as metaphors for how people best deal with major loss. Neimeyer et al. argued cogently that grieving is something people do, not something that is done to them. They suggested that, in the process of grieving, people make hundreds of choices (e.g., whether to keep memoirs of an ended relationship). They, as we, view this process as a dynamic, ongoing venture in constructing new meanings that may last as long as the griever lives.

Among those who grieve there sometimes is a reported appreciation of the ongoing constructive nature of grief. At remembrance events in 1997 for those who died on TWA Flight 800 in 1996, Houston businessman Joseph Lychner, who lost his wife and two young daughters—his whole family—in the disaster was asked by a news reporter whether the memorial events might help him "move on" and achieve "closure." He said that there is no moving on and no closure for him and that he did not want closure. Rather, he wanted to continue remembering and honoring the family he loved so much and to dedicate a significant portion of his life to an area in which his wife had been a leading activist (the criminal justice field). In this commentary Lychner exemplified his commitment to the generative quest of account making and confiding.

Timing of When We Begin to Confide Our Accounts

An interesting dimension of the account-making and confiding sequence concerns when it starts to occur in a substantial way. A current honors project being carried out by Carrie Barnes at the University of Iowa is exploring when World War II and Vietnam combat veterans began to discuss in a substantial way their loss experiences with close others as well as with the general public. As contended by Brende and Parson (1985), U.S. Vietnam veterans were generally silent about their pain for at least a decade after the end of that conflict (around the time of the creation of the Vietnam Memorial Wall in Washington, DC, which opened in 1983). Likewise, many thousands of World War II veterans also had quietly accepted their losses without much sharing with others. In Barnes's honors project, one 73-year-old World War II veteran described this timing aspect of "coming out with their stories":

> For the most part, I have found that most of us W.W.II veterans did not start talking about the war until 40 or so years after the war, in our twilight years of life. Without a doubt it helped; but I feel we dealt with our own individual memories of horror and death, etc. by ourselves, not through any form of therapy. (Barnes, 2000, p. 15)

A similar point about timing and the greater acceptance of confiding about loss in the 1990s as opposed to decades earlier in this century was made by a U.S. woman at mid-life in an unpublished study by Harvey and colleagues, to be more fully described below. At age 48 she wrote about her inconsolable grief at age 13 because of the death of her father:

> At the age of 13, I did not have a good support system. We were not supposed to talk about someone dying like people do now. So I feel it took me a long time to cope with the loss of my father. Only when my sister and I reached our thirties did we really discuss our father's death and how we felt about it.

She commented regarding what she has learned from her loss:

> [I know now] that we can lose the ones we love at anytime and that each person mourns their own losses in their own time. This has helped me be more compassionate with others when they have a loss and allow them to take their time in the process. At times just being with someone and letting them decide if they want to talk about the loss or not may help the person in the healing process.

The Construction of Accounts of Loss: A Cross-Cultural Focus

In an unpublished study of losses experienced by women at the age of mid-life and beyond in the United States and Romania, Harvey and colleagues are interviewing more than 100 respondents in each country about the major losses they have experienced, how they have coped with these losses, and how they have grown and what they have learned because of their losses.

Women were chosen because not only do they tend to be more open in discussing loss events (Harvey, Weber, & Orbuch, 1990), but also because in Romania they have experienced particularly daunting losses. Many of the losses experienced by Romanian women have been associated with the former government's prohibition of contraception, including abortion. This pronatalist policy was developed during the more than 20-year reign of Communist dictator Nicolae Ceausescu. Despite a debilitated economy, Ceausescu decided to try to increase the population in 1965. In this context, which denied women access to contraception and abortion, personal tragedies abounded. Thousands of women had illegal or botched abortions during this period. Mothers and fathers who could not support more children also abandoned children soon after birth, leaving them at hospitals and orphanages. These orphanages now house approximately 100,000 children younger than age 18.

Ceausescu was ousted and executed in late 1989. His policies, however, isolated the country and stifled economic initiative and reform in the 1980s, when other Communist bloc countries, such as Hungary, were moving toward market-based economies. This legacy continues to affect Romania and its leaders. In 1998 the practice of abandoning newborn children by destitute families is directly linked to a harsh, unrelenting economy. For most occupations, including those of highly educated professionals, the average gross monthly salary in 1998 in Romania was around $100 or less. The country had an overall inflation rate that was at 151% in 1997 (compared to less than 4% in the United States). Sixty lei, the Romanian currency, were equal to $1 in 1991. In 1998, 8,400 lei were equivalent to $1.

Despite a standard of living and economy that might seem devastatingly cruel to many Westerners, Romanians complain but do not seem crushed. They often work two or more jobs to make ends meet. Teachers, journalists, professors, and doctors alike take on as many different money-making jobs as they can to scratch together monthly amounts on the order of $100 just to cover housing, food, and transportation expenses. Opinion polls show that one of the "luxuries" desired most by many Romanians is enough money to open a bank account.

Economic struggles affect all parts of Romania, with homeless children, disabled people, and elderly beggars representing particularly salient symbols of loss. With an almost totally collapsed middle class, today's reality is one of steadily growing groups of impoverished people, living in rundown, improvised, and unsanitary conditions. Few people have bank accounts. Few people can afford to eat at restaurants. Many people go to bed and get up hungry. Many people are malnourished.

As we enter the 21st century, Romanians go on without expecting their situation to improve. Vital areas of productivity, such as university research, are virtually invisible because of funding problems. Most Romanians see no end to their economic difficulties in the next 20 years. Stoicism seems to be a national strength—one that has served the Romanians well across centuries of hardship and occupation by outsiders (whether at the hands of the Nazis, Communists, or the Turkish empire).

In this context of a country suffering massive social and economic difficulties, we were interested in whether external, environmental factors would be emphasized in respondents' narratives of loss. Also, would they report different types of coping mechanisms than would the female respondents in the United States?

Illustrative Evidence

A theme running across respondents' commentaries in both countries was the value of telling one's story of loss to close others and friends as a means of coping. In many of these respondents' answers were reports of a long struggle to find meanings in their losses and to redirect their lives to incorporate the new meanings they found. Consider the following accounts.

A 47-year-old U.S. woman wrote of her experience of losing her father when he was age 30 after a 12-year battle with leukemia:

Friends and family were the ones who have brought me through bouts of depression . . . . [My father's death] was everything to me and took away my happiness. I learned after many years that I need to focus on the good things in my life and appreciate the smaller things.

A U.S. woman, age 54, wrote of the loss of her brother in the Vietnam war and, more recently, her parents:

It is always important to have friends and family to talk to, but sometimes it's difficult to talk because that makes me so sad and I cry. . . . I know I can talk to my younger brother [about her other brother's death]. He found relief by talking to the author of a book [who had reported that their brother died in combat after displaying great courage to protect others]. . . losses in your life make you much more compassionate. They also make you realize how important family and friends are, that life is short and time goes by so fast.

In describing the loss of her brother, who died of a heart attack after being mugged, a 51-year-old U.S. woman said,

Loss strengthens a person. You learn to be awake to life and good times. Good times are the calm before the storm. When it hits you, pull together, mourn, and clean up the mess. . . . I will not forget Sandy when Matt died of his heart attack. She is a wife of one of the people I work with. I saw [Sandy], and I cried for the first time. I believe in angels, and she is one.

Similar themes were described by Queen Elizabeth II, who delivered a Christmas message in 1997 that spoke of her family's recent loss of Princess Diana. Her poignant message, delivered at Westminster Abbey, was televised around the world. She opened a book and quoted William Blake's *The Pickering Manuscripts*: "Joy and woe are woven fine, A clothing for the soul divine, Under every grief and pine runs a joy with silken twine." The queen then said,

This interweaving of joy and woe has been very much brought home to me and my family during the last few months. We all felt the shock and sorrow of Diana's death. Thousands upon thousands of you expressed your grief most poignantly in the wonderful flowers and messages left in tribute to her. That was a great comfort to all those close to her. (Associated Press release appearing in *Dallas Morning News*, December 26, 1997, A27)

Romanian women also indicated in Harvey and colleagues' unpublished study that talking and not holding back one's story was a way they dealt with major loss. They advocated telling their stories of loss as a means of clarifying their thinking and feeling. As expected, difficult economic–political conditions in Romania were a focus in many of the stories of loss. Most Romanian respondents also suggested that whining about their suffering was inappropriate in a country where major loss has been so widespread for so long. An accomplished psychologist, age 55, expressed this view in telling part of her own story:

> In 1985, ten years after I received my Ph.D., I was told by the Romanian Communist Party officials that I would be demoted. I gave an interview in Paris in which I discussed transcendental meditation, a topic that I was studying then; they said my interview betrayed state secrets. . . . It was a ruse to show me who was the boss and to punish me for giving the interview.
>
> I was taken out of my university teaching job and given first a factory job, which lasted a short time. . . . Then I was made a janitor in a plant. These jobs lasted about a year and one-half. Then I was allowed to resume my teaching, but I had to start over as if I had just begun.

It is important to recognize that Romanians, by and large, do not readily embrace the idea that they have suffered or are suffering now. The psychologist's story is illustrative. She said that she survived, and it "made for a good story," and besides there were countless others in Romania and eastern Europe locked away in prison by the Communists. She concluded that her suffering was relative to the extensive continuum of different types of suffering she perceived. This unwillingness to accept a state of major loss seems common among today's Romanians.

In our study, Romanians' emphasis on family and friends with whom to share their losses and dilemmas of living was much more pronounced than was such an emphasis among American women. At present, this reliance in Romania is understandable in terms of the difficulty of making a living. Families, which in Romania are even more extended groupings than they are in the United States, have to pool their money just to pay for food, mortgages, automobiles, and children's needs. There is more continuity in extended families out of necessity than is true among families in the United States. Mobility within Romania is limited. Most individuals still live for most of their lives within 100 miles of their place of birth; this facilitates the role of extended families in most citizens' lives.

One Romanian woman in her 60s described her greatest loss as the occurrence of a rare disabling disease experienced by her granddaughter at birth. This disease, *Robert's syndrome*, involves shortened and malformed arms and legs. This woman grieved about the lack of medical facilities to treat this disease in Romania—even though her son and daughter-in-law both were physicians. She grieved that the young girl would grow up in a country with virtually no accommodations for handicapped people. She grieved that the best outcome would be for her son's family to be able to find jobs in the United States and relocate there so that her granddaughter would have a better life, with some possibility of medical treatment. Such a step would likely separate the family for their entire lives.

Family members also serve as confidants regarding loss events in Romania, probably to a greater degree than in the United States. Romania has few, if any, grief support groups. One respondent suggested that such groups were banned in Communist-dominated times (because the Communists believed that they could lead to organized subversion) and that people were reluctant to describe their pain to strangers. She said,

> When I experienced crisis, such as my divorce, I have relied upon my family—my mother, father, and sisters—for support. They understand, accept me, and have observed my life for many years. Friends, neighbors, and slight acquaintances do not understand me nearly as well.
>
> In Romania, we believe in the family and we believe that the family should be there for you when you have trying times. . . . It is true that some people are alienated from their families and may rely upon their friends for support. But for the majority of the Romanian people, the family is vital to their survival and healing from loss.

Overall, both U.S. and Romanian respondents stressed the value of developing and telling their stories to confidants as a way of dealing with various types of major stressors, including death of close others, divorce and dissolution of relationships, rape, loss of children to death, loss of employment, loss of home and major possessions, and political persecution. The Romanian women emphasized family as a source of confidants more than the U.S. women did. The Romanian women also focused their stories to a high degree on the external factors of the harsh economic and political climate in which they have lived. (See Harvey, 2000 for a fuller synopsis of this study of loss in Romania.)

CONCLUSIONS AND UNANSWERED QUESTIONS

In this chapter we have emphasized the value of story development and confiding parts of one's stories in dealing with major loss. The chapter resonates with the overall focus of this book on the role of socially constructed acts in coping. In this constructive activity it is assumed that people vent their feelings of loss, gain feedback and knowledge, and inform others. As much of the literature on false memory suggests (Loftus, 1993), people do not necessarily tell highly accurate stories about their pasts. We argue that, on logical grounds, people's work toward healing will be more effective to the extent that they are concerned with truth and comprehensiveness in their accounts and account-making activities (Harvey, Weber, & Orbuch, 1990). However, like several other assertions of this model, this argument has not been fully tested.

We argued in this chapter that a confidant is critical for account making to be an effective means of coping. Although the work described above attests to the positive qualities of having a confidant in times of loss, the qualities of the confidant that are conducive to adaptation have received inadequate attention to date. Our model suggests that the account maker must have confidence in the confidant's ability to listen and care and be a dependable, discreet friend. The confidant, in turn, needs to care about the account maker and the problem and be there when major loss confronts the individual.

The nature and nuances of the challenging support activity of being a confidant represent an important topic for future work in the loss-and-coping literature. Timing of confiding has been identified in our work as one area requiring attention, but there is a host of questions that deserve further work: Psychologically, what is a "good confidant"? How do we learn to be good confidants? How do we learn to find confidants in whom we can entrust our deepest concerns and fears? How and why do good confidants often persevere in this role and across different confiders and confiding circumstances? Would the study of professional confidants, such as therapists and priests, inform our understanding of the dynamics of being a good confidant? Would we find that such professionals are more effective in their own account making and confiding because of their extensive listening experience? Or are they often "worn out" by the entire process?

We believe that psychology and the social and behavioral sciences in general will be more effective in learning about people's common-sense understanding of their loss experiences to the extent that they value people's stories, storytelling, and the social interaction process that frames storytelling. We also believe that this work will prosper to the extent that it represents an interdisciplinary, internationally oriented, humanistic approach to knowledge about the nature of loss and coping (Harvey & Miller, 1998). Over history, humans have produced a diversity of products, both tangible and symbolic. We submit that, of these many products, the personal story of loss and resilience, like Eugen Zuckermann's story, is one of the world's most cherished products. In a timeless, universal way, such stories educate, inspire, and energize other people to own, tell, and retell their stories of loss, joy, and hope.

REFERENCES

Associated Press. (1997, December 26). Article published in *The Dallas Morning News*, p. A27.

Barnes, C. (2000). *Comparison of narratives of loss of World War II and Vietnam combat veterans*. Unpublished honors thesis, University of Iowa, Iowa City.

Bearak, B. (1997, December 11). Remembering a rememberer. *New York Times*, p. A19.

Brende, J. O., & Parson, E. R. (1985). *Vietnam veterans: The road to recovery*. New York: Plenum.

Coles, R. (1989). *The call of stories*. Boston: Houghton-Mifflin.

Erikson, E. (1963). *Childhood and society* (2nd ed.). New York: Norton.

Harvey, J. H. (2000). *Give sorrow words: Perspectives on loss and trauma*. Philadelphia: Brunner/Routledge.

Harvey, J. H. (1996). *Embracing their memory: Loss and the social psychology of storytelling*. Needham Heights, MA: Allyn & Bacon.

Harvey, J. H., Barnes, M. K., Carlson, H. R., & Haig, J. (1995). Held captive by their memories. In S. Duck & J. Wood (Eds.), *Relationship challenges* (pp. 210–233). Newbury Park, CA: Sage.

Harvey, J. H., & Miller, E. (1998). Toward a psychology of loss. *Psychological Science, 9*, 429–434.

Harvey, J. H., Orbuch, T. L., Chwalisz, K., & Garwood, G. (1991). Coping with sexual assault: The roles of account-making and confiding. *Journal of Traumatic Stress, 4*, 515–531.

Harvey, J. H., Orbuch, T. L., & Weber, A. L. (1990). A social psychological model of account-making in response to severe stress. *Journal of Language and Social Psychology, 9*, 191–207.

Harvey, J. H., Weber, A. L., Galvin, K. S., Huszti, H., & Garwood, N. (1986). Attribution and the termination of close relationships: A special focus on the account. In R. Gilmour & S. Duck (Eds.), *The emerging field of personal relationships* (pp. 189–201). Hillsdale, NJ: Erlbaum.

Harvey, J. H., Weber, A. L., & Orbuch, T. L. (1990). *Interpersonal accounts: A social psychological perspective*. Oxford, England: Blackwell.

Harvey, J. H., Wells, G. L., & Alvarez, M. D. (1978). Attribution in the context of conflict and separation in close relationships. In J. H. Harvey, W. J. Ickes, & R. F. Kidd (Eds.), *New directions in attribution research* (Vol. 2, pp. 235–259). Hillsdale, NJ: Erlbaum.

Lavin, C. (1997, November 1). Tales from the Front. *The Chicago Tribune*, p. B2.

Lawrence, J. (1998, April 6). *USA Today*, p. 1A.

Loftus, E. F. (1993). The reality of repressed memories. *American Psychologist, 48*, 518–537.

Mead, G. H. (1934). *Mind, self, and society*. Chicago: University of Chicago Press.

Neimeyer, R. A., Keesee, N. J., & Fortner, B. V. (2000). Loss and meaning reconstruction: Propositions and procedures. In R. Malkinson, S. Rubin, & E. Witztum (Eds.), *Traumatic and non-traumatic bereavement* (pp. 197–230). Madison, CT: Psychosocial Press.

Niebuhr, Reinhold. (1996). *Promises of a new day*. Kansas City, Mo: Hazelden Meditations Publishers.

Orbuch, T. L. (1997). People's accounts count: The sociology of accounts. *Annual Review of Sociology, 23*, 455–478.

Rando, T. A. (1993). *Treatment of complicated mourning*. Champaign, IL: Research Press.

Weiss, R. S. (1975). *Marital separation*. New York: Basic Books.

13

RESEARCH AS THERAPY: THE POWER OF NARRATIVE TO EFFECT CHANGE

BRONNA D. ROMANOFF

As a practicing psychotherapist, bereavement counselor, and bereaved parent come recently to academia, I now have the opportunity to examine in a research setting a phenomenon that has troubled me clinically and personally: how enduring the grief of parents is and how we struggle to make meaning of our lives. As I conduct research interviews with bereaved parents I sometimes become confused as to setting and purpose: The conversations that we have for research, that I have sought and solicited, are remarkably similar to the therapeutic discourse of clients who seek me out. In this chapter I examine the relation between research and therapy in the telling of stories of loss.

As the 20th century draws to a close, a postmodern consciousness is enriching scholarly inquiry, presenting a forceful, compelling alternative to the logical positivist paradigm that has dominated much of psychological

Portions of this chapter were presented at "Reclaiming Voice: The First Annual Conference on Ethnographic Inquiry and Qualitative Research for a Postmodern Age," University of Southern California, Los Angeles, June 1997. I thank the psychotherapy clients and research participants who shared their stories with me. Thanks are also due to Leslie Grout, my coinvestigator, and Sybillyn Jennings, for their helpful comments on an earlier version of this chapter.

theory, research, and practice since its inception as a discipline (Gergen, 1992). Emphasizing local knowledge and the creation of meaning over "discovery" of broad, generalizable truths that exist in an observable reality (Kvale, 1992), the lines between research and practice are blurred as both come to rely on narrative methods as an important source of data (Hermans, 1995; Polkinghorne, 1992). However, narratives are not only important and fruitful sources of information, but they are also powerful agents of change—in both psychotherapy and, perhaps inadvertently, in research endeavors.

NARRATIVE THERAPY

In psychotherapy practice, clients have always been encouraged to tell their stories. Therapists, whatever their persuasions, have relied on client narratives. Psychoanalysts, with a few notable exceptions (Schafer, 1983; Spence, 1982), treat narratives as the "materials" of analysis (Wyatt, 1986) to be examined for clues to unconscious conflict, which the analyst would interpret for the client. Cognitive therapists listen to narratives to identify and point out logical errors to the client. Behavioral therapists look for evidence in narratives of why planned reinforcement programs fail to produce expected consequences. In sum, modernist therapists, armed with "expert knowledge," comment on the client's inadequacies and replace the client's story with what is taken to be a more accurate representation of reality but may well be the therapist's own story (Gergen, 1996; McNamee & Gergen, 1992). Often, the client's telling of his or her story is considered a necessary precursor to therapy, as in the initial intake interview, from which the therapist derives a treatment plan, or an alcoholic's acknowledgment of his or her powerlessness over the drug.

It is only recently that the telling of the story per se has been recognized as having therapeutic value in and of itself. Constructive and narrative therapies rely on the "narratory principle" (Sarbin, 1986): that "humans think, perceive, imagine, and make moral choices according to narrative structures" (p. 8). Constructive therapists recognize that humans shape experience through narrative meaning (Polkinghorne, 1988, 1991). We know ourselves and our world through the stories that we tell (Neimeyer, 1993, 1995a): "The individual is simultaneously the writer, the written, and the literary critic" (Gonçalves, 1995, p. 197). One's stories confer meaning on one's past and give direction to one's future (Gergen & Gergen, 1986; Polkinghorne, 1988). They note one's triumphs and script one's maladaptations. Because narratives are social and linguistic constructions whose "truths" are measured not objectively but pragmatically, they can be rewritten when they no longer serve a useful purpose or are no longer satisfying (Jago, 1996). By helping clients tell a new story, by listening carefully and suggesting on occasion a narrative turn, or reframing character development, or attending to context, therapists can help clients create a story that aids their adaptation and is more personally satisfying while being no less true or meaningful (Neimeyer, 1995b; White & Epston, 1990). Note that the role of the therapist is not that of the expert, or the prescriber, or the healer. Rather, the therapist is a listener, a witness, a companion on the journey. If the therapist takes an objective role at all, it is as a literary critic deconstructing the text, articulating the thematic subtext, or promoting plot development (Gonçalves, 1995). The healing is in the intersubjective reauthoring of the story (Neimeyer, 1995b).

NARRATIVES OF LOSS

Narratives have long been recognized as an important part of healing from loss. The intersubjective telling of a story, both privately to an imagined other and by confiding in an empathic companion is often thought to be the vehicle through which healing occurs. The narrator tells and retells, "working on" the story and "working through" the loss until the account feels complete and the storyteller recognizes a changed identity. Healing is achieved when the narrator can tell a story of loss that gives meaning to the loss and purpose to his or her life (Harvey, 1996; Harvey, Weber, & Orbuch, 1990). Some individuals who suffer highly severe or traumatic losses are able to construct meaningful accounts readily and with little distress, whereas others who suffer less severe or traumatizing losses struggle with making meaning of their experience and experience high levels of distress (Wortman & Silver, 1989). The difference does not appear to be due to the nature of the loss (Romanoff, Israel, Tremblay, O'Neill, & Roderick, 1999) but rather to the ease with which difficult life events can be incorporated into the individual's view of the world (Braun & Berg, 1994; Janoff-Bulman, 1992; Wortman, Silver, & Kessler, 1993). In other words, some individuals may have to create a different story in order to find meaning once again. This is the goal of narrative therapy following loss (Neimeyer, 1998).

A THERAPY STORY

Let me tell a story that will help explain what I mean. Martha is a middle-school teacher in her 40s who never married. About 10 years ago she began to experience painful, limiting, and debilitating symptoms. She sought medical consultation and intervention, but no objective diagnosis was reached. She was repeatedly told that her symptoms were psychosomatic. After 5 years of searching for an answer, during which she became increasingly depressed and intermittently suicidal from the pain and frustration, Martha's symptoms were diagnosed as a particular chronic inflammatory disease, a disease that affects primarily women and for which there is no highly effective treatment. Martha developed other physical symptoms, unrelated to the first illness, including digestive problems, muscle aches and weakness, debilitating fatigue, and allergic reactions. Again she sought medical advice and again was told her symptoms were without organic basis. Finally, a research physician diagnosed Martha with an autoimmune disorder not widely recognized by the medical community. Throughout the years of symptoms and searching Martha became increasingly depressed and frustrated. She was angry and resentful of her coworkers, physicians, and family, who did not understand or appreciate her pain and suffering and who she claimed treated her like she was faking her illness. It became harder and harder to work at her job, which demanded high energy and enthusiasm.

Martha was the eldest daughter growing up in a working-class, traditional Irish Catholic home. Her mother was sickly for much of Martha's childhood and was chronically depressed, unable to contribute significantly to household maintenance. Martha assumed the role of the parental child, caring for her mother and the younger children. The mother's illness was not taken seriously by the father or the children, and Martha remembers the family openly ridiculing the mother for her limitations. Martha, too, was the object of family ridicule, for she was an obese and unattractive child.

Martha was the first woman in her family to attend college. Over her parents' objections, she became a teacher, putting herself through school. She did not know why she did this, because she was never a stubborn child. Indeed, she saw herself as dependent and powerless, anticipating early marriage and a traditional life as a homemaker. Rather, she entered into a long-term relationship with a married man, aware that she was subjugating her wishes and desires to his but certain that it was her role to fulfill others' needs. As she became sicker, he ended the relationship.

The increasing limitations and physical symptoms frightened Martha and made her desperate. More and more she saw herself as destined to become like her mother, an invalid and the recipient of family contempt. Her frantic attempts to seek support and validation from others failed. The disdain increased when Martha felt forced to take a disability leave from her job because she was too fatigued to function effectively. She thought others saw her as a malingerer and, without a widely accepted and validating medical diagnosis, she wondered if in fact she was "sick enough" to justify early retirement.

Martha mourned the loss of her health, her physical appearance, her job, and the support of friends and family. She anticipated the loss of independence if the progressive course of her illness continued. The only solace Martha received was through her participation in support groups for people with chronic illnesses. Hearing others' stories and reading others' accounts validated her experiences and offered her membership in a community of suffering. But central to Martha's despair was her sense of loneliness, of being cut off from the "normal" world, and this sense, which she suspected was common among those with chronic illnesses, had not been adequately addressed in any of her readings.

Because Martha was articulate and liked to write, I suggested she write a chapter—for an unknown audience—on the loneliness of chronic illness. Writing is a tool often used by narrative therapists (Mahoney, 1991; White & Epston, 1990; see also Richardson, 1994) and has been found to reduce the physical and mental stress associated with loss (Pennebaker, 1990). Martha read me what she had written. I listened. As she felt heard and understood, we sought to identify thematic subtexts in her narrative, of frailty, dependency, and identification with her mother. We then began to deconstruct the text, analyzing the cultural and ecological forces at work in Martha's life.

Revisiting experiences within a cultural context allowed a reframing of actions as duty, not dependency; strength, not stubbornness. Martha began to see herself differently and incorporated these new understandings—and the critical process—into the chapter on loneliness that she was constructing. Analyzing her isolation and understanding her contributing role, she became less isolated. Like a good author, wanting a story with a beginning, middle, and end, she examined and experimented with solutions to her loneliness. The writing task provided a sense of agency and creativity. The chapter became a metaphor for Martha's life narrative. No longer a victim of unfair forces, Martha became busily engaged in the reauthoring of her life.

Martha is simultaneously the author, the protagonist, and the critic of her story. It is through the conscious and deliberate engaging of these multiple roles in the therapeutic process that change has come about. The telling of the story to a compassionate and analytic companion engenders revision. Not all stories will have a happy ending—Martha still has many physical problems—but meanings can be constructed that will lessen suffering. That is the hallmark of a "good" story.

As a psychotherapist, I endeavor to understand in order to facilitate the telling of a good story, one that is coherent and enlarges the domain of experience (Mancuso, 1996; Neimeyer, 1995b). Often this involves a change in the client's story. Narrative approaches view the therapeutic process as a facilitated journey wherein the telling and mutual understanding of the client's story will enable a new coconstructed story to emerge. Although the outcome or goal of therapy is not known at the outset, the desire and expectation of change is an explicit part of the therapeutic contract. Narrative is the vehicle for change.

RESEARCH AND THERAPY

Because narrative methods are increasingly recognized as valid research tools and sources of data in the human sciences, it is useful to compare the functions of narrative in research and practice settings. In both contexts, a narrator tells his or her story to an interested listener. *Narrative* refers to both the product (the story that is told) and the process (the act of telling).

Because all narratives are socially constructed, the story that is told is "a co-constructed product of the interaction between person . . . the subjectivity of the person serving as the object of inquiry and the subjectivity of the researcher [one might substitute "therapist"] are intertwined" (Rennie & Toukmanian, 1992, p. 241). Both research and therapy involve a mutual engagement of the other, linked by the narrative. Because the stories that interest social scientists are often self-narratives, the interaction between the participants is often intense and laden with emotion. The researcher–clinician must be a skillful listener, a "master of the art of conversation" (Goolishian, as cited in Lax, 1992, p. 74), using himself or herself as a tool to direct the flow of the interview in the face of strong affect (Maturana, 1991). He or she must listen beyond the words for the meaning and recognize that which is unspoken (Devault, 1990).

Thus, there is much similarity and overlap between the narratives generated in research and practice settings. However, the goals of narrative research and narrative therapy are fundamentally different. The goal of narrative therapy is to "enlarge the domain of experience" (Neimeyer, 1995b), to help the client to "a different place from where [he or she] began" (Efran & Clarfield, 1992, p. 202). However conceptualized, the goal of therapy is change. At some point in the encounter the therapist interacts "orthogonally" to the client's frame, "changing the rules" and thereby opening up the system to new possibilities (Duncan, Solovey, & Rusk, 1992; Efran & Clarfield, 1992).

In narrative research, however, the goal is not change but understanding human behavior and meaning. Rather than educating our clients, we ask our research participants to educate us about their lives. From the researcher's standpoint this is sufficient in itself. As interviewers we enter our participants' lives in order to understand their constructions of experience. We are aware that our presence in the encounter somehow changes the encounter, and we are sensitive to that and careful when we intrude. Intrusions are not planned for therapeutic effect. We ask broad, unstructured questions so as not to impose our own constructions on our interviewees' experiences; where constructions differ, meaning is negotiated. We empower our respondents to tell their stories with minimal constraint, invite them into the research as informants or collaborators, and let their narratives unfold. As researchers we believe that data collected in this manner best represent our participants' truths (Mishler, 1986).

What if our participants' truths change in the telling of their stories? Because of its reflexive nature, narrative is a powerful vehicle for change. If each time the story is told it changes, then our research product, which may sometimes be based on one iteration, is of necessity ephemeral. It is a given that qualitative research is local and bounded, yielding constructs that cannot generalize across subjects and contexts. Perhaps the constructs cannot generalize across time either.

Change is implicit in the research encounter in other ways as well. Even the agreement to participate in this research demonstrates therapeutic change, as participants agree to a painful line of questioning because they want "to help other parents who are going through it" or because "it's time to give something back." The telling of their stories, then, becomes a means of healing through altruism.

RESEARCH AS THERAPY

Let me tell another story. A colleague and I are investigating the long-term consequences of perinatal and infant loss (Grout & Romanoff, 2000). Specifically, we are interested in how families reconstitute after the death of an infant and how parents' constructions of the dead child and the experience of loss color future family functioning.

In conducting these interviews I have noted two kinds of narratives. Both seem to serve a therapeutic purpose. In most interviews, I have found that participants want to tell their story, one more time, to someone whom they believe will understand. Some interviews seem designed to maintain a connection with the internal representation of the dead child (Klass, 1997; Klass, Silverman, & Nickman, 1996). To the prompt "tell me a little bit about the baby's death and the circumstances around it" many parents have responded with extended narratives of the event, fully formed and uniquely organized around a central theme. The stories seem well rehearsed, as though they have been told many times. The stories are coherent, organized, and logical. The order of the story may not necessarily be chronological, but structure is evident, woven in and around the central construct by which the parents make sense out of what has happened to them. Details are vivid, as many as 10 years after the loss, and narrated with great clarity.

The purpose of the research is to investigate how the families are coping now, many years since the loss. To understand this, their unique history is of course relevant, and I ask the question "tell me about the loss" to set the context. Although the parents understand that the focus of the research is current functioning, most recount their narratives as if the telling is the primary purpose of their participation. Only when they have told their story are they willing to address my questions. These questions are often just as open ended in phrasing, but participants address the current issues that I raise less with extended stories that have a beginning, middle, and an end than with brief, to-the-point responses. For instance, one participant, Ann, spoke for close to 2 hours, with minimal prompting, about her baby's congenital heart disease and death following surgery 8 years ago. Yet her response to the question, "how has this experience changed you?" was brief.

"In the beginning I was bitter, I was angry, I felt the world owed me. Now I think I am a very compassionate person. I was hard, and now I'm softened. It's weird to explain." Despite prompting, Ann felt no need to explain further. Although her brief response contains a narrative structure of beginning and end, it lacks the elaborated detail of an important story. Most parents would rather talk about the central issue that has defined and organized their lives—the death of their child or children—than about how their lives have been changed.

Many studies have shown that the grief of parents who have lost children is enduring (Rando, 1993; Rubin, 1993). My experience in conducting these research interviews supports this finding. Up to 10 years after the death, these parents still need to tell their stories. The therapeutic purpose of these more fully formed narratives about the loss event appears to be to maintain the connection to the dead child. In this sense the research allows them to reconnect with their child in a meaningful context, which appears to be therapeutic in and of itself. Once again, the parents search for, or remind themselves of, the elusive meaning, purpose, or order that the loss gives to their current lives.

For these parents, this result of the narration of the loss event is much more central than my research question "How are you functioning now?" I the researcher serve as an audience, one who has not heard the story before. The parents are not obliged to "get the story right." They will not be challenged on the truth value of the story. They need not protect my feelings, as they might if they were telling the story to a friend or relative. The therapeutic value resides in the telling and listening, the validation of a life lived briefly and known to few and the validation of the parents' continuing struggle to live fully (Harvey, 1996; Harvey, Weber, & Orbuch, 1990). This is the good story that they tell.

A second narrative form noted in the research is the "narrative in formation." Here the parent is dissatisfied with his or her construction of past events and uses the interview as an opportunity to reinterpret what happened, cast the characters differently, and come to a new understanding. The opportunity afforded by the research questions to revise and reconstruct the narrative is clearly therapeutic in that it often allows a more positive adaptation to the loss. The story of Eloise's participation in the research illustrates this.

Eloise, age 35, had experienced the premature birth and death of a daughter, followed by two miscarriages, before successfully giving birth. She used the opportunity of the research interview to revise her understanding of the role her mother played in her marital difficulties following the death of her child. Eloise was less interested in recounting the story of her losses than in recounting the story of her mother's reaction to the loss, the impact of her relationship with her mother on the family, and how she was now beginning to see her mother's role differently. As many times as I tried to refocus her narration to a chronology of loss events, Eloise brought the discussion back to her realization of her mother's negative influence throughout her life. Eloise was doing family-of-origin therapy in the context of a research interview. Her agenda was to use the interview format and narrative process to change her story, to reauthor her relationship to her mother, and thereby hope to reclaim her marriage.

Another participant, Joan, used the research interview to recast her own role in the narrative. Joan had experienced a miscarriage, the death of a newborn daughter, and the death of a multiply disabled year-old son. She was the only parent to ask about the circumstances of my son's death. When she had established some commonality of experience, she spoke of the guilt she carried in wanting to be relieved of the burden of her son's care. In the presence of someone whom she felt could understand and would not judge, she explored the decision she and her husband had made to let their severely neurologically impaired son die. In the course of telling her story she went from characterizing herself as "selfish" to "strong," someone who could make the horribly difficult decision to do what she felt was "best for all of us": "He suffered from the moment he was born. He had a much more peaceful death than he had a life." The research interview became a tool Joan used to explore the purpose of her son's life and construct a new understanding of her role in bringing about a meaningful and peaceful, if not happy, ending.

In contrast to the other research participants, John did not have a highly elaborated narrative about his newborn son's death 10 years ago. This was the first time he had spoken with anyone at length about his son's death, having found it easier to avoid conversation and preoccupy himself with work. Although he was cooperative in answering my questions about the death, the story that John wanted to tell was a story of current grief over the loss of his surviving teenage son to depression and substance abuse. In mourning the deterioration of their relationship, it seemed that indirectly John may have also been grieving the death of his baby years ago: "Every dad wants his son." The therapeutic value of this interview lay in offering a father who had always coped by avoiding strong feelings an opportunity to express his pain and sorrow, to make connections between present and past losses, and to come to a place of hope in a promise to reauthor and repair his relationship with his surviving son.

THE ROLE OF THE RESEARCHER

Eloise and the other research participants who told stories that were "tangential" to the initial research question presented a dilemma for me. In a standard research methodology, I would interrupt the incomplete narratives, redirect and refocus the interviews, and in so doing silence my participants' voices. In a therapeutic interview I would at some point intervene with an interaction orthogonal to the client's frame, suggesting new possibilities. By allowing the participants to direct their own stories I give them permission to reflect and construct new meanings, to tell themselves a new story. Is this research, or is this therapy? And what of the researcher? I can be no neutral observer, no passive listener. Participants know that I am an insider, a fellow bereaved parent. I am privileged to hear their stories and bear witness to their struggles. I do not share my story unless asked, and I have been asked only once. But in the telling and the listening to the respondents, in the space between us (Josselson, 1996), I remember and am once again connected to my own dead child. As Joan recounted the difficult decisions she and her husband faced with their neurologically impaired son, similar painful memories resurfaced for me. By respectful, attentive listening I gave Joan permission to tell her story; in telling her story to me she gave me permission to tell my own to myself in a new, more adaptive way. In these ways, through continuing connection and narrative change, the research process has been therapeutic for me as well.

CONCLUSION

Even in a research setting, narrative can and does have a therapeutic impact. In research on bereavement, the narrative process offers opportunity for both continuity and change. Both have therapeutic potential. Death stories are reiterated to affirm their central meaning in the life course of the bereaved person. This is therapeutic, because contemporary Western culture offers few opportunities to acknowledge the maintenance of continuing bonds with the deceased person (Stroebe, Gergen, Gergen, & Stroebe, 1992). Other stories are efforts to analyze meanings, to revise and reconstruct relationships, and to thereby alter one's life course. These are narratives in formation and will likely be different the next time they are told.

Research participants have varied motivations, including but not limited to the desire to aid in the advance of knowledge. Perhaps we seek out the research experience as an opportunity to tell a story unencumbered by social obligation or a previous relationship, or an opportunity to explore various endings. Investigators studying loss would be advised to attend to the layered nature of the research contract and be sensitive to the use of narrative for therapeutic purposes. A constructivist epistemology can serve as a bridge, uniting theory and practice (Hoshmand & Polkinghorne, 1992).

I do not mean to argue that all storytelling is therapy, and certainly not all stories are therapeutic. However, a story that is told in a research interview is a coconstructed product of the interaction, as it is in therapy. Researchers need to be acutely sensitive to their role in shaping the telling and in shaping the story that is told.

I submit that, in the conduct of narrative research, the lines between therapy and research blur. The process of answering the researcher's questions changes the answer as participants construct their story anew. The process also changes the research question, as together the researcher and respondent create new meanings. Indeed, the form of the research interview much resembles the therapeutic stance in narrative therapy: coinvestigators exploring meaning in the text of a life. Although the explicit purposes of the endeavors differ and should be clearly stated, in actual practice narrative therapy is investigative research, and interview research is often therapeutic. Awareness of the power of the narrative process to effect change and development should inform all our encounters.

REFERENCES

Braun, M., & Berg, D. (1994). Meaning reconstruction in the experience of parental bereavement. *Death Studies, 18,* 105–129.

Devault, M. L. (1990). Talking and listening from women's standpoint: Feminist strategies for interviewing and analysis. *Social Problems, 37,* 96–116.

Duncan, B. D., Solovey, A. D., & Rusk, G. S. (1992). *Changing the rules: A client directed approach to therapy.* New York: Guilford Press.

Efran, J. S., & Clarfield, L. E. (1992). Constructionist therapy: Sense and nonsense. In S. McNamee & K. J. Gergen (Eds.), *Therapy as social construction* (pp. 201–217). Newbury Park, CA: Sage.

Gergen, K. J. (1992). Toward a postmodern psychology. In S. Kvale (Ed.), *Psychology and postmodernism* (pp. 17–30). Newbury Park, CA: Sage.

Gergen, K. J. (1996). Beyond life narratives in the therapeutic encounter. In J. E. Birren, G. M. Kenyon, J. Ruth, J. J. F. Schroots, & T. Svenson (Eds.), *Aging and biography* (pp. 205–223). New York: Springer.

Gergen, K. J., & Gergen, M. M. (1986). Narrative form and the construction of psychological science. In T. R. Sarbin (Ed.), *Narrative psychology: The storied nature of human conduct* (pp. 22–44). New York: Praeger.

Gonçalves, O. F. (1995). Hermeneutics, constructivism, and cognitive–behavioral therapies: From the object to the project. In R. A. Neimeyer & M. J. Mahoney (Eds.), *Constructivism in psychotherapy* (pp. 195–230). Washington, DC: American Psychological Association.

Grout, L., & Romanoff, B. D. (2000). The myth of the replacement child: Parents' stories and practices after perinatal death. *Death Studies, 24,* 93–113.

Harvey, J. H. (1996). *Embracing their memory: Loss and the social psychology of storytelling.* Boston: Allyn & Bacon.

Harvey, J. H., Weber, A. L., & Orbuch, T. L. (1990). *Interpersonal accounts: A social psychological perspective.* Cambridge, MA: Basil Blackwell.

Hermans, H. J. M. (1995). From assessment to change: The personal meaning of clinical problems in the context of the self-narrative. In R. A. Neimeyer & M. J. Mahoney (Eds.), *Constructivism in psychotherapy* (pp. 247–272). Washington, DC: American Psychological Association.

Hoshmand, L. T., & Polkinghorne, D. E. (1992). Redefining the science–practice relationship and professional training. *American Psychologist, 47,* 55–66.

Jago, B. J. (1996). Postcards, ghosts, and fathers: Revising family stories. *Qualitative Inquiry, 2,* 495–516.

Janoff-Bulman, R. (1992). *Shattered assumptions: Toward a new psychology of trauma.* New York: Free Press.

Josselson, R. (1996). *The space between us: Exploring the dimensions of human relationships.* Newbury Park, CA: Sage.

Klass, D. (1997). The deceased child in the psychic and social worlds of bereaved parents during the resolution of grief. *Death Studies, 21,* 147–175.

Klass, D., Silverman, P. R., & Nickman, S. L. (Eds.). (1996). *Continuing bonds: New understandings of grief.* New York: Taylor & Francis.

Kvale, S. (1992). Postmodern psychology: A contradiction in terms? In S. Kvale (Ed.), *Psychology and postmodernism* (pp. 31–57). Newbury Park, CA: Sage.

Lax, W. D. (1992). Postmodern thinking in a clinical practice. In S. McNamee & K. J. Gergen (Eds.), *Therapy as social construction* (pp. 69–85). Newbury Park, CA: Sage.

Mahoney, M. J. (1991). *Human change processes: The scientific foundations of psychotherapy.* New York: Basic Books.

Mancuso, J. C. (1996). Constructionism, personal construct psychology and narrative psychology. *Theory and Psychology, 6,* 47–70.

Maturana, H. R. (1991). Science and daily life: The ontology of scientific explanations. In F. Steier (Ed.), *Research and reflexivity* (pp. 30–52). Newbury Park, CA: Sage.

McNamee, S., & Gergen, K. J. (1992). Introduction. In S. McNamee & K. J. Gergen (Eds.), *Therapy as social construction* (pp. 1–4). Newbury Park, CA: Sage.

Mishler, E. G. (1986). *Research interviewing: Context and narrative.* Cambridge, MA: Harvard University Press.

Neimeyer, R. A. (1993). An appraisal of constructivist psychotherapies. *Journal of Consulting and Clinical Psychology, 61,* 221–234.

Neimeyer, R. A. (1995a). Client generated narratives. In R. A. Neimeyer & M. J. Mahoney (Eds.), *Constructivism in psychotherapy* (pp. 231–246). Washington, DC: American Psychological Association.

Neimeyer, R. A. (1995b). Limits and lessons of constructivism: Some critical reflections. *Journal of Constructivist Psychology, 8,* 339–361.

Neimeyer, R. A. (1998). *Lessons of loss: A guide to coping.* New York: McGraw-Hill.

Pennebaker, J. (1990). *Opening up.* New York: Morrow.

Polkinghorne, D. E. (1988). *Narrative knowing and the human sciences.* Albany: State University of New York Press.

Polkinghorne, D. E. (1991). Two conflicting calls for methodological reform. *Counseling Psychologist, 19*, 103–114.

Polkinghorne, D. E. (1992). Postmodern epistemology of practice. In S. Kvale (Ed.), *Psychology and postmodernism* (pp. 146–165). Newbury Park, CA: Sage.

Rando, T. A. (1993). *Treatment of complicated mourning*. Champaign, IL: Research Press.

Rennie, D. L., & Toukmanian, S. G. (1992). Explanation in psychotherapy research. In S. G. Toukmanian & D. L. Rennie (Eds.), *Psychotherapy process research: Paradigmatic and narrative approaches* (pp. 234–251). Newbury Park, CA: Sage.

Richardson, L. (1994). Writing: A method of inquiry. In N. K. Denzin & Y. S. Lincoln (Eds.), *Handbook of qualitative research* (pp. 516–529). Thousand Oaks, CA: Sage.

Romanoff, B. D., Israel, A. C., Tremblay, G. C., O'Neill, M. R., & Roderick, H. A. (1999). The relationship between differing loss experiences, adjustment, beliefs, and coping. *Journal of Personal and Interpersonal Loss, 4*, 293–308.

Rubin, S. S. (1993). The death of a child is forever: The life course impact of child loss. In M. S. Stroebe, W. Stroebe, & R. O. Hansson (Eds.), *Handbook of bereavement: Theory, research, and intervention* (pp. 285–299). Cambridge, England: Cambridge University Press.

Sarbin, T. R. (1986). The narrative as a root metaphor for psychology. In T. R. Sarbin (Ed.), *Narrative psychology: The storied nature of human conduct* (pp. 3–21). New York: Praeger.

Schafer, R. (1983). *The analytic attitude*. New York: Basic Books.

Spence, D. P. (1982). *Narrative truth and historical truth: Meaning and interpretation in psychoanalysis*. New York: Norton.

Stroebe, M., Gergen, M. M., Gergen, K. J., & Stroebe, W. (1992). Broken hearts or broken bonds? *American Psychologist, 47*, 1205–1212.

White, M., & Epston, D. (1990). *Narrative means to therapeutic ends*. New York: Norton.

Wortman, C. B., & Silver, R. C. (1989). The myths of coping with loss. *Journal of Consulting and Clinical Psychology, 57*, 349–357.

Wortman, C. B., Silver, R. C., & Kessler, R. C. (1993). The meaning of loss and adjustment to bereavement. In M. S. Stroebe, W. Stroebe, & R. O. Hansson (Eds.), *Handbook of bereavement: Theory, research, and intervention* (pp. 349–366). Cambridge, England: Cambridge University Press.

Wyatt, F. (1986). The narrative in psychoanalysis: Psychoanalytic notes on storytelling, listening, and interpreting. In T. R. Sarbin (Ed.), *Narrative psychology: The storied nature of human conduct* (pp. 193–210). New York: Praeger.

V

Renegotiating the World: Meaning Making in Grief Therapy

14

THE LANGUAGE OF LOSS: GRIEF THERAPY AS A PROCESS OF MEANING RECONSTRUCTION

ROBERT A. NEIMEYER

How are we to understand grieving as a process of meaning reconstruction in the wake of loss, and how might we conduct grief therapy in a way that fosters this process? Pursuing these questions has led me toward a more profound appreciation of both the subtle ways in which language and narrative configure our experience and the extent to which our most intimate sense of self is rooted (and uprooted) in our shifting relationships with others. At a primary level, this linguistic–relational approach articulates with recent and emerging theories of grieving that emphasize the bereaved individual's unique quest for a personal narrative that "makes sense" of a changed reality and that finds support in the social domain. At a secondary (but no less important level) this approach also carries implications for the conduct of grief counseling and therapy, conceived as a deep engagement in the client's experiential world as a precondition to its reconstruction. My goal in this chapter is to provide a frame of intelligibility for this approach and to illustrate its application in an actual session of grief therapy.

CONSTRUCTING A WORLD, CONSTRUCTING A SELF

If one traces the history of Western art, one can often discern periods in which dominant discourses about the proper role or function of art struggle to accommodate some bold new vision that breaks radically with traditional views. Sometimes this tension between tradition and innovation is literally visible in the way radical art is *framed* by the contemporary institutions that display it. This jarring juxtaposition is nowhere more obvious than in the incongruity between the vibrant, suggestive, phenomenal dashes of color in Impressionist painting and the baroque, ornate, and delimiting gold leaf frames in which they were (and continue to be) mounted by collectors and museums. Protesting against this incoherence, Impressionist painters, such as Van Gogh, framed some of their own work in simple wooden borders and then continued the painting beyond the canvas to cover the frame itself. The result was a more integrated piece, whose frame resonated with the vitality and nuance of the focal work rather than clashing with it.

At the present historical moment, grief theory finds itself in a similar position. As this volume and other recent works demonstrate, conceptualizations of the role of loss in human life are undergoing a revolution, challenging existing understandings of bereavement in predominantly symptomatic, stress-oriented, and pathological terms (Attig, 1996; Hagman, 1995; Klass, Silverman, & Nickman, 1996; Neimeyer, 1998a). As a consequence, these new views are only uncomfortably accommodated by dominant psychological theories formulated along psychodynamic, cognitive–behavioral, and medical lines. The result is often an awkward attempt to assimilate the innovative theory into a traditional conceptual "frame," as when an existential quest for meaning is construed simply as a "cognitive coping strategy" for dealing with bereavement stress (Gluhoski, 1995). Alternatively, this incoherence sometimes leads to a "stand-alone" theory of grieving, divorced from any broader perspective on human experience (Walter, 1996). In the first instance the significance of the theory is minimized by its procrustean reduction to the dimensions of a dominant traditional model, and in the second by its being decontextualized from a broader perspective on human functioning.

My aim in this chapter is to offer a provisional framing of new trends in grief theory in a way that extends, rather than undercuts, their innovative implications for practice. To do so, I draw on a contemporary constructivist approach to psychology, briefly sketching how it views the human effort after meaning, how it understands the complications introduced into this quest by profound loss, and how we as psychotherapists might intervene to assist grieving people with this essential struggle. Readers who are interested in a more detailed exposition of constructivist and narrative themes are encouraged to consult any of several accounts of constructivism and its clinical implications (Franklin & Nurius, 1998; Neimeyer & Mahoney, 1995; Neimeyer & Raskin, 2000; Rosen & Kuehlwein, 1996).

Narrative Truth

Pervading constructivist metatheory is a position of *epistemological humility*, a recognition that, whatever the status of an external reality, its meaning for us is determined by our constructions of its significance, rather than the "brute facts" themselves. This critical distinction between the *phenomenal* world of human experience and the *noumenal* world of things-in-themselves can be traced back at least to Kant (1787/1965), who emphasized that the mind actively structures experience according to its own principles and procedures. One contemporary extension of this argument is that narrative—the distinctively human penchant for storytelling—represents one such powerful ordering scheme (Bruner, 1986). This further implies that making sense of our lives entails constructing a plausible account of important events, a story that has the ring of narrative truth, regardless of whether it corresponds to a historical truth that would be endorsed by a disinterested observer (Spence, 1982). Because different observers will formulate different stories, theories, or explanations for the "same" event, constructivists view them as alternative constructions that have their own affordances and constraints rather than regarding one as "true" and others in varying degrees of error (Kelly, 1955). Thus, from a metatheoretical standpoint, human beings are viewed as (co)authors of their life stories, struggling to compose a meaningful account of the important events of their lives and revising, editing, or even dramatically rewriting these when the presuppositions that sustain these accounts are challenged by unanticipated or incongruous events.

This metatheoretical frame suggests novel understandings of loss and grief. Significant loss—whether of cherished persons, places, projects, or possessions—presents a challenge to one's sense of narrative coherence as well as to the sense of identity for which they were an important source of validation (Neimeyer, 1998b). Like a novel that loses a central character in the middle chapters, the life story disrupted by loss must be reorganized, rewritten, to find a new strand of continuity that bridges the past with the future in an intelligible fashion. The inability to encompass the loss experience within the "master narrative" of one's life is especially stark in instances of trauma (Sewell, 1996; see also chapter 15, this volume), but the necessity to edit or reauthor aspects of one's life story is present in normative losses as well.

At a practical level this narrative perspective carries implications for both strategy and technique in grief therapy. Perhaps most fundamentally, it suggests that stories are the "heart" of the matter (Attig, 1996), that people seek consultation with helping professionals when they struggle with the meaning of a loss and its significance for their changed lives. Bereaved people often seek safe contexts in which they can tell (and retell) their stories of loss, hoping that therapists can bear to hear what others cannot, validating their pain as real without resorting to simple reassurance. Ultimately, they search for ways of assimilating the multiple meanings of loss into the overarching story of their lives, an effort that professionals can support through careful listening, guided reflection, and a variety of narrative means for fostering fresh perspectives on their losses for themselves and others (Neimeyer, 1998b).

Discourse and Rhetoric

Any narrative, to be intelligible to its author or its audience, must draw on a discursive framework of pre-established meanings that provides a socially sanctioned system for symbolizing events. Stated differently, individuals make meaning by drawing selectively on a fund of discourse that precedes them and that is consensually validated within their cultures, subcultures, communities, and families. In its extreme form this social constructionist argument erodes the individual "self" as an organizing center of experience, insofar as the person can be "populated" by echoes of discordant discourses that struggle for ascendancy, with none achieving full coherence (Gergen, 1991; Neimeyer, 2000). However, in its more moderate forms this constructionist view accords individuals the status of "discourse users," agents who draw on the resources of their cultures and communities in formulating accounts of important life events and seeking their affirmation by others (Harre & Gillett, 1994).

Loss is one such important life event that is given significantly different meaning within alternative discursive frames of reference. For many in the helping professions, grief is understood (and diagnosed) in largely psychiatric terms, as an unwanted constellation of depressive, anxious, or posttraumatic symptomatology. For others, discourses of bereavement draw on conceptions of grief as a presumably universal series of emotional stages of perturbation and adjustment, beginning with shock and denial and progressing through phases of anger, bargaining, depression, and the like before reaching a final stage of acceptance or recovery. These professional discourses further intermingle in complex ways with lay understandings of loss, which themselves draw on a richly varied set of cultural, ethnic, spiritual, and gendered discourses about the meaning of death and the appropriate response of people to it (Doka & Davidson, 1998). Viewed in this light, there is no single "grand narrative" of grief but a panoply of perspectives within which any given family or individual is positioned. Situated at the confluence of multiple discursive streams, each person constructs a unique response to bereavement that distills the meanings of loss current in his or her family, community, and culture. Each of these ways of "languaging" about loss, in turn, provides a partial prescription for how loss is to be accommodated by the individual and the social world.

Viewing bereavement within a discursive frame configures grief therapy as a rhetorical process, with *rhetoric* being understood as the artful use of language to achieve pragmatic ends (Simons, 1989). In this, the language of the client has priority over that of the therapist, as the latter attends to the nuances in the client's way of speaking about loss that suggest critical therapeutic tasks to be addressed in the session. Particularly important in this delicate tracking of client meanings is attending to points of subtle discrepancy between the *content* of a client's discourse and the *emotional modulation* that accompanies it, as when a person speaks of having "moved on" from the loss with a trembling jaw and downward glance. Such moments suggest gaps in the client's story, or instances when the available way of languaging about the loss is inadequate to accommodate its full complexity. Attending to the succession of *quality terms*—phrases or expressions that reveal the client's position with particular power or clarity—in the client's speech helps establish a progressive focus for the therapeutic negotiation of meaning. Allowing the theme of the session to evolve in this way brings forth a therapy that is responsive to the client's shifting processing of experience rather than predetermined by the therapist's conceptualization of the case. For instance, by exploring and elaborating those "frozen metaphors" unreflectively used by a client to convey an experience (e.g., feeling "burdened" or "empty"), the therapist can prompt clients to articulate their meanings with greater precision and move the narrative of their engagement with the loss in new directions (Neimeyer, 1998b).

The Tacit Dimension

The emphasis placed in the foregoing discussion on language could suggest that all meanings are highly explicit, crystallized in words and symbols whose denotative significance is shared by all members of the discursive community. However, in a constructivist view meanings are anchored not only in the linguistic–cultural realm but also in a personal–agentic domain (Mascolo, Craig-Bray, & Neimeyer, 1997) that is partly presymbolic. Put differently, the self-narratives that we construct and perform rely on a field of lived discriminations that are tacit and prereflective, incompletely articulated in symbolic speech (Merleau-Ponty, 1945/1962; Polanyi, 1958). Thus, in contrast to both a psychodynamic view that places meaning "beneath" the spoken word (Freud, 1972), and a social constructionist account that situates it on the "surface" of language (De Shazer, 1994), constructivism links the significance of speech largely to the realm of implicit meaning, which is neither inherently obscure nor obvious. Stated metaphorically, *text has texture*, such that the words we speak are neither misleading nor transparent, but suggestive. Like a richly woven sweater, language is viewed as having a texture that reveals itself to the touch, a partly visible structure that invites further exploration.

Considered from this vantage point, the important losses of our lives disrupt our taken-for-granted narratives, breaking or straining the assumptions that once sustained them (chapter 11, this volume; Janoff-Bulman, 1989; Rando, 1995). Making meaning of these life transitions entails a delicate interplay between explicit redefinition of our identities as spouses, parents, sons, and daughters in light of this dislodgment and an implicit reweaving of our ways of anticipating and engaging the world. Assisting clients with this task requires a way of participating in this reconstructive process that is respectful, resonant, perhaps even reverential. Although this suggests that careful listening will take precedence over leading in the therapeutic conversation, it also implies an active role for the therapist in "sculpting" the dialogue in elaborative directions. Although a number of process interventions can assist with this task (Neimeyer, 1996), at an abstract level all of these entail helping clients more adequately symbolize their experience as a precondition to its reflexive examination (Watson & Greenberg, 1996).

The Relational Self

Situating the self-narrative in language—both public and personal—undermines a traditional view of the self as singular, stable, and fully knowable, insofar as our participation in different relationships fosters a construction of identity that is multiplistic, shifting, and emergent (Gergen, 1991; Neimeyer, 1998c). Because of the frequently competing discourses we take up in our daily lives, no "text of identity" is truly coherent and unambivalent. Instead, it may be more useful to construe the self-narrative as fraught with internal tensions and contradictions, encompassing "fragmented" subsystems of meaning that may or may not be inferentially compatible (Kelly, 1955). However, in contrast to conventional humanistic models of personality, the present constructivist position would not view this internal complexity as inherently problematic, as something to be ultimately resolved or "integrated" (Neimeyer, 2000). Indeed, it may be precisely the features of our experience that fail to fit within the master narrative of our lives that deconstruct its apparent authority (Derrida, 1978) and open our story to new and more complex tellings.

Because we find affirmation for our self-narratives in the responses of significant others, our sense of identity is strained, and sometimes sundered, by the loss of these relationships. In the wake of bereavement, then, we are forced to renegotiate our identity as a survivor in interaction with others, seeking an audience that will validate the new version of self we enact (chapter 4, this volume; Neimeyer, 1998b). This process typically is both conservative and revolutionary, entailing a search for that which remains viable in our previous lives and an invention of new roles and ways of being that are appropriate to our changed worlds (chapter 2, this volume). It is ironic, perhaps, that the audience for our emerging self-narrative often includes the very person or persons we have lost, as our bond with them is transformed from one based on their physical presence to one predicated on their symbolic participation in our lives (Klass et al., 1996; chapter 4, this volume).

At a strategic level an appreciation of the relational basis of selfhood sensitizes us as grief therapists to the bereaved person's struggle to articulate a changed sense of self and to find validation for it in both real and symbolically significant bonds with other people. The reconstruction of identity therefore requires a recursive tacking between the self and social, between sensed and perhaps incompletely symbolized shifts in the client's self-narrative, and the responses of relevant others to these emerging features. Likewise, it involves tacking between the past and present, historicizing preferred developments in the client's story of identity in a way that gives them continuity with an anticipated future (White & Epston, 1990). A further implication of this relational view is that the therapeutic relationship itself provides a vital context for the performance and affirmation of the client's changing text of identity, casting the therapist as an important "validating agent" (Landfield, 1988) for the new narrative.

Evolutionary Epistemology

Although mouth filling as a term and a bit daunting as a concept, *evolutionary epistemology* aptly describes the progressive variation of knowledge structures that characterizes contemporary accounts of science (Campbell, 1987). Applied to the domain of personal knowledge, an evolutionary view implies a natural variation in our self-narratives over time and across contexts. As a function of our positioning in inconsistent discourses and relationships, we necessarily experiment with novel ways of being, and these random variations are selectively retained as facets of our identity to the extent that they prove viable in the social world. Thus, like miniature ecologies, our social environments "select" certain "species" of self-narrative that have sufficient fit with our context to provide a workable script for engaging life. Also like the larger ecosystems of which they are a part, our social ecologies are in constant flux, challenging schemes of personal knowledge that were once adaptive but no longer find a readily available niche to occupy in a changed social world.

Among the most significant changes to our social ecologies are the "exits" of pivotal relationships resulting from geographic separation, job loss, the breakup of intimate bonds, and particularly the death of those we love (Neimeyer, 1998b). Under such circumstances, the bereaved person faces the challenge of either finding ways to preserve cherished features of her or his self-narrative (perhaps through finding new audiences, real and symbolic, for existing self-roles) or experimenting with new identities, in trial-and-error fashion, to find those that are viable. When bereaved individuals are unable to negotiate this transition they may feel constrained by a life story that is radically incoherent, leaves important experiences "unemplotted," is devoid of thematic significance, or is no longer organized around a "fictional goal" that leads toward a meaningful future (Neimeyer, 2000; Neimeyer & Stewart, 1996). However, a progressive evolution of the self-narrative is also feasible, suggesting the possibility of posttraumatic growth (chapter 10, this volume; Tedeschi, Park, & Calhoun, 1998) and the development of richer, more elaborate texts of identity following adaptation to loss. The grief therapist is in a position to foster this evolution, through reflective practices and questioning strategies that help the bereaved person become conscious of the need for narrative restoration, repair, or revision and that provide subtle guidance with this process.

A Grief Therapy Observed

Constructivist approaches like the present one have sometimes been accused of being long on theory and short on practice (Minuchin, 1991). To redress this (partly justifiable) criticism, I provide a verbatim transcript of a session of grief therapy conducted along the lines discussed above, conveying in the left column a turn-by-turn account of the therapeutic conversation. To orient the reader to my own meaning making during the session I also provide, in the right column, some interpretive comments concerning my "read" of the unfolding encounter, my sense of what requires attention, and so on. This attempt to track both the actions and intentions that constitute therapeutic interaction is in keeping with contemporary research in psychotherapy process, especially that conducted within constructivist and narrative paradigms (Levitt & Angus, 1999; Toukmanian & Rennie, 1992). In the transcript, T represents me, the therapist, and C represents Susan, the client.

In offering this illustration, a couple of caveats are in order. First, a printed transcript—even one that contains behavioral annotations like the present one—obviously cannot adequately convey the subtleties of nonverbal and coverbal expression that amplify, modulate, and occasionally nullify the spoken word. Because these interpersonal nuances (on the part of both client and therapist) are especially critical to an approach such as my own, which emphasizes implicit meanings and relational coconstruction of reality, the "thinning" of cues required by a transcript is especially unfortunate. This is particularly so when the client's timing, vocal tone, facial expression, or gesture provide a clear "process validation" (Leitner, 1995) that a particular therapist intervention has touched on or triggered something significant, beyond what might be signaled by the client's saying "right," "yes," or "exactly" in a literal way. However, a verbatim transcript does offer the compensatory virtue of allowing a careful reading and cross-referencing of the verbal "braiding" that constitutes therapeutic exchanges, a consideration of how well or poorly a particular line of intent is pursued, and so on. Perhaps the fullest reading of the transcript would enlist the imagination, much as an actor might try to project herself into a script offered by a playwright.

Thus, it could be helpful to try to visualize and hear the exchange that follows rather than to attend only to the semantic connotations of the printed words themselves.[1]

A second caveat concerns the representativeness of a single session, regardless of the theoretical context in which it is embedded. There certainly is great variation in my own therapeutic interactions across people, and in fact I do not aspire to implement a therapy that is "systematic, predictable, reproducible and rule governed," which some more realist therapists hold as desiderata for scientific psychotherapy (Held, 1995). From my own relational–linguistic perspective, grief counseling, like all forms of therapy, needs to be highly individualized, and the interaction that unfolds between me as a therapist and my client is necessarily a function of the unique coupling of our personal epistemologies (Glover, 1995). This is certainly true of other conversations in our lives, and it is no less true of that specialized conversation that we call grief therapy. Thus, the transcript that follows is not intended to be prescriptive for other grief counselors but rather broadly descriptive of my own practice at this point in my professional and personal development.

Susan, a 42-year-old secretary, volunteered to take part in a demonstration session with me in the context of a full-day professional workshop on grieving as a process of meaning reconstruction. She graciously agreed in advance to our conducting the session on camera in a studio situated in the education wing of a large medical center, with the understanding that our conversation would be broadcast "live" to the 200 participants in the adjacent lecture hall. She also consented to the subsequent use of the recorded session for professional education in grief therapy. I therefore opened our conversation with an invitation for her to share her reactions to the public context of the session, given the potentially intimate content that she had volunteered to explore.

Transcript

T1: Susan, I wonder how you feel about being here in this studio. . . . I know this is an unfamiliar experience for you [**C:** Yes], being in front of a camera and talking about, maybe, some personal experiences.

Commentary

T1: Noticing my own nervousness at conducting therapy in this public arena, I check to see if Susan's reaction matches mine. This seems like a more genuine opening than moving directly into the content of her loss and allows me to get a preliminary reading of her immediate feeling state.

---

[1]A videotape of this session is available from the Department of Psychiatry–CME, UCONN Health Center, 263 Farmington Avenue, Farmington, CT 06030-2945.

C1: I, uh, I am just waiting, I'm just waiting to see how it goes. I really have no feeling about it and I feel comfortable.

T2: Okay. Well, I think some nervousness is, is to be maybe anticipated, and so I'll feel that nervousness for you if you like! [both chuckle]

C2: Okay.

T3: Yeah. Like you, I don't really have any prefabricated design for what we will do here, but my general thought is that we'll take about half an hour to discuss some experience of loss of yours that seems significant to you, um, perhaps one that still feels like it has some unresolved pieces or growing edges to it. And although we haven't had a chance yet to talk about this in any degree, you did mention as we strolled into this studio that just being here in the health center at the university had conjured up some feelings for you that you became aware of.

C3: Umm . . . that's, that's correct. My mother, um, died of lung cancer 3 years ago, and you know, my parents were sepa- . . .were divorced so she had no one really to take care of her, um, when she was dying. My sister and I, also divorced, took her in and took care of her. And we brought her to the health center here twice a week, taking turns for chemotherapy and treatment. And that went on it seemed like years, but it was from October 'til she died in July. And I hadn't been back to the health center till today, [T: Oh my. . .]

C1: Susan responds with a surprising sense of calm and self-assurance.

T2: I acknowledge my own slight anxiety as a way of giving her "permission" to be open as well and to "break the ice" in a nonthreatening way.

T3: I try to convey a "rough sketch" of our session to help Susan anticipate the interaction in a general way. I then invite her to share a loss that may or may not be recent but that still feels "open" and in need of attention. One possibility seems anchored in some unspecified feelings that she mentioned in passing as we entered the studio minutes before.

C3: As Susan opens her narrative of her mother's dying, she alludes to a transgenerational pattern— the divorce of her mother, her sister, and herself—and hints at a potentially "gendered" conception of caregiving that allocates support functions to the women in the family. This catches my attention, but Susan then segues into a more emotionally vivid and present tense "enactment" of her encounter with the "flood" of feelings triggered by finding herself in the very setting in which her mother was treated.

and I wasn't prepared for . . . I didn't think about it 'til I walked down the hallway towards lunch, and realized, "Oh my goodness, this is the same hallway!" [T: "I've been here before."] Yes. Yes. And those feelings kinda, whoa, *flooded* back [Susan pulls back slightly, and raises hands, as if to stem the flood]. Yes.

T4: And so these feelings that sort of flooded in for you were feelings of re-evoking that sense of the loss and the treatment [C: Right], and the women in the family pulling together, you and your sister pulling together to support her or. . . . What was all part of that package of feelings?

C5: Uh, It was reminiscent of the feeling of *powerlessness*, almost *ludicracy*. She was terminal and we were bringing her for chemotherapy. Um, working like crazy, you know, both my sister and I worked full-time, plus we were taking care of my mother at night, plus we had children, plus being single parents ourselves. So it was 16 full, full, full hours a day working very hard. And still at the back of our minds [touching the base of her skull] . . . to what end? You know?

T6: Yeah, so that is the ludicrous element [C: Right] that you brought up [C: Right], that it seemed as if there was no purpose for this in a way, that it was a . . .

C7: But still driven to do it and working very hard at it, and, um, I guess those types of feelings came

T4: I adopt Susan's metaphor of the flood and offer a provisional "unpacking" of the experience that includes both feelings about her relationships with other women in the family and her response to her mother's treatment and death per se. I am seeking her guidance on what is most important to explore further.

C5: Susan makes clear that it is the feeling around the treatment that is most important now, and she offers two poignant terms to describe this: "powerlessness" and "ludicracy," to which she gives added emphasis. These then are the "quality terms" whose meanings require further interrogation.

T6: I reflect the "ludicrous" theme, and Susan gives repeated "on-line" validation that we are on the right track.

C7: Susan completes my thought about the apparent meaninglessness of their efforts and adds

flooding back [**T:** Yeah]. A "What's it all about, Alfie?" sort of thing, you know.

T8: At one level, it seems kind of meaningless, but at another level, there is a driveness to it. [**C:** Yes] What was doing the driving? What was pushing you in the direction of this kind of activity?

C9: I, I kinda wish I knew, I just, I uh. . . [4-second pause]. All right, I guess I *do* know. The need to *do something*, the need not to be powerless in this situation. The refusal to accept being powerless [**T:** um hum] in this situation. I guess that's what was the drive.

T10: "I'm not going to let this leave me incapacitated, I'm going to *do something* [**C:** Right] for my mother," I guess.

C10: Right. "Even if it beats me, I'm going to do my best." Yeah. Yeah. Exactly.

T11: Obviously, as her treatment unfolded across time, [**C:** Um hmm] did it feel like your best was enough? Or did you find that it, uh. . .

C11: No . . . no. I um, that was very disappointing. I, I, even though intellectually I knew, and I was prepared intellectually that. . . . "Doesn't matter what you do, when it's gonna happen, it's gonna happen," um, it was pretty

another frozen metaphor—being "driven" to work at the task nonetheless. She is implicitly requesting my help in finding an answer to this question, thereby establishing our first therapeutic task.

T8: I reflect the ironic tension, and Susan affirms my understanding. I then "thaw" the frozen metaphor of being "driven" to see whether it might lead to fresh responses to Susan's unanswered question.

C9: With the question clarified, Susan uses the metaphor to cut through the ambiguity and find an answer. The driving factor is the need to avoid the "powerlessness" referred to in **C5**.

T10: I underscore her answer, echoing her own intonation.

C10: Susan repeatedly affirms that we have articulated her previously confusing existential position.

T11: I am seeking the unresolved aspect of her experience.

C11: Susan clarifies the problem now: her disappointment that her efforts weren't "good enough" (presumably, to save her mother's life).

much of a blow. . . . (3-second pause) Yeah, it was a blow to know my best wasn't good enough, just plain wasn't good enough [spoken slowly; 2-second pause]. Couldn't be.

T12: That from the outset it was almost preordained that you weren't going to be able to reverse the course of her illness and save her life.

T12: I reflect the implied dilemma to confirm that I grasp the focus of her insufficiency.

C12: No, it had already metasta . . . I can never pronounce that right, metastasized, um and was, yeah. It was really too late. It was terminal from the initial diagnosis.

C12: Susan confirms this interpretation.

T13: So part of you, I guess, lived with the fatalistic awareness that these efforts were going to be for naught. [C: That's right.] But then another part felt driven to nonetheless give it your all, do your best [C: Um hum], make a difference. [C: Absolutely, yes.] Did . . .

T13: I introduce the metaphor of different "parts" of her to capture the tension she feels between the part that struggled to do her best and the part that knew the effort was futile. Susan's response suggests that this language fits her experience.

C14: Well, that's the way she raised me! [laughs]

C14: Susan interrupts with a surprise connection, linking her persistent effort to her mother's upbringing of her. Her positive affect suggests that this is a potential resource in gaining new perspective on her way of responding to her mother's illness and death.

T15: So at the end of *her* life you found yourself being very much her daughter in this [C: Um . . . yes.], enacting the role in a way that was compatible with the way you had been as a child and as a young person in relation to her.

T15: I formulate the implied connection.

C15: Actually (3-second pause) no . . . ? [T: Um hum] Um, I took on a *new* role during all this. I was the middle child, and um, was just kinda there growing up. And so taking charge was kind of a new role for me to take at this point. Yeah [pensively].

T16: So something *new* came out in you that you hadn't known was there in terms of a sort of leadership . . .

C16: But I knew it was something she always *expected* of me and I just never really *did*, and did this time around. Yeah.

T17: Ahh, something she *expected* of you, and then at the end you were able to, to give this to her, I guess.

C17: I guess so, yes. [5-second pause] Yeah, I hadn't thought about that aspect of it before, but yeah. [nodding head pensively]

T18: As you say that, I get some tingles up my spine, as if that's . . . [C chuckles]

C19: Yeah, 'cause I had never been a "take charge" type of person up until 3 years ago [T: Um hm.] And uh . . . [3-second pause]

T20: Now has that carried over in some way? You said up until then it did not seem like that was part of you, but now that has [C: Right], has it *become* a part of you?

C20: Right, right. It has, it has, it has, um. There's a, I think that is true, that is true, yeah, I hadn't thought about *that* either! Um, the positive side I guess, of all this has been that what I've been able to

C15: I have made a tracking error in T15, and Susan corrects me. What emerged during her mother's illness was new for her, different from her role as a child. This had the feel of a fresh insight for Susan.

T16: I reformulate this as a new discovery.

C16: Susan recognizes that her "taking charge" self was rooted in her mother's expectations rather than her own previous behavior.

T17: I resituate Susan's taking charge as a relational act, a gift to her dying mother.

C17: Susan is visibly moved by this possibility.

T18: I disclose that I, too, am moved by Susan's grasping this new meaning.

C19: Susan is reaching for the implications of this.

T20: I look for the durability of this transformation, its implications for the present.

C20: Susan repeatedly validates this new position and further articulates it as a positive acquisition hidden in her loss, an attitude of doing what is right, regardless.

take with me with this experience is a "Damn the consequences, I'm gonna do what's right!" [T: OK] kind of attitude.

T21: Which is in contrast to . . .

T21: I prompt her to verbalize the contrast pole of this newly articulated self-construction, the dimension of movement that clarifies who she was before her mother's illness and who she has become since.

C21: Well *before*, I was in tremendous fear of authority, afraid to step on anybody's toes for anything, you know, um. Afraid to be a mover and a shaker [T: Um hum] before that, and now there doesn't seem to be any *reason* for that fear! [C laughs]

C21: Susan elaborates the contrasting, more fearful pole of the construct, and in her laughter demonstrates that she is no longer constrained by its logic.

T22: Huh [3-second pause, nodding head slightly, maintaining eye contact]. I guess that if you've done battle with death, then the rest does kind of pale by comparison.

T22: I underscore the profundity of this shift in Susan's story of who she is by metaphorically anchoring it again in the context of its transformation—her struggle to care for her mother in the time of her dying.

C22: I guess it does [quietly and thoughtfully].

T23: That's a dramatic shift from sort of being quite cautious and timid about taking action to a position where you feel like now its, "Damn the torpedoes, full speed ahead! I'm going to do what needs to be done" [C: Yep], and . . .

T23: I want to affirm this changed identity, to be an audience for the new story she is authoring.

C23: Exactly. Yes. Exactly.

C23: Susan validates that we have grasped the essence of her shift.

T24: Now, have others in your life noticed this shift?

T24: Tacking from the self to the social, I prompt Susan to recruit a broader audience for the change.

C24: Yes. Yes.

T25: Who are they, and what are their comments on this?

C25: Um, well, at first, my sister and I, um, fought tremendously after my mother's death. Um, and (speaking slowly, deliberately) I suppose, looking back, it could be that she was not able to accept this new *façade* of me [**T:** Um hum] . . . [3-second pause] Yeah. So I'd always taken a backseat to *her* stardom, you know. [**T:** Ah ha] Yeah.

T26: So somehow the limelight shifted, and she wasn't on center stage so much in this production, but *you* were more the leading character in the drama.

C26: It was shared, yeah. I wouldn't say that I was the leading character, definitely *not*, but um, we shared.

T27: So you were not just putting in a cameo appearance as you might have done before, but you were really on stage and had a voice. [**C:** Right, right, exactly]. Its interesting now, of course, we are *literally* on stage, and you *again* have a voice and [**C:** Uh huh] as I asked you about how you were feeling at the very outset of our conversation here, you said that you had no particular fear about that. I wonder if that would have been true 4 or 5 years ago.

C27: Definitely, um, *not*! [laughs] Yeah, definitely, you wouldn't have gotten me up here 4 or 5 years ago! Yeah.

C25: Susan now attributes new meaning to the conflict with her sister after her mother's death—it represented her sister's inability to accommodate Susan's new identity. Susan formulates the change in terms of two new metaphors— her "façade," and "stardom," each a vivid dramaturgical elaboration of the earlier description of her "changed role" in **C15**. These become new quality terms that invite greater unpacking.

T26: I test the elasticity of this new dramatic metaphor, its capacity to order the shift toward Susan's greater prominence in relation to her sister.

C26: Susan corrects my tracking error in attributing too much "stardom" to her but stays within the drama metaphor.

T27: I offer an alternative formulation of the drama metaphor emphasizing Susan's gaining a "voice," which she spontaneously validates. I then tack from this past construction of herself to its present enactment with me. Highlighting her apparent lack of fearfulness in the moment, I ask her to notice her identity shift since her mother's death and to ground it in the immediacy of our relationship.

C27: Susan recognizes and affirms her shift away from fearfulness. This feels good, and fresh for her.

T28: So even in a very concrete way with me now, you're carrying over and exemplifying some of the strength and having a voice that has become part of you since this happened. [C: Right, right. (5-second pause)] You know, when you said one thing your sister resisted was that *façade* of authority, the mantle of authority, that you took on at that point [C: Um hum], the shared control, um "façade," suggests something that is *surface* deep, [C: umm] this doesn't . . .

C28: Did I use that word "façade"?

T28: I further consolidate the shift, and Susan confirms it. I then reintroduce the term *façade*, which Susan used in **C25**, because of its implication that the new role was taken up not in a deep-going way but only superficially.

C28: The metaphor now seems alien to her, it no longer fits her present position, although the term was hers.

T29: I think so.

C29: Yeah . . . wow.

C29: Her use of the term was significant for her, but she is not sure how.

T30: Now, I'm wondering if at that time it felt like it wasn't *fully* you [C: True], that it felt like more of a mask or a role that you were donning.

T30: I inquire whether *façade* was perhaps an apt description of her early attempts at taking up a new identity and try to enliven the concept by speaking of it in more imagistically rich terms, in keeping with our mutually constructed drama metaphor.

C30: That's true. That's true. Umm. . . . It felt like a *new garment*. [T: Ah ha]. . . . Yeah.

C30: Susan validates my understanding, and elaborates it in a slightly revised form; the mask becomes a garment.

T31: And now?

C31: Um . . . sometimes it does too, it still does, but less often, you know. It's more comfortable than it was initially.

T32: So it's a . . . it's a garment that you've worn long enough now that its starting to get broken

T32: I "enact" the metaphor to make it more vivid and again tack from the self to the social to check

in a little bit [adjusting jacket], and feel more like you. [C: Yeah, right. Exactly. Yeah.] Now as it becomes more Susan across time, to be this way, have others also noticed *that*, and have they reacted differently across a period of three years now to the new self that is emerging here?

C32: Ahh, my children have reacted very *positively*, you know, they actually said that they knew that I had it in me! [**T:** Hmmm] Yeah, so I don't know what *that* means, but (laughs) um . . .

T33: So it's as if beforehand they could [**C:** Um hum] forecast the sense of strength that you had that [**C:** Right] wasn't maybe blossoming, [**C:** Right] but it sort of has come forth [**C:** Right, exactly]. . . . Um hum.

C33: They're very strong-minded girls anyway (laughs)! Um yeah, I've had a little bit of difficulty in, well, I wouldn't say difficulty, but it was a little *shock* and *surprise* from my father, and you know, my ex-husband and stuff, but yeah (smiling broadly).

T34: "What do we make of this? [**C:** Yeah] This isn't the girl that I raised; [**C:** "Who is this person?"] It's not the woman I married," right?

C34: Yeah, yeah, yeah, exactly.

T35: How do you feel about that slight shock or shaking up that you're doing in their outlooks?

C35: Good! [**T:** Yeah?] Yeah. Yeah. Good, yeah.

the reactions of others to Susan's transformation.

C32: Like her mother in **C16**, Susan's children were aware of her latent strength and supported the enactment of the new identity.

T33: This historicizing of Susan's emergent strength in her relationship to her children strikes a chord, and she repeatedly validates this anchoring.

C33: The gender theme emerges again, with her receiving direct support for her change from the females in the family while eliciting "shock" from the men.

T34: I spontaneously enact the men, to make their reactions vivid and present.

T35: I check Susan's construction of the men's reactions, to see what they mean for her.

C35: Susan finds the men's shocked reaction affirming, just as

T36: Kind of forcing them to revise their image of you as well . . .

C36: Exactly, yeah. Or maybe see me for the first time [pensively, nodding head, smiling]. Yeah. [**T:** Um hum] Yeah.

T37: So in a sense, it feels like this is very compatible with the *seeds* of something that were planted in your childhood, but that never fully flourished until your mother's death. [**C:** Um hum] As you say that . . .

C37: Um hum, exactly, yeah. Well, um, my mother always recognized that too, and uh, she always did the armchair psychologist, that it was 'cause I was the middle child [smiling]. [**T:** Um hum] Yeah, but um, yeah.

T38: What would she say to you now about this if she were here and able to see, you know, the Susan who sits here and talks about this experience now? What kind of comment do you think that she would make on this person?

C38: Um, I think that she would be very *pleased* [questioning intonation]. Yeah, [**T:** Um hum] yeah. Um, I do [slowly, uncertainly, looking away]. . . . But, yeah, still some of the things of the, um, treatment, the caregiving, where I felt like I couldn't quite do it, that still *haunts* me. Yeah, that I couldn't quite deliver some of the times where the caregiving should have been done. . . . . You know,

she had found the more positive reaction of her girls in **C32**.

T36: I venture an interpretation of Susan's response.

C36: She expands the interpretation: For the first time, they have seen the "real" Susan.

T37: I weave together the strands of this preferred story of who Susan is, tying together her more remote past (sketched in **C16**) and her taking on the "mantle of authority" at the time of her mother's dying.

C37: Susan accepts and extends this weaving, embellishing it with her mother's repeated observation of her family position.

T38: I allow myself to be guided by Susan's reintroduction of her mother into our conversation and wonder aloud about her response to Susan's new role.

C38: Susan's statements function as implicit questions, framing our next therapeutic task, namely, exploring her feeling "haunted" by her insufficiency. This theme had emerged poignantly in **C5** and **C11**, and it re-emerges here with new force.

staying up with her, you know, some of the, um, when we were limited on nursing care because of finances, so I had to do a lot of the nursing for her, and that was difficult because I didn't know what the heck I was doing (laughs uneasily)! Umm. . . .

T39: That's the piece you referred to earlier, of feeling like "your best was not good enough."

C39: Right, exactly, exactly, yeah.

T40: I just had a crazy idea, and that was, um, wondering if in this dual reaction that your mother may have had to that period of time—the sense that on one hand she might have been quite proud of the person that you've become, but on the other hand, you feel a sense of that maybe incompleteness about the level of caregiving that you provided [**C:** Um hum]. . . . The crazy thought was . . . um . . . I wonder if maybe we could invite your *mother* to join us here, to kind of continue the conversation with her, rather than only with me. [**C:** Yeah] (6-second pause) What would that feel like to you?

C40: (Sigh) I don't know if we can succeed on that, but I guess we could try [**T:** OK]; just show me how to go about it. [**T:** OK] (C laughs nervously)

T41: What I'd like to suggest is that (pulling in a third, cushioned chair from across the room, and positioning it opposite to Susan, who sits at a 45-degree angle from me) we maybe place your mother

T39: I echo her phrasing in **C11** to weave back to this theme.

C39: Susan grasps the connection.

T40: I ask Susan's indulgence and permission to pursue the unconventional idea of materializing her mother, figuratively, in session, to address the incompleteness Susan feels about her adequacy in caring for her.

C40: Although unsure how to proceed, Susan gives permission and asks for guidance.

T41: I begin by placing her mother in a chair that symbolically "comforts" this ill woman who consents to join us and position it in a way that invites a direct conversation between mother

in this chair, this kind of comfortable chair, and ask you to really, um, start a conversation with her about that period of time. And it seems like maybe the incomplete part of that experience focused on your sense of inadequacy in providing the nursing care to her. That you might have something yet, if she were here today, to say to her about that [C: Um], and to maybe just to kind of turn to her and express to her some of what feels like it needs to be said there.

C41: Well its kinda difficult to begin, yeah (sigh). Um, I guess that I would just tell her that . . .

T42: "What I want to tell you is . . ." (gesturing to the chair).

C42: Okay. Mom, I really wanted to, you know, take care of you better towards the end there, I just . . . the intentions were all there, but you know, like they say, "the spirit is willing, but the body gets weak," and, uh, I just wore out (laughs uneasily). Um, I *do* wish that we could have provided better for you, so that you could have been more comfortable and, uh, stabilized towards the end. And I do, I do wish that we could have done better for you. (4-second pause)

T43: Could you repeat that: "I wish that *I* could have done better for you, Mom."

C43: I wish I could (stumbles here) have done better for you, Mom, I really do (nodding her head). You *should* have been more comfortable towards the end, and

and daughter, with me serving as a respectful listener. I reinforce the immediacy of their contact by averting my eye contact, which has to this point in the session been quite intense, and instead look and gesture to the chair, as a way of deferring to her mother. I also provide the seed of a conversation, focusing Susan on the sense of inadequate caregiving that continues to trouble her.

C41: Susan hesitates, then begins a third-person, conditional account.

T42: I gently redirect her to her mother and model a first-person, present-tense style of speaking.

C42: Susan reopens the conversation in a more real and present way. I find myself feeling moved and very quiet as she speaks.

T43: I heighten the immediacy of the exchange by prompting Susan to stay in the first person singular.

uh, I wish I could have provided that for you. Yeah (quietly) [6-second pause].

T44: I wonder if you could shift over here now (gesturing to mother's chair).

C44: OK (moving to facing chair).

T45: And now, just lending your mother your own voice, respond to Susan here when she is saying, "I wish I could have done better for ya, Mom. I wish I hadn't worn out as I did."

T45: I indirectly reintroduce the theme of Susan's supporting mother by "lending her her voice" and prompt her to respond as Mom to the heart of what Susan has just said.

C45: Well, Susan, I know you did as best as you could, and sometimes I just wonder, you know, if you put too much of a *burden* on yourself (3-second pause) [**T:** Um hum]. Um, circumstances *were* the way they were. (slight laughter; 5-second pause)

C45: *Burden* is the quality term here.

T46: Could you repeat that? "Stop *burdening* yourself, Susan."

T46: I prompt Susan to say this again, in a first-person, direct way, sensing that she is not fully in the words.

C46: Stop burdening yourself, Susan. [**T:** Um hum (resuming eye contact)]. (6-second pause) Actually . . . (3-second pause) I'm not sure, I'm not sure she would really say that.

C46: Repeated, the words ring hollow for Susan as well. In the silence that follows them, she recognizes this.

T47: Um hum . . . because what you think she would say would be . . .

T47: I prompt a more honest telling.

C48: I think . . . she was a very demanding woman.

C48: Susan begins to tell me in a third-person way about her mother's demandingness.

T49: Demand of Susan (gesturing to other chair). [**C:** Yeah.]

T49: I prompt her to enact, rather than discuss, this pattern.

C49: Um, she kind of had those two sides, and you just never knew (laughs nervously).

T50: Speak from the demanding side.

C50: OK. Um . . . (6-second pause). "I know I fell asleep, but I did *not* want you to turn off the TV!" That would be . . . you know, "I was trying to watch that." Um, (4-second pause) "I know I can't eat anything because, um, the treatment has made me nauseous, but I want you to provide at least *four* meals a day so that I have that option!" [**T:** Umm] (sigh) Um . . . (5-second pause, **C** looks to **T**.)

T51: " I want four meals a day! I want the TV left on!"

C51: Right. Um, "I know that I can't always get out, because I can't walk anymore, and you know, even with a walker it's difficult, um, but I do need to get out, you *have* to take me out of this house!"

T52: "You *have* to get me out of the house" (with desperate intonation).

C52: "You have to get me out of the house," um . . . (3-second pause). "This *wig* is no good anymore, I need a new wig!" You know . . . um . . . (2-second pause)

T53: Why don't you come back over here now.

C49: Susan still speaks about, rather than from within, her mother's position. It is important to her that this is only one aspect of her mother.

T50: I encourage her to enact the more difficult side, now, in session.

C50: Suddenly, there is an affective change: Susan's narrative becomes much more present, concrete, and charged with feeling. These come across as fragments of dialogue vividly remembered but inadequately processed. Susan then hesitates, uncertain whether to continue.

T51: Sensing there is more, I prompt her to stay in role by reiterating mother's concrete complaints.

C51: The demandingness returns and retains its present vividness.

T52: I underscore the demand through restatement.

T53: With her mother's demands vividly before us, I invite Susan to resume her own position in the conversation, gesturing to Susan's chair.

C54: OK (returns to previous seat).

T55: Can you respond to Mom? "I want the TV left on! I want four meals a day! I want to get out of this house! This wig is no good anymore!" (gestures to "mother chair")

T55: Summarizing her mother's demands through first-person enactment, I encourage Susan to respond, perhaps in a way she could not at the time.

C55: . . .Well Mom, I just have to do what I can do for you, I can't do any more. And that's all there is to it. Uh, if you need something, I'm there for you, but I'm only one person, and that's all I can do is just what I can manage. And if I fall short, that doesn't mean that I love you any less . . .

C55: Susan begins to establish some boundaries with her mother, but her statement of positive feeling is indirect, elliptical.

T56: Um hm. Can you repeat that again, with feeling? If I fall short . . .

T56: I prompt a more direct expression of affect.

C56: If I fall short of what you feel you need, it's not because I love you any less, it's only my limitations.

C56: The feeling is still indirect, the self-blame still subtly present.

T57: Um hm. Tell her how you *do* feel about her, now.

T57: I prompt a clear statement of feeling, directly to mother.

C57: I miss you, Mom (3-second pause, smiling genuinely, moisture appearing in eyes). Yeah (nodding head), I miss picking up the phone at any time, and telling you what Katie, my daughter, did and what Regina did today. Um, you know, brainstorming with you, how to handle a certain problem with the kids, um. . . . Even your damned opera (laughs heartily)! I miss that, and uh, since you've been gone, I *love* opera now, umm. . . . But *damn* it, you were difficult

C57: The warmth Susan feels for her mother floods in, anchored in concrete exchanges. Even those things that were irritating about mother's preferences now have become precious. At the same time, however, Susan is able to hold the complexity of her image of her mother and acknowledge the difficulty of their real relationship, affirming it despite (or perhaps because of) this complexity. I find myself tearing up along with her, touched by her palpable love.

(laughs)! She was for me (shaking head), it *was* hard, it was hard. But the best people in life really *are* difficult, yeah, and I miss you (tearing up, but smiling and nodding head). (3-second pause)

T58: Does she have any closing statement to make to you, do you think, for this little piece of the conversation? Could she say something about how. . . .

C58: Yeah (moves to "mother's chair"). I think in closing, she would say, "Susan, I know you did everything you could, you know. You got a long way to go! [both **C** and **T** laugh aloud]. . . . But I'm *proud* of you (nods her head, tearing up). I'm proud of you. [**T:** Um hum (nodding and smiling in affirmation).] I think that would be it (looking up at me, touched, but smiling).

T59: That would be it. Do you want to come back here and be Susan?

C59: Yeah. (moves back to her seat)

T60: [Moves "mother's chair" away] Let me shift this out of our way. How did this feel to you, taking these two chairs? Did that bring forth anything for you worth commenting on?

C60: Well, it's interesting that the chairs are *dissimilar*, 'cause that heightened, um. . . . When I first sat in that chair, I had a little almost shock, like, "This is someone *else*, this is not me (laughs)!" [**T:** Um hmm, um hmm.] You know, so that it was a little easier to extrapolate, and project.

T58: I want to give "Mother" a chance for provisional closure as well, recognizing that more conversations may follow.

C58: Susan, as Mother, forgives herself, while humorously recapitulating her mother's demandingness. The pride Mother feels is nonetheless genuine and provides a sense of completion to the dialogue.

T60: I reconfigure the seating, to again establish the space as ours, in the present, and invite Susan to share what was significant for her in the enactment.

C60: Even the incidental details of the staging supported her leaving her customary role and taking up her mother's.

T61: To project your mother into that seat rather than just Susan.

C61: Right, um. It's a little easier to role play. Normally I find role playing, um, very difficult! (laughs)

T62: Now, as you moved through this, and sort of tacked back and forth between these two seats, did you find the conversation developing in any interesting ways that might not have been completely forecasted?

T62: I am interested in whether enacting the unfinished conversation with mother offered any surprising recognitions to her.

C62: You mean if I hadn't switched seats?

T63: No, if you, if you—yes, if you were just giving a single-person account of the nature of the relationship with your mom. Did anything different emerge enacting it in this way?

T63: I misunderstand Susan's response for a moment, then grasp her meaning, and clarify my request.

C64: Um, definitely, definitely. (Slowly, glancing to the side, enunciating each word:) Although I knew her dissatisfaction, I don't think I would have *expressed* it, even to *myself*. [**T:** Um hmm] (4-second pause) Yeah. So that definitely was helpful. [**T:** Um hm] (3-second pause) I almost *didn't* express it.

C64: Susan reflexively processes the experience, which for her prompted a fuller and more integrated awareness of her mother's dissatisfaction, in place of the partial awareness that she had previously suppressed.

T65: There was this moment of hesitation there for you when it seemed like that [**C:** Yeah, yeah.] what you were saying was ringing hollow [**C:** Right, yeah], and the demandingness wasn't finding a voice.

T65: I index this vacillation between acknowledging and suppressing her mother's dissatisfaction to Susan's hesitation in **C45–C49** as a way of reviving that therapeutic moment for further examination. Susan repeatedly affirms that this was the critical juncture.

C65: Then again even the hollowness was a little bit true too,

C65: Susan grasps and holds the complexity of her mother's because she, as I say, she has those two sides to her.

T66: Just as you have these two sides to you. [**C:** I guess *so* (thoughtfully).] (3-second pause) Quite corresponding sides. [**C:** Um hm] Um hm. [**C:** Right]. (3-second pause)

Part of what I was struck by as you found a point of humor there about her "damned opera," and then finding that you've come to *like* this damned opera some, it's almost as if you've *become* her a little bit.

C66: Hmm. Now *that's* a scary thought! (laughs)

T67: But maybe *selectively*. [**C:** Yeah] That there are portions of her that you have taken into you and other parts that maybe you are not wanting to take in. [**C:** Hmm] Could that fit? Are there good features of her that . . .

C67: Um hmm, *definitely*, definitely that could fit, yeah. Hmm . . . (3-second pause)

T68: Why don't we break out of the this sort of straight talk about this, and just reflect on this process for a minute, and, um, then [**C:** Okay] what we can do, maybe, is move back into the studio and talk with the audience about their perceptions of different features of this. What did you find to be of interest in this, um, 30 minutes or so that we've been talking?

C68: Uh, well, I think that your final comment was something of

image, both the positive and negative.

T66: I provisionally parallel Susan's two sides—the take charge, center-stage Susan versus the powerless, cameo actress of **C15–T37**—to the two sides of her mother, and suggest a connection: Has Susan assimilated some of her mother's identity into her own?

C66: This possibility initially shocks her, perhaps because there are parts of her mother she would rather not incorporate.

T67: I elaborate, allowing her to sort through her identification with her mother, developing a more discriminating sense of connection.

C67: Susan validates and appropriates this idea as an intriguing possibility.

T68: I prompt a shift to metaprocessing of the session as a whole, broadening the frame from the examination of the enacted conversation of Susan and her mother. What has Susan found to be noteworthy in our time together?

C68: The interpretation in **T66** has triggered a significant recon-

interest. (Very slowly, pensively, glancing to the side): I *have* changed since her death. I think I have changed definitely for the *better*. Um, I feel much *stronger*, but I hadn't realized how much of that change was incorporating *her* into *me*. [**T:** Umhm, um hm; 4-second pause] I had never real . . . that's something that I'm gonna need to *chew* on for a while, definitely, 'cause that never occurred to me, and that does seem like worth exploring.

T69: Giving her a kind of continued existence through you [**C:** Exactly], in a way. Really honoring that connection with your life [**C:** Right], not merely with your words. [**C:** Right] Okay.

C69: That definitely deserves a lot of reflection on. I hadn't thought about that at *all*. So that's probably from this thirty minutes what I gained most. Yes (nodding).

T70: For my own part, I have found myself touched by a number of things you said. I found myself chuckling along with you when you reflected on the opera, something that I fully detest! (Both laugh.) Maybe it will take my mother's death to make me love opera as well, I don't know. It will have to be something dramatic! I also was appreciating the way in which you recognized early and deeply that this experience had shaped *you* in some way. That it wasn't just about losing *her*, but about accessing a part of *you* that

struction of Susan's understanding of her adjustment of her mother's death: The valued transformation of her own identity may be in part an incorporation of (the best parts of) her mother. This seems very compelling and fresh to her, something she wants to sift through further.

T69: I frame this newly grasped connection to her mother not as a selfish assimilation but a way of honoring, and extending, the significance of her mother's existence. Susan repeatedly affirms this.

C69: This is the most significant new meaning to emerge for Susan in this session.

T70: I share a humorous disclosure of my own identification with (a part of) Susan, bridging the intensity of the foregoing exploration with re-entry into the social world. I then recapitulate and consolidate some of the themes of our session, using Susan's language to provide anchors for the reconstruction of her identity that she has grasped, explored, and displayed in session. My warmth and admiration for Susan is genuine, and I close by expressing it.

was dormant and recognized in
some sense even by your children.
But it kind of took the event of
your mother's illness to bring
forth a part of you that was willing to share the stage along with
your sister, to not just make a
cameo appearance in your life,
but really to have a voice of your
own, and a presence and authority. And that was very striking to
me. [C: Yeah, for me, too].
[6-second pause] And I *see* that in
you, and I appreciate that in you
(both smiling, with eye contact,
nodding). So . . . (suggesting
standing with a gesture)

C70: Thank you.

CLOSING COMMENTS

From a relational constructivist view, we are shaped and sustained by
our shifting patterns of attachment to people, places, projects, and possessions that largely anchor the meaning of our lives. The loss of these attachments challenges our tacit assumptions about who we are and prompts revisions in our life narratives that can sometimes be deep going. Yet traditional
theories of grief that construe bereavement in terms of simplistic stages of
emotional adjustment, quasi-psychiatric symptomatology, or even common-
sensical challenges to our "coping skills" are poorly equipped to help either
bereaved people or those who counsel them to grasp the subtleties of such
loss and transformation. In my own work I have found a constructivist emphasis on the individuality of meaning making, on the narrative construction
of self, and on the (para)linguistic negotiation of changed meanings to provide a more responsive frame for holding the complexity of loss as a lived experience. In keeping with this view, the grief therapy my clients and I seem
to find most helpful eschews formulaic models that subtly prescribe "normal"
ways of mourning as well as pat reassurance and advice. Instead, I allow myself to be guided by the implicit meaning of what the client says (and does
not say) at each moment of therapy, following his or her lead in giving attention to sensed incompleteness or tension in the client's self-narrative
associated with the loss. Although the resulting conversation focuses on
sense-making, it departs sharply from the disputative, rational, and Socratic
exchanges that characterize contemporary cognitive therapy, instead viewing
therapeutic dialogue as a process of meaning symbolization and experiential

engagement. The goal of such interaction is not a "normalizing" of the client's response or a "correction" of dysfunctional thoughts or behaviors. Instead, a constructivist grief therapy prompts the articulation and elaboration of the client's narrative of loss in a way that promotes a new sense of coherence, continuity, and consensual validation of an enlarged identity.

The therapy with Susan presented here illustrates many of these features. Beginning with an immediate and vivid flood of feelings associated with the death of her mother, I attempted to focus progressively on the growing edge of her story of the loss, an edge that was sometimes sharp and painful to contact. Susan typically led in this process, offering a succession of emotionally evocative quality terms that invited exploration, as well as the seeds of joint metaphors that captured the nuances of her experience better than literal terminology could. As we elaborated these terms and metaphors together in imagistically rich language we more adequately grasped the contrasting features of both her mother's identity and her own and became clearer about the relational tensions that continued to haunt her. This suggested the value of reopening the dialogue with Susan's mother in a direct, present-tense form, leading to a more emotionally resonant and complex enactment of the relationship. As I often do, I then prompted two levels of meta-processing of our work together, focusing in succession on the immediately preceding enactment and then on the session as a whole. My closing comment and disclosure conveyed my genuine respect and appreciation for Susan's work in the session and, more fundamentally, for the person she was becoming as she continued to integrate her mother's death into the narrative of her life.

I hope that this brief discussion and illustration of a linguistic–relational approach to grief therapy offers encouragement to other counselors whose work is carrying them beyond the confines of traditional theories of bereavement. Ultimately, I trust that this combined effort to expand our therapeutic models and practices will enlarge the frame within which bereavement is viewed by both professionals and those who consult them and begin to configure a more adequate response to the process of meaning reconstruction in the aftermath of loss.

REFERENCES

Attig, T. (1996). *How we grieve: Relearning the world.* New York: Oxford University Press.

Bruner, J. (1986). *Actual minds, possible worlds.* Cambridge, England: Cambridge University Press.

Campbell, D. (1987). Blind variation and selective retention in creative thought as in other knowledge processes. In G. Radnitzky & W. Bartley (Eds.), *Evolution-*

ary epistemology, theory of rationality, and the sociology of knowledge (pp. 91–114). La Salle, IL: Open Court.

Derrida, J. (1978). *Writing and difference*. Chicago: University of Chicago Press.

De Shazer, S. (1994). *Words were originally magic*. New York: Norton.

Doka, K., & Davidson, J. D. (Eds.). (1998). *Living with grief: Who we are, how we grieve*. Washington, DC: Hospice Foundation of America.

Franklin, C., & Nurius, P. S. (Eds.). (1998). *Constructivism in practice*. Milwaukee, WI: Families International.

Freud, S. (1972). *The standard edition of the complete psychological works of Sigmund Freud* (J. Strachey, Trans.). New York: Norton.

Gergen, K. J. (1991). *The saturated self*. New York: Basic Books.

Glover, L. (1995). Personal theories in psychotherapy. In R. A. Neimeyer & G. J. Neimeyer (Eds.), *Advances in personal construct psychology* (Vol. 3, pp. 193–227). Greenwich, CT: JAI Press.

Gluhoski, V. L. (1995). A cognitive perspective on bereavement. *Journal of Cognitive Psychotherapy, 9*, 75–84.

Hagman, G. (1995). Mourning: A review and reconsideration. *International Journal of Psychoanalysis, 76*, 909–925.

Harre, R., & Gillett, R. (1994). *The discursive mind*. Thousand Oaks, CA: Sage.

Held, B. (1995). *Back to reality*. New York: Norton.

Janoff-Bulman, R. (1989). Assumptive worlds and the stress of traumatic events. *Social Cognition, 7*, 113–116.

Kant, I. (1965). *Critique of pure reason*. New York: St. Martins. (Original work published 1787)

Kelly, G. A. (1955). *The psychology of personal constructs*. New York: Norton.

Klass, D., Silverman, P. R., & Nickman, S. (1996). *Continuing bonds: New understandings of grief*. Washington, DC: Taylor & Francis.

Landfield, A. W. (1988). Personal science and the concept of validation. *International Journal of Personal Construct Psychology, 1*, 237–249.

Leitner, L. M. (1995). Optimal therapeutic distance. In R. A. Neimeyer & M. J. Mahoney (Eds.), *Constructivism in psychotherapy* (pp. 357–369). Washington, DC: American Psychological Association.

Levitt, H., & Angus, L. (1999). Psychotherapy process measure research and the evaluation of psychotherapy orientation: A narrative analysis. *Journal of Psychotherapy Integration, 9*, 279–300.

Mascolo, M. F., Craig-Bray, L., & Neimeyer, R. A. (1997). The construction of meaning and action in development and psychotherapy. In G. J. Neimeyer & R. A. Neimeyer (Eds.), *Advances in personal construct psychology* (Vol. 4, pp. 3–38). Greenwich, CT: JAI Press.

Merleau-Ponty, M. (1962). *Phenomenology of perception*. London: Routledge. (Original work published 1945)

Minuchin, S. (1991, September–October). The seductions of constructivism. *Family Therapy Networker*, 47–50.

Neimeyer, R. A. (1996). Process interventions for the constructivist psychotherapist. In H. Rosen & K. Kuehlwien (Eds.), *Constructing realities* (pp. 371–411). San Francisco: Jossey Bass.

Neimeyer, R. A. (1998a). Can there be a psychology of loss? In J. H. Harvey (Ed.), *Perspectives on loss: A sourcebook* (pp. 331–341). Philadelphia: Taylor & Francis.

Neimeyer, R. A. (1998b). *Lessons of loss: A guide to coping.* New York: McGraw-Hill.

Neimeyer, R. A. (1998c). Social constructionism in the counselling context. *Counselling Psychology Quarterly, 11,* 135–149.

Neimeyer, R. A. (2000). Narrative disruptions in the construction of self. In R. A. Neimeyer & J. Raskin (Eds.), *Constructions of disorder* (pp. 207–242). Washington, DC: American Psychological Association.

Neimeyer, R. A., & Mahoney, M. J. (1995). *Constructivism in psychotherapy.* Washington, DC: American Psychological Association.

Neimeyer, R. A., & Raskin, J. (Eds.). (2000). *Constructions of disorder.* Washington, DC: American Psychological Association.

Neimeyer, R. A., & Stewart, A. E. (1996). Trauma, healing, and the narrative emplotment of loss. *Families in Society, 77,* 360–375.

Polanyi, M. (1958). *Personal knowledge.* New York: Harper.

Rando, T. A. (1995). Grief and mourning: Accommodating to loss. In H. Wass & R. A. Neimeyer (Eds.), *Dying: Facing the facts* (pp. 211–241). Washington, DC: Taylor & Francis.

Rosen, H., & Kuehlwein, K. (Eds.). (1996). *Constructing realities.* San Francisco: Jossey Bass.

Sewell, K. W. (1996). Constructional risk factors for a post-traumatic stress response after a mass murder. *Journal of Constructivist Psychology, 9,* 97–108.

Simons, H. W. (1989). *Rhetoric in the human sciences.* Newbury Park, CA: Sage.

Spence, D. (1982). *Narrative and historical truth.* New York: Norton.

Tedeschi, R., Park, C., & Calhoun, L. (Eds.). (1998). *Posttraumatic growth: Positive changes in the aftermath of crisis.* Mahwah, NJ: Erlbaum.

Toukmanian, S. G., & Rennie, D. L. (Eds.). (1992). *Psychotherapy process research.* Newbury Park, CA: Sage.

Walter, T. (1996). A new model of grief: Bereavement and biography. *Mortality, 1,* 7–26.

Watson, J. C., & Greenberg, L. (1996). Emotion and cognition in experiential therapy. In H. Rosen & K. T. Kuehlwein (Eds.), *Constructing realities* (pp. 253–275). San Francisco: Jossey Bass.

White, M., & Epston, D. (1990). *Narrative means to therapeutic ends.* New York: Norton.

15

CONSTRUING STRESS: A CONSTRUCTIVIST THERAPEUTIC APPROACH TO POSTTRAUMATIC STRESS REACTIONS

KENNETH W. SEWELL AND AMY M. WILLIAMS

As humans, we move through our world by attempting to accurately anticipate or predict our experiences. Our anticipations range from those that are inconsequential to those that are passionately held. Unfortunately for our short-term comfort (and fortunately for our long-term growth), our experiences often defeat our anticipations. When these losses are dramatic, extreme, and on constructs (dimensions of personal meaning) that are held especially dear, we have encountered a *"traumatic"* experience. An anecdotal vignette follows:

> She, like most of us, moves about the world preferring and anticipating a modicum of personal safety. She anticipates that those she loves will also prefer and participate in her safety. When that dear anticipation is extremely and dramatically invalidated by a sexual assault perpetrated by a family member, she is traumatized.

In this chapter we first outline a constructivist model of posttraumatic stress that has evolved over the past decade, based on research with various trauma populations, including Vietnam combat veterans, sexual assault survivors, murder scene witnesses, and bereaved individuals (Gamino, Sewell, & Easterling, 1998; Moes & Sewell, 1994; Sewell, 1991, 1996, 1997; Sewell et al., 1996; Sewell & Cromwell, 1990; Williams, Gamino, Sewell, Easterling, & Stirman, 1998).[1] The remainder of the chapter is dedicated to outlining a therapeutic approach derived from our current model as well as from other relevant research.

A CONSTRUCTIVIST MODEL OF POSTTRAUMATIC STRESS

We first consider two related questions that will guide the presentation of our model. First, how does one make sense (meaning) of a traumatic event? In answering this question we will outline three alternatives in the construct system for coping with traumatic experiences. The concept of implicit construction will be introduced to help answer this question. Second, what domains of construal are affected by traumatic events? We propose that traumatic experiences disrupt meaning construction in both social and event domains. The nature of the traumatic experience influences the extent to which the event disruption or the social disruption will predominate.

Posttraumatic Alternatives

At least three alternatives are possible for responding to traumatic experiences (or aspects of these experiences). First, in line with Kelly's (1955/1991) notion of anxiety, the individual can experience *constructive bankruptcy*—in other words, there simply are no dimensions of meaning (neither explicit nor implicit) available to the person that allow him or her to place the experience into perspective with other positive and negative life experiences. Imagine a combat soldier encountering the effects of biological warfare for the first time.

Second, the individual might achieve dissociated[2] or cut-off understanding of some or all of the traumatic experience. In *dissociated construction* the person has or creates one or more constructs that are primitively used to construe the trauma. These dichotomies cannot be related in a sophisticated way to the rest of the conceptual structure (Cromwell, Sewell, & Langelle, 1996). Dissociated trauma-related constructions can be problematic, at least in part, because they yield only extreme anticipations and interpretations. As an example, consider a woman who fails to receive an ex-

---

[1]For additional readings on constructivist views of trauma, interested readers are referred to Herman (1992); McCann and Pearlman (1990); Roth, Lebowitz, and DeRosa (1997); and Viney (1996).

[2]It should be noted that the notion of "dissociation" here is descriptive of the ordinal relations within the construct system and does not directly correspond to "dissociative symptoms" sometimes present in PTSD.

pected and routine telephone call. Some months before, this same woman was raped and came to understand her traumatic experience by forming two construct dimensions: (a) "total commitment" versus "in danger of being betrayed" and (b) "in control" versus "harmed by men." When she fails to receive the expected telephone call from her boyfriend, she experiences this as being further harmed and betrayed (i.e., on the same level as the rape).

These first two alternatives following a traumatic experience account for some symptoms of posttraumatic stress disorder (PTSD). Clearly, experiences for which there are no available constructions will trigger subjective anxiety and keep the subjective experience temporally current (accounting for re-experiencing phenomena). Avoidant strategies may temporarily alleviate symptoms, but reminders that invoke the unassigned aspects of the trauma will invariably cause psychological distress. Dissociated constructions, being unstable and usually more extreme, account for the depressive symptoms often observed in PTSD. Finally, the constructive bankruptcy and dissociated construction, when occurring simultaneously with various aspects of the traumatic experience, could feed on each other in a vicious cycle, accounting for volatile mood disturbance (anger, etc.) and the syndromic nature of PTSD (Sewell et al., 1996).

The third constructive alternative following traumatization is elaborative growth. If the individual is quickly able to make only minor adjustments to the overall construct system and rapidly accommodate the experience, then there is—in the subjective sense—no traumatization. On the other hand, if constructive bankruptcy and dissociative construction ensue in order to grapple with the experience, then a posttraumatic stress reaction (or PTSD, if the reaction is persistent and severe) is present. Regardless of the initial reaction, elaborating (extending and reintegrating) one's construct system is requisite to posttraumatic adaptation.

This elaborative process has been refined (Sewell, 1996) to include the notion of implicit constructions. Consider that one end (pole) of a psychological dimension relies on the implicit psychological presence of its other pole to give meaning to the entire construct. When I experience happiness, I must—at some level—consider "sadness" in order to anchor the meaning of my feeling. Of course, we are not usually aware of such construing (thus the term *implicit construing*). Implicit construing is our tool for anticipating invalidation. In other words, we have explicit anticipations that guide and shape how we understand our experiences; the only viable way to attempt an understanding of total invalidation would be to bring forth the opposite poles of our dimensions of anticipation. Take, for instance, a young woman whose childhood sweetheart was brutally murdered several years after they were married. Prior to his murder, she functioned on the basis that they would have children, grow old together, and that one of them would die first of "natural causes" in older age. Although she surely had the concepts of not having children, not growing old together, or losing one's life in an "unnatural" way, they had previously been implicit. Now she has been unexpectedly thrust into anticipating the world from these previously tacit, unelaborated, and less valued poles.

Recovery from PTSD occurs when the traumatized individual develops constructs for the trauma that can be integrated into his or her whole system of meaning. In so doing, he or she must build a network of implicit constructions regarding the traumatic and related experience, such that he or she can both anticipate and understand novel yet nontraumatic experiences.

It should be noted that verbal behavior is likely more closely linked with emergent construction (initial anticipations and understandings). Our focus on the need to elaborate implicit construction would explain why the mere act of talking about a trauma is frequently insufficient to integrate the experience in a comfortable way. It is less the emergent and remembered details of the experience that beg restructuring but more the tacit (Neimeyer, 1981) and implicit details and connections among experiences that must be repaired and rebuilt.

Domains of Anticipation

When traumatization occurs there is a concomitant disruption in at least two different and important domains of construction: events and persons. In other words, the constructional subsystem relevant to events is disrupted, as is the subsystem relevant to the social world. Certainly, a disruption in understanding and anticipating "events" is a central aspect of many presentations of traumatic stress. It has also long been known that social functioning is also often disrupted in traumatized individuals (Figley, 1978; Resick, 1993).

Event disruption occurs when the traumatic experience is characterized by invalidations of expectations regarding "how the world is supposed to work." These types of invalidations are most likely to occur in traumas of horror and violence. Such traumas have been a central focus of the traumatology field in recent years, particularly since the inclusion of PTSD into the *Diagnostic and Statistical Manual of Mental Disorders* (3rd ed., American Psychiatric Association, 1980) in 1980 to account for the postwar syndrome presented by many Vietnam veterans. More recently, similar examples may be found in veterans of the Persian Gulf conflict, participants in peacekeeping missions in war-torn countries, and Bosnian refugees who have survived numerous human rights violations. Central human expectations that bodies remain intact, the world is safe, life is fair, and so on are clearly invalidated by situations of war, terrorism, automobile accidents, and similar such events.

Social disruption involves invalidation of anticipations regarding "with whom and how I am socially related." Previously, social disruption has almost always been viewed as a by-product or sequela of a primary difficulty in construing/processing the event. However, social disruption can be *pri-*

mary in some forms of posttraumatic reactions rather than only secondary to event disruption. Although sexual assault experiences can certainly disrupt event construction, the strong social connotations of sexuality often invoke predominant social disruption. Cromwell et al. (1996) reported two case studies illustrating how children subjected to prolonged sexual trauma can display problematic conceptions of social relations (and thus, problematic conception of the self) well into adulthood. Other types of potentially traumatic experiences would seem also to have predominating social components. For example, the death of an elderly loved one often involves little or no event disruption but can represent profound invalidation in the social domain.

There are almost always problems in *both* event and social domains; singular disruptions are unlikely given that most persons have individual constructs in their repertoire relevant to both domains. Even though the disturbance occurs in both the event and the social domains, one domain will usually predominate in the individual's clinical presentation. However, there are some traumatic experiences that are characterized by high levels of both social and event disruption. When a land mine explodes and the person I see blown to bits is not just another soldier but my best buddy, with whom I have planned an entire life of close relationship, I am likely to be invalidated across both domains. When a wife of many years is ravaged by a disease that disfigures her, makes her no longer recognize her husband, and ultimately kills her, the husband's construction is likely dually disrupted. When a mother and a father see their child dead, they likely experience event disruption ("The world is not *supposed* to work that way–children are not *supposed* to die before their parents!") as well as social disruption ("Who am I without my child?"). No doubt these dual disruptions are the most difficult traumas to transcend—the most difficult to turn into growth.

The foregoing discussion might be interpreted as intending to pigeonhole clients on the basis of the predominantly disrupted domain of anticipation. That would be a mistake. It must be remembered that both event and social constructions are disrupted in the traumatized client. Over the course of psychotherapy the client might vacillate in the predominant presentation, particularly once therapeutic efforts are beginning to ameliorate disruption of any one domain. We highlight the different presentations here to alert clinicians to the likely foci and to guard against the assumption (present in much trauma literature) that social disruption is always secondary.

THE CONSTRUCTIVIST INTEGRATIVE MODEL OF POSTTRAUMATIC STRESS PSYCHOTHERAPY

How does a traumatized person reconstruct his or her construct system to yield new and more adaptive anticipations of experience? What tools are used? Because human beings are seen as complex, self-organizing systems (Mahoney & Moes, 1997), the process must be a recursive one. In other words, the construct system re-creates itself. To conceptualize this process the notion of *metaconstruction* is used.

Metaconstruction

My ability to construe how I thought of myself in the past, and how I might construe myself in the future, involves a human skill known as *metaconstruction*. Indeed, my metaconstructive processes of past and future self-conception, when integrated, can be said to define my current sense of self. As a metaphor of how traumatic experiences can disrupt the sense of self, Sewell (1997) used the experience of sitting in a barber's chair with mirrors in front and behind. The comfortable recognition of all the consistent recursive images represents the untraumatized sense of self. A trauma results when the experience of being in the chair is different from (seemingly discontinuous with) one of the images in the back mirror. When this is the case, predicting what will appear on the front mirror from iteration to iteration becomes troubling and confusing. From the perspective of our model, the images can represent either social or person domains (in other words, what is reflected in the mirrors might be either events or relationships).

Using our model and the mirror metaphor, we theorize that a trauma can initiate a construction subsystem (for the present) that seems dramatically incongruous with how past processes are currently remembered. This incongruity is so extreme that it becomes difficult to see one's present psychological state as having emerged from the remembered past. The ability to metaconstrue the past keeps those processes to some extent current (i.e., they seem to exist alongside the discontinuous trauma subsystem). Consequently, the lack of continuity between metaconstrued present and past impairs the ability to make a coherent future metaconstruction.

The growth alternative, then (and thus the goal of psychotherapy), is elaboration of the present and past metaconstructions, in the predominating event or social domains, such that they are construed as continuously linked. Then, future events, future relationships, and the sense of self can be metaconstructed in a nonfragmented, nonconstricted fashion.

Elements of Psychotherapy

Below we outline what we consider to be the crucial elements of psychotherapy with a traumatized client, as derived from our model of posttraumatic maladjustment. These elements, or foci, should not be viewed as strictly sequential. We list them in order of their likely predominant focus in the therapeutic relationship, but this order is fluid. Human change tends to occur in recursive temporal oscillations (Mahoney & Moes, 1997); thus, even in the most productive of therapeutic encounters the needed foci are likely to alternate in progressive cycles. When a focus shift occurs, movement to a focus on the next element represents legitimate progress; movement to a previous focus need represent not regression but rather a regrouping for yet another push forward in reconstruing the trauma, the social world, and the self in a new and more adaptively satisfying way.

Symptom Management

The first step of symptom management involves an attempt to instill hope in the traumatized client who feels his or her world or self to be irreparably lost or damaged. The most common mode of achieving this is to provide a personally meaningful (for the therapist and for the client) rationale for why psychotherapy might be useful in reducing the pain and disequilibrium following a traumatic experience.

> Christine, I hear what you're saying about being a "different person since the rape." We will work together in decreasing the anxiety and other symptoms you are experiencing. In addition, I want to know more about how you see yourself and those around you. Before the rape occurred, your experiences taught you certain ways of understanding your world and making sense out of what happened to you. You may not have been aware of the "rules" you set up about how to deal with the world, but they probably guided how you approached new experiences, your self, and other people. We are going to work together in exploring not only what it means to have been raped, but also the ways in which your views of the world and yourself have changed. By doing this, I hope we'll find a way to lessen the pain and fear that you've been feeling over the last few months and replace it with a fuller picture of who you are and what you have to look forward to.

Very early, perhaps as early as the first therapy session, the therapist and client must negotiate the client's present metaconstruction. Carrying forward the mirror metaphor, symptom management involves examining, with the therapist, the phenomenology of the chair and what can be done to make the client's position more bearable while working toward long-term resolution. Obviously, the lessening of subjective distress can be, in and of itself, psychotherapeutic. However, we contend that the most important functions of symptom management are the indirect effects of the process and are twofold. First, reducing the distress related to acute symptoms can free some of the client's attentional energies, allowing more productive therapeutic work to be done in the other, reconstructive aspects of therapy. Second, and even more important, symptom management efforts provide a compassionate vehicle for the therapist to join with the client in his or her struggle to deal with the pain and difficulty of adjusting to a trauma. Thus, effective symptom management is a profound demonstration to the client that the therapist is taking the risk to see through his or her eyes, walk in his or her shoes, and share in the pain. This assertive demonstration of sociality from the therapist, particularly when the social disruption is predominating in the client, can dramatically open him or her to the influence of the therapist.

The specific techniques of symptom management are legion (e.g., Meichenbaum, 1994). Some of the most quickly effective are the typically termed *cognitive–behavioral* techniques such as relaxation, thought stopping, self-talk modification and disputation, and breathing retraining (Foa & Rothbaum, 1998; Foy, 1992; Veronen & Kilpatrick, 1983). Grounding techniques, such as focusing on bodily sensations; listening to the therapist's voice; or a touch on the hand, with the client's permission, can be used for dissociative symptoms (Courtois, 1988; van der Kolk, van der Hart, & Marmar, 1996). Even interpersonal skills training (e.g., Linehan, 1993) can be useful in symptom management. Referrals might also be sought for psychopharmacological adjuncts to psychotherapy (particularly antidepressants and sleep aids) to the extent that the acute distress is precluding the development of a trusting therapeutic relationship. Also, assessing for substance abuse can be critical to the success of psychotherapy, given the high rates of self-medication present in PTSD referrals.

> Ashley, a 30-year-old woman who had been sexually and physically abused by her biological father, entered treatment to deal with increasingly intrusive memories of her abuse. She reported emotional and physical reminders being triggered while at her job in a mental health–related field. She was most distressed by dissociative numbing, intrusive thoughts, physiological responding, and lack of concentration. Initial sessions focused on breathing retraining and techniques to avoid dissociation. As Ashley continued in therapy, occasional sessions would serve as "refreshers" for using symptom management techniques. This context allowed Ashley to approach memories of the abuse without the fear that she would become overwhelmed or unable to perform her job in the interim.

Life Review

A client who comes to therapy with an acknowledged trauma history usually will feel compelled to focus on the traumatic experience in the first session (often in the first statements to the therapist). Certainly, a therapist must respect such a client's willingness and desire to self-disclose. However, we never expect that this initial event description is itself therapeutic. It is often a decontextualized story of an experience that the client only partially owns, even if there is explicit recognition that it is the source of great distress. Thus, we recommend informing the client that she will likely need to revisit the memory of the experience in much greater detail later in therapy, after she is more comfortable with the therapeutic relationship and the therapist has gotten to know her better. Instead of immediately targeting the trauma, efforts turn toward a *life review*. A life review involves the evocation of past metaconstruction—exploring the rearview mirror—in order to construe/coconstrue and perhaps construct/coconstruct the context in which the traumatic experience took place.

Life review techniques can be as straightforward as asking the client to talk about his childhood, adolescence, and other periods and significant experiences that preceded the trauma. Although straightforward, this approach is by no means simple if the full context of the client's life is to be explored. One goal of life review is for the therapist to have a sense of knowing the client at various important points in the past. Another goal is for the client to reacquaint himself with his own psychological history (involving effortful reflection, not just remembering a collection of events). "How did you understand that at the time?" followed by "How do you understand that now that you're 35 years old?" are the types of questions that need to be targeted toward episodic remembrances during an unstructured life review.

Because of the difficulty in facilitating an effective life review, some clinicians have developed more structured methods for organizing and coexploring past metaconstruction. Stewart (1995) described one typical method: autobiographical writing assignments. By focusing on him or herself at early and sequentially older life stages, and writing an integrated descriptive story of actions, experiences, stressors, motives, values, and circumstances, the client and therapist are assisted in understanding "who this person was" prior to traumatization. Neimeyer (1995) used the metaphor that stories such as these "yearn for coherence" (p. 233). Thus, the very act of remembering involves restructuring in the here and now the events of the past.

> Teresa, a young woman, entered therapy complaining of re-experiencing, avoidance, and hyperarousal symptomatology. Recent life changes had precipitated her need to understand, and to incorporate, an acquaintance rape in late adolescence in which she "lost her virginity." Initially Teresa maintained that, prior to the rape, she had been a happy-go-lucky, naive, virtuous, and devout Mormon. After the rape, Teresa used alcohol to cope with her assault and later engaged in consensual sex with a boyfriend. After several sessions, Teresa stated that she no longer felt guilt about the rape. However, she continued to experience posttraumatic stress-related symptoms accompanied by low self-esteem and self-derogation with regard to the choices she had made following the rape. Teresa completed an assignment to construct a life review graph from birth to her present age, including negative and positive life events connected to her family, her self, and her relationships with nonfamilial individuals. In the following session Teresa remarked that she had not realized the totality of difficult life experiences she had dealt with prior to the rape, such as the death of her father. She had construed herself as problem free in an attempt to offset her mother's depression following his death and had never allowed herself the freedom of construing an event as negative. From this point on, Teresa used therapy as

a place to explore her ability to persevere through life events in a way that ultimately led to increased self-efficacy. Toward the completion of therapy, Teresa traveled home, to where the rape had occurred, in an attempt to face remaining anxiety connected to her experience but found little remaining fear connected to her memory. At termination, Teresa had remained abstinent from alcohol and was free of both depressive and posttraumatic symptoms.

Trauma Reliving

The element of *trauma reliving* is often presented as a technique necessary to alleviate symptoms in the long term (although it is acknowledged to be painful in the short term). Trauma reliving is the evocation of trauma-related memorial metaconstruction—looking intently and deeply at the discrepant image in the mirror. It is important to realize that trauma reliving is different from symptoms of re-experiencing (e.g., flashbacks), and it is different from relating the event in a cursory way (as clients often do in the initial interview). Re-experiencing symptoms are experienced as outside the person's control; reliving is an intentional process. Talking *about* the event is typical of some traumatized persons; whereas *reliving* means talking from *within* the experience, giving voice to the traumatic story with all its associated pain, confusion, fear, and shame.

A clinician can guide some clients through trauma reliving (after a strong therapeutic relationship has been nurtured by means of symptom management and life review) by instructing the client to take the clinician through the trauma with him or her. It is usually best to encourage the client to move slowly and to focus on as many levels of awareness as possible (sensorial, emotional, stream of consciousness, social, etc.). Sometimes aspects of the memorial construction are suspended, and the client has difficulty building a sequential story. Techniques such as Neimeyer and Stewart's (1996) "jigsaw memories" can be used to help renarrate the story. The jigsaw memories technique involves asking the client to write down fragments of the trauma on separate slips of paper and then to arrange and link them into a coherent story. When the story has been told (and sometimes retold) in a manner that feels "real" or "genuine" to both therapist and client, overt reconstruction processes can begin. Now able to use the accumulated social currency, the therapist can normalize the reaction given the context and the experience. Then the therapist turns the client's attention to ways in which the experience might be viewed differently from the current perspective than from the original perspective.

Trauma reliving is rarely achieved in a single telling of the experience; repetition in the safe and supportive therapeutic context evokes new and adaptive conceptions of the event. Part of the power of reliving the trauma is held in the client's owning of the moment. Often, the traumatized person has forgotten or become numb to the sensory details of the experience—

details that might be intimately connected to important eventual meanings assigned to the event. Reliving the trauma in session, repeatedly, can provide new information in each intentional connection to the remembrance.

> George was unable to realize the full extent of invalidation that occurred when he was raped until, when recounting the event in detail week after week, he realized that his assailants called him a homosexual epithet as they were raping him. This elaboration of his remembrance was pivotal in George's understanding of his omnipresent need to prove his masculinity in the years that followed.

Much like symptom management (but perhaps less obviously), the process of trauma reliving has dual therapeutic status. We argue that trauma reliving is best conceived as an important but incomplete component of effective trauma-related psychotherapy. On the other hand, there is mounting evidence that the processes involved in trauma reliving might independently provoke subjective distress relief. Pennebaker (1993; also Pennebaker & Francis, 1996) has shown that the mere act of writing about a traumatic experience, even outside of the context of therapy, is associated with improvements in subjective and somatic functioning. This is quite encouraging to our perspective, even though the underlying processes we propose might differ from Pennebaker's. Our model suggests that certain psychological processes are logically necessary to adaptively elaborate and incorporate trauma into a person's psychological system. In this chapter we delineate the psychotherapeutic foci to facilitate these processes. However, we do not suggest that all traumatized individuals will need psychotherapy in order to effectively move through these growth processes. Some persons are prompted (by a writing assignment, a research project, a newspaper cartoon, etc.) to engage in a single component of the elaborative process (e.g., trauma reliving). It is consistent with our views to assume that some such persons would then proceed with the other growth-oriented tasks unprompted by therapy or other outside structures.

Constructive Bridging

Constructive bridging is the juxtapositioning of metaconstructive levels—sketching new understandings on the rearview mirror and on the chair—and then finding them to have been preliminary sketches all along.

> Ben, you say you have always felt unmasculine because you were not athletic in high school. At this point in life, you value your role as single parent above all other roles. As a part of that role, you taught each of your boys important athletic skills that they used to enhance their own self-images. Yet you still see yourself as unmasculine. Hold those two pictures next to each other—the boyish sense of unmasculinity and your role as an athletic parent. How do they connect? (Sewell, 1997, p. 229)

Over and over, the therapist pushes the client to provide narrative segues from past–to present/present–to past. By means of this process of self-contextualizing, the client begins to sketch new lines on the mirrors, on the barber's chair, and around the room. The more sketching the client does (i.e., the more of an "as-if" approach he or she adopts), the more he or she internalizes the process of reconstruction. To sketch on the mirror and have it *fit* brings the realization that the image was only a preliminary sketch in the first place.

Intentional Future Metaconstruction

Disruption of the client's future, or of his or her conception of one, is often seen in response to a trauma. If one is left with an invalidated past, present, or both, what is available to project onto the future? Before addressing the future as a therapeutic focus the clinician must assess the client's view of what lies ahead. Stated metaphorically, in what direction is the client looking to protect him or her from the confusion of the front mirror?

> Ronald, a combat veteran, had struggled in therapy whenever the topics of marriage or a future family were raised. Although he emphasized the importance of these aspects of life (especially having children), he did not feel privileged enough to expect them and was not able to envision a future that involved others. He ignored the self-definition based on his experiences before combat: being an older brother and caretaker of his family, working with others, helping his parents provide shelter for the family. Ronald also denied his "traumatized" self, recognizing his experiences in combat only with dissociative responding or as separate from his present self.

What, if anything, does the client see in his future? Ronald saw nothing and hypothesized that he would not live long on the basis of his inability to imagine his future goals. This is often the case with traumatized individuals. Other clients, however, can see only additional trauma. For example, Jane is convinced she will be injured if she engages with others, so she becomes agoraphobic and socially isolated. Intentional future metaconstruction involves first examining the distant iterations in the front mirror and assessing the client's stance. Then the therapist can join the client in beginning to sketch new images on the mirrors with fantasies of possible futures. The therapist can serve as a tool both to help create possibilities and as a sounding board for the client's processing. Instead of this being a finite process, the goal is one of devising, discussing, writing about, and experimentally enacting (by means of role play) new and various futures.

Herman (1992) described this process as "reconciling with oneself." She discussed the need for an understanding of who the individual used to be and the damage done by the trauma. The goal is integration of those elements in creation of "a new self, both ideally and in actuality" (p. 202).

The therapy relationship provides a safe place for the individual to explore possibilities for the new self; specifically, to encourage the person to take initiative in engaging in new activities and fantasy about future selves.

A potential example for future metaconstruction techniques involving both enactment and writing can be found in the Multiple Self Awareness (MSA) self-exploration format (Sewell, Baldwin, & Moes, 1998). MSA involves identifying and anthropomorphizing multiple selves (cf. Mair, 1977). From the perspective of each individual self, therapy group members each write targeted autobiographies that address critical life events, values, and themes. Then, in the group, participants read their autobiographies and engage in a variety of psychodramatic exercises geared toward elaborating their various self-aspects. To adapt the MSA format more specifically for future metaconstruction, the individual selves could all be proposed as possible future selves.

Gonçalves (1995) discussed a series of techniques that guide a client through future metaconstruction. By eliciting recall and elaboration of past narratives, Gonçalves leads the client to "metaphorize" (p. 151) the narratives. Once this skill has been developed and the client can view his or her stories in terms of themes and as-if propositions, he or she is encouraged to explore alternative metaphors. For example, "instead of thinking of relationships as food to be consumed, what might be other metaphors for relationships?" With the therapist's guidance the client might decide to construct a metaphor of relationships as "gifts to be given and received." Following the remetaphorization the therapist and client then project the new metaphor onto anticipated future experiences. By imaginally carrying the new metaphor through future experiences, and then experimentally enacting the metaphor in ongoing experiences, the client and therapist co-construct new modes of being/becoming—modes that can be further reconstructed, given the client's newly acquired skills.

> Ronald began to question whether he would have a career and family. He was encouraged to draw on both positive and negative aspects of his past and present experience. In addition, Ronald began making mental and written lists of how he could offer more to a job or family because of his experiences. In completing this exercise Ronald began to explore the applicability of his past and present selves to a possible future self. Ronald also began to imagine how a family would add to his life and to see it as another experience he could choose to engage.

Constructive Bridging Revisited

Even the slightest amount of success in future metaconstruction opens the door for more elaborated and adaptive constructive bridging. With each new level and content of future possibility that is constructed a new round of bridging becomes available. This process should continue to unfold until the trauma is understood as an important but integrated experience that has changed but not determined the client's life.

> Melissa, 40 years old, was struggling after being assaulted by a romantic partner. When she was growing up, her mother (with whom Melissa was closely bonded) abandoned the family with no explanation. Melissa had a notion of "needing people too much" being connected with later abandonment. She admitted, early in therapy, that she was able to engage in treatment only to the extent that she negated the therapist's identity as a human with whom one could have a relationship. Instead, she saw the therapist as an entity that could be replaced with another "body" if something should happen. In this way, she kept distance and safety while engaging in trauma-focused treatment. This type of stance seemed protective and workable to reduce her event-related PTSD symptoms. But for Melissa to progress toward bridging her current social anxieties with her disrupted past, she had to grant the therapist personhood. The therapeutic work rose to a new level when Melissa allowed herself to care about the therapist and to acknowledge that the therapist cared for her.

CONCLUDING COMMENTS

We believe that the ultimate validation or invalidation of our ideas rests with the "consumers"—those brave individuals who come to therapy to attempt transcendence over their painful pasts. In addition to using theory-based research findings, we have "tested" many (if not all) of our model's components against the shared experiences from our past and current traumatized clients. Assuming we have communicated the overall model and the specific treatment components with some degree of success, we can now hope to have these "experiments" replicated by at least some willing readers.

We acknowledge that embarking on psychotherapy with traumatized clients is personally as well as professionally demanding. We feel it is crucial for psychotherapists to attend to their own reconstructive processes as ways to elaborate their own challenges into growth. In a humble attempt to model this attentiveness, we end this chapter with a personal offering, inspired by a conversation with the senior author's son.

> I hope my son never becomes a philosopher. Because then people will likely attribute his spontaneous wisdom to books or to schools.
> My son, then about 7 years old, was asking about war. I saw it as an opportunity for me both to auger against the glorified media images of combat and aggression as well as to further share with him my work as a psychologist with traumatized patients. So I explained that when people see or must do (in order to survive) horrible things, some cannot go on with a happy life. Sometimes they cannot live with the images. Sometimes a psychologist can . . .
> He listened intently.

Then he said, "Sometimes when you go through something really bad, it helps to talk about it. Sometimes, you'd rather just stick it in the *Junk Drawer* in the back of your mind."

His metaphor left me speechless.

I suppose everyone has a Junk Drawer.

But what is a Junk Drawer? . . . if not a place for things belonging nowhere?

My son's two-sentence sermon provoked an inventory in myself and in my coauthor. Some of the items we discovered are intermingled below.

A single incident of abuse by an uncle who thought it made him more of a man to do an unspeakable thing to a child.

As I inspect this Junk Drawer article, I shake even now. It still belongs nowhere. I still cannot lay it alongside the trust I have in those who were there to protect me . . . who could have protected me . . . who should have protected me. I can neither hate them nor forgive him; I can only shake, and feel embarrassment . . . exposure . . . humiliation.

So back in the Junk Drawer it goes.

I wish for all who have abuse in their inventory that all were only single incidents and that all would fit as neatly into their Junk Drawers as does mine. Many are not so lucky . . . but I can see that only when mine is tucked away.

It didn't feel real. How could I be walking into the funeral home to greet the mourning parents of my first love?

Earlier that day, I had seen the news coverage—a covered body on a gurney being loaded into an ambulance. "Accident victim dies in local hospital," the news anchor stated, with no change of facial expression.

It didn't feel real until I looked down at the face in the casket. The face of the one with whom I had shared countless dreams and hopes for the future. As I looked closer and deeper, I realized it was not that familiar face at all . . . the one I had seen and kissed so many times. Gone were the bright and unforgettable complexion, the laughing blue eyes, and the quick smile. Gone were my dreams of marriage and family growing old with this person who had known me so long and so well. Gone . . .

After many months, I began to make peace with these images. Eventually, I reinvented dreams with another partner; we married and began a family. I even dared to counsel bereaved clients and offer them support through their own experiences of loss. I began to make peace.

Peace, until a young woman walked into my office whose husband had been an "accident victim" some weeks earlier.

After our first session I reluctantly opened the Junk Drawer and began sifting through the odds and ends that remained. I was challenged to re-examine items that had lain hidden for years: the depersonalized media image of the one I had held in my arms and in my heart; the abrupt and wrenching loss of future expectations invested in and by one so young.

I wonder what else remains in my Junk Drawer. Will it stay closed for years, or will I be opening it in the next 50-minute hour?

Watching my father—my face not more than nine inches from his—progress from respiratory distress to strained gasping, to anaphylactic shock, to convulsions, to unconsciousness . . . the images burned into my visual field. Holding him as my mother sped us to the hospital, I held also to a helpless fantasy that by keeping his oxygen tube near his nose, I was prolonging his life. I prayed loudly the entire trip, pleading my orderly ideology not to fail now.

Not yet.

After some medical (and perhaps metaphysical?) miracles, Dad survived the journey. He remembered only the first moments of the ordeal.

But I saw his gray face for months.

Driving alone in my car, I would need to shake my head violently in order to maintain more focus on the road than on his face. Closing my eyes at night would reveal the cinema in living color, spread across my quivering eyelids. I thought surely telling the story to someone trusted would exorcise these sensory demons.

I was only partly right.

I told the story . . . though never with full detail. Like realizing how tired my arms were becoming, and then the mortal guilt for caring about my damned arms. Like staring into eyes that gave no feedback of recognition, and lying to myself that he was still there; that he would still be there.

I can still feel his body convulse inside mine; how can I *tell* that?

So the telling only partly found place for the experience.

Deepening the relationship with Dad—intentionally, and specifically, because we both realize how tenuous life is—has made the story *belong* in my life. Most of the story, anyway. Some details . . . some pictures . . . remain in the Junk Drawer, belonging nowhere.

Other inventory items are smaller and do not press on the drawer's sides, pushing to come out.

At least not now.

REFERENCES

American Psychiatric Association. (1980). *Diagnostic and statistical manual of mental disorders* (3rd ed.). Washington, DC: Author.

Courtois, C. A. (1988). *Healing the incest wound: Adult survivors in therapy.* New York: Norton.

Cromwell, R. L., Sewell, K. W., & Langelle, C. (1996). A personal construction of traumatic stress. In B. E. Walker, J. Costigan, L. L. Viney, & W. G. Warren (Eds.), *Personal construct theory: A psychology for the future* (pp. 173–197). Melbourne, Australia: APS Imprint Books.

Figley, C. R. (1978). Psychosocial adjustment among Vietnam veterans: An overview of the research. In C. R. Figley (Ed.), *Stress disorders among Vietnam veterans* (pp. 57–70). New York: Brunner/Mazel.

Foa, E., & Rothbaum, B. O. (1998). *Treating the trauma of rape: Cognitive–behavioral therapy for PTSD*. New York: Guilford Press.

Foy, D. W. (1992). *Treating PTSD: Cognitive–behavioral strategies*. New York: Guilford Press.

Gamino, L. A., Sewell, K. W., & Easterling, L. W. (1998). Scott & White grief study: An empirical test of predictors of intensified mourning. *Death Studies, 22*, 333–355.

Gonçalves, Ó. F. (1995). Cognitive narrative psychotherapy: The hermeneutic construction of alternative meanings. In M. J. Mahoney (Ed.), *Cognitive and constructive psychotherapies: Theory, research, and practice* (pp. 139–162). New York: Springer.

Herman, J. L. (1992). *Trauma and recovery*. New York: Basic Books.

Kelly, G. A. (1991). *The psychology of personal constructs* (2 vols.). London: Routledge. (Original work published 1955)

Linehan, M. M. (1993). *Skills training manual for treating borderline personality disorder*. New York: Guilford Press.

Mahoney, M. J., & Moes, A. J. (1997). Complexity and psychotherapy: Promising dialogues and practical issues. In F. Masterpasgua & P. A. Perna (Eds.), *The psychological meaning of chaos: Translating theory into practice* (pp. 177–198). Washington, DC: American Psychological Association.

Mair, M. (1977). The community of self. In D. Bannister (Ed.), *New perspectives in personal construct theory* (pp. 125–149). London: Academic Press.

McCann, I. L., & Pearlman, L. A. (1990). *Psychological trauma and the adult survivor: Theory, therapy, and transformation*. New York: Brunner/Mazel.

Meichenbaum, D. (1994). *A clinical handbook/practical therapist manual for assessing and treating adults with post-traumatic stress disorder (PTSD)*. Waterloo, Ontario, Canada: Institute Press.

Moes, A. J., & Sewell, K. W. (1994, July). *Post traumatic stress disorder: A symposium on constructivist findings of combat, disaster, and rape survivors: III. Repertory grid and rape trauma*. Conducted at the sixth North American Conference on Personal Construct Psychology, Indianapolis, IN.

Neimeyer, R. A. (1981). The structure and meaningfulness of tacit construing. In H. Bonarius, R. Holland, & S. Rosenberg (Eds.), *Personal construct psychology: Recent advances in theory and practice* (105–133). New York: Macmillan.

Neimeyer, R. A. (1995). Client-generated narratives in psychotherapy. In M. J. Mahoney & R. A. Neimeyer (Eds.), *Constructivism in psychotherapy* (pp. 231–246). Washington, DC: American Psychological Association.

Neimeyer, R. A., & Stewart, A. E. (1996). Trauma, healing, and the narrative emplotment of loss. *Families in Society: The Journal of Contemporary Human Services, 76*, 360–375.

Pennebaker, J. W. (1993). Putting stress into words: Health, linguistic, and therapeutic implications. *Behaviour Research and Therapy, 31*, 539–548.

Pennebaker, J. W., & Francis, M. E. (1996). Cognitive, emotional, and language processes in disclosure. *Cognition & Emotion, 10*, 601–626.

Resick, P. A. (1993). The psychological impact of rape. *Journal of Interpersonal Violence, 8*, 223–255.

Roth, S., Lebowitz, L., & DeRosa, R. R. (1997). Thematic assessment of posttraumatic stress reactions. In J. P. Wilson & T. M. Keane (Eds.), *Assessing psychological trauma and PTSD* (pp. 512–528). New York: Guilford Press.

Sewell, K. W. (1991). *Conceptual structure of Vietnam combat veterans: Relationship between post-traumatic stress disorder and poorly elaborated trauma constructs.* Unpublished doctoral dissertation, University of Kansas.

Sewell, K. W. (1996). Constructional risk factors for a post-traumatic stress response following a mass murder. *Journal of Constructivist Psychology, 9*, 97–107.

Sewell, K. W. (1997). Posttraumatic stress: Towards a constructivist model of psychotherapy. In G. J. Neimeyer & R. A. Neimeyer (Eds.), *Advances in personal construct psychology* (Vol. 4, pp. 207–235). Greenwich, CT: JAI Press.

Sewell, K. W., Baldwin, C. L., & Moes, A. J. (1998). The multiple self awareness group: Format and application to a personal growth experience. *Journal of Constructivist Psychology, 11*, 59–78.

Sewell, K. W., & Cromwell, R. L. (1990, July). *Personal constructs and post-traumatic stress.* Paper presented at the fourth North American Conference on Personal Construct Psychology, San Antonio, TX.

Sewell, K. W., Cromwell, R. L., Farrell-Higgins, J., Palmer, R., Ohlde, C., & Patterson, T. W. (1996). Hierarchical elaboration in the conceptual structure of Vietnam combat veterans. *Journal of Constructivist Psychology, 9*, 79–96.

Stewart, J. (1995). Reconstruction of the self: Life-span-oriented group psychotherapy. *Journal of Constructivist Psychology, 8*, 129–148.

van der Kolk, B. A., van der Hart, O., & Marmar, C. R. (1996). Dissociation and information processing in posttraumatic stress disorder. In B. A. van der Kolk, A. C. McFarlane, & L. Weisaeth (Eds.), *Traumatic stress: the effects of overwhelming experience on mind, body, and society* (pp. 303–327). New York: Guilford Press.

Veronen, L. J., & Kilpatrick, D. G. (1983). Stress management for rape victims. In D. Meichenbaum & M. E. Jaremko (Eds.), *Stress reduction and prevention* (pp. 341–374). New York: Plenum.

Viney, L. L. (1996). A personal construct model of crisis intervention counseling for adult clients. *Journal of Constructivist Psychology, 9*, 109–126.

Williams, A. M., Gamino, L. A., Sewell, K. W., Easterling, L. W., & Stirman, L. S. (1998). A content and comparative analysis of loss in adaptive and maladaptive grievers. *Journal of Personal and Interpersonal Loss, 3*, 349–368.

16

TRAUMA, GRIEF, AND SURVIVING CHILDHOOD SEXUAL ABUSE

STEPHEN J. FLEMING AND SHERI KATHLEEN BÉLANGER

It is only relatively recently—for example, with the publication of Figley, Bride, and Mazza's (1997) book *Death and Trauma: The Traumatology of Grieving*—that the call has been made to bridge the largely artificial gap between the fields of traumatology and thanatology. It has been argued that these differing modes of response to tragedy are strikingly similar in their defining symptoms and in commonly accepted strategies of intervention. In addition, the search for meaning, and the demands of reconstituting one's shattered assumptive world, represent the core challenges in adapting to loss and trauma. Although all trauma involves loss (e.g., in its most pervasive sense, loss of one's old assumptive world), it must be recognized that not all grief involves trauma. In an attempt to bridge this somewhat curious separation of thanatology and traumatology, in this chapter we conceptually and phenomenologically explore the relation between grief caused by the death of a loved one and a particular type of trauma, namely, surviving childhood sexual abuse (CSA).

We acknowledge the editorial assistance of Kirstin Maxwell and recognize that the order of authorship does not reflect the equal contributions made in the preparation of this chapter.

A GRIEF PROCESS MODEL OF CSA SURVIVAL

The link between grief and recovery from trauma is brought home by an exchange that occurred between Sheri Kathleen Bélanger and her therapy client, a 26-year-old survivor of incest.

> After she had calmly told me about the nights when her father would
> rape her and then leave her alone in a locked room, I, being shocked by
> her steady voice, asked her,
> "But what does your past mean to you now?"
> And she replied as even as before,
> "Oh no. I can't say that."
> To the question "Why?", she answered,
> "Because that would mean I would have to realize all that I have lost."

Survivors of CSA have many things to grieve. They have lost their innocence, their sense of self-esteem, and often their ability to trust. Perhaps, above all, they have lost what should have been, namely, a healthy childhood (Blume, 1990; Hunter, 1990). There are many similarities between surviving CSA and surviving the death of a loved one. First, CSA and death are both events that have happened in the past and cannot be changed. As with any trauma, the acknowledgment, acceptance, and integration of past experience play a crucial role in the survivor's ability to cope within the present and reinvest in the future (Briere, 1989; Fleming & Robinson, 1991; Parkes, 1986). Second, death and CSA are topics generally shunned by society (Butler, 1985; Durkheim, 1951; Kluft, 1990; Russell, 1986; Schoenberg, 1980), often forcing survivors to keep the pain silent and risk complicating the natural healing process (Cook & Dworkin, 1992; Dadds, Smith, Webber, & Robinson, 1991; Schoenberg, 1980; Stroebe & Stroebe, 1987). Third, the closer the relationship between the deceased person (or the abuser) and the survivor, the more intense are the feelings of loss (Finkelhor, 1984; Fleming & Robinson, 1991; Russell, 1986; Rando, 1993; Worden, 1991). Fourth, both attachment theory and object relations theory, which are crucial to our understanding of adaptation to loss (Stroebe & Stroebe, 1987), have been recently applied to the sequelae of CSA survival (Alexander, 1992; Grant & Alpert, 1993).

Finally, many of the popular self-help books on CSA consider "grief work" to be an integral part of recovery (Black, 1990; Blume, 1990; Grubman-Black, 1990; Hunter, 1990; Lew, 1988; Whitfield, 1989). As well, grief work with this population has been documented and shown to be successful in ameliorating the many painful memories and consequences of CSA (Hays, 1985). Furthermore, it has been demonstrated that both clients and therapists concur in their perception of the many losses associated with CSA survival, with the most difficult losses being related to the ability to trust others and to engage in self-love (Bourdon & Cook, 1993). Brown,

Scheflin, and Hammond (1998) clearly referred to the intersection of grief work and trauma mastery when, in referencing Crowder's (1995) work, they wrote

> The patient must *actively mourn* the victim or damaged self-image and must make the transition from survivor to thriver. . . . Overidentification with a victim or survivor self-image at this point may severely limit self development. The patient must also actively mourn the "bad" or "damaged goods" self-image to clear the way for the development of a balanced self-image that shows integration and acceptance of both positive and negative qualities of the self. (p. 493)

The majority of the theoretical frameworks guiding CSA research and practice are "trauma" theories; that is, they generally explain that the adult symptomatology of CSA survivors is, or can be, directly attributed to the sexual abuse acts and the immediate variables surrounding the abuse (e.g., felt stigmatization and the reactions of others after disclosure). Perhaps the most prominent model is that of posttraumatic stress disorder (PTSD), which recognizes that overwhelming life experiences are continually re-experienced, with the ensuing symptomatic behaviors, cognitions, and emotions, until the trauma has been reintegrated into the totality of the survivor's life. The appeal in applying PTSD to victims of sexual abuse is that many of the symptoms—such as flashbacks, amnesia, and hyperarousal—are commonly experienced in survivors of CSA. As well, PTSD attempts to link the severity of trauma experienced with the level or intensity of symptomatology. Thus, the worse the abuse, the poorer the prognosis.

Although the application of PTSD does help one understand and appreciate some of the symptoms of surviving CSA, it does have some limitations, including a too-narrow focus on the affective realm and on physical danger and too little focus on the perceived meaning of the traumatic act, such as "I'm being exploited" (Finkelhor, 1984). In addition, traditional trauma theories do not fully take into account the pretrauma personality characteristics of the survivor, such as his or her attachment patterns or coping styles. The exception is perhaps Alexander's (1992) application of attachment theory to incest.

In contrast, the grief process model developed by Fleming and Robinson (1991) takes into account both the meaning of the event and the pre-event personality and coping style of the survivor. As such, it may be a highly useful model for understanding the process of surviving CSA.

DESCRIPTION OF THE GRIEF PROCESS MODEL

When a death occurs, and a loving relationship is ruptured, there follows a period of pain or grief that is characterized by a host of complex physical, affective, cognitive, and behavioral responses (see Figure 16.1). To

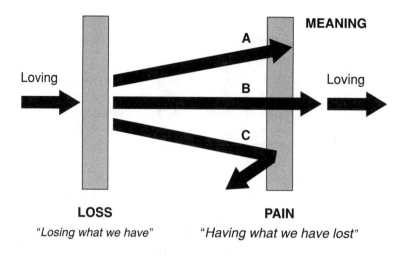

MEANING

Loving

LOSS
"Losing what we have"

PAIN
"Having what we have lost"

A: Chronic Grief Process   **B:** Typical Grief Process

C: Delayed Grief Process

Figure 16.1. A model of the grief process. From "The Application of Cognitive Therapy to the Bereaved" by S. J. Fleming and P. J. Robinson, 1991, in T. M. Vallis, J. L. Howes, & P. C. Miller, *The Challenge of Cognitive Therapy: Applications to Nontraditional Populations*, New York: Plenum Press. Copyright 1991 by Plenum Press. Reprinted by permission.

Fleming and Robinson (1991) grief is not an illness needing treatment, neither is it a pathological or a clinical problem (although it may be); it is simply the price we pay for loving. In this model, to navigate the transition from "losing what you have" to "having what you have lost" the survivor must approach and befriend his or her pain and arrive at some sense of meaning or purpose. Pain is integral to the grieving process; it is in knowing and living the pain that one finds legacy and transformation—where one finds meaning and growth. An individual experiencing an uncomplicated or "typical" grief response ("B," in Figure 16.1) appreciates the full impact of the death on all its levels, effectively working from the end of the relationship back through it in the acknowledgment of what has been lost. Embracing the often soul-crushing pain, the survivor processes the death at a cognitive–affective level and struggles to either assimilate the loss or accommodate it by modifying existing assumptions about one's self and the world.

In this model the struggle for meaning and the deceased person's "legacy" facilitates the transition from "losing what you have" to "having what you have lost." One does not necessarily look for meaning or legacy in the death of a loved one (although one may find it there); legacy is more likely to be culled from the life that was lived. Legacy is a product of the painful encounter with such questions as: What lessons in living has the deceased taught me?, What lessons about loving have I learned?, and How am

I different as a result of knowing and loving the deceased person? This reappraisal of one's relationship with the deceased person is a highly emotionally charged process associated with the acknowledgment of the extent of one's loss. It must be stressed that (a) the personal meaning of the loss can be realized only through processing the affect associated with the loss and that (b) one culls meaning from a variety of differing dimensions, including the personal, social, and spiritual aspects of one's grief; the deceased person's legacy is but one example.

L. B., the mother of a 3-year-old who was killed in a motor vehicle accident, realized the legacy of her son in the following statement:

> Your child now lives within you. Just as you would never let your child go where you have not gone, you go within. You get intimate with yourself, check out your values, the meaning and purpose of things . . . you want your child to live in a warm and nurturing place, not one filled with anger, resentment, and revenge.

L. B. was determined that her son's legacy would not be marked by emotions and sentiments that were inconsistent with his short life and his impact on his parents and sibling.

There are a number of aspects of this model, and of the notion of legacy, that need clarification. First, the graphic depiction of pain in Figure 16.1 is for heuristic purposes only. It is recognized that grief does not have a sharply demarcated beginning and end. Correspondingly, there is no single moment where meaning or legacy is grasped; rather, one negotiates and renegotiates meaning and legacy over time, often precipitated by other losses. Second, consistent with Neimeyer (1998) and Attig (1996), grief is portrayed as an active process; it demands attention. Third, the deceased person's legacy is not simply a collection of images, thoughts, and feelings; it does, however, reflect a form of ongoing attachment (Klass, Silverman, & Nickman, 1996) in that the relationship with the deceased person is reflected in the survivor's transformed sense of self. Legacy leaves the survivor irrevocably changed; it leaves an indelible imprint on the fabric of one's personality such that, in appreciating legacy, we are forever changed and "have what we have lost."

Legacy bears a striking resemblance to an aspect of Attig's (1996) "relearning the world" in which the survivor reinterprets and reshapes his or her life, integrating aesthetic, ethical, and religious meanings embodied in the life that has ended. Attig commented,

> As we survive, we can thrive in an enjoyment and an appreciation of and a heightened sensitivity to life that derives from our having known and loved the deceased. We can sense that we walk in a world as their representatives as they may have wished nothing more than that we would live fully and richly in their absence. As we appropriate some of their values and cares, we can respond inventively to the loss and live

productively in memory of those who have contributed much to our lives. As we continue, deepen, and sometimes transform our caring about what they cared about, we can pay homage to their memory. As we care about what they cared about, we continue to love them. . . . Our relearning of our relationships with the deceased contributes to the emergence of our new personal identities and the achievement of a new wholeness in our current living, personal history, and connection to larger wholes. (pp. 185–186)

Individuals exhibiting a chronic grief response (depicted in Figure 16.1 by "A") continue to display intense reactions for an inordinately lengthy period of time (Leick & Davidsen-Nielsen, 1991; Parkes, 1986; Worden, 1991). Although these responses are typical during the initial period of grieving, if the survivor is unable to assimilate and accommodate to the painful reality of the loss, he or she becomes "stuck." Suggested factors contributing to this response include fear, the nature of the attachment (i.e., highly ambivalent, dependent), the personal meaning of the loss, secondary gain, or concurrent stressors (Fleming & Robinson, 1991; Stroebe & Stroebe, 1987; Worden, 1991).

In contrast to chronic grief is a delayed grief response, represented by "C" in Figure 16.1. Initially the survivor is aware of the loss and begins to embrace the pain; however, he or she backs away and does not exhibit the associated reactions of mourning. Such factors as multiple losses, the presence of concurrent life stressors, lack of social support, and fear of the affective or emotional vicissitudes of grief have been suggested as contributing to a survivor's inability to fully acknowledge the extent of the loss and, thus, the reality of their pain (Fleming & Robinson, 1991).

Although individuals usually adopt a single style of grieving, it is also possible that they experience more than one style in adjusting to their loss. For example, individuals who initially experience a delayed response as a result of multiple losses, or who confront the reality of their pain, may eventually exhibit symptoms suggestive of a chronic response. An advantage of Fleming and Robinson's (1991) model is that it does not assume a linear or fixed process. The model instead recognizes the possibility of different styles of grieving and places the individual in the context of his or her preloss personality, reactions to previous losses, personal meaning of the loss, present social support, current life stressors, and perceptions of the future. Thus, the model acknowledges the variation and uniqueness of survivors' reactions to the death of a loved one while maintaining a clear focus for possible intervention.

Factors Affecting the Grieving Process Following Death and CSA Survival

Using the Fleming and Robinson (1991) model, in the following discussion we present some parallels in the integration of two distinct loss experiences, namely, surviving the death of a loved one and surviving CSA. How a person will react to the death of a loved one, or to being sexually victimized as a child, is determined by a variety of moderating factors. These factors must be examined collectively to assess the possible outcome of the loss. As stated earlier, one particular advantage to Fleming and Robinson's model is that it places the individual in a contextual framework. Consistent with this model, the discussion focuses on factors that regulate the aftermath of loss, incorporating variables before the loss (e.g., preloss personality), during the loss (e.g., who the person was, nature of the attachment, cause of death/abuse-specific trauma, multiple deaths/multiple abusers), and after the loss (e.g., social variables). This discussion is not meant to be exhaustive; rather, it is designed to provoke discussion and consideration of the similarities in modes of response to tragedy.

Before the Loss

Personality factors such as low self-esteem, dependency, or a tendency toward inhibiting or suppressing strong emotions have been linked to a poorer outcome when a loved one dies (Parkes, 1986; Stroebe & Stroebe 1987; Worden, 1991). Parkes (1986) identified a "grief prone" personality, which includes excessive reactions to previous losses, elevated levels of anger or reproachfulness, inability to express emotion, and high anxiety. Linked with an individual's personality is his or her coping style. When overwhelming grief threatens the survivor's coping capacity previous coping styles may not prove adaptive. Whether the individual has traditionally relied on task-oriented coping (i.e., problem focused), or emotion-oriented coping (i.e., seeking reassurance and support from others, cathartic expression of emotions), he or she needs to remain flexible and use different coping styles. One of the unique advantages of Fleming and Robinson's (1991) model is the emphasis it places on the nature of the preloss personality as a moderating variable.

For obvious reasons—it is ethically impossible to control the independent variable—much of the literature on CSA focuses on the possible effects of sexual abuse on the individual rather than the effect of the individual on the outcome (e.g., Briere & Runtz, 1988; Fromuth, 1986). An experimenter cannot divide participants into groups, subject one group to CSA, and then measure the effects. Because of the variability in the symptomatology of CSA, not all of which can be accounted for by external factors surrounding the abuse, other variables, such as preloss personality, must be taken into account when considering outcome.

To this end, a retrospective study examined the coping styles of women who had been sexually abused as children (Leitenberg, Greenwald, & Cado, 1992). Participants responded to questionnaires assessing various coping styles they had used from the end of the abuse until the present. The researchers found that an avoidant and emotionally suppressed style of coping, although rated by the participants as helpful in coping with the abuse, was associated with poorer long-term outcomes. Although this study did not directly address preloss personality, the length of time these coping styles were reported to occur (from the end of the abuse to the present) was sufficient to be indicative of a stable personality trait. It is difficult to assess whether these women had used these coping styles before the abuse; however, Monat and Lazarus (1991) stated that similar coping mechanisms tend to be used repeatedly until challenged. These results, although tentative, suggest that examination of preloss personality in the study of CSA, as it is in bereavement, is warranted. Finally, it is important to recognize that who you thought you were before the abuse, and how you think you coped, is more important than what you were "really" like (or how you "really" coped), as self-narratives about our perceived history are what shape us.

Nature of the Loss

Nature of the Attachment to the Deceased Person/Perpetrator

Numerous authors (e.g., Rando, 1993; Worden, 1991) have commented that the relationship of the survivor to the deceased person is an important influence on the nature and dynamics of the grief response—that is, one's reaction to the death of an aged parent will differ markedly from the anguish experienced at the death of a child (Rando, 1986; Sanders, 1980). Also relevant, of course, is the nature of the relationship between the survivor and the deceased—for conflict, ambivalence, and dependency have been shown to affect the survivor's response to loss (Fleming & Robinson, 1991; Parkes, 1986; Raphael, 1980; Worden, 1991). As the nature and intensity of these factors increase, so too does the potential for a complicated grief reaction.

These interpersonal dynamics also affect survivors of incest and other CSA survivors as they work through the grief process. Perpetrators often occupy a significant position in the victims' lives. It has been documented that approximately 70% of adult survivors of CSA report that the abuse occurred with someone they knew and trusted (Margolin, 1991; Tong, Oates, & McDowell, 1987) and, in one representative study, over 50% indicated that the abuse occurred with a family member (Gale, Thompson, Moran, & Sack, 1988). A child is naturally dependent on adults for nurturance, guidance, and support. This fundamental right of the child is broken when the child is sexually victimized. Consider the varied responses to CSA, such as hyperarousal, anxiety, and the sense of "things not being real" (see Table 16.1)—how many of these would be exacerbated if the abuse occurred within the home? Although much of the literature reveals conflicting data on the severity of outcome of CSA as a measure of the relationship between victims and perpetrators, one consistent finding remains—namely, that survivors of CSA

TABLE 16.1
Common Reactions to Surviving the Death of a Loved One and Surviving Child Sexual Abuse

Death of a loved one	Child sexual abuse
Affective dimension	
Sadness, crying	Sadness, crying
Irritability, frustration	Irritability, frustration
Anger, hostility	Anger, hostility
Guilt	Guilt
Loneliness	Loneliness
Shock, numbness	Shock, numbness
Anxiety, helplessness	Anxiety, helplessness
Yearning, pining for the deceased person	
Cognitive dimension	
Preoccupation with thoughts of the deceased person	Preoccupation with thoughts of the abuse
Denial, disbelief	Denial, disbelief
Obsessive thoughts	Obsessive thoughts
Hallucinations, auditory and visual	Hallucinations, auditory and visual
Difficulties in concentration	Difficulties in concentration
Sense of "things not being real"	Sense of "things not being real"
Behavioral dimension	
Restlessness, agitation	Restlessness, agitation
Social withdrawal	Social withdrawal
Avoiding reminders of the deceased person	Avoiding reminders of the abuse or abuser
Fatigue	Fatigue
Sexual disturbances/fears of intimacy	Sexual disturbances/fears of intimacy
Treasuring objects that belonged to the deceased person	
Physiological dimension	
Muscle weakness, tension	Muscle weakness, tension
Hollowness in stomach, breathlessness	Hollowness in stomach, breathlessness
Difficulty swallowing	Difficulty swallowing
Libidinal changes	Sexual dysfunction
Hyperarousal, startle response	Hyperarousal, startle response
Drop or increase in energy levels	Drop or increase in energy levels

whose perpetrators were fathers or father substitutes report more intense and complicated reactions (Briere, 1989; Dadds et al., 1991; Finkelhor & Browne, 1985; Russell, 1986). Yet it must be noted that the devastating impact of this particular type of incestuous abuse is often confounded by the other characteristics of the abuse (e.g., earlier age at onset and duration).

Cause of Death/Abuse-Specific Trauma

How the death occurred—that is, whether it was anticipated, natural, a suicide, or a homicide—influences the process of integrating the loss. The same holds true for abuse-specific trauma; for example, research has shown that the degree of invasiveness is a potential predictor of future outcome (Finkelhor, 1984; Herman, Russell, & Trocki, 1986; Russell, 1986). Although extremes in the specific mode of death—for example, an anticipated, natural death versus a suicide—as well as in the specific type of abuse—for example, exhibitionism versus penetration—have been reported to have a differential impact on outcome, one must be careful when this becomes the focus of investigation. To a child whose father was killed, what difference does it make if his father was knifed or shot? Or, for an adult survivor of CSA reflecting on her abuse as a 5-year-old girl, what difference does it make whether the abuser had vaginal or anal sex with her? Although these details may be important at some point, questions about them can be distracting from the need to express the emotional impact and the meaning of the loss or betrayal.

As with the cause of death, the degree of assumed preventability, or the survivor's real or believed participation in the event also are important (Fleming & Robinson, 1991; Gold, 1986; Morrow, 1991; Raphael, 1980; Worden, 1991). This is particularly true of survivors of suicide, who often report feeling that they "should have known" and thus entertain feelings of guilt (Fleming & Robinson, 1991; Stroebe & Stroebe, 1987; Valente & Sellers, 1986; Van Der Wal, 1989). Systematic exploration of self-blame—in particular, how "counterfactual thinking" influences such attributions—has been the focus of recent attention (e.g., Davis & Lehman, 1995; Davis, Lehman, Wortman, Silver, & Thompson, 1995). In a study of parents whose children died of sudden infant death syndrome the frequency of counterfactual thinking was directly related to reported feelings of guilt and self-responsibility (Davis et al., 1995). Similarly, the degree of guilt and self-blame reported by many survivors of CSA focuses around the issue of perceived preventability, participation, or both, with survivors often feeling that if they had told someone, or had acted differently, the abuse might have not occurred (Finkelhor, 1984; Kelly, 1986). One must recognize that self-blame has a "positive" role as well; if one blames oneself, then the core assumption that one had control over events that happen to one remains unexamined and intact. For some survivors the belief in control is more precious and integral to the self than the temporary loss of ability or effective functioning. At the very least, if a similar event were to recur, then one can respond to avert it.

Multiple Deaths/Multiple Abusers

As Rando (1993) noted, a survivor of multiple deaths has to cope with simultaneous losses, frequently with fewer sources of strength and support.

In such situations the grieving process is complicated by such predicaments as how one grieves (i.e., sequentially and completely, before moving to the next loss), the related issue of which loss to address first, and how to differentiate among the deaths, particularly when "the pain is not differentiated" (p. 564). In addition, how a person reacted to and coped with a previous loss can determine his or her reactions to future deaths (Parkes, 1986; Worden, 1991). More specifically, experiencing a pathological response to previous deaths indicates a higher likelihood of future pathological reactions.

In the same light, abuse of a child by more than one adult exacerbates the extent of the loss; the child has the added burden of coping with multiple betrayals and has fewer nonaffected areas of his or her life from which to draw energy and support. A child who is sexually victimized is at a potential risk for subsequent revictimization (Brenner & Muehlenhard, 1991; Briere, 1989; Russell, 1986; Wyatt, Guthrie, & Notgrass, 1992). The compounding effects of multiple deaths or abuse can create an overwhelming amount of pain, thus setting the stage for a delayed grief response.

After the Loss

The perceived availability and quality of social support are crucial in the resolution of any traumatic event (Attig, 1996; Brown et al., 1998; Rando, 1993; Worden, 1991). As previously discussed, society's reaction to both death and sexual abuse tends to be one of minimization and denial. On learning that someone we know has suffered the death of a loved one, or has been abused, we first experience shock and then feel our own sense of helplessness, for we cannot change the person's past or remove his or her pain. Having these types of trauma disclosed to us can heighten our own fears of death or abuse (especially if we have children of our own).

It has only recently been documented that the period of grieving is much longer than previously believed (Fleming & Robinson, 1991; Leick & Davidsen-Nielsen, 1991; Worden, 1991). However, society still believes that the "appropriate" period of grieving is approximately 3–6 months (Wortman & Silver, 1991), with most negative affect ameliorating shortly thereafter. It is after this "appropriate" time frame that many friends or relatives frequently withdraw their source of support, feeling as though it may not be necessary or that it may further upset the individual to have the loss verbalized. It is not surprising, then, that survivors often believe their social support network is inadequate. This can be intensified if the survivor feels stigmatized by the trauma, which is not an uncommon situation for adolescents grieving the death of a parent or sibling (Cook & Dworkin, 1992; Fleming & Adolph, 1986) or for parents who have lost a child (Corr, Martinson, & Dyer, 1985).

This, of course, is most often the case with survivors of CSA (Finkelhor, 1984; Tomlin, 1991). Should the survivor feel that there is not an

adequate support system, or is unable to reach out to one, this can compli-
cate mourning and promote a delayed grief response. Although "secondary
gain" in the form of sympathy and increased support has been suggested as a
contributing factor in the development of a chronic response to a loss
(Fleming & Robinson, 1991; Worden, 1991), it can also be said to contribute to a delayed grief response as the survivor receives positive reinforcement from others to "get on with your life" and to "put the past in the past."

GRIEVING STYLES AND CSA SURVIVAL

As discussed earlier, Fleming and Robinson (1991) defined *grief* as the
transition from "losing what you have" to "having what you have lost."
Grieving the death of a loved one, therefore, involves a reassessment of the
past relationship and, borne of the pain of the loss, the reconstruction of
meaning and the appreciation of the deceased person's legacy. It has been argued that the same process is involved for survivors of sexual victimization.
In Figure 16.2, "B," as in Figure 16.1, is representative of a typical grief
process in which survivors successfully integrate the abusive experience,
move through the associated pain, and begin the journey of accepting who
they are. Victims, in working through the pain, reassess the nature of the

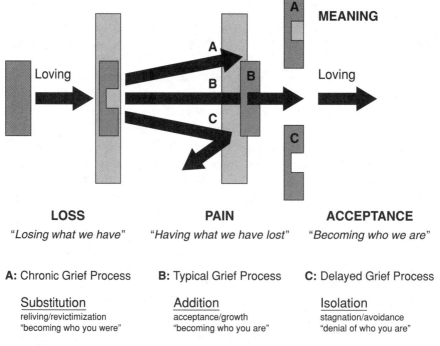

LOSS   **PAIN**   **ACCEPTANCE**

"Losing what we have"   *"Having what we have lost"*   *"Becoming who we are"*

A: Chronic Grief Process   **B:** Typical Grief Process   **C:** Delayed Grief Process

Substitution	Addition	Isolation
reliving/revictimization	acceptance/growth	stagnation/avoidance
"becoming who you were"	"becoming who you are"	"denial of who you are"

Figure 16.2. A model of surviving childhood sexual abuse.

past relationship with the perpetrator and its impact. In understanding what has been lost and accepting this reality, the survivors move on to "having what they have lost." Although they may not have had control as a child, they do now, as an adult. In this respect, when survivors move through the pain they are able to take control of the past, which involves directing the blame and anger appropriately at the perpetrator, thus releasing the guilt and internal anger that can often prevent survivors from healing. Although there has been relatively little research into the search for meaning and CSA survival, Silver, Boon, and Stones (1983) did study survivors of father–daughter incest and reported that finding meaning in one's victimization was related to less psychological distress, better social adjustment, and increased self-esteem.

Because of the unique dynamics of CSA, there is a greater potential for survivors of such trauma to have complications in their grieving process. In adjusting to the death of a loved one, pathological grief is often a function of the amount of ambivalence in the relationship and the presumed degree of preventability and/or participation in the death (Fleming & Robinson, 1991; Parkes, 1986; Worden, 1991). For the survivor of CSA, however, the relationship between the abuser and the victim is often one of ambivalence. Abuse was disguised as "love," and what "should have been" (i.e., a healthy relationship), was not. Often the victim was a child who depended on the abuser, as children naturally do with adults. Furthermore, because of the profound sense of secrecy and shame surrounding sexual abuse, many survivors feel that they cannot reach out to anyone. A further complication in CSA is that the perpetrator may still be alive; deny any wrongdoing; or continue to abuse someone the victim knows and loves, for example, a sibling.

After the loss, CSA survivors who exhibit intense reactions (i.e., intense flashbacks, nightmares, thoughts or actions of self-harm, self-blame) for an extended period of time are said to be experiencing a chronic grief reaction ("A" in Figure 16.2). These reactions are typical during the initial period of loss and, as in the case of abuse, the initial period of becoming aware of the past. When these reactions dominate the individual's present situation the person reacts as if the abuse were still occurring. This has been identified as *reliving* (Blume, 1990; Briere, 1989; Jehu, 1989). Unfortunately, for some survivors of CSA reliving the past abusive situation can become literal as they become involved in abusive relationships as adults. In Russell's (1986) community survey, between 38% and 48% of CSA survivors were or had been involved with physically abusive husbands, whereas 17% of nonabused women reported such relationships. As "A" in Figure 16.2 illustrates, individuals who experience this pattern of coping to some degree "become who they were"—that is, a victim. Attachment characteristics of these women developing a chronic response can be said to be the same as those of the "preoccupied" and "fearful" adult (Alexander, 1992). These survivors may simultaneously seek social ties yet avoid intimate contact.

Depression and anxiety could be the manifestations of some of the individuals who experience this form of grief.

Bereaved people as well as survivors of CSA who exhibit a delayed grief response begin to experience the pain of their loss, but they turn away from befriending it and realizing its meaning (depicted as "C" in Figure 16.2). The variables that are said to contribute to this type of response are multiple losses, the presence of concurrent life stressors, lack of a social support system, and the fear of the negative emotions and affect associated with mourning (Fleming & Robinson, 1991). There is a great potential for survivors of CSA to initially exhibit a delayed response. Being subjected to sexual victimization entails many losses—for example, loss of trust in an adult, which may be generalized to others; loss of self-esteem; and loss of innocence. Because of the shame and secrecy surrounding abuse, many survivors do not reach out for support. As well, because of the pain, humiliation, and sheer sense of betrayal that CSA involves, the urge to suppress these volatile feelings is strong. It must also be recognized that it is difficult to change core assumptions, even if they reflect a mistrust of the world and others. Movement to appreciating the world as safe and reliable means the abandonment of assumptions that, however ineffectual, are nonetheless familiar and, to some extent, have helped the individual survive.

Common techniques used to avoid the memories and the associated feelings of abuse are "blocking out," repression, and dissociation (Braun, 1990; Briere, 1989; Coons, 1986; Leitenberg et al., 1992). Many survivors who exhibit a delayed grief response are likely not to have integrated the trauma in part because the extent of the trauma remains unavailable in their conscious memory. Alternatively, they may be able to recall the event (perhaps trivializing the abuse) but are unable, for reasons mentioned above, to accept the painful feelings associated with the trauma. Isolating themselves from their emotions, these individuals may be subsequently unable to express emotion in future relationships. Similar to the avoidant attachment patterns of adults proposed by Alexander (1992), these survivors may idealize their childhood, the abuser, or both. Yet when these women and men avoid meaningful contact with others they further isolate themselves and thus are unable to obtain future assistance or support should they begin to experience the intense upset and pain from the past. Indeed, some may rationalize that "I don't need help anyway." Individuals experiencing this form of grief in surviving CSA are individuals who deny who they are. For example, they may deny their sexuality, their right to happiness and love, their feelings of integrity and, often, their sense of self.

In addition to delayed and chronic grief reactions, Worden (1991) identified a "masked grief reaction" whereby the survivor either displays physical symptoms similar to those of the deceased person or engages in maladaptive behaviors (e.g., acting out). Either way, the survivor experiences the pain but does not recognize that the symptoms are associated with the loss. Thus, in avoiding working through the pain of the loss, the grieving process is delayed. It is for this reason that the masked grief response has been subsumed under a delayed style. Just as repression is related to a delayed grief response, so dissociation is related to a masked grief response. Both styles serve to avoid the true meaning of the loss and its associated pain.

SUMMARY AND CONCLUSION

The focus of this chapter involved applying Fleming and Robinson's (1991) model of the grief process to both grief per se and to adjustment to a particular type of trauma, namely, surviving CSA. We illustrated that the losses suffered by victims of CSA are profound and that integrating the experience of sexual victimization involves many elements of the grief process. We discussed the determinants of grief (i.e., preloss personality, the perpetrator's identity and the nature of the attachment, cause of death/abuse-specific trauma, multiple deaths/multiple abusers, and social variables) and their impact on adjustment to both CSA and the death of a loved one. We examined three grieving responses (i.e., chronic, delayed, and uncomplicated) as they related both to surviving a death and surviving CSA.

In spite of the striking similarities between adjusting to the death of a loved one and adjusting to a traumatic stressor, in the *Diagnostic and Statistical Manual of Mental Disorders* (4th ed. [*DSM–IV*]; American Psychiatric Association, 1994) bereavement was not included in the definition of a traumatic event. Consideration of deficiencies in *DSM–IV* is considerably beyond the scope of this chapter; however, we hope that future revisions of the *DSM* reflect the similarity between PTSD and grief in (a) their symptomatology; (b) their oscillating modes of intrusion, avoidance, and arousal; and (c) their strategies to facilitate trauma mastery and the integration of loss. Including a separate diagnostic category that reflects the relation between traumatic death and grief complications (e.g., death-related PTSD) would not only reflect the clinical reality but also significantly bridge the chasm that currently exists between the fields of thanatology and traumatology. We hope this chapter has made a contribution toward spanning this chasm for, as Simpson (1997) stated, "Ignoring the trauma component of grief, or the grief component of trauma, is surely negligent" (p. 6).

REFERENCES

Alexander, P. C. (1992). Application of attachment theory to the study of sexual abuse. *Journal of Consulting and Clinical Psychology, 60,* 185–195.

American Psychiatric Association. (1994). *Diagnostic and statistical manual of mental disorders* (4th ed.). Washington, DC: Author.

Attig, T. (1996). *How we grieve: Relearning the world.* New York: Oxford University Press.

Black, C. (1990). *Double duty: Help for the adult child who is also sexually abused.* New York: Ballantine.

Blume, S. E. (1990). *Secret survivors: Uncovering incest and its aftereffects in women.* New York: Ballantine.

Bourdon, L. S., & Cook, A. S. (1993). Losses associated with sexual abuse: Therapist and client perceptions. *Journal of Child Sexual Abuse, 2,* 69–82.

Braun, B. G. (1990). Dissociative disorders as sequelae to incest. In R. P. Kluft (Ed.), *Incest related syndromes of adult psychopathology* (pp. 227–245). Washington, DC: American Psychiatric Press.

Brenner, L. M., & Muehlenhard, C. L. (November, 1991). *Women sexually abused as children and their patterns of sexual re-victimization in adolescence and adulthood.* Paper presented at the annual meeting of the Society for the Scientific Study of Sex, New Orleans, LA.

Briere, J. (1989). *Therapy for adults molested as children: Beyond survival.* New York: Springer.

Briere, J., & Runtz, M. (1988). Post sexual abuse trauma: Data and implications for clinical practice. *Journal of Interpersonal Violence, 2,* 367–379.

Brown, D., Scheflin, A.W., & Hammond, D. C. (1998). *Memory, trauma treatment, and the law.* New York: Norton.

Butler, S. (1985). *Conspiracy of silence: The trauma of incest.* Volcano, CA: Volcano Press.

Cook, A. S., & Dworkin, D. S. (1992). *Helping the bereaved: Therapeutic interventions for children, adolescents, and adults.* New York: Basic Books.

Coons, P. M. (1986). Child abuse and multiple personality disorder: Review of the literature and suggestions for treatment. *Child Abuse and Neglect, 10,* 455–462.

Corr, C. A., Martinson, I. M., & Dyer, K. L. (1985). Parental bereavement. In C. A. Corr & D. M. Corr (Eds.), *Hospice approaches to pediatric care* (pp. 219–240). New York: Springer.

Crowder, A. (1995). *Opening the door: A treatment model for therapy with male survivors of sexual abuse.* New York: Brunner/Mazel.

Dadds, M., Smith, M., Webber, Y., & Robinson, A. (1991). An exploration of family and individual profiles following father–daughter incest. *Child Abuse and Neglect, 15,* 575–586.

Davis, C. G., & Lehman, D. R. (1995). Counterfactual thinking and coping with traumatic life events. In N. J. Roese & J. M. Olson (Eds.), *What might have been: The social psychology of counterfactual thinking* (pp. 353–374). Mahwah, NJ: Erlbaum.

Davis, C. G., Lehman, D. R., Wortman, C. B., Silver, R. C., & Thompson, S. C. (1995). The undoing of traumatic life events. *Personality and Social Psychology Bulletin, 21,* 109–124.

Durkheim, E. (1951). *Suicide: A study in sociology.* New York: Free Press.

Figley, C. R., Bride, B. E., &. Mazza, N. (Eds.). (1997). *Death and trauma: The traumatology of grieving.* Washington, DC: Taylor & Francis.

Finkelhor, D. (1984). *Child sexual abuse: New theory and practice.* New York: Macmillan.

Finkelhor, D., & Browne, A. (1985). The traumatic impact of child sexual abuse: A conceptualization. *American Journal of Orthopsychiatry, 55,* 530–541.

Fleming, S. J., & Adolph, R. (1986). Helping bereaved adolescents: Needs and responses. In C. A. Corr & J. N. McNeil (Eds.), *Adolescents and death* (pp. 97–118). New York: Springer.

Fleming, S. J., & Robinson, P. J. (1991). The application of cognitive therapy to the bereaved. In T. M. Vallis, J. L. Howes, & P. C. Miller (Eds.), *The challenge of cognitive therapy: Applications to nontraditional populations* (pp. 135–158). New York: Plenum.

Fromuth, M. E. (1986). The relationship of childhood sexual abuse with later psychological and sexual adjustment in a sample of college women. *Child Abuse and Neglect, 10,* 5–15.

Gale, J., Thompson, R. J., Moran, T., & Sack, W. H. (1988). Sexual abuse in young children: Its clinical presentation and characteristic patterns. *Child Abuse and Neglect, 12,* 163–170.

Gold, E. R. (1986). Long-term effects of sexual victimization in childhood: An attributional approach. *Journal of Consulting and Clinical Psychology, 54,* 471–475.

Grant, S., & Alpert, J. L. (1993). The core trauma of incest: An object relations view. *Professional Psychology: Research and Practice, 24,* 330–334.

Grubman-Black, S. D. (1990). *Recovery from childhood sexual abuse: Broken boys/ mending men.* New York: Ballantine.

Hays, K. F. (1985). Electra in mourning: Grief work and the adult incest survivor. *Psychotherapy Patient, 2,* 45–58.

Herman, J. R., Russell, D., & Trocki, K. (1986). Long-term effects of incestuous abuse in childhood. *American Journal of Psychiatry, 143,* 1293–1296.

Hunter, M. (1990). *Abused boys: The neglected victims of sexual abuse.* New York: Fawcett.

Jehu, D. (1989). Sexual dysfunctions among women clients who were sexually abused in childhood. *Behavioral Psychotherapy, 17,* 53–70.

Kelly, S. J. (1986). Learned helplessness in the sexually abused child. *Issues in Comprehensive Pediatric Nursing, 9,* 193–207.

Klass, D., Silverman, P. R., & Nickman, S. L. (Eds.). (1996). *Continuing bonds: New understandings of grief.* Washington, DC: Taylor & Francis.

Kluft, R. P. (1990). On the apparent invisibility of incest: A personal reflection on things known and forgotten. In R. P. Kluft (Ed.), *Incest related syndromes of adult psychopathology* (pp. 11–34). Washington, DC: American Psychiatric Press.

Leick, N., & Davidsen-Nielsen, M. (1991). *Healing pain: Attachment, loss and grief therapy.* New York: Routledge.

Leitenberg, H., Greenwald, E., & Cado, S. (1992). A retrospective study of long-term methods of coping with having been sexually abused during childhood. *Child Abuse and Neglect, 16,* 399–407.

Lew, M. (1988). *Victims no longer: Men recovering from incest and other sexual child abuse.* New York: Harper & Row.

Margolin, L. (1991). Child sexual abuse by nonrelated caregivers. *Child Abuse and Neglect, 15,* 213–221.

Monat, A., & Lazarus, R. S. (1991). Stress and coping: Some current issues and controversies. In A. Monat & R. S. Lazarus (Eds.), *Stress and coping: An anthology* (3rd ed., pp. 1–15). New York: Columbia University Press.

Morrow, K. B. (1991). Attributions of female adolescent incest victims regarding their molestation. *Child Abuse and Neglect, 15,* 477–483.

Neimeyer, R. A. (1998). *Lessons of loss: A guide to coping.* New York: McGraw-Hill.

Parkes, C. M. (1986). *Bereavement: Studies of grief in adult life* (2nd ed.) New York: Tavistock.

Rando, T. A. (Ed.). (1986). *Parental loss of a child.* Champaign, IL: Research Press.

Rando, T. A. (1993). *Treatment of complicated mourning.* Champaign, IL: Research Press.

Raphael, B. (1980). A psychiatric model for bereavement counseling. In B. M. Schoenberg (Ed.), *Bereavement counseling: A multidisciplinary handbook* (pp. 148–172). Westport, CT: Greenwood.

Russell, D. E. H. (1986). *The secret trauma: Incest in the lives of girls and women.* New York: Basic Books.

Sanders, C. M. (1980). A comparison of adult bereavement in the death of a spouse, child, and parent. *Omega, 10,* 303–322.

Schoenberg, B. M. (1980). When a friend is in mourning. In B. M. Schoenberg (Ed.), *Bereavement counseling: A multidisciplinary handbook* (pp. 239–249). Westport, CT: Greenwood.

Silver, R. I., Boon, C., & Stones, H. (1983). Searching for meaning in misfortune: Making sense of incest. *Journal of Social Issues, 39,* 81–102.

Simpson, M. A. (1997). Traumatic bereavements and death-related PTSD. In C. R. Figley, B. E. Bride, & N. Mazza (Eds.), *Death and trauma: The traumatology of grieving* (pp. 3–16). Washington, DC: Taylor & Francis.

Stroebe, W., & Stroebe, M. (1987). *Bereavement and health.* New York: Cambridge University Press.

Tomlin, S. S. (1991). Stigma and incest survivors. *Child Abuse and Neglect, 15,* 557–566.

Tong, L., Oates, K., & McDowell, M. (1987). Personality development following sexual abuse. *Child Abuse and Neglect, 11,* 371–383.

Valente, S., & Sellers, J. R. (1986). Helping adolescent survivors of suicide. In C. A. Corr & J. N. McNeil (Eds.), *Adolescence and death* (pp. 167–182). New York: Springer.

Van Der Wal, J. (1989). The aftermath of suicide: A review of empirical evidence. *Omega, 20*, 149–171.

Whitfield, C. L. (1989). *Healing the child within*. Deerfield Beach, FL: Health Communications.

Worden, J. W. (1991). *Grief counseling and grief therapy: A handbook for the mental health practitioner* (2nd ed.). New York: Springer.

Wortman, C. B., & Silver, R. C. (1991). The myths of coping with loss. In A. Monat & R. S. Lazarus (Eds.), *Stress and coping* (pp. 388–405). New York: Columbia University Press.

Wyatt, G. E., Guthrie, D., & Notgrass, C. M. (1992). Differential effects of women's child sexual abuse and subsequent sexual revictimization. *Journal of Consulting and Clinical Psychology, 60*, 167–173.

17

VIDEOGRAPHY: RE-STORYING THE LIVES OF CLIENTS FACING TERMINAL ILLNESS

SANDRA A. RIGAZIO-DIGILIO

This chapter offers a coconstructivist approach to working with clients facing terminal illness using narrative therapy and videography. These creative media can provide therapeutic environments and between-session experiences that help clients construct stories, enact new stories, and re-experience older stories at different times along their developmental journey. A clinical example is described to demonstrate how videography can enhance the overall transformational value of storytelling, story enactment, and story reconstruction.

THERAPEUTIC NARRATIVES, TERMINAL ILLNESS, AND VIDEOGRAPHY

Coconstructivist psychotherapies use the dialogic process of therapeutic narratives to help clients expand individual and collective meaning systems that have heretofore influenced the parameters within which they function (Anderson & Goolishian, 1992; Bruner, 1986; Harre, 1983; Martin, 1994; McNamee & Gergen, 1992; Neimeyer & Mahoney, 1995; Polking-horne, 1992; Rigazio-DiGilio & Ivey, 1991). As clients share their stories during the dialectic exchange, they construct, extend, deconstruct, and re-construct personal histories and current worldviews. In this regard, clients and clinicians use the therapeutic conversation to realize alternative poten-tialities for change.

> It is through stories that we obtain a sense of the unfolding of events of our lives through recent history, and it appears that this sense is vital to the perception of a "future" that is in any way different from a "present." (Epston, White, & Murray, 1992, p. 97)

Although people who are dying may lose physical and cognitive abili-ties, many seem to find an intuition that healthy individuals capture only later in life. They have an incredible capacity to connect to others, to be hu-morous, and to be wise. Their spirituality connects them to a plane beyond life as we know it and draws others who are significant to them to this plane. The understandings and connectedness that emerge when hearing their sto-ries about life, dying, death, and life beyond are heartfelt. Significant others stretch to listen to the worldviews held in the mind of individuals who are dying and to express themselves during these intimate encounters.

The grieving process spans a phase of life including caring for a dying member through many iterations of illness, accepting the dying process, the death itself, bereavement, and reorganization. During this journey clients often need to retell portions of life and of this life phase and to reorganize how they understand and operate under quickly changing circumstances. The community of support that may be active at the beginning of this process tends to dwindle. Family members find it difficult to provide a source of support because of the immensity of care each member needs, the differ-ent grieving processes each one goes through, and the demands on contin-ual family reorganization and maintenance. Therapy offers a place for clients to tell and retell their stories and to reorganize their worldviews across all phases of the grieving process.

Many believe that client stories are enhanced through the use of visu-alization processes (e.g., Ivey, 1995; L'Abate & Bagarozzi, 1993; McGoldrick & Gerson, 1985). Creative media such as therapeutic graphics, artwork, and photography add new layers of meanings to client stories by providing visual prompts that stimulate alternative points of reference. In addition, the use of such media permits the sharing of client narratives across time and with different people. Adding visual complements to our client's narrations can enhance the creative possibilities for clients, clinicians, and current and fu-ture intended audiences.

Videography is one visual medium that is rich and fluid enough to as-sist clients in telling stories, to enact new stories, and to re-examine and reinterpret stories with different groups at different times. Although it has not been extensively explored in professional literature, introducing video as an adjunct to the oral rendition of client stories has tremendous potential in narrative psychotherapy. Videotaping stories offers opportunities for individuals, families, communities, and others to focus on an event that seems untenable and to find a way to define it, experience it, and interpret it. Videotaped stories offer unprecedented opportunities for clients and significant others to construct, deconstruct, and reconstruct the storylines and symbols represented within an individual or collective narrative and to understand how this narrative fits within, influences, and is affected by the immediate surround.

THERAPEUTIC OBJECTIVES CORRESPONDING TO THE GRIEF PROCESS

All families will deal with dying, death, and bereavement several times over the course of life. How they choose to work through this task often enhances this period, during which what is considered important dramatically changes. However, many do not develop collective meaning structures around this life phase that facilitate open communication, preparedness, or frames of reference that emphasize issues such as spirituality and generativity.

Using videography with individuals who are terminally ill and their significant others is influenced by five therapeutic objectives that correspond with general phases that may occur during dying and bereavement. These can be used as a guiding framework to tailor the therapy to the unique needs of each client.

- *Finishing unfinished business.* When families enter into the dying process, it often happens that members believe it is too late to address issues heretofore left for a later time. However, some unfinished business, if unattended to, can promote a maladaptive script related to the dying process now and in the future.
- *Using this time to live.* Coconstructivist therapy and videography provide a way for clients to fully experience and embrace the remaining time in their life journeys as this particular living system to enjoy precious moments; to tell, retell, and package memories; to move through a grieving and celebratory process in their own way; and to provide all family members a sense of accomplishment and immortality.
- *Creating an atmosphere in which to say goodbye.* When a strong foundation is established by working through the first two objectives, families are more ready to accept the dying process. Often, they see themselves as a bridge to a life beyond and

embrace the task of building this bridge together for the sake of one another and the dying member.

- *Fostering an atmosphere for bereavement.* Coconstructivist therapy and videography offer an environment for individuals and collective systems to grieve, to celebrate, to make sense of their experience, and to reorganize their collective system.

- *Prompting re-examination along the developmental journey.* Videography offers a future time for significant others to re-view and retell stories using the videos as a point of departure. Watching videos from a different place in one's developmental journey permits significant others to re-examine, laugh, grieve, forgive, and more fully embrace and understand the experience. In addition, this environment allows survivors an opportunity to reconsider multiple facets of the deceased member that might have been previously overlooked or interpreted from a different perspective and to re-examine themselves under these alternative frames of reference.

The final value of using videotape transcends the epistemological foundations of coconstructivism and the grieving process and touches the creative spirit. Kübler-Ross (1984) devised a way to use pictures and storytelling to assist people at the end of their lives and those who survived beyond this life. Using video, people who are dying have found the most creative ways to leave lasting impressions for others, and those left behind have found many creative ways to remember, re-experience, and prepare for future events. Clients and significant others are proud of their work and eager to share it with others. This, in and of itself, is a valuable outcome of using video with people who are terminally ill. No matter what cultural, religious, or spiritual background they represent, all feel a sense of immortality in the leaving and receiving of messages that will always be available to simply watch, or to rediscover something that may have been missed.

THE THERAPEUTIC PLATFORM

Videography helps humanize a technology that, unfortunately, is all too often more alienating than relational. However, the careful introduction and use of video within a coconstructivist framework can be creatively linked to work with clients dealing with terminal illness. It is in the careful synthesis of coconstructivist principles and videography that clients and psychotherapists can experience and capture precious moments of this life phase.

An essential prerequisite to exploring personal narratives is understanding the point(s) of view of the storyteller and the audience. What is the importance of the story? What themes, ideas, images, feelings, and relationships are intended to be portrayed? What is the purpose underlying the construction of this story? Knowledge about issues of importance and intent establish a framework to begin the construction, deconstruction, and reconstruction process.

The use of videography is guided by four principles of coconstructivist therapy.

1. *Clients construct their own meanings.* Although therapists assist in the coconstruction of meaning through the therapeutic dialogue it is, ultimately, the personal meanings clients carry away that matter most. Videos are intended to be the client's production and cannot be made to fulfill the expectations of the therapist.

2. *Personal and collective meaning making is mediated by social interactions.* As clients test alternative ways of experiencing, understanding, and operating in their world and in response to specific life tasks, the feedback they receive will influence and modify their experiences, perceptions, and behaviors. The feedback generated by the clients and others during the production and viewing of videos influences the interpretations they, and others, will construct.

3. *Personal and collective meaning making, generated through reflection and elaboration, can lead to alternative solutions.* Alternative ideas and insights from multiple viewings of videos can lead to changes in client worldviews. Such modifications or innovations can lead to expanded solutions regarding the issues that prompted treatment. In addition, clients can generalize from this work to adapt to upcoming developmental and contextual demands.

4. *Alternative meanings can generate changes that reverberate in wider social and community contexts.* Videos can be viewed by wide audiences. Actions based on the reactions and alternative meanings generated by audience members can instigate changes at levels of organization far beyond clients and their immediate circle of family and friends.

INTRODUCING VIDEOGRAPHY TO CLIENTS

When dying clients reach a stage in the process where they are reflective about their life experiences they may be open to suggestions about using videotape to capture their personal stories. The therapist can offer this medium as one way the client can share his or her reflections with significant others.

In introducing the process the therapist should keep in mind that each client may choose to use this medium differently. Some wish to structure the process and take full charge over video production, directing who will be there, who will talk and about what, and who will view the video and when. Others prefer to simply use the videotape to record spontaneous family conversation. Clients can be presented with several options, and the therapist then proceeds accordingly.

Metaphors can be useful in describing this process to the client (Bruner, 1986). Video production metaphors help provide a sense of collective direction for the dying individual and his or her family. Producer, writer, choreographer, designer, and consultant are some metaphoric roles that the family members relate to in discussing the video project.

The analogous relationship between making therapeutic videos and production roles open new possibilities for narrative therapy. By choosing a role, individuals facing death can view the video as an opportunity to cast, direct, script, and/or orchestrate the story of their lives and the legacies they hope will live beyond their physical presence. Their sense of power and direction becomes the focus, while less attention is paid to the technical aspects of "acting the part" or "directing competency." Significant others often choose roles as well, either as part of central videos or by creating videos to enhance the immediacy of the moment bringing parts of the world no longer available to their dying member into the therapeutic environment. These adjunct videos often represent ways to finish unfinished business.

Clients dealing with terminal illness who enter treatment with me for the purpose of videotaping memoirs begin the process of increasing power and collective direction at first contact. To coconstruct an environment that enables their natural healing process, I learn about their experiences with the dying process; styles of coping; individual and collective developmental trajectories; and rules, rituals, and assumptions. At the same time, I complement their style, assure them that others have gone through this process and survived, and relay stories of others dealing with similar issues.

Regardless of the metaphorical language used, a significant aspect of videography is the alternative meanings clients construct during the process. Making videos is transformational. Alternative stories are generated as clients make decisions about how to communicate or how to use video to actually enhance an immediate wish or experience. In the following section I describe this process with one client as a way of illustrating the various purposes and processes involved in using this medium.

VIDEOGRAPHY WITH A DYING ADOLESCENT AND HER FAMILY

Christina Gerelli, a 13-year-old with terminal cancer, requested that I meet her, her parents Maria (45) and Robert (48), her sister Catherine (10), and her brother Anthony (15). During hospital stays, she met a child who had discussed his work with me. When we met, Christina wondered if I had "what it takes" to make videos with her and her family without "getting too sad and bringing everyone down." Once assured, she opened the floor to a family dialogue. Maria and Robert told of their history as a family and, in particular, the in-home care of Maria's mother throughout her dying process, 4 years previous. Christina mentioned her desire to make videos and was clear that she wanted to be involved in how the videos were arranged. Color coordination was particularly important, as she had viewed one of the boy's tapes and noted that his shirt clashed with his father's. Catherine was at first teary but then excited about being on the "big screen" with her sister. She was especially energetic when Christina suggested that Catherine could determine what items would be placed on the table for the video (she did not like what she saw on the table in the boy's video and wanted her sister to make it look more like home). Anthony was reluctantly and peripherally involved at this point.

An area of unfinished business was the family's recollection of Nonni's (maternal grandmother) dying process. Christina and Catherine remembered Nonni being left alone in a dark room. Christina wanted to be sure that this did not happen to her as her illness progressed. She and Catherine remembered Nonni as having an unpleasant smell. They "hated" when mom made them kiss Nonni's hand. As these recollections were shared, Christina asked that her bedroom be moved closer to family living areas so she would not be alone. She also asked that no one be "made" to kiss her. One might imagine how the visions the girls held affected the family. They were inspired to retell the story of Nonni's dying process, her caretaking, and the parents' attempt to shelter the children from the cognitive effects of her illness. They also retold stores of various gatherings with Nonni. We viewed videos with Nonni where she was the family historian and where the children touched her on their own initiative. Through dialogue and visual memory prompts the Gerellis reconstructed the story of Nonni's caretaking and used this to live a different experience in the moment. This aspect of therapy not only provided a window into the daughters' minds, and helped the family recollect special memories, but it also helped set a direction for guided caretaking of Christina that would not isolate her from the family.

Conversations rallied members to create a desired environment for Christina. A family project involved decorating a new room for her. When the room was finished, Christina placed a picture of her Nonni—as a healthy woman—on her nightstand. Anthony worked with Robert to build shelves that could be adjusted to accommodate Christina's wheelchair. Catherine placed chairs in the room for company to sit upon.

As clients receive feedback about their words, the creative lenses they used in production, and their stage personas, new ideas about the meaning of their lives, the ways in which they have helped one another, and the legacies they leave behind surface and are explored in the therapeutic setting. Screenings of past or current videos seem to have a motivational effect. Clients are excited about reviews and are frequently moved to make more tapes.

The building of the shelves for Christina's room prompted a second area of unfinished business to emerge: Christina's feeling of being left out of her dad's and her brother's lives. This led to stories about the peripheral nature of the males in the family, focusing on the fact that Christina had not been invited to her father's work, as she had asked, and the fact that her brother had not taken her for the hiking trip he had promised her before her illness became so advanced. Building on this, Robert took Christina to his workplace and videotaped her as she wheeled around to meet everyone. She used the taping scenario as reason to interview her father's coworkers, learning what they did and what they thought about her dad. She entitled the tape "My Dad's Other Life." Anthony, following his father's example, took a walk in the woods, videotaping the scenery for Christina. It was both serene and humorous, letting two parts of Anthony fully emerge in the therapeutic encounter. Christina entitled this tape "My Walk With Anthony—and I Did Not Even Have to Lose My Breath." These tapes, and one made of a gathering in Christina's room (choreographed by Anthony and Catherine) were shown in therapy and used to continue the re-storying process by deconstructing the peripheral nature of the males and by making it possible to live out this dying process differently than the images previously locked within the minds of the girls. Experiencing and telling stories offers a sense of power clients thought had been extinguished. This storying process helps them make sense of this stage of life, in the immediacy of the moment, and afterward.

Messages Before and Beyond the Grave: Sharing Stories for Posterity and Reinterpretation

The value of videography is that stories can be shared at specified times and locations, and decisions about such issues pulls the re-storying process into the future. The term *re-storying* captures the idea that, although stories placed on video tell a particular story, future narratives of how the video will be viewed and interpreted are just as important. Such decisions empower and direct clients throughout the dying and bereavement process.

For example, making videos helps people who are dying integrate their sense of mortality and use this new sense of self to resolve past conflicts. Their decision to share certain tapes during the dying process and some after death has been extremely useful in helping all involved work through the grieving process and begin to integrate this experience into their own healing journey.

At any screening, videos trigger reflections and questions. These musings are opportunities for new elaborations and interpretations for all who are present. In addition to the myriad questions that are prompted by the viewing, personal insights and emotions are evoked. These feelings, impressions, and interpretations can be processed by the assembled group and often lead to new meanings for all present, in relation to the dying member, the death, someone's role in the process, or future anticipated events.

The Gerelli family videotaped two therapy sessions. In the first, Christina interviewed the family, basically getting a historical account of how the family came to be—how her parents met, what having three babies was like, what it was like to live so close to so many relatives, and so forth. She asked her brother about his most humorous memories of his family, and she asked her sister the same. Then the whole family began to tell funny stories from both the past and present. This tape would later be part of the grieving process after Christina's death.

Communion around videos with cherished friends and family can transform anticipatory grieving and postdeath grieving into celebrations of life, love, and story. The search to make sense out of the death of a loved one can be enhanced by the messages captured on tape. Directing the actual production and viewing schedule allows clients to, in some ways, prewrite the future. The story on tape and the story of making these tapes will live long after the individual's passing. Both the stories and the surrounding interpretations will help survivors generate new understandings and personal meanings about this person, this life and death, their role in this dying process, and future passages they are certain to confront.

In the second video made during therapy the family simply had a dialogue that was to be an open conversation geared to the benefit of their significant others. It included topics such as their love of their extended family, funny stories about certain extended family members, and the family's appreciation for all the assistance they had received since Christina's diagnosis. This second tape was copied for various extended family systems. With the help of Catherine, Christina painted cards and wrote little notes to these families. The cards and videos were then given to each extended family when they came to visit.

Creating Legacies: Multiple Stories Toward a New Sense of Self, Family, and Future

Using the same videos over a series of sessions before, during, and after a person's death promotes the sharing of new perceptions. This iterative process allows participants to integrate new insights into the purpose and meaning of the client's life, story, and death.

For people who are dying, how they hope to be remembered is important. Having the opportunity to construct stories and direct video production increases the likelihood that their legacy will be shared. For survivors these tapes represent transitional objects that help them cope with tangible loss. Oftentimes, screenings become family rituals that creatively assist in the healing process. Bereaved family and friends see new meanings and more deeply understand certain messages. Some families invite new persons to see tapes, and these persons inevitably see things from differing vantage points, helping survivors continue to develop a full image of their loved one. These new ideas can lead to personal and collective solutions that might not have been explored had it not been for the messages of and on the tape.

On Christina's death, Robert edited some portions of videos he had along with the tapes made in therapy, while Catherine made a montage of her sister's life. The montage was placed by her casket, and the video played in the Gerelli home for people who visited after the service.

Before Christina's death, she made a tape with her parents in which each person spoke into the camera at a generation of Gerellis yet to be born. In this tape the parents spoke of their love for Christina and for this part of their life as a family. The parents ended this tape by stating that they hoped future Gerellis learn from this tape about the precious girl named Christina who will be an aunt, in heaven, watching out for them.

Christina also asked to make a short tape, to be given to her paternal grandmother and grandfather for their 50th wedding anniversary. In this tape Christina remembered some funny stories about her grandparents and talked about how these stories filled days when she was stuck at home with good and loving thoughts. She ended by saying that although she knew they were sad, they should remember that she was with God now, and very happy.

Both these tapes were meant to leave a living legacy of Christina's life and her impact on the family. In the years since her death, these and other tapes have been used in subsequent therapy sessions to remember, relive, and reinterpret what occurred, who Christina was, and the role each person played in her life and her caretaking.

Ultimately, sessions end, but stories live on. The tapes, and how they were made, shared, and discussed become the living legacy. This legacy can be shared with future generations to create a sense of continuity of family. These videos become cherished gifts for clients, friends, and current and future family members.

Recently, Anthony wrote me a letter, telling me of his son Christian and his glee at seeing his dad on Christina's videotapes when he was just a boy. Anthony wrote

> I knew I was too young to understand or accept what was happening to my sister. I was angry. I have felt that perhaps I did not do enough to make her feel I loved her. However, when I watched my son laugh at my video of the woods, I knew I must have had an impact on Christina. A memory from so long ago leaves me with a precious thought of how hard I tried to be there, using the resources I had. Obviously, I did a good job.

PHOENIX RISING: THE POSTSTORYING PHASE

Videos have the power to affect community and wider social contexts. Some clients construct videos to maximize community and public impact. These video projects help clients experience a deeper sense of generativity. Their cause may be related to issues such as their particular illness, concepts of dying with dignity, or spirituality.

The distribution of tapes is a decision that can be made before or after the passing. The tape itself takes on a "life of its own." Someone may view it and feel that it would be very helpful to share with a community group or in an educational setting. The final path the tape follows will not be fully evident during its construction.

For example, clients have distributed tapes to be used to stimulate policy initiatives, such as support for victims of AIDS. Other tapes are intended to stimulate discussion among others working though similar illnesses, such as self-help groups or family support networks. The spirit of deceased members will be used to create a better place after their passing.

Very near to Christina's death, she asked her parents if she could make a tape alone with me. She said it would be a Christmas gift for them and the final tape she wanted to make. This tape was made in the hospital, where Christina and I spoke together. She started the tape by saying that she knew she would not be returning to the room created for her. When I asked her how she knew, Christina said that

> Since I have been in the hospital this time, I am having a very pleasant dream—or it maybe is not a dream. All I know is that my Nonni is holding me, and she is strong, and she does not smell. And she kisses my hand.

And with this, Christina gave a brief message to each family member. She told Anthony to remember her each time he looked at the freckle on his hand that was in the same place as her freckle. She told her sister that she would be a fine artist some day and that she hoped Catherine would make cards for others who needed them. She also bequeathed all her artist equipment to Catherine. She told her mom and dad she loved them and knew, because she looked so much like them, that they would not forget her. She left some happy memories to friends and schoolmates and, in fact, she herself became quite humorous. Then, just as smoothly, she said "Okay, Sandra, shut the tape now." And when I did, she asked me to "give the tape to my parents when I die, and ask them to play it at my memorial service." I asked about her choice of where the tape would be played. Her response was

> Remember when I wanted to be sure you could handle all this and make it fun. I have been to my church many times, and it is not a fun place to be. And they make dead people seem so big and kind of frightening, actually. I just want people to remember me like this and to think of

church as a fun place to come and celebrate things. I think I would have liked church more if someone did this for me.

And that was it. I sat quietly with her for a moment. She said "It was nice meeting you—and I am happy you did not make these tapes too sad or scary. But one thing—you really need better decorations in your office." Christina died 5 days later in the hospital with her family by her side.

CONCLUSION

The production of personal videos, the use of active metaphors, and the process of narrative therapy are all consistent with coconstructivist philosophy. All three are about helping individuals make new meanings from their experience. The concrete gift of videos is enormously powerful for both the givers and the receivers. Client-directed videos, first and foremost, create a new medium for the reconstitution of the story of their lives that can be processed in treatment. These videos also allow the client's story to live on, even for family members not yet born, thus reinforcing the continuity of family history. For friends, cherished memories and images of the departed, or of a particular collection of individuals, will be preserved throughout their lifetime. And for the community, new persuasive ideas might be encapsulated in these videos.

Videography connects the internal struggle of people dealing with terminal illness to the outside reality of family, friends, and community in a concrete fashion. It is a way of helping clients re-story their lived and living experiences, as individuals and as a particular collection of individuals, not just for themselves but for wider audiences. The acknowledgment of this audience and the actual sharing of tapes reinforce the social ties that add meaning and value to a life.

REFERENCES

Anderson, H., & Goolishian, H. (1992). The client is the expert: A not knowing approach to therapy. In S. McNamee & K. J. Gergen (Eds.), *Therapy as social construction* (pp. 25–39). London: Sage.

Bruner, J. (1986). *Actual minds, possible worlds.* Cambridge, MA: Harvard University Press.

Epston, D., White, M., & Murray, K. (1992). A proposal for re-authoring therapy: Rose's revisioning of her life and a commentary. In S. McNamee & K. J. Gergen (Eds.), *Therapy as social construction* (pp. 96–115). Sage: London.

Harre, R. (1983). *Personal being.* Cambridge, MA: Harvard University Press.

Ivey, A. E. (1995, March). *The community genogram: A strategy to assess culture and community resources.* Paper presented at the American Counseling Association convention, Denver.

Kübler-Ross, E. (1984). Unfinished business. In T. Frantz (Ed.), *Death and grief in the family* (pp. 27–49). Rockville, MD: Aspen.

L'Abate, L., & Bagarozzi, D. A. (1993). *Sourcebook of marriage and family evaluation.* New York: Brunner/Mazel.

Martin, J. (1994). The construction and understanding of psychotherapeutic change: Conversations, memories, and theories. In A. Ivey (Vol. Ed.), *Counseling and development series.* New York: Teachers College Press.

McGoldrick, M., & Gerson, R. (1985) *Genograms in family assessment.* New York: Norton.

McNamee, S., & Gergen, K. J. (Eds.). (1992). *Therapy as social construction.* London: Sage.

Neimeyer, R., & Mahoney, M. (Eds.). (1995). *Constructivism in psychotherapy.* Washington, DC: American Psychological Association.

Polkinghorne, D. E. (1992). Postmodern epistemology of practice. In S. Kvalve (Ed.), *Psychology and postmodernism* (pp. 146–155). London: Sage.

Rigazio-DiGilio, S. A., & Ivey, A. E. (1991). Developmental counseling and therapy: A framework for individual and family treatment. *Counseling and Human Development, 24,* 1–20.

SUBJECT INDEX

Meaning making, 34, 55–56. *See also* Dual process model
    constructivist view of, 215–216
    and definition of meaning, 143–144
    family, 97–107
    and finding benefits, 145–147
    and making sense of loss, 144–145
    by mothers of children with developmental disabilities, 126–127
    need for, 142–143
    and purpose of grief, 78
    as response to loss/trauma, 142–148
    and typology of meanings, 106–107
Memories, 47–48
Metaconstruction, 298–306
Metaphors, 224–226, 265
Milan circular questioning, 96, 100
Mirror metaphor, 298, 299, 304
Mothers of children with developmental disabilities. *See* Developmental disabilities, bereavement over death of children with
Mourning. *See also* Bereavement; Grief
    definitions of, 16, 24
    new psychoanalytic model of, 19–29
    stage model of, 16
    standard psychoanalytic model of, 14–19
    treatment of pathological, 25–29
Mourning and Melancholia (Sigmund Freud), 13–15, 20
Multiple Self Awareness (MSA), 305
Mystery, accommodation to, 45–46

Narrative(s), 231–242
    and account-making model, 234–236
    and confiding, 236–237
    coping with haunting loss via, 233–234
    cross-cultural approach to, 237–241
    and generativity, 235–236
    in grief therapy, 263–268
    of loss, 247
    and purpose of grief, 78
    research on, 249–254
    and self-construction, 216–218
    therapeutic effect of, 245–255
Narrative therapy, 246–255
    example of, 247–249
    goal of, 247

and research, 249–254
Narratory principle, 246
Neimeyer, Robert, 69, 301–302
New model of grief, 56
"New wave" (of grief theory), 5–6
Niebuhr, Reinhold, 234
Noumenal world, 263

Occasions, recurrent, 39
Old Testament, 157
On Death and Dying (Elizabeth Kübler-Ross), 3, 16
Openness, 99–100
Oscillation, 58, 60, 67

Pain, 37–38
    of child, 83–84
    in standard model, 18
Parental grief, 77–93
    developmental disabilities, children with. *See* Developmental disabilities, bereavement over death of children with
    and initial response to death of child, 79–82
    and inner world of parent, 79–87, 89–91
    "moving into," 82–86
    and purpose of grief, 78–79
    relative resolution of, 89–92
    and social world of parent, 81–82, 85–89, 91–92
    "well along in," 86–89
Pennebaker, J., 60–61, 303
Persian Gulf conflict, 296
Personality, and posttraumatic growth, 163
Phenomenal world, 263
Photographs, 67, 69
Physical surroundings, 39–40
Places, 39
Polkinghorne, D. E., 216
Pollock, G., 23
Positive outcome(s), 191–206. *See also* AIDS, bereavement over death of partner from; Posttraumatic growth
    emotional expressiveness as, 194–195
    factors leading to, 195–196
    feelings, positive, 64–66

AUTHOR INDEX

Finkenauer, C., 61, *72*
Finucane, R. C., 78, *93*
Fischer, L. R., 98, *111*
Fisher, R. H., 146, *152*
Fiske, S. T., 174, *188*
Fleming, S. J., 56, *70*, 312–314, 316–318, 320–325, *327*
Foa, E., 300, *309*
Folkman, S., 56, 58, 64–67, *70, 71*, 139, *152*, 175, 181–183, *188, 189*, 194, 195, *207*
Foote, C., 18, *29*
Fortner, B., 69, *71*
Fortner, B. V., 195, *208*, 216, *229, 243*
Fortunato, J. E., 175, *188*
Fowler, J. W., 174, *188*
Foy, D. W., 300, *309*
Francis, M. E., 60, *72*, 303, *309*
Frank, A., *29*
Frank, J. D., 174, *188*
Frankl, V. E., 97, *111*, 143, *151*, 174, *188*
Franklin, C., 262, *291*
Frantz, C. M., 148, *151*
Frantz, T. T., 193, 198, *207*
Frazier, P. A., 168, *171*
Freud, S., 13–15, 20, *30*, 57, *70*, 265, *291*
Friedman, S. B., 142, *150*
Friese, S., 176, *190*
Fromuth, M. E., 317, *327*
Furman, E., 14, 20, *30*

Gaines, R., 15, 20, 21, 24, *30*
Gale, J., 318, *327*
Gallagher, D., 205, *207*
Galvin, K. S., 234, *243*
Gamino, L. A., 294, *309, 310*
Garnick, G., 234, *243*
Garwood, N., 235, *243*
Gass, K., 191, *207, 208*
Geertz, C., 78, *93*
Gergen, K. J., 4, *11*, 246, 254, *255–257*, 264, 266, *291*, 332, *343*
Gergen, M. M., 4, *11*, 246, 254, *255, 257*
Gerson, R., 332, *343*
Gibran, K., 205, *207*
Gibson, A., 216, *229*
Gilbert, K. R., 83, *93*, 143, *151*, 193, *207*
Gilham, A. B., *70*
Gillett, R., 264, *291*
Glaser, B. G., 3, *11*, 78, *93*, 117, *134*
Glaser, R., 60, *72*

Gleicher, F., 141, *150*
Glesne, C., 118, *134*
Glover, L., 269, *291*
Gluhoski, V. L., 137, *151*, 262, *291*
Goenjian, A., *153*
Gold, E. R., 320, *327*
Gonçalves, O. F., 216, *229*, 246, 247, *255*, 305, *309*
Goolishian, H., 332, *342*
Gottlieb, B. H., 139, *151*
Grant, S., *327*
Grayson, C., 138, *153*
Greenberg, L., 266, *292*
Greenberg, M. A., 61, *70*
Greenwald, E., 317, *328*
Greger, H., 191, *209*
Grout, L., 251, *255*
Grubman-Black, S. D., 312, *327*
Guthrie, D., 321, *329*

Haase, J., 116, *134*
Hagman, G., 14, 18, 20–22, 24, 28, *30*, 262, *291*
Haig, J., 233, *243*
Hainer, J., 194, *207*
Hall, A. D., 99, *111*
Hamburg, D. A., 142, *150*
Hammersley, M., 78, *93*
Hammond, D. C., 313, *326*
Handel, G., 96, 97, *111*
Hanley-Dunn, P., 205, *207*
Hansson, R., 7, *11*, 191, 196, *207, 209*
Harre, R., 264, *291*, 332, *342*
Harvey, J. H., 7, *11*, 232–235, 237, 239, 241, 242, *243*, 247, 252, *255*
Hays, K. F., 312, *327*
Hays, R. B., 175, *189*
Held, B., 269, *291*
Helmruth, T., 116, *134*
Helmruth, T. A., 193, *207*
Herman, J. L., 160, 165, *170*, 214, *229*, 294n1, 304, *309*
Herman, J. R., 320, *327*
Hermans, H. J. M., 216, *229*, 246, *256*
Herth, K., 191, *207*
Hess, R. D., 96, 97, *111*
Hodgkinson, P. E., 158, 165, *170*
Hoffman, L., 96, *111*
Hogan, N., 4, *11*, 194, *207*
Holahan, C. H., 139, *154*
Holen, A., 62, *70*
Holmstrom, L. L., 142, 143, *150*

Lloyd, D. A., 137, *154*
Loftus, E. F., 241, *243*
Loos, M. E., 164, *170*
Lopata, H. Z., 159, *170*
Lovett, S., 205, *207*
Luckman, T., 98, *110*
Luminet, O., 61, *72*
Lund, D. A., 192, 195, *208*
Lyddon, W. J., 216, *228*
Lyubomirsky, S., 142, 149, *152*

Mahoney, M. J., 5, *11*, 215, 216, 226, 228, 229, 249, 256, 262, *292*, 298, *309*, 332, *343*
Mair, M., 305, *309*
Mancuso, J. C., 249, *256*
Mandel, D. R., *152, 170, 208*
Manjikian, R., *153*
Manoukian, G., *153*
Margolin, L., 318, *328*
Marmar, C. R., 300, *310*
Marmor, C., 83, *93*
Marris, P., 6, *11*
Martin, J., 332, *343*
Martinson, I. M., 321, *326*
Mascolo, M. F., 265, *291*
Maslow, A., 185, *189*
Maturana, H. R., 250, *256*
Mauger, P., 116, *134*
Mazza, N., 311, *327*
McAdams, D. P., 149, *152*
McBride, A., 144, *153*
McCann, I. L., 215, *229*, 294n1, *309*
McDannell, C., 78, *94*
McDowell, M., 318, *328*
McGoldrick, M., 332, *343*
McIntosh, D. N., 142, 143, *152*
McKillop, K. J., 62, *71*
McMillen, J. C., 146, *152*
McNamee, S., 246, *256*, 332, *343*
Mead, G. H., 97, *111*, 235, *243*
Meichenbaum, D., 300, *309*
Merleau-Ponty, M., 265, *291*
Mesquita, B., 61, *72*
Metalsky, G. I., 138, 150, *152*
Miles, M. S., 118, *134*, 193, *208*
Miller, E., 242, *243*
Miller, W. R., 149, *152*
Millison, M., 173, *189*
Milo, E. M., 194, *208*
Minuchin, S., 268, *291*
Mishler, E. G., 250, *256*

Mitchell, J. T., *71*
Mitchell, S., 20, *30*
Moes, A. J., 215, 216, 226, 229, 294, 298, 305, *309, 310*
Mollica, R. F., 214, *229*
Monat, A., 318, *328*
Moore, B. E., 16, *30*
Moos, R. H., 58, 69, 139, 143, 146, *152–154*
Moran, T., 318, *327*
Morrow, J., 138, *153*
Morrow, K. B., 320, *328*
Morse, J. M., 194, *207*
Moskowitz, J., 65, *71*
Moss, M., 191, *208*
Moss, S., 191, *208*
Muehlenhard, C. L., 321, *326*
Murch, R. L., 139, *153*, 163, *171*
Murray, E. J., 61, *71*
Murray, K., 332, *342*
Murrell, S., 191, *208*
Muxen, M., 99, *111*

Nadeau, J. W., 56, *71*, 96, *111*
Neimeyer, R. A., 3–6, *11*, 18, *30*, 69, *71*, 78, *94*, 142, 149, *152, 153, 170*, 195, *208*, 216, *228, 229*, 230, 236, *243*, 246, 247, 249, 250, 256, 262–267, *291*, 292, 296, 301, 302, *309*, 315, *328*, 332, *343*
Nickman, S. L., 78, *94*, 251, 256, 262, *291*, 315, *327*
Nolen-Hoeksema, S., 63, 65, 66, *71*, 138–140, 142–147, *151, 153*
Norris, A. S., 159, *169*
Norris, F. H., 137, *153*, 191, *208*
Notgrass, C. M., 321, *329*
Nunn, K., 57, *72*, 195, *208*
Nurius, P. S., 262, *291*

Oates, K., 318, *328*
Ochberg, R., 217, *230*
Ohlde, C., *310*
O'Leary, V. E., 158, *170*
Olshansky, S., 114, *134*
Oltjenbruns, K. A., 193, *208*
O'Neill, M. R., 247, *257*
Orbuch, T. L., 232, 235, 237, 241, *243*, 247, 252, *255*
Overcash, W. S., 160, *170*
Oxford English Dictionary, 53

Veronen, L. J., 300, *310*
Viney, L. L., 294n1, *310*
Vittinghoff, E., 65, *71*
Volkan, V., 16, *31*, 81, *94*

Walsh, J., 174, *190*
Walter, T., 18, *31*, 56, *73*, 78, *94*, 262, *292*
Wass, H., 3, *11*
Watson, J. C., 266, *292*
Wax, R., 78, *93*
Wayment, H. A., 139, *152*
Webber, Y., 312, *326*
Weber, A. L., 214, 232, 235, 237, *243*,
        247, 252, *255*
Wegner, D. M., 142, *154*, *155*
Weintraub, J. K., 139, *150*
Weiss, R. S., 61, *71*, 140, 142, 153, *155*,
        173, 175, *189*, *190*, 235, *243*
Wells, G. L., 235, *243*
White, M., 247, 249, *257*, 267, *292*, 332,
        342
Whitefield, C. L., 312, *329*
Whyte, W. F., 78, *94*
Williams, A. F., 137, *152*

Williams, A. M., 294, *310*
Williams, D. A., 142, *152*
Wills, T. A., 139, *150*
Wilner, N., 83, *93*, 182, *189*
Wimberly, D. W., 194, *207*
Wood, J. V., 142, *154*, 192, *209*
Worden, J. W., 185, *190*, 312, 316–318,
        320–324, *329*
Wortman, C. B., 57, 61, 63, 65, *73*, 137,
        140–142, *150–152*, 170, 195,
        208, *209*, 247, *257*, 320, 321,
        326, *329*
Wright, S., 100, *111*
Wrubel, J., 181, *189*
Wurthnow, R., 160, 166, *172*
Wyatt, F., 246, *257*
Wyatt, G. E., 321, *329*

Yalom, I. D., 146, *155*, 160, *172*
Yancey, D., 191, *209*

Zech, E., 61, *72*, *73*
Zimpfer, D. G., 192, 194, *207*, *209*
Zisook, S., 173, 184, *190*

ABOUT THE EDITOR

Robert A. Neimeyer, PhD, holds a Dunavant University Professorship in the Department of Psychology, University of Memphis, where he also maintains an active clinical practice. Since completing his doctoral training at the University of Nebraska in 1982, he has conducted extensive research on psychotherapy from a constructivist or meaning-making perspective, with a special interest in issues related to death, grief, and loss.

Dr. Neimeyer has published 17 books, including *Constructivism in Psychotherapy, Constructions of Disorder, Lessons of Loss: A Guide to Coping*, and *Dying: Facing the Facts*. The author of over 200 articles and book chapters, he is currently working to advance a more adequate theory of grieving as a process of meaning reconstruction.

Dr. Neimeyer is the editor of the international journal *Death Studies* and served as president of the Association for Death Education and Counseling (1996–1997). In recognition of his scholarly contributions, he has been granted both the Distinguished Research Award (1990) and the Distinguished Teaching Award (1999) by the University of Memphis; elected to the International Work Group on Death, Dying, and Bereavement (1993); designated Psychologist of the Year by the Tennessee Psychological Association (1996); made a Fellow of the Clinical Psychology Division of the American Psychological Association (1997); and given the Research Recognition Award by the Association for Death Education and Counseling (1999).